D0041538

GREEN SISTERS

Sarah McFarland Taylor

GREEN SISTERS

A Spiritual Ecology

Harvard University Press

Cambridge, Massachusetts

London, England

2007

Copyright © 2007 by the President and Fellows of Harvard College
All rights reserved
Printed in the United States of America

Library of Congress Cataloging-in-Publication Data

Taylor, Sarah McFarland, 1968–
Green sisters : a spiritual ecology / Sarah McFarland Taylor.
p. cm.
Includes bibliographical refrences (p.   ) and index.
ISBN-13: 978-0-674-02440-3 (alk. paper)
ISBN-10: 0-674-02440-0 (alk. paper)
1. Human ecology—Religious aspects—Catholic Church.
2. Catholic women—Political activity.   3. Nuns—Political activity.   I. Title.
BX1795.H82T39 2007
261.8′80882719—dc22   2006041343

To my sisters, Anne and Martha,
and to all Sisters of Earth

CONTENTS

ILLUSTRATIONS

PREFACE

This book is an invitation to journey into the fascinating world of "green sisters" as they cultivate a new variety of religious culture on the North American landscape. Often referred to as "green nuns," "eco-nuns," or "green sisters," these environmentally activist Roman Catholic vowed religious women and their emergent movement complicate conventional categories of "liberal" and "conservative" within American Catholic history. In a political climate that has polarized religious traditionalists and religious innovators, green sisters are both. Their movement is one that "reinhabits" culturally resonant heirlooms of Catholic tradition and vowed religious life, while opening up those traditions to new and imaginative interpretations. Their movement is fundamentally countercultural but is so on many fronts at once and in complex ways. These women bring together and successfully blend Catholicism and environmentalism, orthodoxy and experience, institutional authority and grassroots innovation, abstract theory and on-the-ground application. A close examination of these new missionaries to the planet demonstrates the role that today's religious women are playing as active producers and transformers of new varieties of culture and spiritual expression.

A brief word about terminology: technically, according to canon law (the law that governs the Catholic Church), the term "nun" is specifically used to refer to vowed religious women who are cloistered from the outside world. But in commonly accepted vernacular, "nun" is also used more generally to mean all women who are vowed members of Roman Catholic religious orders. In this book, various sources use the terms "sisters" and "nuns" fairly interchangeably and reflect their common usage. I, however, have chosen primarily to use the term "sisters" because the majority of women in the movement are "sisters" but not "nuns" in the technical sense. I also use "green sisters" because of the three common shorthand terms used to denote "ecologically concerned and environmentally activist Roman Catholic vowed religious women," it is the one preferred by the religious sisters themselves.[1]

Immersing myself in the study of green sisters for more than a decade has been the most challenging and rewarding commitment of my life. It has come with periods of tremendous self-doubt and confusion as well as periods of great joy and satisfaction. Over the years, I have developed strong bonds with green sisters, becoming what Linda Archibald and Mary Crnkovich refer to as an "intimate outsider"—one who is never fully part of the community but, at the same time, is intimately tied to it.[2] Feminist scholars from a variety of disciplines now frequently speak about the importance of the "view from below," a research approach that focuses not on an elite class occupying the realms of hierarchical or institutional power but on those operating at the grassroots of society.[3] In this approach, the researcher also strives to create alternatives to the traditional vertical relationship in academic scholarship between researcher and researched in favor of a more horizontal and reciprocal relationship. In doing so, the researcher works to replace "spectator knowledge" with active participation in the life events and concerns of those she seeks to understand better. With this in mind, I want to be careful to make the distinction that throughout this book, my intent has been to speak about green sisters, not for them. My knowledge of the sisters' lives and communities has been filtered through my own experiences and perspectives.

The very fact that I am not a vowed member of a religious order, or even a Roman Catholic, builds in a certain amount of distance to this work. In several consultations with sisters over the years, I have questioned very carefully whether I should be doing this project at all. "Is this intrusive or unwanted?" I have asked. The responses I have received from sisters have been overwhelmingly positive, articulating the importance sisters themselves place on the documentation of women's history and their conviction that a scholarly secondary source, produced by a women's historian who has spent a number of years getting to know sisters and their ministries, would indeed be a contribution to scholarship on women and their religious lives.

As an "intimate outsider," and particularly as a scholar-researcher, I offer analysis and critique not endemic to the movement. In doing so, I certainly do not seek to supplant green sisters' own stories but instead to offer a different lens through which to view the movement both historically and culturally. I hope that such a lens will be beneficial for both those within the movement and the uninitiated. Ideally, by focusing more attention on this compelling movement of religious women, this book will also help to create greater interest in sisters' own autobiographies and self-written narratives. Some of those are already in process, and I am committed to supporting these efforts.[4]

Catholic Ecology on the Ground

My research initially began in 1994 with a study of the Dominican-sponsored earth literacy center and community-supported garden at Genesis Farm in western New Jersey. Cofounded by Dominican Sister Miriam MacGillis in 1980, Genesis Farm has become an important "seed community" within the movement, providing critical earth-literacy training, informational resources, and networking support, all of which have helped other sisters' earth ministries to germinate. After spending two summers at Genesis Farm volunteering and attending programs, I expanded my research to cover the propagation of sisters' earth ministries, organic farms, and ecological centers across the United States and Canada. I have made field visits to more than a dozen of these ministries, farms, and centers across the country (in states as diverse as Indiana, New Jersey, Vermont, Colorado, Ohio, California, and Texas). I have also attended four of the five most recent international conferences of Sisters of Earth, an international network of environmentally active sisters that meets every two years, as well as other informal gatherings of sisters.

In the course of my field visits to sisters and their ministries, at various times I have dug potatoes, shucked garlic, cut brush, mulched, weeded, harvested, and double-dug vegetable beds for intensive planting. Between the fall of 1994 and the summer of 2006, I conducted both formal and informal interviews in person and by telephone, in addition to sixty-five standardized but open-ended interviews conducted electronically via the internet, for a total of more than one hundred interview contacts. I also collected and made a comprehensive study of a wide variety of primary source documents, including newsletters, pamphlets, poetry, cookbooks, audio- and videotaped lectures and courses, workshop curricula, fundraising materials, garden handbooks, correspondence, and community statements. Additionally, I studied green sisters' artwork, crafts, music, performance, prayer and prayer tools, rituals, and ceremonies.

My approach to this research has been dictated by a commitment to studying "religion on the ground" or what Danièle Hervieu-Lèger calls *religion veçue* (lived religion). Hervieu-Lèger argues that attention to "lived practice" is critical to shedding light on what religion really is because it gets at the often obscured dimension of how the faithful organize their daily lives and actively put beliefs into practice.[5] Catholic historian Robert Orsi similarly focuses on "lived religion" or "religion on the ground" because he finds it reveals the dynamic integrations of religion and experience, and it is "through such dynamic processes of engagement that religion takes life."[6] Because my primary subject of study is women, I would add that this kind of approach has been vital to exploring and understanding women's religious lives and experiences, especially since women have seldom been in hierarchical positions of religious authority "off the ground."

In shedding light on the obscured corners of religion as it is actually practiced, we discover that women, especially those marginalized by mainline religions, are the principal occupants of such hidden corners.[7] In drawing theory and method from religious history, feminist ethnography, and cultural studies, my aim has been to produce a contemporary ethnographic history of green sisters that illuminates their active production and shaping of religious culture. In presenting the research in this book, I have cross-referenced data from written materials, such as newsletters or correspondence, with telephone communications, personal interviews, electronic interviews, and field journals. Not wanting to fall into the classic anthropological fallacy "In Africa, women carry water on their heads, at least the one I saw did," I have drawn my conclusions from "interlocking sources" (a term borrowed from the legal world, in which one presents overlapping evidence from multiple domains in order to build a more solid case).[8] That is, I have consciously avoided offering broader analysis based on one instance or one source of information, and instead have given such analysis only when patterns emerged across multiple sources. Guided, in part, by Robert Orsi's history of contemporary devotions to St. Jude in conjunction with Thomas Tweed's ethnography on the Cuban-American shrine to Our Lady of Charity in Miami, I have also experimented with interlocking methodologies—that is, with combining historical, ethnographic, and gender-studies approaches. In the challenges I faced in my own research, it quickly became evident that history and ethnography need one another and that both benefit from an analysis of gender as it relates to religion and culture.

Sister Disciplines

Traditionally, history and anthropology were considered to be "sister disciplines," and they have indeed functioned as close siblings in my study of green sisters.[9] Historical anthropologists John and Jean Comaroff advise that "no ethnography can ever hope to penetrate beyond the surface planes of everyday life, to plumb its invisible forms, unless it is informed by the historical imagination—the imagination, that is, of both those who make history and those who write it." The Comaroffs issue the caveat that "neither imaginatively nor empirically" can the ethnographer ever "capture the reality" of those she researches.[10] While recognizing the subjective and imaginative quality inherent in any ethnographic enterprise, I have still worked to create a balance between the subjectivity of the ethnographer's lens and a strong commitment to approximate as closely as possible the texture, depth, and detail of this movement, while considering its historical and cultural implications. I have not (intentionally) taken creative license with details, created "composites," or intertwined field experiences with fictional narrative, as is now popular in contemporary ethnography. This is not to say that some ethnographers do not have very good reasons for using such tactics. In an era of postpositivist ethnography, anthropologists tell us, there is no such thing as "getting the story right."[11] Still, with all the flaws and contradictions inherent in this process, I have tried very hard not to get it wrong.

The purpose of my research has been primarily historical, and this has made my research questions and concerns differ in some ways from those of the social scientist. From the beginning, I have viewed green sisters not simply as social actors but also as historical actors within the larger schemata of American religious history and women's religious history; thus the details of identity and the contexts of timeframe and place were too important consciously to fictionalize. The politics of erasure have also been prominent in my mind throughout the composition of this book. Consequently, in consultation with sisters themselves, I have not changed the names, geographic details, or backgrounds of the women involved with this movement in order to make them anonymous. Sisters who were interviewed for this study were of course given the option of total anonymity, but only eleven respondents of the sixty-five interviewed electronically requested it, and those with whom I met in person either agreed to a more informal conversation in which their names would not be cited or agreed to a more formal interview (often audiotaped) in which their names would be identified. For the women who chose anonymity, I have carefully coded and filed all their responses separately from any identifying information. When referring to the majority of those who did grant permission to be quoted, I have (as much as possible) indicated the earth ministry with which they are involved, including information about the state or region of a ministry's location to provide a better sense of the national scope of the movement. When conducting field work and conducting interviews in person, I always openly identified myself, gave my academic affiliation, asked permission to use the material I gathered in this study, and explained my purpose ahead of time. I have also stood up and publicly introduced myself and the nature of my project during the "open microphone" period of the three Sisters of Earth conferences I have attended. Rather than being put off by these announcements and declarations, sisters were generously receptive, asked to hear more, and offered to help. I found that the religious sisters I encountered had a strong sense of the important role that history has played in their own lives and were especially supportive of women's scholarship. Repeatedly, they cited the important legacy for women today, especially for religious women, of historical figures such as Hildegard of Bingen (an accomplished scholar and German nun of the twelfth century whose life and achievements were until recently largely obscured).[12] As did Virginia Woolf in her day, green sisters remarked in conversation that "for most of history, 'Anonymous' was a woman" and observed the perils faced by social groups that are denied their past.[13]

When Ann Braude writes that "women's history *is* American religious history," she points out that women constitute the majority of participants in religious activities and institutions, and yet much of religious history has focused on the lives of men.[14] To find material about women's religious lives, often one must pick through the refuse of history. American women's religious historians such as Braude herself, Mary Farrell Bednarowski, Catherine Brekus, Jean Humez, Elizabeth Reis, and a growing number of others have definitely made such "historical dumpster diving" to retrieve the stories of religious women much easier than it used to be.[15] Despite this progress, women continue to be dismissed and relegated to the subordinate or "left hand" of the academic study of religion.[16] Part of my decision to work on a contemporary historical ethnography of this movement stems from wanting to bring to light an important phenomenon in the present, but I also hope that when, years from now, a religious studies, history, or women's studies professor wants to teach about the green sisters movement at the turn of the twenty-first century, this book may in some small way contribute to the resources enabling him or her to do so more effectively.

Surveyed to Death

Religious ethnographer Meredith McGuire has argued that "we need less emphasis on quantitative methods such as surveys, opinion research, and formal organizational analysis, because these methodologies presume a relatively fixed, institutional form of religion."[17] The notion of "fixed" religion also tends to marginalize the study of women's religious experiences, which when taken in the context of a presumed institutional orthodoxy have often been dismissed by scholars as "superstition" or "folk practice."[18] By placing a strong emphasis on qualitative research and participant observation in this study, I have sought to focus instead on what McGuire calls "the *ongoing processes* by which believers create, maintain, and change their symbols for making sense out of their worlds."[19]

Before I embarked on the formal electronic interview component of my research, I thus first had conversations with several sisters involved with the Sisters of Earth network to find out what features they would want to see in an interview, and what they might want to learn from other sisters who are involved in earth ministries and active in environmental issues. From the field work and face-to-face interviews I had already conducted, I most definitely had a sense of the kinds of questions I was interested in asking, but I also wanted this research tool to reflect sisters' own input and interests. The overwhelming message I received from these contacts was that this interview should be "tree-free" (it should not be paper-based and should use as few of earth's resources as possible) and that it should be as little like a survey as possible. More than one sister whom I consulted used the same phrase: "Sisters have been surveyed to death." And it is true that religious sisters have had their lives statistically combed over, from sociologist Marie Augusta Neal's surveys in 1965, 1980, and 1989; to major surveys by more sociologists in 1993 and 1994; to a 1994 *Los Angeles Times* poll; and to, more recently, "The Nun Study" (2001), which literally surveyed sisters to death by tracking their cognitive and lifestyle patterns to study the onset of and mortality from Alzheimer's disease.[20]

Based on my own experiences working in election polling for the national primaries in the 1980s, I was well aware of survey respondents' frustration with a pat selection of responses from which to choose. I was continually asked by respondents for more context and asked questions like, "In what way do they mean that?" I was often told, largely by female respondents, "None of those answers applies to me" or "My answer's not there." In the electronic interview, my goal was instead to create open-ended questions that would allow respondents to, in feminist theorist Bell Hooks's terms, "talk back."[21] At the suggestion of Sisters of Earth cofounder Toni Nash, I also implemented a system whereby sisters could answer the questions they felt drawn to and which they had prioritized as important, instead of conforming their responses solely to my interests. As long as sisters completed the short-answer demo-graphic background information at the beginning and the short-answer questions on vegetarianism, farming, and lifestyle habits, they were invited to pick and choose which of the other questions they wanted to spend time on, or simply to write their own comments. The format of the long-answer questions also allowed unlimited space for response and individual expression. At first, I worried that they would skip the more "edgy" questions, as when I asked sisters if they had experienced hostile reactions to their ecological practices and beliefs (for instance, whether they had been labeled pantheistic, un-orthodox, heretical, or un-Christian), and if so, how they dealt with these accusations. As it turns out, sisters tackled these difficult questions directly, with thoughtful answers that I was able to incorporate into this book. Sisters who responded to the electronic interview also took me up on the opportunity provided to make additional comments and to critique the structure and framework of questions, word choice, and other elements of the interview. For instance, when I asked sisters to rank in terms of importance the issues or experiences that had first drawn them to the movement, one sister responded, "This idea of 'ranking' really doesn't work for me" and proceeded to create her own system. Or, for instance, when sisters felt I had worded a question skewed toward the U.S. context, they would answer, "Don't forget our Canadian sisters!" Many times these metacritiques were more valuable than the answers themselves because they expanded my own perspective and framework for analysis, causing me to reconsider fundamental assumptions I had made. I have included these critiques throughout this work, as well as others that sisters offered after reading various sections of this book.

Positionality and Voice

As a feminist researcher, a white heterosexual woman, a mother, a cradle Episcopalian, and a North American scholar of religion, I naturally bring my own set of cultural, academic, and experiential lenses to this book, as would any researcher. As ethnographer Lorraine Code points out, there is "no view from nowhere."[22] One element that has certainly shaped the interpretive nature of this study is that, unlike many who have written about Catholic religious sisters, I have not grown up with romantic images of Catholic nuns or visions of them as quasisupernatural creatures. At the same time, unlike those individuals who sport "I survived Catholic School" buttons, I have never felt frightened or intimidated by religious sisters or associated them with punitive treatment or sadistic guilt. As a Catholic friend of mine remarks incredulously, I "missed the whole nun head trip."

Reading a special insert in the January 2002 *Atlantic Monthly* entitled "Women of God" signaled for me just how different my images and experiences of North American religious sisters have been from those of Catholic writers such as Mary Gordon. Gordon writes about the Hollywood images she grew up with of long-suffering saintly nuns, such as those played by Ingrid Bergman in *The Bells of St. Mary's* (1945) or by Audrey Hepburn in *The Nun's Story* (1959).[23] I come from a very different generation from Gordon, so the first cinematic image of nuns I can recall was from *The Sound of Music.* The sisters I know bristle at the stereotype of sappy singing nuns, but the scene that always resonated for me was when Maria's former sisters from the convent sabotage two Nazi SS cars by concealing the distributor caps under their habits. This early image of subversive (and capable) nuns working for justice in the world was later followed by my encounter with the film *Dead Man Walking* in the 1990s. Susan Sarandon plays the role of Helen Prejean, a very practical and down-to-earth death row counselor and Sister of St. Joseph of Medaille. If I had any Hollywood images of nuns in mind, they were these two.

The first sisters I ever met were environmental-activist, ecophilosophy-reading, farming sisters teaching on the staff or participating in the earth literacy programs at Genesis Farm, an organic farm and earth ministry in New Jersey. I very likely had encountered other religious sisters before the fall of 1994 when I first visited the farm but simply was not aware of it, since most religious sisters look just like everybody else. My first conscious encounter with religious sisters, then, was with contemporary, active, nonhabited, well-educated, savvy, professional peers. Whereas Mary Gordon comments that she realized by the eighth grade that the nuns teaching her "weren't very smart," the nuns I've encountered have been passionate intellectuals, scientists, artists, and philosophers. Of the sixty-five green sisters I interviewed electronically, only four did not have an advanced graduate degree and several held more than one master's degree. Out of the eight who held doctorates, one sister actually had two doctorates. Sisters were continually recommending a wide variety of scholarly books for me to read, and when I was not doing field work, it was a challenge to try to keep up with this list. My intellectual discussions with green sisters about environmental philosophy, spirituality, and theology have greatly enriched who I am as a scholar and a person. In the course of walking "earth meditation trails" and "cosmic labyrinths," and participating in ecospirituality retreat weekends, earth literacy courses, geology workshops, natural foods cooking classes, and seasonal liturgies, my own relationship to the natural world has also been unquestionably deepened.

Reciprocally, I have become aware of the small ways in which I have inadvertently shaped the movement just by my very contact with green sisters. Traveling from one earth ministry to another has meant that the stories of approaches and developments at a number of other sisters' ecology centers have traveled with me. At various times, I have been a carrier for the cross-pollination of small bits of liturgy, philosophies, programs, and curricula. Because I have shared drafts of my work with sisters and requested their response, some of my analysis ends up inadvertently returning to the movement in a feedback loop. For example, when working on a draft on the concept of "reinhabiting religion," I made sure to point out to readers that when I spoke about sisters' "reinhabiting spiritual landscapes," I was using the bioregionalist term "reinhabiting" in a metaphoric way. I carefully explained that I was taking some liberty, because sisters themselves used this term in a topographical sense but (as far as I knew) did not refer specifically to the concepts of "reinhabiting religion," "reinhabiting tradition," or "reinhabiting spiritual landscapes." I was concerned about being presumptive and putting words in their mouths, so I made sure to identify this as the researcher's analytical construct.

Shortly after I mailed a draft of that section to the Green Mountain Monastery, I received a gracious note back from monastery prioress Gail Worcelo indicating that she had very much liked this use of "reinhabiting" and had incorporated the phrase "we are reinhabiting the spiritual landscape of the Catholic monastic tradition" into the Green Mountain Monastery's Rule of Life (a religious community's set of guiding principles). Were this book project a laboratory experiment, this kind of feedback might indicate that I had contaminated the research sample. But I am not dealing with bacteria in a petri dish. Religious movements are not closed systems, and historical ethnography is not a hard science. These women are people with whom I have an ongoing relationship, and that relationship is fundamentally based on exchange. The Heisenberg uncertainty principle from quantum mechanics (sometimes dubbed by ethnographers the "ethnography uncertainty principle") teaches us that we cannot study something without changing it in the process, and this has also been true to a greater or lesser degree in the course of my research.

In many ways, I took the fact that the metaphor had resonated with

Worcelo as a positive sign that I was on track in terms of my interpretive analysis and that sisters were indeed able to see themselves in my work. No doubt there will be some areas of the book in which, despite my best efforts, my interpretations or use of analytical metaphor will not ring true. One of my goals, however, has been to include as much as possible what Elaine Lawless and Jeffrey Titon call "reciprocal ethnography," in which they urge scholars to include "the informant's interpretations of our interpretations."[24] Anthropologist Bernard McGrane, by contrast, cautions against any illusion of reciprocity and ethnographic "dialogue" since the author always has the last word.[25] As imperfect and incomplete a strategy as it may be for addressing problems of voice and authority, soliciting and including sisters' reactions to what I have written is a practice that stems from my own recognition of the situatedness and mutually negotiated nature of knowledge.[26]

In terms of voice, I interject the first person to provide further explanation and context at various points in the text, to indicate further how I came to know things, or to relate certain salient direct experiences. At other points, I stay mostly to one side, acknowledging that this is never possible in a real sense, since the text itself is always a narrative as seen through this particular researcher's eyes. My interjections in some areas and not in others are not meant to imply that some parts of the text are "objective" and free of "standpoint." I have sought to avoid what Donna Haraway has called "the God trick," in which the researcher's pseudo-scientific presentation of information about a cultural group bears the god-like *(deus ex machina)* quality of having been dropped from nowhere.[27] Not unlike the green sisters who cultivate creative combinations of tradition and change within their own lives, I steep my narrative in both the old and the new, creating a fusion of traditional and experimental approaches to religious ethnography.

In various sessions on ethnography at meetings of the American Academy of Religion, I have repeatedly listened to researchers speak about the traditional "extrication process" once research has been completed within a community. But the idea of such a process is antithetical to the way I have approached this project. It seems strange to me that I would simply be a "squatter" in these women's lives, extract what was needed, and then move on to tap a new resource. I further cannot imagine simply ending the relationships I have built with these women over a dozen years. We have shared what goes on in each others' lives from job changes to health concerns, news of parents and siblings, the births of nieces and nephews, and my own pregnancy with my first child. I am in regular e-mail communication with sisters about concerns ranging from peace actions and environmental petitions to course syllabi and persons in need of prayer. As Karen McCarthy Brown has said, "A true friendship is not over just because a writing project is done."[28] This particular book project may be concluding, but the relationships built over more than a decade continue. Furthermore, the living history of green sisters is still being written, and I have made both a personal and professional commitment to keep documenting this movement as long as I am welcome to do so. The religious sisters I have met through this project have been some of the most candid and forthright women I have ever encountered, so I trust them to let me know if I should in fact "extricate" myself and cease my involvement, a decision by which I would respectfully abide.

The period of work leading up to this book has come to a close, but I feel that my commitment to working with green sisters has only just begun, especially in the movement's international dimensions. While the subject of this book is the green sisters of North America, there is still much to be learned about the religious sisters around the globe who are addressing issues of globalization, sustainability, and environmental problems, especially as they affect children everywhere and the world's poor and marginalized.

INTRODUCTION

Planetary Call and Response

It would be an understatement to write that the last few years have been particularly troubling ones for the Roman Catholic Church in the United States. Widely publicized abuses within the male hierarchy have created an atmosphere characterized largely by divisiveness, betrayal, and the violation of trust. But amid the painful furor over sex scandals and lawsuits, a much quieter movement is now beginning to garner notice. At the very grassroots of the Church, Catholic religious sisters have faithfully and steadfastly taken up the mission to heal and restore the life systems of the planet.[1] Beginning with the communal lands in their own backyards, sisters are extending their ecological repair efforts from their local bioregions to those of the world's poor, who are disproportionately affected by environmental pollution and resource depletion. Popularly referred to as "green nuns," "green sisters," or even "eco-nuns," a growing number of Roman Catholic vowed religious women have committed themselves to addressing the most pressing environmental concerns confronting both human and nonhuman life communities. In this book, I refer to these women by their preferred name of "green sisters" and focus predominantly on groups in the United States and Canada, acknowledging that there are now green sisters attending to issues of ecojustice and ecosystem repair all over the world.[2]

In the North American context, these women are building new "earth ministries" and finding greener (that is, more ecologically friendly) ways to reinhabit their communal lands.[3] Some sisters are sodbusting the neatly manicured lawns surrounding their motherhouses to create community-supported organic gardens where they engage in "sacred agriculture" and "contemplative gardening." Others are building alternative housing structures and hermitages from renewable materials, using straw bale, rammed earth, and cob materials instead of forest products. They are building composting

1

toilets, heating their buildings with solar panels, installing compact florescent light bulbs, cooking with solar ovens, and replacing old "gas-guzzling" automobiles with new, efficient electric-hybrid vehicles. They are putting their community lands into land trusts and creating wildlife sanctuaries on their properties. They are disrupting shareholder meetings of corporate polluters, contesting the construction of garbage incinerators, and leading struggles to stop the proliferation of suburban sprawl, genetically modified organisms, and irradiated food. They are developing "green" liturgies that honor the whole life community, and they are adopting environmentally sustainable lifestyles both as daily spiritual practice and as models to others.

Historically, when orphanages were needed in North America, religious sisters' communities built orphanages. When hospitals were needed, sisters built hospitals and staffed them. When schools were needed, sisters built schools and taught in them. When peace and social justice concerns intensified, especially in the context of the Vietnam War, the civil rights movement, the political violence in Central America, and the widening economic disparities between wealthier countries and the world's poor, sisters formed ministries to respond, including commissions on peace and justice that took sisters' lobbying efforts to Congress and the United Nations.[4] Today, sisters are hearing and answering a call from the earth, and it is to these needs that they are directing their efforts.

Founding numerous ecological learning centers, community-supported farms, and other earth ministries on their lands has been one such response to the call. Data from personal interviews, telephone interviews, field research, and sixty-five electronic interviews of religious sisters indicate that at least fifty of these centers and ministries are now active in the United States and Canada.[5] Data gathered from field work, literature review, interviews, and the directory produced by a major network of green sisters show that Dominican Sisters, Sisters of St. Joseph, Sisters of Loretto, Franciscan Sisters, Sisters of Charity, Sisters of Notre Dame, Servants of the Immaculate Heart of Mary Sisters, Sisters of the Humility of Mary, Medical Mission Sisters, and a wide variety of Catholic women religious are actively involved in ecological centers, community gardens, or other earth ministries. At a variety of sisters' earth ministries, such as Genesis Farm in New Jersey, EarthLinks in Colorado, and Earth Home in California, the founders and staff are intercongregational, combining participation and sometimes support from multiple Catholic women's religious communities. Although the bulk of these ministries are located either in the Midwest or on the East Coast, every region of the United

States is represented, as are some parts of Canada.[6] (A listing of these earth ministries is provided in the section of this book entitled "Critical Mass.")

A Green Blade Rising

For centuries, women religious have periodically created movements to reinvent and reinvigorate religious life.[7] The culture of green sisters is arguably one of these movements. During more than a decade of studying green sisters and their ministries, I have come to know contemporary women religious who are radically different from the portraits of nuns in a variety of popular books. Lucy Kaylin's *For the Love of God: The Faith and Future of the American Nun* (2000), for example, opens with a scene of an aging motherhouse of feeble nuns, many of whom are confined to the infirmary or suffer from Alzheimer's disease. Kaylin depicts a very real and depressing scene of atrophy and decay, where sisters dial up Mass on their closed-circuit television sets because they are too frail to leave their rooms.[8] In remarkable contrast, I have been privy to a world of athletic, denim-clad, suntanned nuns out digging vegetable beds, pruning fruit trees, building ecovillages, launching clean-water campaigns, and celebrating planetary seasons and cycles. These are also not the nuns of the "doom and gloom" academic studies on dying religious communities.[9] Undeniably, many communities of Catholic sisters have been devastated by a lack of new vocations in recent decades, but in the process of finding new ways to reinhabit their community lands, sisters are also creating more sustainable ways to "reinhabit" the spiritual landscapes of Catholic tradition and vowed religious life.

Dominican sister Mary Ellen Leciejewski, the ecology program coordinator for the California-based Catholic Healthcare West, initiates and implements waste reduction and mercury- and PVC-free purchasing programs that mitigate hospitals' negative effects on the environment. Leciejewski observes: "Earth ministry has changed the way I think, the way I love, the way I live. I've been blessed with a lot of energy, but this has tapped a reservoir of energy that baffles me. This call beckons me to grow, search, forgive, let go, accept, appreciate, question assumptions I grew up with regarding my place in the world and my connection to all creation. I have experienced a profound calling that I dare not ignore and for which I am grateful."[10]

Leciejewski's level of energy, like that of sisters across the spectrum of this movement, is palpable and bespeaks a strong sense of spiritual renewal and reinvigorated mission, a "green blade rising" amid what other authors have characterized as the rubble of the Church after the Second Vatican Council (1962–1965), also known as "Vatican II."[11] Carole Rossi, a Dominican sister and a cofounder of Crystal Spring Earth Learning Center in eastern Massachusetts, echoes the energizing effect this movement has had in the lives of women religious: "I think it's amazing the way this consciousness has *bubbled* across women's religious congregations . . . I mean, I think this is at a time when it seems most of us would be sort of pulling in, you know, pulling the shades down and closing the back door and saying, "Well, it's all over." But there are people who are moving ahead and willing to say, "This is something important. This is what we've given our lives to." I think that's pretty intriguing."[12]

Not only is it intriguing; ultimately the way in which green sisters answer "the call of the earth"—by reinhabiting both their communal lands and the spiritual landscape of religious life—provides powerful insight into religion and culture as inherently organic, dynamic processes at work in the North American context.

Working with the Landscape: Ten Responses to the Call

Poet-farmer Wendell Berry observes: "It is the nature of soil to be highly complex and variable, to conform inexactly to human conclusions and rules. It is itself easily damaged by the imposition of alien patterns. Out of the random grammar and lexicon of possibilities—geological, topographical, climatological, biological—the soil of any one place makes its own peculiar and inevitable sense."[13] For Berry and others who subscribe to small-scale, nonindustrial cultivating methods, working with the landscape means getting to know that landscape's own composition, patterns, and propensities, then adapting one's own methods accordingly.[14] It means that before introducing new elements or frameworks, one first walks the landscape, carefully observes and gets to know it, listens to it, and then asks oneself, "What already likes to grow here?" Sustainable land-use designer Bill Mollison writes that through careful observation, one can discover important "landscape indicators"—embedded patterns and processes that demonstrate how each element of the landscape serves multiple functions.[15] Contemporary historical religious ethnography must do this as well, attending to the contours of a living landscape of religion and culture much as a biogeographer would. I have similarly tried to discern and work with the contours of the religiocultural landscape that sisters have created and continue to cultivate.[16] "Good ethnography," as sociologist Meredith

McGuire defines it, "tries to represent the voices and the meanings of the participants themselves. It attempts to derive analytical categories from the culture itself rather than impose ideas, including the researcher's scientific meanings."[17] Acknowledging that the researcher's frameworks of analysis are always in some way alien, I have looked and listened over time for intrinsic ways to talk about how green sisters are actively engaging the living and lived processes of religion and culture in order to address ecological concerns.[18] As it turns out, this is not a movement that lends itself to one overarching analytical model; instead it is best described with a multiplicity of interlocking models that reflect the movement's own complex and varied dimensions.

As I have come to know green sisters better and to learn more about their movement, ten major categories of "response to the call of the earth" have organically emerged. Each one functions on a variety of levels and simultaneously takes on cultural, spiritual, and topographical significance within the context of the movement. These ten categories of response become most apparent within the seven focused areas that make up the main chapters of this book: greening the religious vows (Chapter 2), ecologically sustainable living as daily spiritual practice (Chapter 3), the reinhabiting of Western monasticism (Chapter 4), ecological food choice and contemplative cooking (Chapter 5), sacred agriculture (Chapter 6), seed saving (Chapter 7), and the "greening" of prayer and liturgy (Chapter 8). Each one of these chapters demonstrates how one or more of the following ten conceptual categories of response have been translated by green sisters and put into practice "on the ground," both in their personal lives and in their public ministries.

1. "Telling the Story" Overwhelmingly, the most visible theoretical influence on the green sisters movement has come from the work of the Passionist priest Thomas Berry.[19] His work is indispensable to understanding the growth and development of an ecological ethos among green sisters in North America. In *The Dream of the Earth* (1988); *The Universe Story* (1992), a later work coauthored with cosmologist Brian Swimme; and more recently, *The Great Work* (1999), Berry argues that contemporary environmental destruction is symptomatic of a culture that no longer possesses a "functional cosmology."[20] For Berry, a functional cosmology is one that, by providing a meaningful sense of the nature of the universe, helps us know who we are, where we are, and what our relationship is to the created order.[21] Building on comparative religionist Mircea Eliade's classic premise that, cross-culturally, cosmology provides the central and fundamental psychological and conceptual orientation that undergirds all major institutions in a given society, Berry champions a conscious shift in cosmology as the best strategy for the kind of global cultural transformation that would solve our environmental problems.[22] The telling and retelling of the creation story through performance and ritual, Eliade argues, is a critical means of affirming, transmitting, and reinforcing a collective ontology (philosophy of the nature of being).[23] Berry similarly emphasizes that it is the telling of the origin story of cosmic evolution, emphasizing its sacred dimensions, that will establish, affirm, and reinforce a collective notion of cosmic communion or interrelatedness of all things.[24]

As a disciple of the French Jesuit paleontologist and theologian Pierre Teilhard de Chardin (1881–1955), Berry contends that the Western philosophical divisions between religion and science and between humanity and creation must be mended by recognizing the cosmic evolutionary epic as the sacred story of our time.[25] The Genesis story of Jewish and Christian traditions, argues Berry, has failed to provide modern humanity a sense of communion and kinship with a universe that is alive, sacred, intelligent, and still being created.[26] He also finds that Western science's evolutionary narrative, when told in a context detached from spirituality, fails to capture the intrinsic mystery and sacredness of the cosmic evolutionary process. "What we have to understand," says Berry, "is that the scientists are correct in their data, but wrong in their interpretation. The universe is a psychic-spiritual reality from the beginning, as well as a physical-material reality."[27]

Berry, who describes himself not as a theologian but as a "geologian," speaks of the need for a common creation story that understands the human not only as an intimate part of a sacred, evolving universe, but also as the being in whom the universe has become conscious of itself.[28] A failure of cosmology, argues Berry, produces the ultimate crisis in identity. To know who we are, he says, we must know where we are. Like children, says Berry, "we've become lost, adrift in a society that has lost its guidelines, its rudder," and it is this loss of guidelines that has had dire consequences for the life systems of the planet.[29]

Berry's prescription for regaining that rudder is for those peoples who have grown away from the planet, and who have forgotten their fundamental connection to the mystery at the heart of the universe, to begin "telling the story." (Berry primarily directs this message to Western cultures and exempts indigenous peoples of the world, who presumably practice earth-based traditions that conceptually imbed the human in the natural world and whose worldviews recognize sacred interrelationships among all living things.)[30] Berry explains that "at the present time we are in between stories. Since our traditional creation story no longer carries meaning for many people, we need another story that will educate, heal, guide, and discipline us, just as the Genesis story once did."[31]

This "new" story, handed down from cosmological physics and evolutionary science (yet infused with a message of the mystical oneness of the cosmos) has resonated strongly with religious sisters who are now bringing this "gospel" to others through their ministries. Indeed, many green sisters speak of their mission to bring to others the "New Story": to create centers for exploring it; to experiment with ways of putting its principles into practice; to teach it to children; to build communities for "living" it; to create art, music, and rituals that celebrate and describe it; to develop ways of producing food in harmony with it; and so forth.[32] Sisters frequently begin talks, workshops, discussions or interviews with the obligatory "First, I want to say that I am indebted to the work of Thomas Berry," or "I want to acknowledge Thomas Berry as having provided the context for what I'm about to say," or "Immediately, I should clarify that here at our center, we are operating out of the insights provided by the 'New Story.'"

In fact, at various times, I would ask sisters about their own work and accomplishments, and immediately they would refocus the conversation on what a powerful prophet Thomas Berry has been and on all that he has done on behalf of the earth. In more than a few cases, I have asked a sister what she thought of a particular issue, and she has answered me by asking if I have read Thomas Berry's new book. At first, I interpreted this phenomenon solely in terms of devoted female followers sacrificing their own voices in favor of a male leader or prophet. I eventually realized, however, that part of this refocusing of the conversation might be tied to the "culture of humility" among sisters, in which one deflects attention from one's own accomplishments and praises those of others. Undeniably, however, it has also communicated to me what a pivotal role Berry's philosophies have played in the development of this movement. Drawing from Berry's message of the power of cosmic narrative for effecting cultural transformation, green sisters have taken up the dual mission of both telling the "New Story" and putting that new story into action.

In my interviews with green sisters, there were those who also cited other key sources whom they credit with having helped to catalyze and crystallize their own growing ecological awareness and activism on behalf of the earth. These sources most frequently include Dominican sister Miriam MacGillis, a disciple and important interpreter of Thomas Berry within the green sisters movement. In fact, more sisters listed MacGillis as the primary source for first introducing them to the "New Story" and awakening them to environmental concerns than listed Thomas Berry. (Contact with MacGillis's work through audiotapes, articles, workshops, or retreats made at Genesis Farm garnered thirty-three mentions out of sixty-five, whereas Berry's work was cited as the first point of entry into greater environmental awareness nineteen times.) As a student of Thomas Berry, MacGillis is still transmitting and interpreting Berry's work, but she and other sisters are also contributing their own unique interpretations, which they have developed after applying his principles on the ground. (In the case of green sisters' sacred agriculture, this is literally so.) Sisters also mentioned others influential to their growing ecological consciousness, such as theologians Sallie McFague, Elizabeth Johnson, and Ivone Gebara; ecofeminist Charlene Spretnak; Sisters of Earth cofounder Sister Mary Southard; earth activist and futurist Sister Paula González; Jesuit priest Al Fritsch; antiradiation activist Sister Rosalie Bertell; and Indian physicist-philosopher Vandana Shiva.[33]

In their history *The Transformation of American Catholic Sisters* (1992), Lora Ann Quiñonez and Mary Daniel Turner point to ample survey research demonstrating that ideologically, American sisters are by no means a monolithic group.[34] And even though the influence of Berry's work is widespread within the movement, I want to stress that green sisters are also not a monolithic group—some describe themselves as feminist and others specifically do not, some are vegetarian and some are not, some are more politically liberal, others are more conservative, and still others challenge both those political terms and refuse to subscribe to either. Some align themselves with Berry's philosophies, and others prefer to glean inspiration elsewhere. That diversity is honored by Sisters of Earth, the major network of green sisters in the United States, even as the network itself recognizes what Sisters of Earth organizer Mary Ellen Leciejewski, a Dominican sister, calls "common ground."[35] In her video documentary of the same name, Leciejewski shows that even across diverse communities of women religious there is a recognition that the earth is in trouble and that there are ways that sisters can work together to answer this call. The theme of "telling the story" as one means to answer the call continues to appear in various forms throughout green sisters' ministries, and I conclude this book with a look at the role of story and prophecy as they relate to the possibilities for green sisters' own continuing story.

2. Companion Planting   I first learned about "companion planting" from organic-farming sisters who explained this technique by which organic growers interplant species that possess special affinities; the proximity of one plant to the other ultimately strengthens both. Unlikely combinations, such as cabbage and mint, and potatoes and horseradish, as it turns out, display traits or properties that harmonize well with one another and help both plants to flourish. Apparently, carrots love tomatoes. Who would have known? Some plants put back into the soil nutrients that other plants extract, thus creating a symbiotic relationship. Because companion planting reduces the need for fertilizers or pest control, it is especially prized by organic gardeners. In effect, the gardener interplants diverse species in such a way that the design itself, although it may appear arbitrary, actually possesses an internal logic directed toward creating a healthier and more sustainable garden overall.

When I first learned about companion planting, I was trying to map out all the different theological, ideological, and social movements that sisters responding to my interviews had credited with influencing their thought and practice. The confluence of American Catholic liberalism, liberation theology, perspectives from Berry and de Chardin, feminism, the Grail movement, the women's spirituality movement, the Second Vatican Council, Creation-Centered Spirituality, the Catholic back-to-the-land movement, the peace and social justice movements, the civil rights movement, the Catholic Worker Movement, the Catholic rural life movement, aspects of neotraditionalist movements, mystical and meditative practices from the Middle Ages, and renewed interest in monasticism, environmentalism, natural foods cooking, organic farming, world hunger, and food security—in addition to many other elements—was staggering for me to behold. How, I wondered, might sisters' participation or simply their interest in these movements have helped to "prepare the soil" for this most recent development? And how did all of these elements make sense together, if they did? I kept asking sisters about the Catholic Church, social movements, and the effects of the reforms brought by the Second Vatican Council, and they did speak about these things, but they also kept talking to me about "earthy" matters such as organic gardening, sustainable agriculture, companion planting, and composting. I read the books they suggested to me on organic gardening, and over time I myself began to see the religious culture that sisters are currently cultivating in terms of gardening, with the tangible acts of planting and composting helping to articulate the sisters' philosophies and worldviews.

I began asking what made the legacies of some social movements grow well together in the newly created culture of green sisters and why. What made some unlikely combinations of elements "work" in the context of green sisters' ministries? What affinities are there between certain varieties of "green culture" and varieties of American Catholicism? Conversely, which "old" and "new" varieties do not grow well together and why? How do sisters deal with aspects of Catholicism and environmentalism that are not a "natural fit," and how do conflicting or even hostile combinations get resolved, if indeed they do? What creative solutions do sisters devise? And are "transplantations" necessary when certain combinations fail? What historical elements have given rise to and nourished the green sisters movement in North America at this particular time, and what elements provide obstacles or inhospitable conditions to its existence and growth? What are some of the tensions between top-down institutional greening efforts and grassroots greening efforts?

In Chapter 1, using "companion planting" as a framework for discussion, I situate the contemporary movement of green sisters within the broader context of the American cultural landscape, attending to the affinities and conflicts inherent in sisters' cultivation of greener varieties of religion and culture.

3. Reinhabiting Earth, Religion, and Culture   Reinhabiting the landscape is another theme that pervades green sisters' earth ministries and community-supported farms. "To reinhabit" is a phrase used by bioregionalist environmental philosophers to signify a process of relearning how to "live in place."[36] Adding to this definition, earth activist Stephanie Mills says that bioregionalism also "holds up the hope of learning to live more lightly on the Earth, of developing communities integrated in their local ecosystems—creaturely associations that can carry the lifesome ethic forward through generations."[37]

Bioregionalists view reinhabitation as a primary means to make that hope manifest.[38] Instead of abandoning and "moving on" from a certain geographic region, no matter how damaged that place has become, one instead makes the conscious decision to stay in place, to repair the damage that has been caused there, and to devise ways to make that place habitable in a way that is more ecologically sound. In essence, then, reinhabitation is about staying home and "digging in" where you are; it is the antithesis of using up local resources and then moving on to colonize anew.[39] As green sisters dig in and commit to reinhabiting Catholic religious life rather than moving on, they are also devising new and greener ways of "living in place."

Drawing from the theoretical work of historians of religion Jonathan Z. Smith and Charles H. Long, Thomas Tweed identifies religions as "ongoing cultural processes whereby individuals and groups map, construct, and inhabit worlds of meaning."[40] If so, then green sisters work to reinhabit their worlds of meaning as they physically reinhabit their surrounding landscapes. In Chapter 2, I focus on the ways in which sisters are reinhabiting the framework for the vows of religious life by espousing a more ecologically conscious context for the vows while also greening the content of those commitments. In Chapter 3, I consider this notion of reinhabitation inasmuch as it is made manifest in various greener daily practices adopted by religious sisters. The data presented in these two chapters point toward a few perhaps unexpected insights, such as that the intense challenges demanded by ecologically conscious living actually infuse new energy and commitment into religious life. Because "it isn't easy being green," answering the call of the earth demands real sacrifice, which constitutes part of its appeal.

Discussion of reinhabiting daily practices leads into an examination of the comprehensive ecorenovation of the motherhouse of the Monroe, Michigan–based Sisters, Servants of the Immaculate Heart of Mary (Monroe IHMs).[41] This section of the book delves into the simultaneous spiritual and physical transformations that are occurring in one community as sisters reinhabit their motherhouse. The outside structure of the motherhouse has largely remained the same, but the interior has been transformed into a model of ecologically sustainable living. As the IHM sisters continue to remodel their motherhouse into a greener dwelling, they describe their building as a visible sign of their commitment to answering the call of the earth.

4. Modeling Sustainability   The term "sustainability," as it is used by environmental philosophers, denotes the actual human use of natural resources at a rate or volume of use that does not outstrip the ecosystem's capacity to renew and replenish those natural resources.[42] On a very simple level, "sustainability" is the opposite of depletion. As green business entrepreneur Paul Hawken defines it, sustainability is about leaving the world a better place for future generations by not using up the earth's resources.[43] David Orr's work on sustainability adds the dimension of a "careful meshing of human purposes with the larger patterns and flows of the natural world, and careful study of those patterns and flows to inform human purposes."[44]

By living lightly on the earth and consciously harmonizing their ways of life with nature's ways, green sisters have made "modeling sustainability" a priority in their ministries. The Monroe, Michigan, IHM sisters, for example, as part of their long-range plan, will create what they call a "center for modeling sustainability."[45] Chapter 3 also contains examples of other earth ministries in which sisters model for others how humans can live in true communion with creation. The ministries partner with their surrounding communities to build with renewable materials like straw, implement renewable energy source heating and cooling systems, and practice agricultural methods that renew instead of deplete the soil. In doing so, they have also created a new, energized context for the commitments and challenges of vowed religious life. That is, as ecological sustainability has become a part of daily spiritual practice, and sustainable ways of life have become a form of spiritual discipline, sisters in effect have consciously created what is for them a more sustainable religious life—one that is constantly being renewed and replenished and is consequently depleting neither to the spirit nor to the life systems of the planet.

An examination of the new Green Mountain Monastery in Chapter 4 highlights the ways that the traditional charge for Western monastic communities to "model the Kingdom of God" has been rediscovered and adapted to the charge of modeling ecological sustainability. Green sisters who are monastics deftly draw on the Benedictine tradition, in particular, to guide their sensitive relationship with the land, their renewed appreciation of stability of place and community, and their efforts to lead balanced lifestyles that consume few of earth's resources.

Chapter 5, which begins with a window into the sacramental food culture of the green sisters movement, highlights how practicing sustainability has become a rich medium for contemplation, communion, and a daily creation-centered practice. More than any other aspect of the movement, the food culture of green sisters has been central to their harmonizing of internal and external landscapes. Sisters' innovative rituals surrounding food choices, preparation, and consumption reflect an ideological "healing" of the divisions between both matter and spirit, and body and earth.

5. Cultivating Diversity and Biodiversity   Specifically identified by the Texas-based Santuario Sisterfarm as one of that community's central and sacred tenets, "cultivation of diversity and biodiversity" is another common ideal put into practice in sisters' earth ministries across North America.[46] In Chapters 6 and 7, I consider the connections between the actual work performed in sister's organic-farming ministries and sisters' active cultivation of a new religious culture. How, for instance, might the relationships that green sisters negotiate with the institutional Church change as the sisters cultivate a new relationship with the land and as they come to new cosmological and ecological understandings of Christianity and traditional Catholic teachings? How are contested meanings negotiated between what constitutes life-giving tradition and what constitutes sustainable spiritual practice?

First, I examine notions of "sacred agriculture" and the gender dynamics involved in recasting farming as a kind of "priestly practice."[47] Second, I look at the manifestation of an ecological diversity ethic within sisters' farming practices as they reject industrial "monocropping" (planting one uniform crop across a wide range of acres) in favor of fields bearing a "pluraculture" of diverse interplanted species. In Chapter 8, I consider the possible connections between championing biodiversity in agriculture and the active combination of eclectic ecumenical elements embodied in sisters' greening of public and private prayer.

6. Conserving "Heirlooms"   The theme of conservation is often connected to the work of nineteenth-century conservationist John Muir (1838–1914), who fought against mining and deforestation and for the preservation of America's wild lands.[48] It is in this "Muirian" sense that green sisters speak about themselves as "conserving" and as being "conservative."[49] For instance, Sister Miriam MacGillis, a key prophet and teacher within the green sisters movement, remarks, "Each year, I become more and more conservative. I want to conserve more and more."[50] Other sisters have used similar language when discussing the conservation of habitat, farmland, or heritage seeds through their ministries. Put another way, sisters do not "give ground" to interpretations that might cast their efforts as being radical or extreme. For example, from an ecologically conservative perspective, "extreme" would describe allowing untested genetically modified organisms to permeate the food chain with unknown results, "extreme" would describe testing how far humans can deplete the ozone layer before triggering the direst effects of global warming, and "extreme" would be standing by as the planet experiences the largest extinction of species in the Cenozoic era. Taking action to redress each of these problems and others like them, however, is viewed as both prudent and ideologically conservative.

Political theorist Andrew Dobson declares, "Green thinkers like to define their political position as 'beyond left and right,'" and the rhetoric and practice of green sisters indicate a similar effort to transcend conventional ideological categories.[51] Conscious conservation of various "heirlooms" of vowed religious life (albeit in modified forms and greener contexts) does bespeak a kind of conservativism. Elements of monasticism, mysticism, spiritual discipline, more challenging rules of religious life, an emphasis on sacrifice for the larger community, geographic stability, fasting and food restrictions, chant, contemplative labor, and even (in some cases) the wearing of ecologically friendly religious garments, all are enjoying a renaissance in a new ecologically aware religious culture being cultivated by green sisters. There are, of course, some aspects of religious tradition that have not been conserved. Aspects of Catholicism that are regarded as not being "life giving"—for instance, patriarchal norms, abuses of hierarchy, notions of humans' divinely sanctioned right (or indeed mandate) to dominate and subdue the earth, and associations of women's bodies with sin, to name a few—are permitted to pass away, much in the way that, in sisters' organic gardens, the death of diseased vegetation makes room for new and "healthier" growth.

In fact, sisters' complex combinations of traditionalist and progressive political and lifestyle approaches make categorizing the movement along conventional notions of "left" and "right" a challenge. Author and Sister of Our Lady of Sion Mary Jo Leddy has sharply criticized what she has called "pluralism without purpose" in contemporary religious life in North America. She has instead advocated "loosening the bonds of liberalism" in order to reweave and repair religious life.[52] But one would be hard-pressed to apply Leddy's definition of "liberalism" to the green sisters movement. The green sisters have neither returned to a traditional (that is, pre–Vatican II) way of religious life in North America nor abandoned traditionalism altogether in favor of radical pluralism; instead they have chosen a third and alternative path that integrates parts of both the preconciliar and postconciliar cultures. As sisters retrieve, conserve, and then reinhabit (in greener ways) aspects of Catholic religious life that precede the Second Vatican Council, they continue to defy ready-made political boxes. Thus, throughout this book, I trace the motif of "heirloom seed saving," examining the ways in which sisters negotiate the tensions between conserving "heirlooms" from the past while supporting the interplanting of new and old in the present.[53]

In Chapter 7, which features an heirloom seed-saving ministry run by religious sisters in Canada, I explore the ways that sisters are creating "seed sanctuaries" to protect nongenetically engineered seed stock, while also identifying themselves as "seed keepers of the heirlooms of the Catholic Church," particularly its mystical and creation-centered traditions. Inherent in sisters' harmonizing of internal and external landscapes are, of course, the tensions between the dynamics of conservation and preservation versus "natural" evolutionary changes in faith, community, belief, and practice. As sisters work to reconcile simultaneous commitments to honor both tradition and change, we see the creative process of religious meaning-making in action.

7. Providing Sanctuary   One of the analogies used throughout the green sisters movement is that, much as monasteries in Europe provided haven for the classical texts during the Middle Ages, ultimately enabling their rediscovery in the Renaissance, sisters today are providing sanctuary to myriad threatened species during the dark times of genetic engineering and rapid habitat destruction.[54] In addition to following Noah's lead by providing "botanical arks of biodiversity" for nonpatented seeds (the genetic "classics" of our time), green sisters' ecological centers, organic gardens, and communal lands conserve open space, which provides a safe haven for wildlife.[55]

In response to the creation of the federal Department of Homeland Security, Miriam MacGillis countered in a fall 2002 letter to the friends of Genesis Farm that every being has a fundamental right to "homeland security." Adapting this phrase from the nationally patriotic context to the planetary context, she wrote: "Every being needs a homeland on this fragile, loving planet, which, in this solar system, appears to be the only homeland that exists and upon which all smaller regional homelands depend . . . conserving the commons, supporting local communities and economies, rather than incurring debt, waste, and contamination, is the cornerstone of patriotism, both regionally and globally."[56]

The practical planning involved in providing such homeland security is discussed in a section of Chapter 3, where I discuss sisters' involvement with land trusts. Specifically, I examine how efforts to shelter needy "refugees" of all species by preventing the development of community lands bears parallels to sisters' involvement with the sanctuary movement of the 1980s that provided refuge to those fleeing the political and economic violence of Central America.[57]

Exploring a variety of the meanings of "sanctuary" brings to light the role played by sisters' earth ministries in providing sanctuary to those who fundamentally disagree with the dominant capitalist consumer culture in North America. As green sisters work with surrounding communities, their gardens, ecology centers, and common lands become refuge for those who have be-

come disenchanted with the "American Dream" and the planetary consequences of unchecked wealth accumulation and unlimited progress.[58] Attracted by sisters' own countercultural lifestyles, earth liturgies, and larger
commitments to earth concerns, different groups of laypersons have linked
with women's religious communities.[59] As volunteers, cooks, farmers, event
organizers, and shareholders in community-supported gardens, neighboring
community members have not only sought spiritual sanctuary at sisters' earth
ministries, but also become part of an extended ecumenical community that
helps support and extend the reach of sisters' efforts. Green sisters are thus
creating integrated spaces to bring together religious sisters with what American religious historian Martin Marty has called "countercovenanters"—those
who have historically challenged the dominant covenant made by America, a
covenant they view as obsessed with unlimited production, achievement at
all costs, and national superiority. Marty says that historically, countercovenanters—many of them Transcendentalists—urged that Americans "make
contracts with nature, produce only what harmonizes with it, achieve without
grim competition."[60] In the broader context of earth ministries, green sisters
(practicing their own countercultural lifestyles) and neighboring contemporary "countercovenanters" come together to pool labor, strategies, prayer, and
educational and financial resources, all in the service of a common call.

8. Celebrating the "Cosmic Liturgy"   One of the key areas where green sisters put various ecotheological philosophies or ecospiritual principles into
practice is liturgy. This is yet another place of integration where sisters worship together with laypeople. Regarding terminology, I should mention that
when I was wording the questions for the electronic interview with green sisters, two sisters suggested that I use the term "public and private prayer" in
place of "liturgy" or "ritual." They explained that "liturgy" connoted "Church,"
and "ritual" sounded too much like it might be associated with New Age spirituality or something like Wicca. When I use the word "liturgy" in the context
of religious sisters, I use it in a nonecclesiastic context to refer to regular, cyclical, and usually communal public or private prayer performed by sisters.
When I use the term "ritual," it is in the context of places and times when sisters themselves have referred to their public or private prayer as "ritual," as in
Sisters of Earth conferences, where "morning ritual" is listed in the conference
program.

In this book, I feature four major kinds of liturgy created and celebrated by green sisters. The first is the diurnal "cosmic liturgy" of dawn and dusk as marked in special ways through both body prayer and spoken word.[61] The second is the set of seasonal "cosmic liturgies" of solstices and equinoxes, when many green sisters observe and celebrate as holy events the celestial cycles of the sun, earth, and moon. The third kind is the body of liturgies that retrace and mark the "universe story," celebrating major events in the course of cosmological evolution and the connection of both individual and community to a common cosmic origin. The fourth kind of liturgy is performed at special community gatherings, such as the Sisters of Earth conferences. In these special liturgies, sisters celebrate the universe story, recognize the oneness of humans and the cosmic community, and affirm and solidify the community of green sisters as they seek to serve the whole life community. Integral to the creation of these new ritual expressions is the sisters' goal of establishing new forms of spiritual observance that embody a dawning era of an integrated human-earth-cosmic consciousness. In Chapters 3 and 5, I also discuss sisters' daily prayerful practices of food preparation and consumption, conscientious water use for bathing and washing dishes, conscious cleaning with nontoxic compounds, and other mindful expressions in the practice of everyday life. Once again, the power of many of these expressions lies in sisters' ability to conserve spiritually resonant frameworks of Catholic liturgical and contemplative traditions while infusing those traditions with "greener" content. Sisters' innovations in prayer and liturgy reclaim a kind of pre–Vatican II delight in a "liturgy of the senses" and in the powerful spiritual substance of symbol and image, while still bringing worship into what they identify as a new prophetic moment. When faced with the modernist choice between the intellectual and the rational versus the mystical and embodied, green sisters have chosen both.

9. Creating Space for New Growth   Using an image that would likely delight philosopher Gilles Deleuze, some green sisters have invoked the metaphor of "rhizomes" to describe the decentralized quality of their work on behalf of the earth.[62] The rhizome is a classification of plant that propagates horizontally by sending out a network of multiple shoots and lateral branches just under the soil's surface. As explained by Gilles Deleuze and his colleague Félix Guattari, one of the basic characteristics of the rhizome—examples of which include iris, ginger, pachysandra, and couchgrass—is its ability to embody both multiplicity and unity. It is part of a common yet heterogeneous network.[63] Although the rhizome is strong and tenacious, its strength does not emanate from a central source; instead it comes both from its organic decentralization and lateral structure, which provide it with flexibility, and from its ability to adapt quickly to new conditions. That green sisters have adopted the image of the rhizome as a metaphor for their movement poses a striking contrast to the centralized, hierarchical "taproot" power of the institutional Church.

Part of the power and productivity of rhizomes lies in their ability to re-inhabit damaged spaces—train tracks, vacant lots, and stripped land. Rhizomes transform such places, loosening hardened, inhospitable soil and making way for the softer shoots of new plants. Rhizomes thus aerate the soil with their system of offshoots and make room for a diversity of new species to plant themselves. Yet rhizomes also conserve the soil, holding it in place with lateral networks of roots that prevent erosion. Similar connections can be made between the image of rhizomes as they grow in the ground and that of the growing network of green sisters as they continue to extend their lateral, decentralized network.

Deleuze points to a distinctive and important feature of rhizomes. Unlike the single central taproot of a tree, rhizomes have "multiple entryways."[64] These entryways mean that not only can the rhizome draw sustenance and support from a multiplicity of sources; it is also part of an open system, perpetually in process of becoming and reconfiguring along the lines of varied schemata. Lacking the strength, size, or vertical stature of the tree, the rhizome instead draws advantage from the diffusion and mutability of its structure. And unlike a tree, which is vulnerable to an axe taken to its trunk, the rhizome is particularly difficult to uproot and eradicate.[65] Deleuze and Guattari remark that "a rhizome may be broken, shattered at a given spot, but it will start up again on one of its old lines, or on new lines."[66] Thus one can pull up one visible part of the rhizome, or even remove all its visible parts, but seemingly never quite eliminate its subterranean network. In other words, rhizomes are tenacious. Regardless of ruptures in various lines, the network itself continues and simply extends around the broken spot to expand further. In fact, ironically, rather than weakening the network, destroying visible manifestations of the rhizome simply stimulates new growth.

In the Conclusion, I consider what sort of obstacles this movement of green sisters might face in the years ahead and how the movement's rhizomorphic structure might or might not work to the sisters' advantage. How might sisters continue to balance tradition and change, orthodoxy and experience, institutional authority and grassroots practice, as they face new challenges?

10. Living the Vision   A fundamental faith in the power of the prophetic imagination for effecting positive planetary transformation pervades the work of green sisters. Drawing inspiration from Thomas Berry's vision of the "Great Work" and Buddhist antinuclear activist Joanna Macy's vision of the "Great Turning," among others, sisters have consciously embarked on a collective journey into a new way of being. For Berry, the Great Work of our time is for humans to turn away from a "Technozoic" era of ecological destruction and despair and to turn toward a new "Ecozoic" era, in which human beings live in harmony with the natural world.[67] Joanna Macy similarly envisions the transition from an "Industrial Growth Society" to a "Life-Sustaining Society" as our only truly viable path into the future. She prophesies that "when people of the future look back at this historical moment, they will see, perhaps more clearly than we can know now, how revolutionary it is. They may well call it the Great Turning . . . While the agricultural revolution took centuries, and the industrial revolution took generations, this ecological revolution has to happen in a matter of a few years. It also has to be more comprehensive—involving not only the political economy, but the habits and values that foster it."[68] As religious sisters cultivate green habits, they commit themselves to "living the vision" of this new mode of being. Berry's conviction that shared dream experience, collective stories, and artistic and scientific visions will lead the planetary community out of a destructive relationship and into a mutually enhancing one has become integral to the very foundations of these sisters' ministries.[69]

I conclude this book by considering sisters' use of the power of prophecy and their potential efficacy in extending the lateral reach of this movement into otherwise ecologically unreceptive areas of American culture. Jon Butler writes that "heterodoxy is crucial to understanding both Americans and Catholics."[70] Does the prophetic imagination of green sisters have the potential to garner significant appeal beyond Catholic religious orders? And if there is potential for successful wider evangelization, what then are the implications of the broader cultural and even ecological effects of this movement? And as sisters increasingly respond to the call of the earth, what will be the institutional response? Will the sisters' movement reap greater approval and recognition by the institutional Church? Will religious women's dedication and service to the planetary community be touted as "good news" about publicly vowed members of the Church restoring goodwill at the grassroots level, offsetting some of the recent scandal and shame brought about by those in the male hierarchy? Or will sisters' greater successes necessitate increasingly delicate negotiations with the hierarchical Church? I explore both the potential demise and the potential survival of the green sisters movement should an authoritarian backlash occur.

Corresponding Landscapes: Ecospiritual Mimetics

In planting earth ministries across the North American landscape and growing a new way of life in their own spiritual backyards, green sisters are contributing something unique to the work of putting theory into practice. They may draw from the work of Thomas Aquinas or Thomas Berry, Pierre Teilhard de Chardin or Vandana Shiva, but in their practice they show themselves to be anything but "passive receivers."[71] Sometimes sisters prune from overarching theories or theologies those elements that are not deemed useful or "life-giving" on a practical level. At other times, they generate new combinations of elements that help abstract theories take root and thrive in real-world contexts. In essence, green sisters' earth ministries are the "test plots" for concepts and perspectives from ecospiritual philosophy. To use Michael Taussig's term, sisters "tangibilize" their combined inheritance from Catholic religious life, American intellectual thought, contemporary spirituality, and environmentalism.[72] On an experiential level, they find out what works and what does not and then proceed to make necessary readjustments. In their earth literacy centers, community-supported gardens, and ecologically sustainable ways of life, we see green sisters putting the authority of experience into action.

A close look at sisters' approaches—to liturgy and the daily nature of vowed religious life, to cultural tradition and religious heritage, and to the cultivation of both land and community—also suggests the creative development of what I have come to identify as a kind of "ecospiritual mimetics." In other words, there are dynamic correspondences between the spiritual and biophysical landscapes, which green sisters seek to harmonize. "Mimesis" simply refers to the phenomenon by which cultural forms, such as art and literature, mimic life. There is a similar mimetic quality to the evolving culture of green sisters, in which the spirituality and ways of life of ecologically minded sisters embody the earth's own patterns of diversity, pluraculture, planting, conservation, renewal, and growth.[73] Sisters' "green" ideals and values reflect their spiritual ideals and religiocultural values, which in turn are reflected in their ecologically sustainable practices made manifest on the physical landscapes of their communities. Valuing and cultivating "biodiversity" on their lands, for instance, becomes integral to a spiritual life that also honors diverse elements of "earth wisdom" from a variety of religious traditions. The bioregional ideal of reinhabitation, that is, of staying in place (stability) and finding new and more sustainable ways to live in that place, is also reflected in green sisters' commitment to stay with Roman Catholicism but to find new ways to live with, and within, its traditions. Similarly, as green sisters model sustainability by incorporating more ecofriendly practices into daily life, they also strive to create a more ideally sustainable or renewable religious life in both its external and internal dimensions. In many ways, green sisters' mission to heal and restore the life systems of the planet parallels the split between spirit and matter in Western philosophical consciousness that sisters themselves already seem to have "healed" within their own consciousnesses.

The Roman Catholic Church has a long history of being energized by those who challenge and extend its boundaries.[74] Even if temporarily vilified, grassroots movements such as the one that has been launched by green sisters are often later embraced and touted as examples of the Church's vitality and relevance. Cultural theorist Susan Mizruchi writes: "Religions are, by definition, 'polythetic' as opposed to 'monothetic': they are amoebas not clams, which is to say that their survival depends on their capacity for transformation and incorporation, to borrow, influence, and be influenced, to maintain coherence in the face of diversity and crisis."[75] As green sisters explore ways to maintain coherence in the face of increased cultural diversity and ecological crisis, the historical movement they have created merits our keen attention. In their harmonizing of institutional and personal authority, in their transformation and conservation of religious symbol and practice, in their reinhabitation of tradition and everyday life, and in their mystical embrace of both cosmic unity and multiplicity, these North American Catholic sisters provide unique and rich insights into the intersections of women, religion, ecology, and culture.

1. THE GREEN CATHOLIC IMAGINATION

Varieties of Companion Planting

It is Sunday morning, August 4, 2002, at the fifth annual international conference of Sisters of Earth in Holyoke, Massachusetts, and about 150 women are gathered together in two concentric circles, waiting to begin the morning ritual. At the center of the circles, a multilevel altar has been constructed to the "Great Mystery" at the heart of the universe. Brightly colored scarves of fiery reds and yellows are draped across several platforms, which are covered with symbols of the evolution of the earth and cosmos and with corresponding symbols of the unfolding of human history. Atop the very highest riser sits a large blue sphere representing the earth. It is flanked by lower risers containing prayer beads, a blue ceramic chalice, and a bowl of water, along with various forms of the four elements—earth, air, water, and fire. Fossils and shells, flowers and leaves, dried braided grasses and rocks are intermingled with symbols of the ancient cultures of the world and cross-cultural images of the divine feminine. The entire altar is surrounded by candles, and a white cord spirals out from the altar itself, marking the major evolutionary events in the history of the cosmos. At one of the long ends of the altar, there is a large icon of the Virgin Mary situated between a bouquet of flowers and a prayer candle. Entitled "Mary as Cosmos," the icon shows Mary bearing the earth and cosmos inside her womb.[1]

The ritual itself begins with chanting, prayer, and meditation and leads into liturgical dance, more chanting, and colorful dramaturgy, all of which express in a sensory and bodily active way the mystical oneness of creation. There is a colorful processional collage dedicated to the community of life, featuring whales, wolves, geese, and polar bears, among other creatures. An "all-species" dance celebrates the sacred interconnections between the human community and the larger community of life. Among the various chants included in the liturgy, sisters sing, "There is one breath. There is one life. There is one Earth.

Room set up for opening ritual, 2002 conference of Sisters of Earth.

There is one chance. All is holy, so holy. All is sacred, so sacred. All is one."[2] As the liturgy draws to a close, themes and images of cosmic oneness take a less abstract and more practical form—volunteers with clipboards form stations where participants are invited to approach (if they choose) and sign their names in support of the "Earth Charter," an international declaration on environmental protection, human rights, peace, and equitable human development that has been proposed for endorsement to the United Nations General Assembly.[3] Long lines form at each of the stations as sisters "walk their talk" by signing the petition. As they do, they sing their spiritual intention by repeating, "Reverently, consciously, compassionately, I want to walk, I want to live within the Earth community."[4] Finally, the morning ritual concludes with the "Ecozoic dance," a simple circle dance of embodied prayer for the transition of the life community to an era when the human species ceases to be a destructive force on the planet and becomes instead "present to the planet in a manner that is mutually enhancing."[5]

In 1993, Mary Southard, a Sister of St. Joseph of La Grange, Illinois, and a few other Roman Catholic religious sisters concerned about ecological devastation founded a decentralized network called Sisters of Earth.[6] In reading and responding to this statement about the network's beginnings, Southard qualified my use of the word "founded" and offered more organic language to describe the beginnings of Sisters of Earth, saying, "It was more like noticing a seed, and planting it, and seeing it grow."[7] Out of this seed planted by Southard and others, Sisters of Earth held its first international conference in 1994 at St. Gabriel's Monastery in Clark's Summit, Pennsylvania. Fifty women attended that first year, but at the next Sisters of Earth meeting in 1996 at Grailville in Loveland, Ohio, twice as many sisters attended. The 2002 meeting in Holyoke attracted nearly 150 Sisters of Earth members, although the actual number of sisters actively affiliated within the network is more than double that number.[8] In an effort to minimize the effect of travel miles on the environment, the network rotates its meetings among different regions of the country, making the composition of attendance mostly local. (Participants do, however, come from as far away as the Netherlands, Nigeria, and the Philippines.) Sisters' communities or ministries will sometimes fund one representative to attend the conference; she will then brief others back home on new information gleaned from seminars, discussions, and activities. This minimizes both cost to communities and the amount of fossil fuel burned in order to connect with others in the network. Still other connections between Sisters of Earth are conducted largely via e-mail exchanges, and my study has purposely made use of that lively network of communication.[9] Not all green sisters are members of Sisters of Earth, but many of them are, and the network itself is one of the more visible manifestations of the larger movement of ecologically active religious sisters in North America.

The Sisters of Earth biennial conferences serve, in particular, as gathering sites where sisters (and a few laywomen) can share information, ideas, and a common spiritual sense of earth's sacredness. A section of the conference called "Sharing the Wisdom" features reports from different sisters' earth ministries, followed by an open-microphone period during which sisters involved in many different forms of earth activism—such as organic farming, land trusts, antitoxics work, ecojustice, ecorenovation, farmland renewal, food safety, heritage seed conservation, earth literacy education, and ecospirituality—can network with one another. Mary Southard, Toni Nash, and others involved with Sisters of Earth have stressed the "informal nature" of the network and its aim to provide support and informational resources for ecologically concerned sisters (and some laywomen) "without becoming yet another centralized hierarchical institution."[10] There is no headquarters for Sisters of Earth, no president, and no central leader. The rhizomorphic configuration of Sisters of Earth comprises a lateral grassroots network that is noninstitutional, nonhierarchical, nondogmatic, and egalitarian; its rotating facilitation replaces fixed positions of authority. Although there is a rotating conference-planning committee, it issues no policy statements and does not require that members adhere to a particular set of tenets. Before the close of the 2002 conference, however, the membership of Sisters of Earth voted to send a letter on behalf of the network to the Leadership Conference of Women Religious of the USA (LCWR), encouraging the LCWR to focus its next national assembly on an environmental theme.[11]

In contrast to Sisters of Earth's smaller-scale network of several hundred sisters, the LCWR membership comprises more than a thousand elected leaders (principal administrators) of religious orders who represent about 76,000 Catholic sisters in the United States. To play upon Mary Southard's imagery, if Sisters of Earth is a new "seedling," then the LCWR can be considered a mature, hardy plant. Originally founded in 1956 under the title "Conference of Major Superiors of Women," the organization received canonical status by decree of the Vatican in 1959, maintains a strong governing structure, and remains the major recognized national body for collaboration and dialogue among Catholic women's religious congregations. LCWR Executive Director Carole Shinnick (SSND), a School Sister of Notre Dame who administers the

LCWR national office, shared the Sisters of Earth letter with the National Board of LCWR during the planning process for the 2003 assembly, and the conference that emerged indeed focused on ecology.

Themed "Tending the Holy," the 2003 National Assembly met in August in Detroit, where nine hundred sisters from across the United States took up issues of earth, cosmos, creation care, ecojustice, and ecospirituality for discussion, prayer, and collaborative action. The LCWR assembly invitation and literature publicizing the conference bore a logo containing an icon of planet earth with the words "Tending the Holy" below and a stream of water underneath the title. A preassembly field trip took LCWR members to the Servants of the Immaculate Heart of Mary Sisters in Monroe, Michigan, where the "IHMs" are involved in a total "ecorenovation" of their motherhouse and surrounding lands. A follow-up workshop discussed the process of sustainable construction, building reclamation, and ecorenovation, building on the Monroe IHMs' model. Other workshops covered topics such as permaculture (a kind of sustainable agriculture and landscape design), ecospirituality, creation, and the cosmos, and even a session on the same "Earth Charter" that had been a program feature at the Sisters of Earth conference.

The opening ritual of the assembly included prayers offered by representatives from each of the LCWR's fifteen different regions. Each sister presented a symbol of her bioregion as she made her prayer of petition.

Region one (Connecticut, Maine, Massachusetts, New Hampshire, Rhode Island, and Vermont):

> That like the cranberry plant, which takes its name from the crane—a bird of peace, we draw nourishment from the balance and harmony of the earth, that we bear fruit that brings the gifts of unity, healing and peace to our world, we pray . . .

Region two (New York):

> That we commit ourselves to do all that we can to insure that the poor and most vulnerable have access to this precious gift of clean water both now and for future generations, we pray . . .

Region three (New Jersey and eastern Pennsylvania):

> That just as our rivers have their own life and also flow into the greater sea, we may be vibrant as the Hudson, the Delaware, and the Susquehanna as we flow out to God's people. That we may be refreshed by winter snows and summer showers and pool into the great Atlantic of peace, we pray . . .

Region four (Delaware; Maryland; North Carolina; western Pennsylvania; South Carolina; Washington, D.C.; and West Virginia):

> That our efforts for a sound ecology blossom for the people and all of created life that is found in Region 4, a place rich in beauty with its mountains, Great Lake, ocean coasts, forests, Appalachian trail, large municipalities, small cities, farms, villages, and the capital of the United States, we pray . . .

Regions five through fourteen continued to pray for things such as "bayous free of contaminants so that all life in them may flourish and give glory to God," respect for Native American land rights, all those suffering from problems of polluted air, the restoration of the life-sustaining waters of the Rio Grande, and the commitment to live in harmony with all creatures. The representative sister from Region Fifteen—which includes Alaska, Idaho, Montana, Oregon, and Washington—concluded with the following prayer: "That by tending to our contemplative practices, we may be empowered to leap towards YES and be like salmon who, against all obstacles, follow an internal force that compels them to swim upstream to birth something new, we pray . . ."[12]

Cranberries and cranes, salmon and air-pollution sufferers, rivers and bayous, mountains and oceans; it may be fairly easy to dismiss the importance of the relatively smaller gatherings of groups such as Sisters of Earth and their prayerful invocation of earthy images, but it is much more difficult to deny the pervasiveness and significance of a "greening" movement among U.S. Catholic sisters when themes and prayers such as these take center stage at the major national gathering for leaders of women's religious orders. In her presidential address to the assembly, "Tending the Holy through the Power of Sisterhood," Mary Ann Zollmann, a member of the Sisters of Charity of the Blessed Virgin Mary, spoke of sisters' "aching for creation, salvation, and resurrection" and of her own intimacy with the earth, an intimacy she identified as born of the realization that "we women religious are living out of and growing more deeply into an ecofeminism that is a communion of companionship, responsibility, and accountability to the whole web of life."[13] In the spirit of such communion and responsibility, LCWR members—like Sisters of Earth members—focused not simply on prayer but also on practical action. Among the resolutions to action proposed by the LCWR Global Concerns Committee following the 2003 assembly was a commitment by women's religious communities to replace old failing automobiles (once their lifespan had come to an end) with high-efficiency, ultra-low-emissions, hybrid vehicles. Making this shift from being, as one of the committee publications phrased it, "dominators of creation" to "participants in a cosmic story" takes on a profound sacred dimension in the committee literature, and this theme is repeated throughout conference proceedings and publications.[14] Much like the Sisters of Earth conference participants, LCWR members combined public prayer, ritual, and reverence for creation with practical ecological strategies and measures that leadership could carry back with them to their communities. Throughout the LCWR assembly, sisters also repeatedly sang a unifying chant that called forth their collective purpose and resolve to communion, commitment, and responsibility: "Sacred is the call, awesome indeed the entrustment. Tending the Holy. Tending the Holy."[15]

Preparing the Soil

There is a popular chant sung at Sisters of Earth conferences, green sisters' earth literacy workshops, and in the context of public and private prayer at Catholic ecology centers: "Everything before us has brought us to this moment / Standing at the threshold of a brand new day." What are some of the things that have brought sisters to this moment? What has created a hospitable environment today for the germination and growth of Sisters of Earth and the larger green sisters movement? How might some historical movements have "prepared the soil," as it were, for the more than fifty earth ministries run by religious sisters that now dot the North American landscape? How have the changes to the religious lives of Catholic vowed women in North America over the course of the twentieth century, and into the first years of the twenty-first, contributed favorable conditions to the newly formed culture of green sisters? And how have a variety of historical currents in the history of American Catholicism and American culture helped to shape the religious imagination of green sisters, even as they themselves now shape the North American religious landscape? Drawing from a gardening approach called "companion planting," favored by organic gardeners in general and used by organic-farming religious sisters, provides a fertile framework for looking at how sisters combine varieties of Catholicism, contemporary spirituality, environmental thought, and "green culture."

In her now classic book, *Carrots Love Tomatoes: Secrets of Companion Planting for Successful Gardening* (1975), Louise Riotte reveals what she calls "the magic and mystery" of companion planting that has "intrigued and fascinated humans for centuries."[16] By studying the various properties of plants and how they positively or negatively react with one another, contends Riotte, a gardener can design and plant a multipurpose community of life that is both strong and functional. The keys for Riotte are diversity, intensive interplanting, and compatibility. "The upright leek finds room near the bushy celery plant," advises Riotte, and "radish will grow extra well and especially tender near lettuce."[17]

Before discussing the actual implementation of such a design, however, Riotte points to the critical role played by a succession of cover crops for creating a milieu conducive to the new planting project. Alfalfa, she confides, is one of the most powerful nitrogen-fixers of all legumes and can take 250 pounds of nitrogen per acre from the air each year. A good crop of rye, continues Riotte, will choke out chickweed, creating ideal soil conditions for strawberries.[18] Preparing the soil, then, is important for creating conditions that encourage new growth and an enriched medium from which new plantings can draw sustenance.

Several historical movements and developments might be similarly credited for having "prepared the soil" well for the seeding and growth of the green sisters movement. Certainly the Sister Formation movement of the 1950s may be recognized as having helped to create a pool of religious women better educated, more confident in their intellectual capabilities, and trained in the arts of critical thinking. This movement, which pushed for greater time and support for religious sisters' education, succeeded in keeping young sisters from teaching in schools until they had completed their bachelor's degrees. Today, religious sisters are some of the best-educated women in America, and the group of green sisters I interviewed for this book, with their multiple advanced degrees, reflects that status.[19] Together, the establishment of the Sister Formation Conference in 1953, and the creation three years later of the group that would later become known as the LCWR, fostered an environment of greater collaboration among women's religious communities. The creation of intercommunity initiatives and cooperation within LCWR strengthened bonds and communication among communities, redressing the relative isolation that the women had previously experienced.[20] Early LCWR assembly themes, such as "revitalization of religious life," enabled religious women to engage in collective examination of and reflection about their ways of living and knowing. Once they were able to share information and ideas, women's communities could focus on addressing particular issues and problems, providing organizational and planning support for one another.[21]

Dominican sister Mary Ewens recounts that by the time Pope John XXIII convoked the Second Vatican Council (October 11, 1962–December 8, 1965), sisters were more than ready for it. "As the various documents appeared," she writes, "sisters read them eagerly and discussed their implications with growing excitement." When communities were specifically asked to "renew their lives by returning to the charisms of their founders, studying the signs of the times, and reflecting on ways of living gospel values in the contemporary world, they set about the task with great seriousness of purpose."[22] The "aggiornamento" or "bringing up to date" of Vatican II resulted in Church reform and renewal. It also created a tremendous opening for a reexamination of religious life, especially by women's communities, which eagerly seized this opportunity. As several primary-source accounts tell us, this intense period of questioning and reassessment surrounding Vatican II was exhilarating for some, although traumatic for others.[23]

The profound effect that the women's movement and other social justice movements had on women's congregations also opened channels for sisters' questioning of dominant social structures, cultural paradigms, gender relations, and dynamics of power and authority. In a variety of ways, these movements have created fertile ground for the growth and development of Sisters of Earth and the larger movement of green sisters. Chris Loughlin, of Crystal Spring Earth Learning Center in Plainville, Massachusetts, reflects that it took all the activist movements in which sisters have been involved to build the foundation for the new ecological awareness that is flourishing today. Loughlin says, "We experienced the Civil Rights Movement, the Anti-War Movement, and certainly the Women's Movement . . . So our lives became *practiced* at bringing about change through personal experience and through communal experiences."[24]

In 1968, the widely reported clash between the Immaculate Heart of Mary (IHM) Sisters in Los Angeles and the incumbent archbishop of the Archdiocese of Los Angeles, James Francis Cardinal McIntyre, over reforms related to contemporary dress, religious life, and governance (reforms that are now routinely accepted) brought to light increasing tensions between sisters' greater shift toward self-governance and the control asserted by male Church authorities.[25] In 1970, rather than repeal the changes that had already been approved by their general chapter, 90 percent of the almost four hundred IHM sisters requested release from their vows and reformed into the "Immaculate Heart Community," an ecumenical community of laywomen.[26] In 2000, thirty years after this incident, the Immaculate Heart Community hosted the Sisters of Earth conference at La Casa de Maria interfaith retreat center located on the community's property in Santa Barbara, California. As sisters from all over North America and from as far away as Africa and Europe met together under the community's California live oaks, there was a fitting connection between those who had stood their ground on matters of conscience nearly a genera-tion ago and those who are now standing their ground on matters related to the life systems of the planet.

In the span of three decades, of course, the religious landscape has shifted. During the 1980s and 1990s, for example, there was a popular "rediscovery" and valuing of contemplative life and monasticism in American spirituality. Various musical recordings of monastic men and women in chant gained tre-mendous popularity, such as *Chant: The Benedictine Monks of Santo Domingo* (1994), produced by Angel Records. In the same year, another of Angel's re-cordings, called *Vision* and featuring the music of twelfth-century German nun Hildegard of Bingen (1098–1179), spent fourteen straight weeks at the top of *Billboard*'s chart for classical crossover music. In 1996, Kathleen Norris's *The Cloister Walk,* in which the South Dakotan poet and author re-counts her experiences as an oblate in a Benedictine monastery, became a best seller. Spurred in part by the success of Norris's book, monasteries have now become popular vacation destinations, with many visitors now booking res-ervations more than a year in advance.[27] Much as trends in American spiritu-ality in the 1960s were marked by a turn toward the East by those seeking countercultural alternatives, so current trends point to a turning back toward the West to revisit sources of mysticism and spiritual gnosis from medieval Europe (as read, of course, through the lens of the present). Interest in such things as the use of labyrinth-walking from the Middle Ages as a "spiritual tool," particularly the use of replicas of the design imbedded in the floor of Chartres Cathedral in the twelfth century, has made its way into Catholic sis-ters' communities as well as into a variety of Christian churches across North America.[28] A bumper crop of discussion groups devoted to American Trappist monk and mystic Thomas Merton (1915–1968), an icon of American reli-gious thought for more than thirty years, has also sprung up on the spiritual landscape in the past decade, as new monographs on his work continue to feed a growing audience.[29] Merton shares this attention with rediscovered Eu-ropean Catholic mystics, particularly women mystics such as Hildegard of Bingen, Julian of Norwich (ca. 1342–ca. 1420), and Mechthild of Magdeburg (1212–ca. 1299).[30] There are monastic soup books, recipe books, and even dog-training books.[31] And in 2002, a *New Yorker* magazine article was devoted to the little-known "underground" of U.S. monastic cheese makers.[32]

While much of this fascination with monasticism could be dismissed as merely "trendy," for women who are actually living the vowed life on a daily basis, the greater receptivity in American culture to things both mystical and monastic has affirmed their reconsideration and revisiting (on sisters' own terms and in differently situated contexts) of many of the aspects of Catholic religious life that were "modernized" in the process of Vatican II updating. As a young nun in 1976 grappling with the then Renewal movement in religious life, Patricia Lucas wrote in her diary, "God, when Mother Loretta Theresa reads this she is going to think I flipped, but somehow I have to make her realize that we must be women of vision, not clinging to the old, beautiful ways of the past but rather seeking the precarious new and frightening path that will lead us into the 21st century."[33] Now, in the twenty-first century, green sisters seem to embrace the paths of both tradition and innovation.

The legacy of sisters' activism during the 1960s and 1970s to the green sisters movement becomes apparent as one traces the personal histories of women now active in Sisters of Earth. For example, in Ann Patrick Ware's *Midwives of the Future: American Sisters Tell Their Story* (1985), Sister of Loretto Maureen McCormack described the 1960s and 1970s period of reexamination and renewal in sisters' communities as a turbulent but exciting time, a process of uprooting and rerooting that changed religious life forever. McCormack recounts her own experience:

> Now we were marching in the streets, going to jail, creating our own liturgies, designing our own jobs, living in Third World countries, becoming radicalized, challenging the institutional church and making headlines. We prayed in our rooms instead of the chapel, did our yoga, Tai Chi and Zen sitting, used a mantra and spontaneous prayer. We were fasting in order to highlight injustices, giving homilies in church, working against the Vietnam war, counseling draft resisters and cheering the Berrigans [antiwar activist priests]. Some people were calling us communists. We socialized with men, gave retreats, called ourselves feminists, held press conferences, promoted women's ordination, criticized the U.S. Government, rejected our middle-class upbringing, wore jeans, gave workshops, associated with hippies and read questionable books and articles.[34]

Today, McCormack is both an active member of Sisters of Earth and a founding member of the Loretto Earth Network, a group begun by the Sisters of Loretto in 1991 that engages in earth study, educational programs, and activism on behalf of the planet.[35] McCormack is still reading "questionable books and articles," although now she does so on slightly different topics. A former Loretto Community president for eight years, McCormack, who holds a Ph.D. and is a practicing psychologist in Colorado, was a featured presenter at the 2002 Sisters of Earth conference. McCormack shared with other Sisters of Earth her training in the "Natural Step," a process created by Swedish cancer researcher Karl-Hendrik Robert for promoting ecological sustainable decision-making in the realms of government, business, health, and community planning.[36] As I hiked in the mountains of Vermont with McCormack and a handful of other Sisters of Loretto during a visit to the Green Mountain Monastery in July 2002, McCormack stopped to appreciate plants along the trail, and her face lit up as she spoke about the great work of bringing about a time when humans will live sustainably and harmoniously with and within the life community. Navigating steep slopes in a plain pair of sneakers (I wore hiking boots and still found the terrain tricky), McCormack was a long way from "marching in the streets," but her perseverance and resolve toward this latest mission appeared no less strong.

Like McCormack's history, Dominican sister Carol Coston's life journey also shows how sisters' involvement in movements for peace and social justice have prepared the soil for their current involvement with issues of ecojustice and environmental sustainability. Coston was the cofounder and first director of Network, a Catholic social justice lobby founded by forty-seven Catholic sisters in 1971. Often referred to as "the peace movement's voice on Capitol Hill," Network's mission is to lobby for a social, economic, and political order that, according to its literature, "supports and builds political will to develop a just, participatory and sustainable world community."[37] Back in the mid-1980s, Coston wrote an account of the ways in which the post–Vatican II renewal had affected her life: "The whole painful and energizing renewal process which led us Adrian Dominicans to critique every part of our congregational life—rule, constitutions, original charism, customs, works, history, relationship with the hierarchical church—led me to reject much that was no longer valid or life-giving and to reaffirm or discover anew other aspects."[38] Today, Coston is cofounder and codirector of Santuario Sisterfarm, an ecological learning center, organic farm, and women's sanctuary in the Texas hill country dedicated to "cultivating diversity: biodiversity and cultural diversity."[39] The community describes its mission in the following way: "Santuario Sisterfarm inspirits the work of transforming human relationships with Earth and among ourselves, by moving from dominance to co-creative partnerships, drawing on insights from wisdom traditions, nature, the new science, and women's ways."[40] By creating Sisterfarm, Coston and cofounder Elise D. García, a former vice president of Common Cause who in 2005 entered the Adrian Dominican Sisters' novitiate, have strengthened their commitment to peace and social justice for the human community but have continued to cultivate this commitment within a context in which justice for humans and justice for the whole earth community are inextricably linked.[41]

Although there are many points of entry into the green sisters movement—from social justice and peace activism to agricultural issues—the effect of the women's movement, in particular, on women's religious congregations created an acceptable environment for questioning the relationships of power, authority, and hierarchy. By inviting opening and change in the 1960s and 1970s, women religious did in fact, as Ann Ware has said, "midwife" the future. Their work ultimately "prepared the soil" for places such as Genesis Farm, Crystal Spring, Santuario Sisterfarm, and the Green Mountain Monastery to grow and flourish.[42]

Feminism's critique of mechanisms of domination and oppression in its various forms easily lent itself to discussions of human domination of the earth. When the green sisters I interviewed ranked from most important to least important the issues that called forth their commitment to earth concerns, "feminist concerns" ranked last (behind, in descending order of importance, concerns about peace and justice, world hunger and food supply, and poverty and globalization).[43] This is not to say that feminist concerns were unimportant to those I interviewed, only that they felt other issues were more important or pressing. As I mentioned earlier, some of the "talking back" in responses to my interview questions told me that, for some women, ranking these things "didn't work for them." Others filled in the rankings but then wrote below their response that they thought "all" of these things were important. And one sister declined to rank their importance because they were "all connected" and she found listing them as separate (and "hierarchically ranked") issues to be a false construction on my part. In face-to-face interactions, a few sisters made a point of specifying that they do not identify with the label "feminist" per se or consider themselves to be ecofeminists. In other contexts, such as the Sisters of Earth conferences or the 2003 LCWR National Assembly, the term "ecofeminism" has been readily and comfortably used to characterize green sisters' perspectives on the environment, as in Sister Mary Ann Zollmann's aforementioned 2003 Presidential Address, in which she spoke of women religious growing more deeply into ecofeminism.

Whether or not individual green sisters choose to identify themselves as feminist, ecofeminist, both, or neither, the green sisters movement itself has foundationally benefited from the infrastructure, sensibilities, pathways for questioning, and language introduced into women's congregations through both the renewal process and the women's movement. Nourished by this fertile soil, women's congregations have become ripe for today's "greening" environment.

The Legacy of Catholic Rural Life

In August 1996, the National Catholic Rural Life Conference (NCRLC) issued a publication entitled *Religious Congregations on the Land: The Practical Links between Community, Sustainable Use, and Spiritual Charism,* which features thirty-one case studies of Catholic religious communities involved in some kind of ecologically sustainable land use.[44] Of the eighteen primary case studies, fifteen featured women's religious communities that have specifically created earth ministries such as earth literacy centers, ecojustice centers, ecological learning centers, ecospiritual retreat centers, or community-supported organic gardens. One community featured, the Franciscan-sponsored Michaela Farm in Indiana, had even put into place an "office of sacred agriculture." Only three of the communities featured in the case studies are Catholic men's religious communities, and, although the men's communities reported involvement in efforts to manage their lands more sustainably (better management of timber harvesting on their lands and reducing the need for mowing on their grounds were two cited examples), none of the men's communities listed had created ecological learning centers or related earth ministries.[45] The shorter case studies in the same publication feature the work of a dozen communities involved in additional earth ministries, but none of these communities is headed by male religious. Rather, all have been founded and continue to be administered by sisters.

At the 1998 conference of Sisters of Earth in Sinsinawa, Wisconsin, Sandy LaBlanc, then director of communications for the NCRLC, stood up at the open-microphone portion and instructed: "Take a good look at where the women religious are today, and that's where you'll see the Church ten years from now."[46] From organic farmers to food safety advocates, and from earth literacy educators to those involved in setting up land trusts, green sisters and their ministries have in part had the opportunity to take root and grow because of the space created for such ministries by the NCRLC, the Catholic back-to-the-land movement, and the experimental ethos created by the Grail movement in the United States.

Founded in St. Louis, Missouri, in 1923 by Father Edwin O'Hara, the National Catholic Rural Life Conference is an organization made up of bishops, priests, and laypeople. Historically, the NCRLC has been an advocate for Catholic agrarianism, bringing attention to the plight of the small farmer, placing ministries in rural areas, and providing education to rural Catholics.[47] In 1923, O'Hara passionately preached his conviction that "the farmer pursues the most fundamental, the most dignified profession in the world."[48] O'Hara was convinced that there was something intrinsically virtuous and salubrious for the spirit about the farming life, remarking how "the hearts of the people in the fields were naturally open to God."[49] Sixty years later, Genesis Farm founder Sister Miriam MacGillis wrote: "If we were to accept the Earth on the terms and under the exquisite conditions in which it continues to evolve, the role of the farmer would be raised to a most honorable and sacred human profession. Relieved of the illusions that they are manufacturing food, or that they are worthy of success to the degree that they are also economists, cosmeticists, and managers, farmers might understand themselves as acting in something akin to a prophetic and priestly role."[50]

In 1927, NCRLC president Father W. Howard Bishop publicly championed farming as a sacred profession, proclaiming, "Next to the priesthood there is no calling in the world so full of romance—the quality that grips the imagination and fires the will—as the profession of agriculture."[51] Bishop's 1927 address to the NCRLC championed something akin to the "earth literacy" message now promoted by green sisters and their earth ministries. Bishop advocated "nature study" as both an important cultural activity and something very practical, and he sought to cultivate "an intelligent love of the land" among Catholics, especially children. Like O'Hara, Howard Bishop also criticized the advance of big business into the rural sector and encouraged Catholics to return to the land to engage in small-scale farming as a solution to problems of poverty and unemployment.

This faith in the salubrious effects of the land was shared by Catholic Worker cofounder Peter Maurin (1877–1949), whose vision of a "Green Revolution" in the 1930s and 1940s advocated a Catholic back-to-the-land movement. Maurin argued that the escape from the ravages of industrialism lay not in socialism or sovietism but in agrarianism. He wrote: "The answer lies in a return to a society where agriculture is practiced by most of the people. It is in fact impossible for any culture to be sound and healthy without a proper respect and proper regard for the soil."[52] Just like the programs in which green sisters teach about ecologically sustainable living, self-sufficiency, and earth literacy, Maurin conceived of Catholic Worker communes as "outdoor universities" where those educated with college degrees would learn to use their hands and their heads while learning "how to build their houses, how to gather fuel, how to raise their food, how to make their furniture, that is to say, how to employ themselves."[53] Catholic Worker farms would thus be places of labor as well as arenas for study and the exchange of ideas.

In the 1930s and 1940s, the NCRLC fueled an energetic wave of Catholic agrarianism and homesteading. Founded as an experiment in Catholic lay-women's community, Grailville came into being when Lydwine van Kersbergen and Joan Overboss, who established the American Grail movement in 1940, created a center for their movement in the rural Midwest.[54] Originally located in the Chicago Archdiocese, the American Grail moved its headquarters in 1944 to a large farm in Loveland, Ohio, with the encouragement of the then-executive secretary of the NCRLC, Monsignor Luigi Ligutti. Much like the centers now run by green sisters, Grailville quickly became a center for liturgical innovation, or as historian Debra Campbell has said, "a laboratory for the development of new rituals and new attitudes."[55] Early on, Grail members were referred to in the press as "silk stocking nuns," but members themselves stressed the "down-to-earth" nature of their programs and the wholesome labor of rural life.[56] Mary Jo Weaver writes that some of the most innovative books on feminist ritual were produced by Grail members.[57] Like the liturgy performed at Sisters of Earth described earlier, the liturgical experiments at Grailville combined a plurality of elements from a variety of traditions, emphasizing inclusivity and ecumenism. In her essay "Living the Liturgy: The Keystone of the Grail Vision," Janet Kalven (one of the original members of Grailville and Grailville's chief historian) describes Grailville celebrations as "created out of the old and new, drawing on traditional texts and forms and augmenting them with other spiritual wellsprings."[58] She refers to Grail members as "liturgical pioneers" who understood ritual as "the energizing transformative contact with the holy in itself and in one another."[59]

In the 1940s, liturgy at Grailville, just as the liturgies of green sisters do now, reflected a renewed interest in the medieval monastic link between work and prayer, embodied ritual, and daily spiritual practice. Debra Campbell reports that the two-week summer course at Grailville in 1943 included "sessions on liturgy and plainchant, and featured specialists such as the Benedictine Dom Ermin Vitry on plainchant and Luigi Ligutti on rural life, along with Lydwine van Kersbergen [the co-founder of the American Grail] on women and agriculture."[60] Then as now, there was an interest in unifying labor and contemplative prayer and in combining ritual innovations with the spiritual traditions of the past. After attending a two-week intensive course at Grailville in 1943, Catholic Worker Movement cofounder Dorothy Day (1897–1980) gave a report that sounds as if she had made a retreat at Crystal Spring, Michaela Farm, or the Green Mountain Monastery. Day chronicled: "We have learned to meditate *and* bake bread, pray *and* extract honey, sing *and* make butter, cheese, cider, wine, and sauerkraut."[61]

In a treatise published by the NCRLC in November 1944, Grail member Janet Kalven uses poetic imagery to communicate what would today signal themes of ecofeminism. Kalven prescribed: "Like Anteaus, the mythological hero, modern society must renew its strength by contact with the earth. Women have an essential role to play in that renewal."[62] On the porch of the old Victorian main house at Grailville in the summer of 1997, Kalven spoke with me about Grail members' early interest (in the 1940s) in organic gardening and the philosophies of sacred agriculture and biodynamic farming theorized by nineteenth-century Austrian mystic Rudolf Steiner.[63] She explained (in part because of this interest) that the garden directly outside what is now the community dining hall has been cultivated organically since its inception in the 1940s. She also spoke of how Grail members performed rituals in the fields and in the vineyards, claiming nature as their sanctuary, ritually observing the seasons and reveling in the bounty of the land. "We had a liturgical approach to rural life," recounts Kalven. "We had the idea that you understood the symbolism of the Grapevine more if you had actually pruned a grapevine."[64] Barbara Ellen Wald's 1943 essay "Grail Adventure" similarly brims with excitement about her first year with the Grail and evokes seasonal themes and imagery similar to those now found within the culture of green sisters. Wald writes: "The beautiful rhythm of the Church year with its cycles and seasons has never before had such a deep significance for me . . . [At Advent] we eagerly counted the hours until 'the earth would open and bud forth the Savior.'"[65]

Kalven also recounted that in the 1970s, Grailville—a haven for prominent Catholic liberals—welcomed the new philosophies of Thomas Berry. When I went through the Grailville archives, I immediately recognized Berry's now-famous "blue books"—the original early mimeographed installments of Berry's academic papers (before the advent of the photocopier) that were circulated to his various students, supporters, and colleagues. There was also a flyer from a 1981 workshop weekend that Berry had conducted at Grailville, entitled "The New Creation Story."[66] According to notes recorded from the weekend, the program featured a "particularly resplendent" Sunday morning liturgy, led by Berry, called "A Celebration of the Cosmos."[67] Notes from the weekend also show that "bioregionalism" was a major theme, discussed in conjunction with themes of earth, cosmic evolution, and "the ecological age."[68] What was then called the ecological age, Berry now terms the Ecozoic era (a time of mutually enhancing relations between humans and the earth), a concept that has resonated strongly in the ministries of today's green sisters.

Debra Campbell argues that the pioneering activities and programs at Grailville during the 1940s and 1950s were what created a path for later countercultural experiments and movements in American Catholic culture. It is no coincidence, then, that the second meeting held by Sisters of Earth was hosted at Grailville in the summer of 1996. The historical and cultural connections between Sisters of Earth and the legacy of Grailville are meaningful. In its most recent incarnation, Grailville is now an ecumenical retreat and learning center, rather than an intentional community, but the interplantings of women, spirituality, agriculture, and community are still evident decades after the community's founding. When invited to participate in the communal garlic shucking on the porch of the old Victorian main house (during a brutal Ohio heat wave), I joined thirty other women—some in chairs, some sitting cross-legged, and some perched on the front steps. Surrounded by thousands of cream- and purple-colored bulbs, all were laughing, talking, and telling stories. Our hands turned the shade of earth, and the perfume of garlic seemed to create a festive bond as our small paring knives and fingernails meticulously pulled and stripped away the outer layers of bulb after bulb. If not for the clothing and hairstyles, it could just as easily have been 1947 as 1997.

Compatible Plantings

A variety of movements in contemporary North American spirituality have also nourished the culture of green sisters and their spiritual expressions. In the Sisters of Earth conference morning ritual described earlier, the images of the divine feminine on the altar, as well as the colorful use of costume and dramaturgy, dance, chant, and body-active prayer in the ritual, reflect a dynamic cross-fertilization between the rise of the women's spirituality movement in the latter decades of the twentieth century and the contemporary spiritual practices of religious sisters.[69]

Sacramental objects, home altars, chants, incense, liturgical costume, sacred iconography, and performance of sacred story—elements embedded in Catholic liturgical and paraliturgical traditions—are all significant components of the women's spirituality movement.[70] Kay Turner's study of women's home altars demonstrates how Mary-centered Catholic home altars in America became important models for and precursors to goddess altars dedicated to "the Great Mother" in the 1970s and beyond.[71] Turner observes that both Catholic home altars and goddess home altars are almost always mother-centered. She finds that a common appeal for both kinds of altars has been that Mary as well as the goddess, when situated in the home (a space traditionally identified as "women's domain"), are essentially freed from the presence of a priest or other male authority. Images and objects symbolic of divine immanence, as well as objects representing the four elements—chalice (water), candles (fire), air (incense), and bread or food (earth)—are also shared by both traditions. One of the reasons such images are common to both movements is that many of those who first helped shape the women's spirituality movement were feminist women who had migrated from Roman Catholicism.[72]

Green sisters, like many other religious sisters, have borrowed back elements of their own tradition now employed by women's spirituality circles and in turn adopted some of the structural elements associated with the women's spirituality movement. Examples include the nonhierarchical liturgical configuration of the circle, in which there is no "head" and in which all participants are on the same level; the rotation of liturgical leadership tasks rather than the creation of a presiding "authority"; and the importance of women being active participants (often bodily so) rather than passive receivers in the ritual process. In the prayer and liturgy of green sisters, these egalitarian elements are combined not just with images of the divine feminine, but also with the many faces of the divine in creation (shells, rocks, flowers, food, water, fire), demonstrating a pronounced sense of Catholic sacramentalism.

Aspects of women's spirituality (with its emphasis on "women's spaces" for "women's ritual," images of divine immanence in its feminine manifestations and in various aspects of earth, a liturgy of the senses, and nonhierarchical understandings of community and power) bear a strong affinity to green sisters' own practices. Sisters' own rituals also embody ethics of social justice, nonhierarchical organizational practices, an affirmation of the divine feminine (especially through images such as the "Cosmic Mary" and "Wisdom / Sophia"), and the recognition of the sacramental presence of the divine in creation. In other words, these two movements "grow well together" as companion plantings, and that symbiosis can be seen throughout the lived practices of green sisters.

The very structuring of the 2002 Sisters of Earth conference program further reflected characteristics of companion planting. Sisters of Earth cofounder Toni Nash, a Sister of St. Joseph of Carondelet, made clear in her opening statements that the proceedings of the conference, especially the open-microphone period, would be conducted in such a way as to acknowledge the "wisdom within" each woman. In her comments, Nash went on to replace conventional distinctions at conferences between experts and non-experts with an honoring of the wisdom that each participant had to offer.[73] As each speaker came to the podium, she was blessed by the entire room of participants, who raised their arms in unison and held their hands up to her while singing, "Bless the women / Light the Fire / Share the Wisdom / Burning Deep Within."

This emphasis on honoring "women's wisdom" and the importance of sharing women's wisdom for the healing of the planet echoes mutual affinities present in the discourses of the women's spirituality movement, Christian feminist theology, and (not surprisingly) the work of Thomas Berry. For instance, ecofeminist and literary activist Charlene Spretnak (who was also the keynote speaker for the 2002 Sisters of Earth conference) has written extensively on women's spirituality and the connections among women, nature, and the sacred. Spretnak, both a Catholic and a central figure in the women's spirituality movement, has published several books on green politics, spirituality, and the environment. In the 1980s, she articulated physiological, psychological, and cultural connections linking women, nature, and wisdom in a way that was characteristic of ecofeminist discourse of the time. She wrote, "The spiritually grounded transformative power of Earth-based wisdom and compassion is our best hope for creating a future worth living. Women have been associated with transformative power from the beginning: we can grow people out of our very flesh, take in food and transform it into milk for the young. Women's transformative wisdom and energy are absolutely necessary in the struggle for ecological sanity, secure peace, and social justice."[74] More recently, such arguments (which are usually labeled as examples of "cultural feminism") have come under fire by other branches of feminism for "essentializing" women (promoting the claim that there is some universal essence to being a woman that all women share).[75] Ecofeminists, in particular, have been taken to task for asserting some sort of privileged "natural" connection between women and the earth.[76] Those who speak from a cultural feminism perspective are less concerned with deconstructing and neutralizing the differences between men and women, and more focused on valuing, reclaiming, and affirming culturally negated aspects of the feminine (however this may be defined). This branch of feminism still forms much of the philosophical basis for literature related to women's spirituality and the environment.[77] Yet despite cultural feminism's predominantly falling out of favor in current feminist theory and critique, narratives that make strong linkages among women, nature, and the ultimate destiny of the planet have struck a chord with many North American women, including green sisters.[78]

Reclaiming the "wisdom within women" and "Sophia" as an archetype of women's wisdom is also a current that runs through the work of major Christian feminist theologians such as Elizabeth Schussler Fiorenza and Elizabeth Johnson. In the early 1980s, Schussler Fiorenza's work, in particular, set about reclaiming the biblical image of Sophia or "Lady Wisdom." In her discussion of the pre-Pauline missionary movement, Schussler Fiorenza pointed to conceptions of Jesus as "prophet and child of Sophia."[79] Similarly, Elizabeth Johnson fleshed out the figure of "Sophia" as a powerful female image of the incomprehensible mystery of God, embedding Sophia in the generative life force of the planet and the cycles of the universe. "Creating and vivifying the natural world," says Johnson, Sophia "knows the ways of equinoxes, wild animals, and herbs."[80] In this way, Sophia has also become an important image for green sisters within their new ministries and communities. The first draft of the Sisters of the Green Mountain Monastery's Rule of Life, for instance, stated: "Our deepest longing lies wholeheartedly in our single hearted desire for God, in following Jesus, Icon of Wisdom Sophia as he continues to IN-BREAK [meaning "insert itself"] in our time and in giving ourselves unconditionally for healing of the Earth."[81] In her address to the 2003 environmentally themed National Assembly, LCWR President Mary Ann Zollmann used similar language, urging that "like Sophia-God, incarnated in Jesus, we set wildly inclusive tables in the household of God where our friends on the margins find a place of honor."[82] Thus, both varieties of wisdom—the notion of the internal "wisdom within every woman" and the powerful image of "Sophia" as feminine-identified mystery of God who creates the natural world—find fertile ground to take root within the discourse of green sisters.

In calling for the emergence of a "fourfold wisdom" to bring about the "Ecozoic" era, Thomas Berry lends yet another dimension to the popular discourse on women, the earth, and the sacred that has informed the culture and content of the green sisters movement. One of the wisdoms Berry believes must return to the earth is the "wisdom of women," which Berry identifies with the capacity to "join the knowing of the body to that of the mind, to join soul to spirit, intuition to reasoning, feeling consciousness to objective distance."[83] Berry makes an argument similar to that made within the women's spirituality movement. He speaks of the lost wisdom of Neolithic cultures that identified women's maternal nurturance with the primordial creating and sustaining of the universe.[84] These goddess-based cultures, writes Berry (citing the work of archeologist Marija Gimbutas) composed a cosmology of woman that was also a cosmology of mutual nurturance between humans and earth.[85] Although Berry does not go so far as to claim that these cultures were matriarchal (as some interpreters of Gimbutas's work have implied), he does point to them as having been more peaceful. Berry also asserts that the surfacing and returning of this revelatory wisdom of women found in goddess cultures must play a critical role in healing planetary destruction. His statements echo the basic arguments made by goddess spirituality authors such as Merlin Stone and Riane Eisler.[86] This recurrent prophetic narrative—that a positive outcome for the earth depends on the return of the wisdom that women bear because of their special connectedness to the earth and their capacity for greater connectedness with others—finds ideal conditions for nurturance and growth within the green sisters movement.

The Green Catholic Imagination

An evening portion of the 2002 Sisters of Earth conference, entitled "Being Earth's Imagination," was specifically designated for singing and chanting, dancing, drumming, drum making, and visual and verbal reflections. The "Catholic imagination," sociologist and Roman Catholic priest Andrew Greeley has said, is if nothing else fundamentally "sacramental"—that is, it views created reality as a sacrament that is a revelation of the presence of God.[87] What are some of the affinities between what Greeley has defined as the "Catholic imagination" and what we might call "green culture" in America, a culture that arguably can be found embedded in the notion of "being Earth's imagination"?

In combination, green culture and the Catholic imagination "grow well together" and give rise to a kind of hybrid "green Catholic imagination" that the green sisters movement exemplifies. Green culture in America can be exemplified by five core characteristics, each of which has helped nurture the "green Catholic imagination" of today's religious sisters.[88] The first is an aesthetic appreciation of the natural world that can, for example, be associated with the work of iconic figures such as landscape painter Thomas Cole, photographer Ansel Adams, or more recently through popular television shows such as *Northern Exposure* or films such as *A River Runs through It*.[89]

The second characteristic of American green culture is an admiration for the awesome complexity and functional "interconnected workings" of nature, the life community, or the ecosystem, especially as represented by such images as the "web of life." The green poet, green mystic, or green philosopher includes himself or herself in this unitive reality, in a manner reminiscent of Emerson's woodland realization that he is a "transparent eyeball," "a part and parcel of God," and that there is an "occult relation between man and the vegetable."[90] This second aspect of the green cultural imagination may also be associated with the work of scientific nature writers such as Loren Eiseley, E. O. Wilson, Rachel Carson, and more recently, cell biologist Ursula Goodenough.[91]

The third characteristic of green culture is an affective sense of the "spirit in nature," as culturally represented in the experiential narratives of figures ranging from Jonathan Edwards to John Muir, Chief Seattle to treesitter Julia Hill, and Aldo Leopold to Annie Dillard.[92] The fourth characteristic of green culture in America is an association of nature, and especially wild places, with a capacity to soothe and heal, as when poet Wendell Berry "comes into the peace of wild things," or when Emerson in the woods "returns to faith and reason" and finds that there is no calamity that "nature cannot repair."[93] This same inspirited nature also invigorates and revitalizes, as it does in the writings of Edward Abbey and Dave Foreman, or even in the images of the urban escapee or "weekend warrior" portrayed in contemporary sport utility vehicle (SUV) commercials.[94] Conversely, the absence of such regular doses of nature as "tonic" is thought to result in a weakened character in both the individual and the nation.[95]

Fifth and finally, green culture is characterized by a civic sense of the "good planetary denizen" who strives to live "the simple life," as exemplified in the American cultural imagination by such iconic examples as Thoreau's experiment on Walden Pond, Helen and Scott Nearing's homesteading "good life," and even Gary Snyder's green Buddhist asceticism.[96] More recently, the launching of popular magazines such as *SimplyCity*, which markets "life in the slow lane"; *Real Simple*, which runs articles on how to eliminate bathroom clutter and organize your linen closet; and *Simple Living: The Journal of Voluntary Simplicity* suggests that the ideal of living "the simple life" continues to have considerable resonance in American culture. Not surprisingly (and not insignificantly), the ideal of living simply also "grows well" together with religious sisters' vows of poverty and commitments to a nonmaterialistic lifestyle, as I explain more fully in Chapter 2.

The Holy Lurking in Creation

In companion planting terms, Greeley's self-described Catholic imagination and green culture share considerable affinities. The most pronounced of these appears in the area of sacramentalism. Greeley points to the imaginative ability of Catholics to see the sacred in the material world: "Catholics live in an enchanted world, a world of statues and holy water, stained glass and votive candles, saints and religious medals, rosary beads and holy pictures. But these Catholic paraphernalia are mere hints of a deeper and more pervasive religious sensibility which inclines Catholics to see the Holy lurking in creation. As Catholics, we find our houses and our world haunted by the sense that the objects, events, and persons of daily life are revelations of grace."[97] In the hybrid "green Catholic imagination," there is an affinity between the concept of a sacramental universe in which God's presence is visible in the created gifts of nature and the aesthetic appreciation of an inspired nature espoused by green culture. Both the incarnationalism that theologically unites spirit and flesh and the Catholic ethic of "sacred reverence for all life" create more ideal exchange points between Roman Catholicism and American green culture. Catholic theologian John Carmody's work provides yet another example of this exchange. He argues that the very basis of an ecological Christian theology is found in the doctrines of incarnation and creation, which "inevitably affirm the goodness of material creation, the Goodness of God himself affirmed when he gazed upon what he had wrought."[98]

The structure outlined by the U.S. Catholic Conference of Bishops' 1991 statement *Renewing the Earth,* which addresses environmental ethics in light of Catholic social teaching, also provides fertile ground for the growth and development of a "green Catholic imagination." The document embraces ethics based on the notion of a sacramental universe, respect for life, the collective planetary good, a valuing and recognition of the web of life, and a commitment to solidarity with the poor through, among other things, reduced consumption and voluntary simplicity.[99] John Tropman's *The Catholic Ethic in American Society* (1995) further suggests characteristics of American Catholic culture that may be seen as having affinity with the values and principles of the environmental movement and American "green culture."[100] In contrast to Max Weber's 1930 articulation of a "Protestant ethic" of work, wealth, achievement, and self-reliance in American society, Tropman argues for the existence of an American "Catholic ethic" that holds fewer individualistic and more community-oriented values.[101] He identifies the American Catholic ethic as one of "sharing" that "supports interdependence and communalistic orientation, and that views work and money simply as tools through which the needs of life are met." The green cultural affirmation of notions such as the web of life and the interdependence of ecosystems corresponds well with a Roman Catholic communalistic ethic and an emphasis on what Tropman calls Catholicism's "culture of cooperation."[102] Ultimately, in the green sisters movement, we see a companionable interplanting of the Catholic imagination, green culture, Catholic social teaching, and environmental ethics (which have only been partially enumerated here) to such a degree that they constitute what Louise Riotte might call a strong and functional natural partnership in which there is mutual benefit.

The Tensions of Hostile Plantings

Not all combinations, however, are so "friendly," warns Riotte. Beets, she cautions, are "turned off" by pole beans; wild mustard and kale are frequently troublesome and intrusive in oat fields; and pumpkins are perilously hostile toward potatoes.[103] Similarly, despite numerous companionable affinities, there are areas of conflict and disharmony between the institutional Roman Catholic Church and certain aspects of environmental thought and green culture. Various "unfriendly" combinations are necessarily dealt with very carefully by green sisters. For instance, the Church hierarchy's anxieties about associations between environmental consciousness (especially the environmental philosophy of biocentrism) and paganism present serious tensions and suspicions.[104] In 1989, Pope John Paul II issued his much-cited World Day of Peace message, "The Ecological Crisis: A Common Responsibility," in which he defined the ecological crisis as being categorically a moral issue.[105] This message was marked as a major shift in magisterial (official) teachings on the environment. Four years later, however, John Paul issued a condemnation of "nature worship" by feminist Catholic groups in America, highlighting tensions in the relationship of faith to nature. In a statement that communicated a distinct nervousness about currents in the United States, Pope John Paul warned that "the Christian faith itself is in danger of being undermined. Sometimes forms of nature worship and the celebration of myths and symbols take the place of the worship of the God revealed in Jesus Christ."[106]

Thomas Berry, who has played a pivotal role in the rise of the green sisters movement, has said that to achieve better relations between humans and the planet, there needs to be a shift in consciousness from an "anthropocentric norm of progress to a biocentric norm of progress." "Our challenge as humans," says Berry, is to "create a new language, even a new sense of what it is to be human. It is to transcend not only national limitations, but even our species isolation, to enter into the larger community of living species."[107] Berry recognizes a "special role" for humans on earth but stresses that humans are not separate from the earth and that the "Earth's story *is* the human story."[108]

Not everyone is as enamored of this perspective as Berry's supporters are. A November 1997 issue of the *National Catholic Register* featured a front-page article, for instance, that struck quite a different note. The headline proclaimed: "Despite Growing Environmental Threats, 'Green' Catholics Remain Few in Number." The article begins with a pro-environmental premise that there should be more "Green Catholics." In fact, the reporter wonders why, despite Pope John Paul II's "strong statements regarding pollution and conservation" made in his World Day of Peace Message on December 8, 1989, the "environment" has not become a greater issue of concern for Catholics. In answering his own question, the reporter proposes that Catholics are alienated from environmental issues not because of a lack of leadership from the church, but rather due to "a growing pantheistic, naturalistic element in the environmental movement, as well as an increasing focus on population control through abortion and contraception by many who profess to be concerned with the environment."[109] The reporter then suggests that many of these pantheistic, naturalistic dynamics may have crept into the environmental movement precisely because the Church's absence has left the door open to ideas and philosophies not guided by appropriate Christian beliefs.[110]

The same "Green Catholics" article quotes Walter Grazer, then director of the Environmental Justice Program for the U.S. Catholic Conference (USCC), who explains to the paper's readers that as the environmental movement developed, "it became easy to identify the movement with naturalism (the doctrine that all religious truths are derived from nature and natural causes and not from revelation)." In this passage, Grazer carefully identifies "nature" as distinct from "revelation" and reminds the paper's readers that regarding nature as a source of revelation "is not in accord with Catholic teaching."[111] Needless to say, Grazer's perspective does not form a "companionable relationship" with Thomas Berry's work, which casts the natural world as God's "primary revelation" and all other forms of revelation as derivative of this primary revelation.

In my own visit with Grazer at the USCC Office of Environmental Justice (which has now been absorbed under the administrative umbrella of social justice concerns), his passion and industriousness in putting out letters, green parish kits, editing books, and setting up conferences to, as he says, "get the environmental question on the map of the Catholic Church in the United States" were pronounced.[112] During our discussion, it also became evident that he cares deeply about the well-being of the environment, and that the institutional change he has worked for has required a great deal of delicate diplomacy.

From the early 1990s at the start of the National Religious Partnership for the Environment—an ecumenical coalition of religious groups addressing environmental concerns—Grazer has produced environmentally related materials for about eighteen thousand parishes. These materials provide what he calls a "sacramental, down-to-earth approach" while laying out "the Catholic case" on the environment. Grazer contends that the Roman Catholic Church is a large umbrella organization with room for diversity and variation, but in doing his job of representing the bishops and the USCC as an official body, he is meticulous about making sure anything generated from his office is both Christ-focused and human-focused. "We have a person-centered theology," he explains. "It's person-centered because God is a person, and a human person has a special role in creation."[113] In contrast, he finds figures such as Thomas Berry "too far left" to reach the mainstream of American Catholics. "He [Berry] wants to put scripture on the shelf for a while. Well, we can't do that. You can't put scripture on the shelf, at least from my perspective. I mean, that's what most Catholics and Christians, at least, struggle with—scripture. And so if you can't make scripture make sense here, we are in serious trouble."[114] Here, Grazer makes reference to Berry's suggestion that we "put the Bible on the shelf for at least twenty years and get on with reading the primary scripture which is the scripture of the world about us."[115] Grazer also warned that any hint of impropriety among Roman Catholics working on environmental issues gives license to "Catholics on the right" to launch attacks toward environmental efforts. "Then they [Catholics on the right] don't have to deal with the environment because they've labeled it as pagan," he explained.[116]

In the course of our conversation, Grazer referred to Thomas Berry as a "poet" but carefully and politely steered me away from his work. (I had specifically asked about Berry because his writings are so popular among green sisters.) In his comments, Grazer communicated that there are definite boundaries between Roman Catholic belief and practice in relation to the environment, boundaries marked by clear dangers of biocentrism, naturalism, and the kind of spontaneity that forms spiritual beliefs about nature without the guidance of scripture and Church-based authority. Grazer is not alone in his concerns, and others are not quite as diplomatic as Grazer was when he discussed Berry. Clearly Berry's work has been a major catalyst for the "greening" of Catholicism in general and Catholic sisters' mission to heal the planet in particular, but it has also been a lightning rod. The embrace of Thomas Berry as an inspirational and guiding figure by a sizable group of ecologically activist sisters does potentially pose a certain delicate political situation. Repeatedly, Berry is either dismissed or vilified by his right-wing Catholic opponents for being a "New Age guru" and a member of the so-called Catholic New Age heresy.[117] Green sisters who support Berry may dismiss such criticisms, but their own support and close association with Berry mean that they are at times confronted with similar accusations or assumptions.

When considering sisters' dealings with the Church (or avoidance thereof, as the case may be), it is important to keep in mind that they are no strangers to hostile ground, controversial combinations, or unpopular perspectives.[118] Sisters' historical involvement in peace and justice concerns, civil rights, women's rights, and antiwar efforts have given rise to an American Catholic sisterhood practiced at being what environmental author and naturalist Terry Tempest Williams calls "edge walkers."[119]

In *Tomorrow's Catholics, Yesterday's Church* (1988), Eugene Kennedy speaks to such "edges" within American Catholic culture and the line between them, arguing that there are two cultures of American Roman Catholicism, each one embodying a different notion of what faith and religion truly mean. The first culture is the "organizational culture of the institutional church," which looks to the Council of Trent for its decrees. The second is the culture of "the church as a community of vital believers." In this second culture, according to Kennedy, Roman Catholics "do not accept the controlling, authoritarian style of institutional bureaucrats as an adequate or healthy substitute for generative authority."[120] In effect, sisters walk the edge between both the culture of institution and the culture of grassroots religious practice as they continue to answer the call of the earth, providing further support for David Tracy's assertion that "the only people not afraid of the Catholic Church are Catholics."[121] And yet, in none of the interviews and in none of the encounters I had with green sisters did they display disrespect toward the Church. On the contrary, the older green sisters today are among the women who, amid the defections of the 1960s, made the conscious decision not only to stay within the Church, but to remain as publicly vowed members. The younger green sisters, who in the 1980s and 1990s were drawn to join religious orders—sisters such as former Passionist nun and current Green Mountain Monastery cofounder Gail Worcelo—also express a continued commitment to the Church.

In the formation of the Sisters of the Green Mountain Monastery, for instance, Worcelo easily could have decided not to seek "canonical status" (authorization from Rome) for the new monastery, but she did so anyway because it was important to her to work within the framework of the Church and to be recognized by the institutional hierarchy. Carole Rossi of Crystal Spring Earth Learning Center similarly balances what Eugene Kennedy identifies as two cultures, institutional and lived church, as she negotiates tradition and change. She says, "We have to recognize the tradition [Roman Catholicism] for what it is. It got us where we are, and so we don't want to haul off and say, 'I'm not part of that anymore.'" And yet, she says, "it's not going

Greening Marian cairn at Genesis Farm.

to take us into the future in the way we need to go into the future. We need a new story in order to do that."[122]

Miriam MacGillis of Genesis Farm similarly affirms the tradition of the Church while edging its living and lived aspects in new directions, saying, "I think we carry the *entire* past. We're not cutting ourselves off from the past, as though the past were wrong, and we're making an enormous corrective that disconnects us from it. The past has made it possible for us to have these kinds of insights."[123]

Up past the highest hill at Genesis Farm, tucked away at the very end of a corridor of cedar trees, stands a unique image of the convergence of tradition and change within the faith as it has been institutionalized and as it is practiced "on the ground." Nestled into the landscape at the end of the cedars, one finds a "cairn" of prayer stones surrounding a sculpted relief of the Virgin Mary. Visitors place candles and wildflowers on the rocks in front of the stone Virgin. Her upturned palms hold a birthing cloth in her hands, and her womb is filled with a triple spiral drawn from Celtic symbols. When the grasses are at their tallest in the upper meadow of the farm, one cannot find her. The subtle opening to the cedar corridor disappears and remains hidden until the grasses are either cut back or die back on their own in the autumn.

It had been a wet summer when I first discovered this cairn at the farm, so much so that a soft layer of green moss had begun to work its way up the Virgin's belly and lightly surround her halo and upturned palms. Over the course of several weeks, the greening spread. Each day that I hiked up to the cairn, more and more of her body was clad in moss, until finally all of the spirals in her belly were covered, and the Virgin sported a pea-green halo. As I touched the thin layer of green covering her belly, I found that insects had taken up residence in the covering of shallow soil and a small leafy plant had somehow managed to root itself in the stone of the Virgin's side. It is this greening cairn of Mary that comes to mind when I reflect on the various aspects of environmental consciousness, green culture, and Catholic sensibilities that "grow" well together. Green sisters have become faithful tenders of that growth as new green shoots somehow manage to embed themselves in stone.

2. STANDING THEIR GROUND

From Pioneering Nuns to Bioneering Sisters

 On April 22, 1998, Dominican sister Patricia Daly and then-CEO of General Electric John F. ("Jack") Welch, Jr. exchanged words at a General Electric Company shareholders' meeting. In this excerpt, Daly refers to an Environmental Protection Agency order that General Electric clean up polychlorinated biphenyl (PCB) contamination from its Pittsfield, Massachusetts, plant.

Sister Patricia Daly: Good morning, Mr. Welch, members of the board, and fellow shareholders. My name is Pat Daly. I am a Dominican sister, and I am here representing the Interfaith Center on Corporate Responsibility. ICCR has been raising very critical issues before U.S. corporations for almost thirty years. We represent about $90 billion of investment money.

Today, I would like to discuss the resolution on the necessity for public education about General Electric's pollution around the Hudson Valley. The Hudson River is the largest PCB spill on the planet. It is also the largest Superfund site in the country. Most of those PCBs are in the river because of the past practices of General Electric. We also have been contacted by G.E. employees in the beautiful Berkshires and along the Housatonic River watershed who are facing similar situations. This is a serious concern for people who have given their lives to General Electric and have been very grateful to be a part of the G.E. family.

Mr. Welch, we will probably never agree on the science of PCBs. We did agree last year that certainly PCB-contaminated fish should not be eaten by people along the Hudson Valley. We have asked, and we continue to ask, General Electric to work with us on a public-education program. So many people along the Hudson Valley depend on the river to feed their families. It is not common knowledge that people should not be fishing and feeding their families on a regular basis from the Hudson. So we are asking again that you join us in educating people about the hazards they face.

John F. Welch Jr.: Thank you. Before we have any more comments on this, I would like to put the company's position on PCBs in perspective for all of you.

PCB use by General Electric has always been lawful. It is critical to know that our use of PCBs, every day we ever used them, was lawful. We did not manufacture PCBs; we bought them. Starting in the 1940s, General Electric and every electrical manufacturer used PCBs in electrical equipment for a very important reason: safety. PCBs were used in capacitors and transformers to prevent fires. Government codes mandated the use of PCBs in electrical equipment. In the mid-1970s, the government changed its position and banned the continued production and use of PCBs. Your company complied immediately.

PCBs do not pose health risks. Based on the scientific evidence developed since the 1970s, we simply do not believe that there are any significant adverse health effects from PCBs. More than twenty studies show absolutely no link between workers and others with elevated PCBs in their blood, and cancer and other adverse health effects.

I want to make it very clear to all of you that we, your company, will base our discussion of PCBs, as we have for twenty years, on science, not on bad politics or shouting voices from a few activists. Science will decide this issue. Advocates can shout loudly. They can say anything. They are accountable to no one.

Daly: Mr. Welch, you are right. We are all accountable, and you know who I am accountable to.

Welch: No, I do not. I would like to—

Daly: I truly think my accountability is ultimately to God, which is why—

Welch: And I think mine is also.

Daly: I am not judging that. What I am saying, Mr. Welch, is that this is an issue of public education.

Welch: Sister, why not take public education right to the government and have them educate the public on the situation? It is not our job to educate.

Daly: It is, however. Let's get this absolutely straight. The EPA continues to list PCBs on its suspected-carcinogen list. For you to be saying that PCBs are perfectly harmless is not true. I really want our company to be a credible mover on this. We all remember the images of the CEOs of the tobacco companies swearing that they were telling the truth. Do they have any credibility in the United States today?

Welch: That is an outrageous comparison.

Daly: That is an absolutely valid comparison, Mr. Welch.

Welch: It is outrageous.

Daly: Mr. Welch, I am sorry, but we need to have the independent scientific community decide this, not the G.E. scientific community.

Welch: Twenty-seven studies, twenty-one of them independent, have concluded that there is no correlation between PCB levels and cancer, Sister. You have to stop this conversation. You owe it to God to be on the side of truth here.

Daly: I am on the side of truth. The other consideration here is that this is not just about carcinogens. We are talking about hormonal disruptions, fertility issues, and developmental problems in children. Those are real issues, and certainly those are the issues that my sisters are seeing in schools all along the Hudson River. That is exactly what is going on here.

Welch: Thank you very much for coming, Sister. Let's move on to the next agenda item.[1]

Patricia Daly's strategy for effecting greater corporate responsibility is considered in some environmental circles to be somewhat heretical. Much of the movement toward enforcing greater corporate responsibility has focused on divesting from "dirty stocks," such as timber companies, chemical and weapons manufacturers, petroleum companies, and so forth, and investing instead in "green funds" that reward more ecofriendly and socially responsible companies. Daly's approach is bold and controversial—work from within, speak truth to power, and hold enough of a stake in the institution that your message becomes difficult to ignore. Daly's organization buys stock in large corporations and then uses the power and clout of that investment to pressure those entities from within to "clean up their act."[2] Daly, who is professionally dressed and well-spoken, has become a compelling force in her capacity as a top executive with the Interfaith Center on Corporate Responsibility (ICCR). Now managing over $100 billion in investments from faith-based institutions, ICCR makes portfolio decisions that carry substantial weight. In 2002, Daly filed shareholder resolutions with both General Motors and Ford Motor Company that would require the auto manufacturers to reduce carbon dioxide emissions significantly over the next decade. She has also taken on what some environmentalists dubbed "the filthy five," the worst carbon-dioxide-polluting utility companies at that time in the United States (American Electric Power of Columbus, Ohio; Southern Company of Atlanta; Cinergy Corporation of Cincinnati; Xcel Energy of Minneapolis; and TXU Corporation of Dallas). Under Daly's direction, the ICCR has requested that these companies implement and enforce scheduled plans for reducing greenhouse-gas emissions.

What is not immediately apparent from reading the transcript of the exchange between Daly and Welch is that, despite his reference to "shouting advocates," it was Welsh who raised his voice and was ruffled that day, which happened to be Earth Day.[3] Shareholder activist Daly continued to respond throughout the exchange with an even voice resonating with steady determination. Daly has learned how to stand her ground with calm and resolve in front of some of America's toughest and most intimidating business executives. She sees her work with corporate responsibility as an integral expression of her core values as a Dominican sister and her publicly made vows. When I asked her what motivates her involvement with environmental concerns, Daly responded: "I celebrated my final vows in the context of my understanding of baptismal commitment to social and ecological justice—[and] a preferential option for the poor includes the earth."[4]

Know Where You Stand and Stand There

Like Daly, Dominican sisters Ardeth Platte, Carol Gilbert, and Jackie Hudson have also made a firm commitment to "defending the earth" through activist efforts, yet their approach differs from Daly's "work from within" strategy. On Sunday, October 6, 2002, the three members of the Grand Rapids, Michigan, Dominican congregation dressed up in toxic-waste mop-up suits labeled "Citizens Weapons Inspection Team" and cut through a chain-link security fence to gain entrance to a national N-8 nuclear missile silo site near Greeley, Colorado. Using their own blood, they painted a cross on the silo and then struck the silo with small hammers in an act of symbolic sabotage and disarmament. The sisters then held a protest prayer service and sang hymns until Air Force personnel arrived in Humvees and surrounded them with machine guns. Facing the guns head on, the sisters quietly and steadfastly refused to tell the men anything but their names. Instead, they simply carried with them a statement that read (in part):

> We, women religious, naming ourselves "SACRED EARTH AND SPACE PLOWSHARES II," come to Colorado to unmask the false religion and worship of national security so evident at Buckley AFB [Air Force Base], in Aurora, the Missile Silos, and in Colorado Springs . . . We come in the name of Truth, an-Nur, the Light. God alone is Master of Space, of the heavens that

'pour forth speech or language where their voice is not heard' (Psalms 19:2), a voice that proclaims world community, not domination of the world's economy; peace and not planning for space warfare . . . We reject the U.S. Space Command Vision for 2020 to dominate space for military operations; to exploit space as a U.S. 4th frontier, making all other nations vulnerable to U.S. conventional and nuclear attacks; to integrate space forces for warfighting; to abuse the Aleutian Islands and other lands with interceptors and spy satellites and to waste more billions and billions of dollars and more human and material resources, causing the destruction of Earth and desecration of Space.[5]

On July 25, 2003, the three sisters were sentenced in a Denver federal court to two-and-one-half to three-and-one-half years in prison and ordered to pay restitution to the U.S. government. Ardeth Platte and Carol Gilbert are both residents of Jonah House, a Baltimore community for pacifists that was cofounded by famed anti–Vietnam War activist and priest Philip Berrigan. (In a 1968 protest, Philip Berrigan and his brother Daniel Berrigan [also a priest] destroyed Vietnam War draft records in Maryland and subsequently went underground to avoid prosecution.) Plowshares peace activists take their name from the instructions in a biblical passage (Micah 4:3) to "hammer swords into plowshares that nation will not lift sword against nation nor will they ever again be trained to make war." It is this symbolism that inspired the sisters' use of hammers to "sabotage" the missile silo. In late December 2005 Platte was released from prison (Gilbert was released the previous May), and shortly afterward, in early January 2006, I spoke with both Platte and Gilbert about their actions and why they chose to call themselves "Sacred Earth and Space Plowshares." Platte replied, "All violences to the Earth and creation are connected . . . Our peace activism is deeply connected with environment in every dimension. The injury to Mother Earth is universal. And now we are doing the same thing to outer space. We are now dominators of land, water, air, and space. That's how far our greed has taken us . . . We see these things as all connected and so we named ourselves based upon this."[6]

As Platte spoke to her fellow activists the morning of her sentencing, she reassured them: "Whatever sentence I receive today will be joyfully accepted as an offering of peace. I will remain with you in prayer and walk together with you for the good of all humanity and creation."[7] Here, Platte articulates her commitment to the authority of conscience over manmade laws and affirms the call to be responsible for the good of both the human and nonhuman life of creation.

In press releases, the sisters spoke of their protest as an act of "joyful disobedience" in the spirit of their deeply held vows. According to the Sacred Earth and Space Plowshares official statement, the sisters declare that, as women religious, they "choose to open obedient ears to what justice requires: to act to unmask the heresy which equates power with violence and rejects the essential relationship between humanity and God's universe."[8] When I spoke with Gilbert, she emphasized, "We really see the connection between war and war-making, the use of nuclear weapons, and the destruction of the earth, so we do direct active resistance."[9] In Gilbert's sentencing statement, she specifically spoke of "obedience to conscience," invoking the language of the social justice documents of the Catholic Church, which instruct the faithful to uphold the law that has been "inscribed on their hearts by God."[10] She also asked that the federal judge, himself a Catholic, abide by these social justice documents. Gilbert concluded her statement by recounting a story about activist priest Daniel Berrigan, who had been asked to give the commencement address at a prestigious university graduation. Apparently, Berrigan simply walked up to the podium, declared "Know where you stand and stand there," then returned to his seat. Gilbert repeated this line for emphasis to her fellow activists before entering the courthouse to receive her sentence: "Know where you stand and stand there."[11]

Whether facing shouting CEOs, men with machine guns, federal court judges, or agribusiness companies, religious sisters "standing their ground" in the face of daunting circumstances is certainly nothing new. It was perhaps fitting that the meetings for the 2002 Sisters of Earth Conference were held in the Le Puy Room at the Sisters of St. Joseph of Springfield's Mont Marie Conference Center and Motherhouse in Holyoke, Massachusetts. Information posted in the motherhouse tells the history of the eighteenth-century Josephite sisters guillotined in Le Puy, France, during the French Revolution for defying the Law of Suspects (a 1793 law that indiscriminately identified and persecuted "enemies of the Revolution"). The sisters in Le Puy risked (and ultimately lost) their lives for sheltering persecuted clergy in their convent and encouraging popular resistance to the reign of terror. A century earlier, as historians Carol Coburn and Martha Smith point out, "In spite of a storm of opposition from church authorities and social elites, legions of Catholic women responded to the social and religious exigencies of seventeenth-century Europe by becoming religious activists."[12] Ursuline and Visitandine nuns (forerunners to the Sisters of St. Joseph) "expanded options for women religious by becoming 'active contemplatives,'" serving the poor in the community outside the convent. Later in the seventeenth century, the Sisters of St. Joseph in Le Puy administered hospitals, taught children, and provided houses of refuge for the poor. During a particularly gruesome epidemic in 1691, all of the sisters from Le Puy who were staffing a hospital in the French Alps lost their lives in their efforts to care for the sick.[13] The guillotining of Josephite sisters in the eighteenth century followed a trajectory of sisters' active service and commitment to conscience over convention. More recently, modern historians have brought to light the untold stories of nuns from a variety of orders who in twentieth-century Europe jeopardized their own safety to shelter Jews, especially children, from the Nazis during the Holocaust.[14]

Beyond events of activism and resistance chronicled in the histories of women's religious orders in Europe, sisters on the North American continent have a rich history of not shying away from desperate situations and dire need, despite threats of violence, intimidation, or personal peril. For example, in the 1830s, when able citizens fled Philadelphia during a series of devastating epidemics, it was the Sisters of Charity who stayed, entering the most disease-ridden buildings, tending to survivors, and preparing the dead for burial. Similar scenes played out during yellow fever and cholera epidemics in Augusta (Georgia), New Orleans, Indianapolis, and many other cities stricken by disease and disaster in the nineteenth century. Repeatedly, where others abandoned the most devastated locations, sisters entered the scene and stood their ground.[15]

During the Civil War, sisters again risked their lives, this time to nurse the many wounded soldiers on both sides of the conflict. During bombardments when regular medical staff fled field hospitals, the sisters continued to attend the wounded, dead, and dying. Observing the women continuing to work under fire from Union forces, a wounded Confederate soldier at Galveston reportedly remarked, "My God, look at those women. What are they doing down there? They'll get killed." To which another soldier responded, "Oh, those are the sisters. They are not afraid of anything."[16]

Accounts such as these testify to sisters' steadfast commitment to attend to the worst crises despite personal consequences, yet such characterizations also run the risk of overly romanticizing sisters, at times casting them as superhuman creatures. On the contrary, from what I have witnessed in my own research, there are indeed many things that green sisters are afraid of, not the least of which is what they recognize as the increasingly devastating effects of environmental destruction on the life community of the planet and the ramifications of the ecological crisis for all species. These activist sisters feel fear; they simply consider it an inadequate reason for ignoring need.

In the nineteenth century, frontier nuns in North America confronted violence and bloodshed of the "Wild West," often putting themselves in harm's way for the protection of ordinary citizens. Based in Colorado in 1874 and just twenty-four years old, Italian-born Sister Blandina Segale, for example, faced down a lynch mob of armed men in order to escort a prisoner across town. Two years later, having become known for her "pluck" and perseverance, she faced Billy the Kid himself and his gang to negotiate for the lives of four local doctors.[17] In the twentieth century, sisters took up different struggles but continued to face down injustice. In 1960s civil rights marches, sisters faced riot police armed with batons, attack dogs, and high-pressure fire hoses.[18] Margaret Ellen Traxler, a School Sister of Notre Dame from Minnesota, recounted her experience in the famed protest march in Selma, Alabama, during 1965: "Ten of us sisters were ushered out into the street where rows of state troopers stood with their billy clubs in front of them. We formed a line, the sisters in front all the way across the street. People began to sing freedom songs and lined up behind us. The troopers stared at us, their necks red in the sharp March winds. I think of our singing now for there was a touch of prophecy, 'No man's gonna turn us 'round.'"[19] In the late 1960s, marching in Vietnam antiwar demonstrations, sisters similarly faced state and National Guard troops who greeted them with guns and tear gas. And in the 1970s, sisters joined the struggle for farm workers' rights. Two organic-farming green sisters I spoke with from Southern California recounted their transformative experiences of sleeping on the dirt floors of impoverished migrant workers' shacks as they came to learn more about the plight of the families who lived in them. The sisters spoke passionately of linking arms with Dorothy Day and Cesar Chavez and of marching in solidarity with the farmworkers. One of the sisters still had a picture of Dorothy Day posted in a place of honor in her room.[20]

Sisters' calling to be active in social justice concerns took new directions in the 1980s but did not diminish. A watershed event for many communities was the December 1980 murder in El Salvador of two U.S. Maryknoll sisters and one Ursuline sister for their continued sympathetic stance toward "liberation theology" and their opposition to the Salvadoran government and its death squads. In 1985, religious sisters in Arizona who were active participants in the sanctuary movement (1982–1992) committed acts of civil disobedience, violating federal and state laws by hiding refugees fleeing the political violence in Central America. School Sister of St. Francis Darlene Nicgorski made the cover of *Ms.* magazine as "1986 Woman of the Year" after she was convicted in federal court of conspiring to smuggle and harbor illegal aliens. Rather than shrinking from participation in the sanctuary movement and being discouraged by the conviction, she found that it merely strengthened her resolve to continue her work counseling refugees.[21]

More recently, Dorothy Marie Hennessey and Gwen Hennessey, siblings and vowed members of the Dubuque, Iowa, Franciscan community, were sentenced to prison in 2001 for trespassing on the property of the U.S. "School of the Americas" in Columbus, Georgia. (The sisters were protesting the school's training of Central American military dictators.) This is just a small sampling of U.S. sisters who have been involved in countless contemporary protest actions at government buildings, nuclear power plants, military installations, draft boards, manufacturing sites of industrial polluters, and other significant locations.

In sociologist Marie Augusta Neal's 1989 survey of 139,000 U.S. Roman Catholic religious sisters, she found that more than 80 percent of her respondents identified "social justice as their primary mission in religious life."[22] Perhaps it is not surprising, then, that in my interviews with green sisters, "peace and social justice concerns" were the most often cited "entry points" for sisters' work in ecological activism, ecojustice issues, and earth ministries. Where once pioneer nuns stood up to the likes of Billy the Kid, now "bioneer" nuns stand their ground and confront the CEOs of giant agribusiness companies, toxic waste producers, polluting power companies, auto manufacturers, and those producing and wielding the tools of war.[23] Considering the historical involvement of Roman Catholic religious sisters in daunting causes, Daly's refusal to back down when facing former General Electric CEO Jack Welsh should be seen as part of a longstanding tradition of steadfastness and courage.

A Third Way: Both "In" and "Out"

It is important to recognize that religious sisters employ a multiplicity of activist approaches, working from within authority structures and institutions of power, or working from without, and sometimes doing both at the same time. This multiplicity also characterizes contemporary sisters' dealings with and varied relationships to authority within the Roman Catholic Church. Women have a long and rich history of functioning as what historian Mary Farrell Bednarowski calls "simultaneously outsiders and insiders" to American religious institutions. This phenomenon has arguably strengthened since the broader feminist consciousness was raised in the 1960s and 1970s, a movement that also coincided with the Second Vatican Council's profound effect on Catholic women's religious orders in North America. In the decades since Vatican II, sisters' fundamental questioning and reexamination of all dimensions of religious life and its relevance to the needs of the times has laid the foundation for the growth of the green sisters movement. According to Bednarowski, more recent trends in women's "theological creativity" and women's "growing confidence and delight in the play of religious ideas" have helped to "ameliorat[e] some of the more polarizing choices" with which women have traditionally been faced: "Be silent or get out; give up or get out; work from within or get out; be a radical (which meant getting out, usually) or a reformer (which meant staying in)." In her study of American women and religious imagination, Bednarowski finds instead that women are innovating "more subtle ways to stay in and out than had previously been supposed."[24]

Balancing the interests of both religiocultural conservation and innovation, green sisters have in effect rejected the polarizing choice between "in or out" and instead made space for a third way. In their devotion to ecologically sustainable living, earth renewal, and ecosystem repair, sisters continue to craft new definitions, terms, and meanings of religion and tradition, including meanings of "Church" as both institutional structure and "the people of God."[25] Sisters bridge conventional dualisms and integrate unique combinations of old, new, and old made new again. A particularly vital framework for this third way is evident in sisters' efforts to reinhabit the vows of religious life in ecologically conscious ways. That is, sisters work from within their location as publicly vowed members of the Roman Catholic Church to revive the seeds of ecologically friendly thought and practice embedded in their native heritage, while integrating elements drawn from outside sources.

Reinhabiting the Vows

"Reinhabiting" is a term that has been developed and theorized within the context of bioregionalism, an ecological philosophy that attends to the fundamental importance of place in human-earth relations. Bioregionalism is concerned with developing new systems of government, law, farming, commerce, consumption, education, and culture that are geared toward living and working with the features and within the resources of a particular region or place. Bioregionalists Peter Berg and Raymond Dasmann, for instance, define the practice of reinhabiting in terms of a commitment to relearn how to live in a place that has been disrupted and injured through past actions and policies. Those who set out to reinhabit a particular place work to restore its health and wellbeing, often using creative and unconventional strategies. In ecological terms, reinhabitation is fundamentally about attending to a place that has been wounded rather than leaving it behind for newer and fresher territory. Instead of becoming pioneers of new lands, those who choose to reinhabit view themselves more as "bioneers," discovering new ways to live sustainably within the local resources at home and to rectify or mitigate past injury.[26] More specifically, reinhabiting is about engaging the features of the landscape, the climate, and all the interconnected ecological variables of place in order to reshape culture and society and, ultimately, the ways of being in or relating to that place. Poet-philosopher and self-described bioregionalist Gary Snyder identifies an intrinsically spiritual dimension to bioregionalism's emphasis on a deep sense of belonging to place and "homecoming."[27] Similarly, one of the better-known and well-published female bioregionalist thinkers, Stephanie Mills, declares that bioregionalism is more than simply a philosophy; it is a spiritual practice that is about "growing a lifeway." Chosen as the keynote speaker at the 1998 Sisters of Earth international conference in Sinsinawa, Wisconsin, Mills (who is not a nun or religious sister) has cast the commitment to reinhabit as being itself both "a vow" and "a devotion."[28]

Mills drew widespread media attention in 1969, when her "barn-burning" college graduation speech at Mills College thrust her into the national spotlight. Inspired by Paul Ehrlich's 1968 sermon at Grace Cathedral in San Francisco, "The Population Explosion: Facts and Fiction," Mills addressed the relationship between unchecked human population growth and ecological crisis, publicly vowing to do "the most humane thing" she could and commit herself to a nonprocreative life—a vow that she has upheld to this day.[29] Nearly thirty years later, as Mills stood in front of an audience of Sisters of Earth, women who had each made a vow of chastity (and thus nonprocreation), there must have been a mutual understanding of what it meant to make a lifelong commitment and hold it sacred. Over those three decades, Mills's youthful commitment to the well-being of the earth and sisters' own commitment to the earth and its life communities had converged.

Today, as a growing number of Catholic sisters reexamine the vows of religious life (more formally known as "the evangelical counsels") from the perspective of a unified and interconnected human-earth story," they are reinhabiting those vows from greener perspectives. Ecologically sustainable living, for instance, has become a form of daily spiritual discipline in which vows of poverty, chastity, and obedience take on new meanings. Sisters strengthen existing frameworks of vowed religious life, while infusing those frameworks with ecospiritual content. This process of green sisters looking critically at the vows and experimenting with how the vows might be lived in ecologically mindful practice constitutes an outgrowth of what is often referred to as the Renewal movement, a reform movement spurred by the October 25, 1965, publication of the Second Vatican Council's *Decree on the Renewal of Religious Life.* In this document, religious congregations were invited to adapt and renew consecrated apostolic religious life to meet "the needs of our time."[30] In *From Nuns to Sisters* (1990), Sister Marie Augusta Neal argues that since this process of "renewal," it has become vital to understand sisters' vows not in isolation but specifically "within the context of mission."[31] The review and renewal of the vowed life continues today in various forms and shapes the emergence of new interpretations of religious life and new concepts of mission. Sisters' earth ministries, ecospiritual expressions, environmental activism, and the greening of religious life are prime examples.

"Digging In"

Sisters' vows have traditionally been considered to be the core of religious life, and green sisters maintain this core. Sisters at work in earth ministries today are those who have decided to "dig in" and reinhabit the structures and traditions of religious life and community according to what they identify as the most pressing needs of the day. Also working in today's earth ministries are sisters who have been drawn to religious life since the Second Vatican Council, sparked in some way by the rich framework and purpose offered by a spiritually motivated countercultural lifestyle. Canadian Sister of Charity Maureen Wild is just one example of a contemporary religious sister who has placed her perpetual (lifetime) vows in the context of planetary commitments and a deepened consciousness of the sacredness of creation. Here is an excerpt from Wild's vows upon becoming a recognized permanent member of her religious community, the Sisters of Charity of St. Vincent de Paul, Halifax, Nova Scotia, on August 5, 1990. Note how she casts each of the traditional vows within the broader context of earth, cosmos, and creation.

> Loving Mystery of Life
> you whose presence pervades the natural world
> in the grandeur of the universe

and the splendid modes of earth's expression,
I am impassioned by your divine revelation in all of creation
through the faith of my parents.
I was covenanted closely with you in the mission of Jesus
through the waters of life in Baptism.
I desire to remain faithful to your presence
working through me.
Loving God, today I, Maureen Ann Wild, profess my love
for you through perpetual vows.
I profess a life commitment to poverty
by striving to become more and more creatively simple in my living;
learning to live appropriately within the limitations
of the earth-life process.
I profess a life commitment to chastity
acknowledging the sacredness of my own relational, sexual being
and desiring to relate to all of life as sacred.
I profess a life commitment to obedience
by listening to the needs of life within and around me
and responding with my gifts.
Sister Louise, I ask you to accept these vows that I make
according to the Constitutions of the Sisters of Charity
of St. Vincent de Paul, Halifax.
I have professed myself to them publicly as a member of this congregation.
I believe that the living of these counsels is about the death it takes to create
　　life;
that they are essential to the mission of bringing about the reign of God.[32]

In preparation for her final vows, Wild made clear her intent to dedicate herself freely in service not simply to God but also to the whole life community through which God expresses divine revelation. She identified her mission thus:

Standing at this time in history, on this very beautiful but fragile and endangered planet—seeing and hearing the cries within the community of life—I desire nothing more than to be part of the mission of the Divine Mystery: bringing life more fully by learning to live graciously with all creation, and helping others to live with courtesy, respect and reverence before all of life. And so it is to the trees and birds, the water, the air and land, to all of you, to all the children of the earth that I am making this commitment.[33]

Wild, native to Canada and a former director of Genesis Farm in New Jersey, is now working with an earth ministry in British Columbia. The text of her vows provides an ideal illustration of how green sisters are simultaneously conserving the traditional ritual profession of vows but reinhabiting that ritual in innovative ways that extend the scope of those commitments. As she directs her vows to the "Loving Mystery of Life . . . whose presence pervades the natural world / in the grandeur of the universe / and the splendid modes of earth's expression," Wild finds new, sustainable ways to live within the vows. Notice that she speaks of the vow of poverty in terms of "simple living" that respects the limits of the "earth-life process." Wild also speaks of the vow of chastity not in negative or restrictive terms but as embracing the desire to "relate to all life as sacred"—that is, she does not confine or focus her sacred relationality on one specific being. In this way, Wild extends the more common understanding of the vow of chastity as "freeing one to love all people with an undivided heart" or "promising to love all people without distinction" to freeing one to love all beings in the life community—human and nonhuman—in those meaningful ways. Similarly, whereas the vow of obedience is often defined as having to do with "listening to God's voice," Wild articulates her commitment to obedience in terms of "listening to the needs of life."[34] Toni Nash, also a Sister of Earth and a Sister of St. Joseph of Carondelet in Los Angeles, expressed a similar reading of the vow of obedience. Nash posits "obedience" as an act of worship in which one vows to listen to the "voice of the Spirit of the whole Earth community." Obedience, says Nash, is a vow of obedience to "the Community of Creation."[35]

Both Wild's and Nash's understanding of "obedience" stands in marked contrast to what Marie Augusta Neal identifies as the (pre–Renewal movement) institutionalization of "obedience" as "irresponsible submission" or "uncritical submission" to the will of an appointed superior.[36] The kind of "obedience" Neal describes stems from a more literal reading of the Roman Catholic Church's Canon 601, which specifies that sisters are to be "obedient to their legitimate superiors in areas relating to their Constitutions." ("Legitimate superiors" in the context of the canon conventionally refers to the superior general, who is the congregation's president and chief executive.)[37] Wild instead opens up the interpretation of obedience and consequently the notion of to whom "obedience" is vowed beyond the strict Canonical confines. In doing so, she provides a prime illustration of the kind of creative engagement that Bednarowski finds so key to North American women's religious imagination.[38]

Both Wild's conception of obedience to the needs of life and the Plowshares activist sisters' understanding of obedience to justice and the authority of conscience reflect a framework based on personal responsibility and mature discernment of legitimate authority as an expression of God's will. That is, both of these frameworks presume sisters to be adults capable of reasoning, evaluation, and analysis, instead of unquestioning "children" dictated to by their superiors. This is no insignificant shift in a culture that, as psychologist Eugene Kennedy has said, once prized sisters as "little girls" within infantilizing institutions. As Jeannine Gramick has pointed out, before the movement of Vatican II–inspired reforms within religious life, even sisters' private mail could be routinely opened, read, screened, and sometimes even withheld (a federal offense) by the mother superior, the sisters' "legitimate authority" and guardian.[39] Green sisters, like the majority of North American women religious, have rejected these infantilizing dynamics and cast themselves instead as responsible self-managers as well as effective organizational managers—of institutions as diverse as ecological learning centers, nongovernmental organizations such as Network, and Patricia Daly's Interfaith Center on Corporate Responsibility. Today no one would presume to withhold or read Patricia Daly's mail, and this greater degree of autonomy within religious communities and greater respect for sisters as capable adults have made possible the kind of entrepreneurial and organizational work conducted in the green sisters movement.[40]

The Three-Ply Cord

When a postulant (a "sister in training" who may or may not go on to make final vows) goes through formation (spiritual education within the religious community), she is often taught that the vows are like a three-ply cord and that "no vow stands alone; they are all related and intertwined."[41] In her book *Sisters: An Inside Look* (2001), Kathleen Rooney of the Sisters of St. Joseph of Philadelphia provides to those discerning a possible calling to religious life a broad but concise explanation of the meaning of these three publicly made vows: "Obedience is the commitment to listen to the voice of God; poverty commits a sister to the freedom to respond to that voice; and chastity—a passionate love for God—motivates her listening and her doing."[42] When a basic articulation of the vows, such as that offered by Rooney, is applied to social justice concerns, ecological concerns, or any number of areas in which sisters act and serve "out, in, and among the world," the possibilities for interpretation and lived practice of these vows are abundant and diverse. As Carol Coburn and Martha Smith point out, Catholic sisters in the United States have historically "learned to utilize their three vows (poverty, obedience, chastity) to justify, create and control space for their public endeavors."[43]

Even though Rooney is writing for a more general audience of the uninitiated, she includes a significant amount of material connecting the vows to ecological responsibilities. When explaining the vow of poverty, for instance, Rooney suggests that sisters can practice a simple lifestyle "by honoring the earth and by prudently using and preserving the earth's resources." Rooney herself is not focused explicitly on environmental concerns and came to religious life through the Catholic charismatic Renewal movement, a contemporary spiritual movement with connections and alliances with conservative evangelical Protestant groups.[44] Nonetheless, the environmental content of her book is "mainstreamed," as when she stresses that the vow of poverty is knit up with "a sister's growing awareness and commitment to care for the earth."[45] The fact that ecological values make frequent appearances in Rooney's general primer for those considering the vocation, even though she herself is not identified with the green sisters movement or its goals, demonstrates in part the extent to which "green" ethics and concerns have pervaded the discourse of women religious.

Sister of Loretto Elaine Prevallet has been particularly prolific in her work of exploring the connections between the three-ply cord of the vows and what she terms "earth spirituality." The author of several books and a frequent speaker in women's religious communities, Prevallet has a self-described goal "to place the vows of religious life—poverty, celibacy, and obedience—within the broad frame of our participation in the very large process of planetary life."[46] In *A Wisdom for Life* (1995), for instance, Prevallet reconceives the vow of "obedience" within an ecological framework to mean learning how to live "within one's niche" and within the bounds of the local ecological resources without encroaching on the habitats of others.[47] The vow of poverty, according to Prevallet, is connected to the recognition that "creation is governed by the law of reciprocity." More simply put, "Community of goods is a cosmic law." In this way, Prevallet draws on the tradition in religious communities that all things be shared in common and applies it to an ethic of fairly shared life-sustaining resources such as air, water, land, and energy.[48] Prevallet's explication of the "community of goods" as it relates to the earth's resources also parallels the dynamics of recycling resources through ecosystems, in which all material becomes food for something else and nothing is wasted.

A commitment to live "in solidarity with the poor" translates in Prevallet's work to a commitment to humility, which recognizes humans' total interdependence with all other creatures and beings. "At the Source," says Prevallet, "the dependence is absolute. We *own* nothing, not even our lives."[49] She identifies this dimension of the vows as being in keeping with the mystical tradition of Roman Catholicism and in keeping with the tradition of Catholic commitments to social justice—both of which she says speak to the truth of "our radical poverty." This last point of attribution is an important one because in it Prevallet conveys the message to her audience (made up largely of Catholic sisters) that guidance and wisdom about the ecological relevance of the vows can come out of their own tradition. Prevallet has long been interested in the study of Buddhism, and this interest informs her work, but ultimately she makes the case that connections between sisters' religious commitments and "earth spirituality" are natural outgrowths of Catholic identity and faith—"grounded in the gospel of Jesus" and deeply rooted in "the mystery of the Life of God that draws all things together in unity."[50]

I have asked green sisters about Buddhist or other Eastern influences on their language of "interdependence," "interrelatedness," and the "unity of all things." In large part, they have responded that, whereas this language does contain concepts and sensibilities common to Eastern philosophies (with which they are familiar and for which they express deep respect), these wisdoms can also be found much closer to home, embedded in the cultural soil of their own religious "backyards."[51] The concept of a "sacramental universe," for instance, which is central to Catholic sensibilities and heritage, easily lends itself to ecological interpretation. Catholic sacramentality, as theologian Susan Ross succinctly puts it, "takes physical reality very seriously" and "affirms that all of created reality reveals God."[52] And it is this sacramental view of the physical world, of an "enchanted cosmos," that permeates the "Catholic imagination," as described by Andrew Greeley in Chapter 1. The centrality of sacramentalism moves Catholic theologians, poets, artists, and philosophers to emphasize "the presence of God in the world" and the visibility of God in creation.[53]

As Prevallet and other green sisters talk about "webs of life," "interconnectedness," and "the sacred Earth," one can discern themes from environmental science, Eastern philosophy, American transcendentalism (the "oneness" and "manyness" of Emerson's "Oversoul," for example), and even Native American philosophies. To be sure, the discourse and practice of green sisters is informed by multicultural and multireligious currents, reflecting their own ecumenical bent, as well as the breadth of their reading and study of other religions. In the spirit of poet-philosopher Johann Wolfgang von Goethe's observation that "He who knows one, knows none," sisters educate themselves about other religious traditions and engage in comparative religious and philosophical study. Goethe's statement refers to languages, but (as Friedrich

Max Müller famously argued) the same principle applies to the study of religions, and the libraries at the various earth literacy centers I visited demonstrated evidence of sisters' comparative study.[54] Each library or book collection had a substantial selection of books, videotapes, audiotaped workshops, lectures, poetry, and other materials that address issues of nature and environment from non-Western religious perspectives. Some of these materials, such as videotapes, were included in earth literacy workshops, where sisters made a conscious effort not to be "parochial" in their approach, especially when students came from a variety of backgrounds. Other resources, such as educational audiotapes, were played during the evening meal as sisters ate in silence and listened.

Sister Miriam MacGillis once told me that when one studies other religions, such work must be respectfully approached as the study of "sacred Torahs." She said that one can learn a great deal from this study, but cautioned that each "sacred Torah" is most respectfully approached when the student first has a solid grounding in her own religious foundation.[55]

In this vein, sisters consciously make a point of rooting discussions of ecospiritual practice, earth ethics, and creation care in a Catholic milieu, careful not to abandon the fertile soil that originally nurtured their spiritual awareness and growth. In interviews, sisters, especially those active with social justice concerns among native peoples in North America, stressed the importance of "looking to one's own tradition" rather than appropriating those of others. This was also a topic that came up at the 2002 Sisters of Earth conference, where in discussions following a presentation on the ecorenovation of a motherhouse in Michigan, sisters again voiced the adage that ecologically conscious practice begins first at home and within one's own backyard.[56] Their discourse once again favored the image of the "bioneer" who stays at home and digs in, rather than the "pioneer" who moves on to colonize new ground. The reinhabiting or bioneering approach is also a way that sisters distance themselves from what might be called New Age religion, a religion viewed to be in some of its forms exploitative of other religious traditions, superficially engaged in spiritual exploration, and mercenary in its quest for material gain.

Sisters' Gift to the Earth Community

Prevallet provides yet another example of sisters' conserving traditional frameworks while infusing those frameworks with greener content in her exploration of the ecological relevance of "consecrated celibacy," a central part of the public profession of vows for Sisters of Loretto. Prevallet connects the practice of celibacy to a moral commitment to ease ecosystem stresses caused by a burgeoning human population, citing wildlife studies that show that, under certain environmental conditions, a significant nonbreeding portion of the adult population is the norm for many species. "When food and territory become scarce," says Prevallet, "some individuals in the species become non-breeders." Prevallet is intrigued, for instance, that many bird species keep a reserve of nonbreeders in the population that "promote the good of the species in time of need." With this in mind, she considers whether "the impulse to conscious choice of celibacy in human species might not be the counterpart of that instinct in non-human species, to serve the good of the whole."[57] She further reasons that women religious, as celibates, in addition to easing population pressures on the earth's resources, contribute to the earth's well-being in other vital ways: "Celibates, not having a brood of their own, can use their life-creating sexual energies for the other-than-biological preservation of the species of the earth community."[58] Some sisters I spoke with indeed referred to celibacy (and a lifetime commitment not to be "fruitful and multiply") as a gift that sisters have given the earth community throughout the history of religious orders.[59]

When I spoke with Genesis Farm's Miriam MacGillis in the spring of 2004 about celibacy, however, she made a strong qualification to my treatment of the subject. She interjected that just because sisters' vows result in a lifestyle that does not contribute to population growth, this does not mean that she or other ecologically concerned sisters are in any way negative toward human procreation. "Celibacy is a gift to the earth, but each child is *also* a gift to the earth," she told me emphatically.[60] MacGillis was concerned that I not misconstrue sisters' views on celibacy and the environment as being somehow against the birth of human children. Our ensuing discussion highlighted the tensions that sisters face and the delicate balance sisters must maintain between the ethics of ecological responsibility, the need to address the effects of a burgeoning human population on the earth's limited resources, and the "hot button" issue of population control within the Roman Catholic Church. MacGillis articulated a "third way" that acknowledged both the sacredness of sisters' gift of nonprocreation to the earth and acknowledged each child as another kind of sacred gift.

Offering still another perspective, Sisters of Earth organizer and cofounder Toni Nash, who is a Sister of St. Joseph of Carondelet in Los Angeles, proposes that the vows be understood within a larger commitment to creation and a positive approach to the discipline of learning to live within certain limits: "God, present in the community of creation, could use persons who were committed to really living the laws of nature . . . the true 'Natural Law' . . . and who [are] therefore vowed to live sustainably, who showed by their lifestyles that they hold the community and its integrity as the highest good, and who were willing to live within the limits of the community to which we all belong."[61]

Celibacy, says Nash, is one of the spiritual disciplines that "wakes one up" to hear the voice of the life community and to become alert to its needs. Like medieval hermits who practiced a variety of spiritual disciplines, Nash says, "We also need spiritual practices like fasting from that which anesthetizes us . . . noise . . . over-eating and drinking, TV, acquiring, over-working."[62] (Prevallet sounds a similar note by referring to the "collective narcoticization" of our culture and suggesting ways to resist this phenomenon in one's everyday life.)[63] Specifically, Nash approaches the issue of celibacy from the perspective of psychologist and author Father Diarmuid O'Murchu, a Missionary Servant of Christ, who defines celibacy as being "caught by God."[64] Nash explains: "One may choose to have children and raise them to see God, another may chain herself to a tree to keep it from being cut down, another vows to never again eat the flesh of an animal . . . This is not done to enter an elite group, nor to be revered. These are the responses of the heart to being 'caught' by a communication with the Holy."[65]

For Nash, this being "caught" can lead to positive and needed cultural change. Catholic vowed religious women, as persons on the margins engaged in a "liminal vocation" and countercultural lifestyle, play a critical role in being a voice and witness for this kind of change. Nash continues:

> Diarmuid O'Murchu, in *Religious Life, A Prophetic Vision*, describes our societal role when he sets religious life within the liminal nature of the shamanic tradition, that is, a tradition of persons "on the edge of a society and living values needed by that society for its evolution." David Abram in *The Spell of the Sensuous* describes such people as ones who derive their ability to cure ailments from their more continuous practice of "healing" or balancing the community's relation to the surrounding land. These shift me from seeing my role only in terms of influencing our church sub-culture, to recognizing my place in a larger societal picture, to questioning whether my vows are a gift God could really use today.[66]

The process of reinhabiting the vows is thus both practical and mystical, conserving not only a sense of prayerfulness, contemplation, and cosmic mystery, but also a focus on what is useful for this day and age. In fact, the Vatican II language of responding to and addressing "the needs of the times" constitutes a major theme repeated throughout the literature produced by sisters' earth ministries. The Sisters of the Humility of Mary who run EverGreen, an ecology center in Villa Maria, Pennsylvania, also invoke language from the Second Vatican Council. They describe their ministry this way: "At Ever-Green, a place of Earth-centered awareness, we invite others to share in our heritage of being connected to the land. In the spirit of humility and hospitality, we welcome others to join us in responding to the needs of the times by living a simple life of interdependence with all life communities."[67]

Poverty and Voluntary Simplicity

EverGreen's literature also makes repeated and significant connections between the sisters' vow of poverty and a commitment to "voluntary simplicity." The sisters specifically describe EverGreen as "a place to explore Earth Spirituality and to experience Divine Presence through simple living." This sacramental sensibility has translated into living what historian David Shi has called the "not-so-simple" simple life: the sisters at EverGreen have put into place a composting toilet to recycle human waste, solar ovens to cook food for center programs, water catchment to supply their herb garden, and they continue their dedication to vermicomposting (using worms to eat organic wastes), which they have now practiced for more than a decade.[68] The sisters are also in the midst of exploring wind and solar options to meet their energy needs. Again, the vow of poverty as lived through "voluntary simplicity" rises to the fore as EverGreen Director Barbara O'Donnell discusses her community's commitment to ecologically sustainable ways of life. "Simple living and sustainable choices are expression[s] of spirituality," says O'Donnell. "These kinds of choices are a part of our daily existence now."[69]

It may seem somewhat redundant or obvious to speak about Catholic religious sisters and nuns working diligently to "live simply." After all, the lives of women religious are vastly less materialistic and are filled with far fewer consumer items than are the lives of most North Americans. And yet, within today's consumer-driven culture, sisters often find that maintaining a "simple" lifestyle requires struggle and vigilance. Dominican Carole Rossi of Crystal Spring Earth Learning Center in Massachusetts observes that, as with the rest of America, the dominant culture of consumerism has influenced women religious, who have tended to become more individualistic and consumer-oriented, often without really realizing it:

Everybody drives home in her own car and then maybe goes to her own room where there is her own television set. I mean, that is not too far-fetched. And they are good women, you know. They are not people who want to live a selfish way of life. It is the function of having lost, sort of thrown away all the structures, and then having become subsumed in the culture that we said we were somehow different from—not better than, but different from. But we are *just like it*. And I think many women in religious congregations are realizing that is *not* what the call is. The call is to something different from that.[70]

Crystal Spring cofounder Dominican Chris Loughlin spoke of the ways in which getting caught up in a consumer lifestyle can produce feelings of emptiness:

It's just not satisfying. It's not spiritually nourishing, it's not nourishing for other humans' lives, it's not nourishing to the earth, and I think a lot of women religious came to religious congregations with a sense of really being more in tune with a simple way of life. And [back] then, a simple way of life was more . . . of a simple way of life for its own sake, which didn't really have the context that we're talking about here. But I think many of us have had that experience, that lived experience, and now we're saying we don't like what has become of us.[71]

Rossi's and Loughlin's comments address the consequences of the more liberalizing post–Vatican II changes in religious life—changes that affirmed self-determination, sisters' identities as adults and individuals, and the importance of human service out, in, and among "the world" but that also left some sisters feeling increasingly isolated, as well as lacking community, prayer life, and opportunities for contemplation. Now she and other green sisters speak of achieving more of a balance and of bringing the old structures into "a new moment" or "new context."

Author Mary Jo Leddy, a Sister of Our Lady of Sion, has called for the "reweaving of religious life" to reintroduce the kind of vital structures that Rossi identifies. Leddy's imagery is powerful, provocative, and tactile, but the ministries and ways of life of green sisters go far beyond the mere reintroduction of "old threads" into threadbare patterns. By actually reinhabiting many of the aspects of religious life associated with pre–Vatican II customs and culture, green sisters find creative ways to conserve meaningful religious practices that deepen their spiritual lives, while still updating those practices in ways that engage with the present culture and respond to the current needs of the earth community. The process of reinhabiting the vows involves a marriage of both a valuing heritage and a faithful openness to experimentation within that heritage. Far from finding this an onerous or dour task, the green sisters' enthusiasm further demonstrates Bednarowski's observation of women's "growing confidence and delight in the play of religious ideas."[72]

"Greening the Vows"

After hearing the phrase "greening the vows" used at a Sisters of Earth conference, I asked a number of sisters what that phrase meant to them. In response, Sister of Loretto Cathy Mueller, the cofounder of EarthLinks, an urban earth ministry in Denver, Colorado, spoke of how she now "see[s] the vows in a broader perspective—that our connections are not just with humans, rather with the whole web of life." She also characterized the vows as "patterns that are reflected in nature" and "natural choices that enhance Earth." Her image of patterns reflected in nature is evocative of not only philosophies of "natural religion" but also the language of ecodesign (or more formally, "biomimicry"), in which buildings, systems, and organizations consciously draw their structure from the patterns of nature. Mueller also pointed to growing innovations in the vows themselves, citing the example of a Loretto comember (someone who is affiliated with the community but who has not taken final or permanent vows) who had specifically added a vow of "ecological sanity" to her yearly renewal of vows.[73]

When Sister Joellen Sbrissa of the Community of St. Joseph of La Grange, Illinois, was asked what form "greening the vows" might take for her and her community, she responded that "care for the Earth is part of our religious life and witness."[74] Sisters of Earth cofounder Mary Southard, who belongs to Sbrissa's community, responded that to her, "greening the vows" means "seeing the vows within the context of an evolutionary universe, and the kind of values and dynamics which we observe in the community of life on earth. It is an ever-deepening adventure into the heart of God."[75]

For Janet Fraser of the Congregation of St. Joseph of Toronto, greening the vows meant "seeing the Earth as primary and learning to live in relationship with the Earth. This is the basis for our Religious commitment to the vows." Fraser added, "Doing earth-friendly practices has given me a growing awareness of being one with 'all my relations.' Alienation or disconnectedness has disappeared for me. I believe that earth and the cosmos are the Body of God [a concept theorized by theologian Sallie McFague] so there is an inner motivation to live this way."[76] When contemplating the meaning of the phrase "greening the vows," Barbara O'Donnell of EverGreen places a similar importance on interconnection and a holistic connection between individual and community: "[It means] living in ways that are compatible with Earth's story—making Earth's story our story. Deepening consciousness of all life communities as being part of my life and my life being part of the interdependence of all . . . [I] see the vows as a relationship with the Divine Presence and the whole Earth community—as service to church and world and planet."[77]

Language of interconnectedness and oneness with creation, relationality and community, mutuality and interdependence, common cause and the "family of life" pervaded sisters' responses to my questions about the vows— responses that significantly seemed to have been drawn from diverse sources. In Fraser's comments, for instance, she rearticulated the Native American belief that the earth's life community constitutes "all our relations" (in Lakota, "Mitakuye Oyasin"), but she just as easily drew from Protestant ecotheologian Sallie McFague's image of the "earth as God's body" as explained in McFague's book *The Body of God: An Ecological Theology* (1993). Southard's response, framed by the context of the "evolutionary universe," conjures the language of Father Thomas Berry and scientist-philosopher Brian Swimme in their work on the sacred dimensions of the unfolding "Universe Story."[78] Sbrissa's choice of language evokes the work of Sean McDonagh, an Irish priest in the Columban order, environmentalist, and author of *To Care for the Earth: A Call to a New Theology* (1987) as much as it does the peace and social justice tradition's consistent emphasis on "bearing witness."[79] And O'Donnell's comments are evocative of Teilhard de Chardin's emphasis on the shared earth story and human story, as read through a number of thinkers, from Thomas Berry in his *Universe Story* to James Conlon in his *Earth Story, Sacred Story* (1994).[80] Motivated by a common concern, sisters' "greening the vows" calls to mind myriad interpretations and sources of inspiration that in turn become manifest in sisters' individual and unique spiritual expressions.

I should mention that two sisters who responded jointly to interview questions for this book, but who asked that their names and community not be cited in this instance, took issue with the phrase "greening the vows." They told me that it was "too narrow" and "didn't mean very much" to them. Instead, they explained that they were currently working on a "rearticulation of the vows to match [their] current lived understanding of life." As they explained, "We would look at it [the reexamination of the vows] more from the understanding of the wholeness of life, and what orientation or vowed life would most foster this."[81] This feedback communicated vital information to me that spoke to a broad plurality of interpretation. It also told me that, for some sisters, it felt much more comfortable to speak more broadly of commitments to "life" than to speak explicitly of ecological or "green" contexts. Using the language of "life" also effectively taps into an entire discourse on the "respect for life," the "defense of life," and the "culture of life" within a Catholic idiom that is already well established. Pope John Paul II's 1995 *Evangelium Vitae* is probably the best example; here the Pope makes at least fifteen references to the importance of building or establishing an authentic "culture of life."[82] Although the *Vitae* primarily addresses issues related to abortion and euthanasia, the language is sufficiently broad that it may be read to apply to social justice issues, struggles for peace, or even to the kind of "culture of life" that would holistically respect and defend the "life systems" of the planet. Keying into the language of life may lend stronger legitimacy to sisters' earth ministries; more importantly, it rings true for those who reject a "culture of death" (as it affects all species) in favor of a more ecologically sustainable "culture of life."

Intergradations

In the audio series *Re-Visioning the Vowed Life*, an intensive retreat program for vowed members of religious congregations, Miriam MacGillis explicitly conserves and retains the import of the vows while, as she says, exploring them "within a broader, ecological dimension of community and ministry."[83] The actual hyphenated term "re-visioning," used in this sense, originated with feminist poet Adrienne Rich, who spoke of re-visioning as an act of "survival, a looking back and seeing with free eyes, in which one enters an old text from a new critical dimension."[84] MacGillis enters the territory of the "old text" with exacting care, repeatedly emphasizing what a "precious, precious legacy" it is. She quickly adds, however, "But it cannot be freeze-dried!"[85] She finds that not even the vows can be freeze-dried in a universe that is "in process and that will continue to unfold its understandings."[86]

Here again, the bioregionalist principle of reinhabitation can offer insight into the simultaneous constancy and shifting dynamics of the green sisters movement. Bioregionalist philosophers Peter Berg and Ray Dasmann point out, for instance, that as flora, fauna, and features of topography change and shift over time, so do attitudes about place, its boundaries, and its definition profoundly influence how a region comes to be inhabited and reinhabited over time. Bioregions, as with "regions of religion," clearly have some distinguishing features—coastal marshlands are not rocky mountains, Buddhism is not Christianity—though the boundaries of what does or does not belong to a particular region shift in accordance with a living religious landscape and the sensibilities of its inhabitants. What biogeographers call "intergradations" from one region to the next are fundamentally fluid, complex, overlapping, and dependent on the perceptions of those who, as Berg writes, live "in-place." In the "intergradations" of Catholic vowed religious life and the culture of American environmentalism, green sisters in effect simultaneously embody resistance toward and creative affirmation of both tradition and change, reconciling the inherent conflicts between institutional heritage and grassroots community adaptation. Martin Heidegger defined inhabitation in terms of "der Aufenthalt bei den Dingen," literally, "staying with things."[87] In practicing reinhabitation, sisters are indeed "staying with things" (their vows, their communities, their Church, their landscapes), yet they are dwelling quite differently—they are self-consciously and earth-consciously considering what it means truly to dwell in place and in a way that is mindful of past actions and attitudes as well as present and future needs.[88]

According to U.S. Census Bureau statistics, more than 40 million Americans moved between 2002 and 2003, a slight decrease from previous years, but at 14 percent, still the highest rate of any industrialized nation.[89] Moving, bioregionalist Deborah Tall contends, has been a means of "remaking and reinventing the self."[90] Nature writer Terry Tempest Williams has similarly observed, "As Americans, we have always left when the land became degraded, moved on to the next best place. Walked west. Now, our continent is inhabited. There is no place left to go."[91] In the wake of defections of sisters and nuns from the vowed life in the 1960s and 1970s, the landscape of women's Catholic religious congregations in North America looks quite different from what it once did.[92] Still, green sisters stand their ground instead of "walking west," choosing in the twenty-first century to reinhabit the religious landscape rather than move on to the "next best place."

3. IT ISN'T EASY BEING GREEN

Habitat, Habits, and Hybrids

In one of her many books exploring the spiritual dimensions of nature, Annie Dillard remarks, "It is madness to wear ladies' straw hats and velvet hats to church; we should all be wearing crash helmets."[1] I am reminded of Dillard's line as I follow my hardhat-clad tour guide, Janet Ryan, around the construction site of the motherhouse ecorenovation project being conducted by the Sisters, Servants of the Immaculate Heart of Mary (the "IHMs") in Monroe, Michigan. Ryan points out a gray-water system, geothermal heating tanks, sustainable cork flooring, and recycled window materials. She provides me the specifications on the low-VOC (volatile organic chemical) composition of the motherhouse's ecofriendly paint and the high-efficiency performance specifications regarding lighting, low-flush toilets, aerated faucets, and showers. She explains the flexibility of the wiring and functioning of the new thermostat system that will enable sisters to tailor heating and cooling to specific needs and to reduce energy waste.

Before arriving for my appointment with Ryan, I had prepared for my visit to the motherhouse by reading *Building Sisterhood* (1997), a collaborative feminist history of the IHM sisters. The beginning of this book is illustrated with an icon of the rather unusual IHM founder, Mother Theresa Maxis Duchemin. Born in the early part of the nineteenth century, Duchemin was a multiracial woman (her mother was a native of Haiti and her father, British), who was born out of wedlock and had risen to be elected superior of the Oblate Sisters of Providence (the first community of African-American sisters in the United States). She left the Oblate Sisters behind in 1845 to plant a new religious community in the "wildness" of the Michigan frontier. Insufficiently deferential to male clergy and those who would challenge her vision for the nascent community, Duchemin was eventually dismissed by the local bishop and sent into an eighteen-year exile from the community she founded.[2]

Yet Duchemin's pioneering influence and penchant for risk-taking persisted in various forms and can still be found in the ethos and values espoused by the IHM sisters today. The icon of Duchemin (the 1995 rendition of artist and IHM Sister Nancy Lee Smith) depicts the founder in full habit holding a ball of fire in her hands. I look at Ryan in her business blazer and hardhat, her eyes lively and spirited as she explains the ecological principles behind heating a large-scale institutional building such as the motherhouse with the use of geothermal dynamics, and I can't help but think of Duchemin's fireball.

The IHM sisters' "Mission for the Millennium" project in Monroe is the largest environmentally sustainable building renovation project of its kind in the United States. Registered with the U.S. Green Building Council and dubbed the "Motherhouse of Reinvention," this project has become a principal model in North America for green building design, materials conservation, green product use, energy and water efficiency, sustainable site planning, and wetlands restoration.[3] A motherhouse is the home base or headquarters for a religious congregation's leadership and is often the site of the novitiate as well as elder care for retired sisters. Faced with the problem of meeting the needs of an aging community of sisters, the IHM sisters had the option of tearing down their current facilities and building a new structure more suitable to the needs of their current population, or gutting the existing structure in a costly renovation. After several years of prayer, study, and discernment, the sisters chose a third way—a "greener path." Originally built in the 1930s, the motherhouse has eighteen-inch-thick concrete and brick walls. Although the basic structure was in need of repair and renovation, the sisters realized that it was extraordinarily solid. Instead of building something new, they decided to conserve the structure of their 376,000-square-foot home and set about recycling the valued contents of the building, reusing these materials in new, creative, and environmentally friendly ways.

"The Motherhouse stands as a physical symbol of a deeper transformation for us—a transformation that is changing the way we live," states the IHM sisters' literature on the ecorenovation project.[4] The sisters' decision to conserve the container for their religious community, while "greening" its contents, mirrors sisters' ongoing conservation of institutional structures of religious tradition while infusing those structures with content that is more ecologically conscious, more "sustainable." "Our IHM community considers sustainability a moral mandate for the 21st century," proclaims the sisters' Mission for the Millennium statement. "Our growing ecological consciousness places all humans in interdependent relationships to one another and all life on the planet." In defining "sustainable living," the sisters use the World Commission on Environment and Development's definition—that the needs of the present are met "without compromising the ability of future generations to meet their own needs."[5]

Faith under Construction

What does a serious commitment to ecological sustainability look like in practice? For the IHM community it has meant reusing eight hundred wooden windows, five hundred cherry wood doors, wooden trim, and wainscoting. It has meant salvaging marble pieces for use as windowsills and countertops, retrofitting over one hundred period fixtures to be energy efficient, and outfitting them with compact fluorescent bulbs. It has meant using only low-VOC paint to reduce toxic off-gassing of paint fumes, as well as recycling 45,260 square feet of carpeting and many miles of duct work and wiring. The sisters have also reduced consumption of the earth's resources in the present in order not to compromise the needs of future generations, by installing a recycled (or "gray") water system. The system takes water used in the motherhouse sinks and showers, funnels it through a constructed wetlands purification system, and then pumps it back into the motherhouse for use in flushing toilets. By combining the gray-water system with the installation of high-velocity low-flow structures, the sisters have reduced their freshwater consumption by over 50 percent. To reduce even further their ecological "footprint" (the measure of a community's effect on the earth's resources), the sisters have installed a geothermal heating and cooling system, which uses the earth's reasonably consistent 55-degree underground temperature to maintain a comfortable building temperature in a highly energy-efficient manner. In fact, the IHM motherhouse's geothermal field is the largest of its kind in the country.[6]

In an ironic twist, the same workmen who decades ago constructed the cooling tanks for the nearby "Fermi 2" nuclear reactor came to the motherhouse to build the community's industrial-sized, ecologically "sustainable" heating and cooling system. My tour guide, Janet Ryan of the IHM leadership team, smiled down on the geothermal tanks in the basement of the motherhouse while she pointed out this fact and subsequently explained how the system cleverly makes use of the earth's steady temperature as a "natural radiator." As we continue to walk through the inner workings of the motherhouse, I ask Ryan whether she thinks the workmen had a qualitatively different experience of their work while constructing the sisters' "green" heating and cooling system versus constructing the cooling tanks for the nuclear power plant. She responded, "I think so . . . We really give them [the workmen] the sense that this is a sacred enterprise." She explained that when the workers arrive at the job site each day, two sisters go out to meet them and proceed to bless both them and their tools. One of the workmen had told her how previously he used to throw his tools in the back of his truck at the end of the day, but once they had been blessed by the sisters, he began carrying them inside the cab with him and taking better care of them. "It [the blessing and sacred context] has really raised the quality of the workmanship," says Ryan, pointing out the quality of various joints and fittings in the plumbing, heating, and cooling system.[7] Later, we pass two Latino workmen on stilts spackling a ceiling. They focus intently on their work and paint with great care but stop and smile with pride as Ryan comments on the progress they have made.

This motherhouse will also serve as a teaching center for tradesmen in the area so that they can learn alternative and more ecologically sustainable methods of construction and renovation. The project itself has been so large that it has indeed created a market for green construction among local tradespeople. At the 2002 Sisters of Earth conference, IHM Sister Paula Cathcart reported that the construction company the sisters used for the renovation is now implementing recycling policies in all its jobs. The civil engineer who helped the sisters with their gray-water system is now promoting gray-water designs throughout Michigan, and the project's geothermal engineer has taken the principles learned from building the large-scale geothermal field at the Monroe motherhouse and brought them to bear on government projects.[8] The influence of the IHMs' motherhouse ecorenovation has thus extended far beyond the immediate religious community.

The Blue Nuns Go Green

As the IHM sisters reinvent their motherhouse, they are at the same time reinventing themselves, a case of what the sisters have called "the Blue Nuns Going Green" (a reference to the IHM's signature blue habits).[9] About this transformation, Janet Ryan comments, "We have always been committed to social justice and advocacy for the abandoned and the poor. Our founders' call was to respond to the needs of the world. In this century, we have come to understand the Earth is abandoned in many ways. People don't realize that it's a living organism and must be treated with care."[10] Working as a team and forming discernment groups, visioning groups, prayer groups, and study groups, the sisters committed to a lengthy in-depth process. In visiting the motherhouse, I heard the metaphor of "journey" used at least a half a dozen times to describe the renovation undertaking and the movement through its various stages of progress. Renovation Director Danielle Conroyd remarked, "We have been challenged and stretched and changed as much by the process as by the work . . . We have become a learning community and have told others about what we are doing. Many others have already come here to see this landmark project and to learn from our experience."[11]

What sparks this kind of affirmation and commitment to sustainability among the Monroe IHMs? It has clearly been a confluence of factors. The first step involved the community's "Theological Education Process" (a communal education and learning experience held between 1994 and 2000). This process included a section on "Science and the New Cosmology," which largely focused on the philosophies of Father Thomas Berry and Brian Swimme, author of *The Universe Is a Green Dragon* and coauthor with Berry of *The Universe Story*. By the time the IHM community took the next step and went into the 2000–2006 "Learning Process," they were focusing on "sustainability, advocacy and action for eco-justice, corporate responsible investing, organic gardening, and community supported agriculture." What had been the IHMs' Environment Committee developed into an Eco-Justice Office, and the Eco-Justice Office in turn evolved into the Center for Justice, Peace, and Sustainable Living. Paula Cathcart notes that all of these developments were accomplished through participatory processes, like "creative thinking days," discernment groups, and incubation groups. In other words, the process itself was one of grassroots consensus, collaboration, and cooperation, rather than top-down decision-making.[12] As Cathcart explains,

> Each phase—data gathering, recommendations and implementation—included many and varied opportunities for participation such as surveys, written feedback, consultation, regional meetings, education days, creative thinking days, justice and values days, project team, advisory group, incubation group, bridge group, and the discernment group. We were mindful of our heritage. We used existing organizational structures. We accompanied each other by connecting sister to sister. Symbol and ritual marked the entering into and letting go at various steps. We tapped into both right- and left-brain energy. Communication was a priority. We listened, welcomed questions, and shared information.[13]

Despite all the attention to "group process," this has not been an easy transformation for the IHMs. There has been apprehension about the coming changes, which the community has dealt with continually in their visioning groups, discernment groups, and feedback meetings. At first the older sisters were very anxious about any changes to the chapel at the motherhouse and requested that it be left out of the redesign plan. During the renovation process, however, the sisters began meeting in an alternative liturgical space where for the first time they were all able to face each other in a three-quarter-round configuration that allowed them to interact during worship. When faced with the prospect of going back to the rigidity and impersonality of the original chapel's linear pews, the older sisters softened their stance and began exploring ways to modify the chapel.

What is perhaps most extraordinary about the Monroe IHMs' commitment to sustainable renovation is that 71 percent of its members are over the age of sixty-five. With over six hundred vowed sisters and more than one hundred associate members, 50 percent of the community is retired or infirm. How to provide for elderly sisters is a pressing concern for the Monroe IHMs, to say the least—and their situation is similar to that of many other Catholic religious women's communities in America. With limited resources and fewer younger sisters bringing in salaries to the community, the financial challenges to such a project are daunting. And yet, after much prayer, reflection, and visioning as a community, the sisters decided that the only way to keep their community "moving forward" was to invest in the future.[14]

"My community is being called to respond to the plight of the Earth," IHM Sister Paula Cathcart told an audience of Sisters of Earth in the summer of 2002. She added that throughout the renovation process, her community has remained "open to the spirit working among us" and has approached the process "with reverence for the gift we were being given."[15] Cathcart spoke about how her community realized that the only way to move was forward, and that meant challenging themselves to "walk their talk"—to trust and live their commitments. "It was about entering into and letting go," says Cathcart. Revitalization of IHM identity and mission is a bold commitment to the future. If the sisters had decided to "calcify" and avoid risks, who would want to join them, she asked, remarking that in reading the "needs of the times," the community had to respond with changes in ministry that would "connect to the whole Earth community." IHM vice president Mary Katherine Hamilton extends these sentiments further by evoking the well-known Six Nation Iroquois Confederacy ethic for decision-making that takes into consideration the well-being of future generations: "Perhaps more than ever before, IHMs today are becoming aware that the difference we need to make includes a commitment to the seventh generation—those whose very future depends on today's choices and actions."[16]

The renovation project includes more than simply the physical structure of the motherhouse. The IHM comprehensive integrative plan calls for prairie restoration, for replanting native hardwood trees as the pines on the property die, and for restoring wetlands. Swales (landscaped depressions) have already been created adjacent to parking lots and planted with native aquatic plants that will absorb and eliminate run-off from the property. The master plan also calls for creating a more contemplative landscape with places for prayer, reflection, and meditation. Already, garden meditations are held in the morning at the community-supported organic garden. The IHMs, whose charism is rooted in the "liberating mission of Jesus," have liberated their landscape from the strict confines of the suburban Midwestern lawn and restored the land to its indigenous meadow savannas, planted with wild native grasses.

In their work with the community-supported organic garden (or CSG) called St. Mary Organic Farm, the sisters are quite cognizant of their history of self-sufficiency and rootedness in the land. Like many communities of Catholic religious, the IHMs were largely able to provide food for themselves from the bounty of their communal land. This history is made visible on the St. Mary Organic Farm CSG official T-shirt. The front of the shirt features a photo taken in the 1940s of a group of IHM novices in a pickup truck on their way to harvest the community's fields. The back shows a photo of current sisters and CSG members in a pickup truck on their way to work in today's organic garden. Under both photos the same line appears: "Caring for the land. Building Community."[17] In the design of the shirts, the IHMs have made a strong statement about continuity with their history and heritage, honoring the old while going forward, once again, "into a new moment."

Moving Forward: Symbols in Action

The cover of the Fall 2002 issue of *IHM Journal* shows the IHMs' new logo—a green planet earth with a green cross integrated into one side of it and the "IHM" letters (in "habit blue") interwoven into the bottom of the planet. This logo is then superimposed against a picture of an open road surrounded by green hills and farmland. The message is one of boldly moving forward into what the IHM literature characterizes as a new moment. The open road again evokes the metaphor of journey and of IHM sisters on the move toward their mission for the millennium—a mission to bring about the dream of God on Earth. Coincidently, I picked up this 2002 issue of *IHM Journal* shortly after rereading Helen Rose Fuchs Ebaugh's *Women in the Vanishing Cloister* (1993). Fuchs Ebaugh begins her book by "sounding the death knell for religious orders of women in the United States," arguing that they are a dying institution. "I feel like the doctor facing the challenge of telling a patient that she has terminal cancer and needs to prepare for the end," she writes. Within the green sisters movement, though, is the cloister "vanishing" or merely "morphing" into a spiritual ecovillage? It is uncanny how so much of the imagery among green sisters concerns "planting anew," "breathing new life into," "reviving," "renewing," "resurrecting," and "creating a place for new green shoots of growth." More than a decade after Fuchs Ebaugh's book, could it be that as old ways are either "composted" and "recycled" or (in the case of the IHMs) undergo ecorenovation, new growth has begun?

Transformation is a major theme in IHM literature. The IHMs' Mission for the Millennium reads: "The entire Monroe Campus is, at this moment, evolving as a center of growth and learning—of transformation. This sacred space expresses our value for all of life as God's good creation—a place to meet not only our needs, but also the needs of future generations . . . With joy and anticipation, we invite you to experience this transformation with us, to embrace an expanded family of kinship and to discover your own sense of place."[18] Throughout the renovation process, the IHMs' mantra has been a simple chant: "Everything before us has brought us to this moment, standing on the threshold of a brand new day."[19] And indeed, this chant is an accurate representation for the philosophical underpinnings of the movement—a movement that does not reject or deny the past but "owns" it and acknowledges it for having brought them to this current moment of understanding.

And what has brought them to this moment? Janet Ryan explains to me that IHMs have always been risk takers and cites the challenges that founder Theresa Maxis Duchemin faced on the frontier, including racism and bigotry. She also points to the fact that the IHM community pushed for sisters to get advanced degrees back in the 1920s and 1930s, well before the Sister Formation movement encouraged this effort in the 1950s. "Now we are risking again," says Ryan, "but this is the core of who we are."[20] Like other green sisters, the IHMs stand on the threshold of a new beginning, fully knowing that for better or worse, they rely on the foundation of what has come before them in contexts of Church, religious community, women's history, movements toward peace and justice, and human relations with the planet.

In considering what would be best for their renovation project, the IHMs have been keenly aware of the symbolism of their decisions. The group's vision of sustainability pointed toward renovating instead of building a new structure, conserving the strength of the building, whose thick brick walls provided strength and durability through past generations and would endure into the future. In addition, by reusing and recycling materials, adapting the structure for greater flexibility while maintaining its essential integrity, the sisters have been able to remodel and reinhabit the structure more sustainably. Not surprisingly then, this project has been cast repeatedly in terms of the IHMs' commitment to honor their "heritage" while promoting more flexible alternatives for present and future. This combination is as true in the building as it is in the community. New flexibility has created space for new growth in different ways. Many of the new sisters and lay associates have been specifically attracted by the community's move into environmental concerns and its efforts to address interlocking issues holistically. The IHMs' commitment to sustainability has been successful in energizing and retaining younger vowed members who might otherwise have moved onto external opportunities for work related to social justice, peace, economic, and environmental issues. These days, the IHMs bring all of these concerns under one roof.

Indeed, discernment groups are now studying the possibility of creating a model ecovillage on the Monroe campus that would include members from diverse ethnic groups, ages, and economic levels. The campus itself would be not only a place to model sustainable living, but also an educational center for teaching about spirituality, theology, ecology, social justice, public policy, organic agriculture, sustainable methods of energy generation and land use, holistic health care for the aging, and intergenerational living. In its project vision statement, the IHM community envisions the Monroe Campus as "a CENTER of new growth and new learning, of transformation of consciousness through transformation of land and building use and through personal, corporate and systemic conversion of mind and heart. It sees the CENTER as a SACRED PLACE actualizing the faith dimension of the core value of SUSTAINABILITY of life in all its forms."[21]

At the end of my tour of the ecorenovated motherhouse, I reflected on how, in literary terms, the house is a metaphor par excellence for a life. I think about what I have just witnessed means in terms of the life of this religious community, and perhaps that of others who follow in their footsteps. I also ask and then circle the question in my field notes, "Is nature reclaiming this house?" But this is not the kind of reclaiming we encounter, for instance, in the deterioration of the Ramsey house as nature reclaims it in Virginia Woolf's *To the Lighthouse*. Here, in Monroe, nature is taking a very different approach. This old motherhouse has had new life breathed into it. It has had a fresh beginning and is barely recognizable except for its basic structure— which is still familiar and solid to its inhabitants. If nature is reclaiming this motherhouse and its surrounding grounds, it is doing so through restored swales, wetlands, native grasses, nature-mimicking gray-water systems, eco-friendly geothermal power, and ecologically friendly renovation and recycling. With their cultivated earth-consciousness, are the IHM sisters themselves in a sense acting as agents of nature in reclaiming, recycling, and resurrecting this motherhouse? And how might sisters be modeling this collaborative enterprise between "mother nature" and motherhouse for others beyond religious communities? As Janet Ryan speaks with me about the motherhouse as a "symbol of transformation," she adds, "We're *all* going through this." I ask her to clarify if by "all" she means her religious community, the larger Monroe community, humans in general, or the entire planet. I have my pen poised over paper as she pauses to consider a moment, smiles, and then simply answers, "Yes."[22]

Greener Habitats and Sacred Homemaking

Bioregionalist Stephanie Mills identifies the processes of reinhabitation as "finding a home, knowing a home, making a home, feeling at home, and staying at home."[23] Much of this focus on home within the bioregional movement consciously invokes the etymology of "ecology," in which the Greek root *oikos* refers to house or home. In his essay "Ecology: Sacred Homemaking," Thomas Moore views "ecology" as "the mystery of home." Playing on the more mystical associations of the other root of "ecology," *logos* ("words, stories, logic, nature") to mean the "mysterious essence" of a thing, Moore argues that, in its essence, the pursuit of ecology is about a deep, heartfelt spiritual longing for home that is the opposite of the hero's journey. "Saving the planet" as a call to action, says Moore, is too abstract. "Healing the environment" is too externalized. Taking care of homes and neighborhoods, "sacred homemaking," is intimate, attached, and speaks to us where we live.[24]

The Monroe IHMs serve as a prime example of how green sisters are putting their vows into action and modeling sustainability through sacred home remaking. But there are many more small-scale projects in which sisters are moving in the same direction. Alternative housing construction is one way that sisters are creating greener "habitats" for themselves while respecting the habitats of other species. Straw-bale hermitages in particular have become quite popular with green sisters as a way to build long-lasting, well-insulated structures without the use of wood products that contribute to forest habitat destruction. In New Jersey, while giving guests a tour of Genesis Farm's straw-bale hermitage, one of the farm's cofounders, Dominican sister Miriam MacGillis, advised: "We need to look to the Earth to see how it shelters and provides, in order to see how humans should shelter and provide. The Earth's ways are our models."[25] This kind of ecodesign housing ethic is yet another way to reinhabit both the physical landscape and the landscape of religious life. Ecological designers Sim Van der Ryn and Stuart Cowan explain that, in construction design, "a building should itself become, in Gregory Bateson's words, a 'pattern that connects' us to the change and flow of climate, season, sun, and shadow, constantly tuning our awareness of the natural cycles that support all life. A wall should be not a static, two-dimensional architectural element but a living skin that adapts to differences in temperature and light."[26]

Green sisters' choice of straw-bale construction as a medium for hermitages and other housing needs reflects a conscious effort to live "simply," use few resources, and practice a more ecologically sustainable lifestyle. Made of assembled straw bales that are bolted into place and then covered with a nontoxic stucco-plaster, straw-bale structures use inexpensive, (ideally) locally grown straw—an easily renewable alternative to timber that does not contribute to deforestation. The energy efficiency of straw-bale structures also contributes to its popularity with green sisters. The thick insulation of the straw-bale walls, about two feet wide, means that, on cool nights, a small wood stove is usually all that is necessary to heat the entire living space.[27] The energy-efficiency rating for a straw-bale house, according to design experts, is about three times greater than that of even the most thoroughly synthetically insulated modern wooden or brick houses, and five to ten times greater than that of older homes.[28]

For the most part, straw that is left out in the field after the harvest of major grains such as wheat and rice is eventually burned by farmers as a waste product. In California alone, for instance, almost a million tons of rice straw is burned each fall, contributing significantly to air pollution in that state.[29]

*Straw-bale construction: Sisters of the Presentation "Green Welcoming Center"
and dining hall under construction, Los Gatos, California.*
(Photo courtesy of Daniel Smith & Associates Green Architecture, Berkeley, California.)

Sisters who favor straw-bale building stress the importance of turning waste products such as straw into usable resources that provide shelter in an affordable and aesthetically pleasing way. Straw-bale structures are also often spatially configured to be in harmony with the seasons and integrated into the surrounding habitat. In fact, placement has been a critically important component of green sisters' straw-bale structures. Genesis Farm's MacGillis, for instance, had originally planned to erect the farm's straw-bale "hermitage" on another part of the property until, after lengthy observation, she discovered that it was a key habitat area for wildlife. Rather than encroach on other creatures' space, she turned the area of the initial site into a sanctuary where humans are requested not to go. A different, lower-impact location was chosen in an area nestled at the edge of the woods, in order to take advantage of deciduous trees to the south and coniferous trees to the north, which provide the structure with cooling shade throughout the summer and warming southern exposure in winter.

Dominican Sisters' straw-bale hermitage at Santa Sabina Retreat Center, San Rafael, California.
(Photo courtesy of Daniel Smith & Associates Green Architecture, Berkeley, California.)

In discerning a low-impact, energy-efficient, wildlife-sensitive location for the straw-bale hermitage at Homecomings, a center for ecology and contemplation founded in the 1990s at St. Gabriel's Monastery in Pennsylvania, Gail Worcelo engaged a similar process consciously aimed at working with (instead of against) the designs of nature. An important component of the straw-bale construction project for Worcelo and her building partners was that trees not be felled to construct the house. In her remarks at the beginning of the straw-bale hermitage guest book, she writes: "We did not impose this structure on this spot, but spent months walking the land and asking for permission and an invitation from the natural world. This spot was given as a gift. Not one tree was taken down (although a small sapling was removed and transplanted)."[30] In building straw-bale structures, sisters are thus mindful of the green version of the vow of obedience, in which one has committed to listening to and abiding by the needs of the whole community—in this case, the designs of nature.

In the Midwest, Prairiewoods Franciscan Spirituality Center in Hiawatha, Iowa, offers use of not one but two straw-bale hermitages on its property. These structures were built to provide "sacred space for stillness and solitude . . . quiet prayer and contemplation." Those at the center say the atmosphere of a straw-bale hermitage, with its natural materials and simple beauty, helps to "nourish what is deep within the self." Center literature points out that one of the key benefits of the straw-bale hermitage is that it "allows one to quiet down—in the company of God and all creation, in the beauty of the woods and prairie, in the touch of the earth, in the songs and sounds of creatures."[31] Thus, the straw-bale structure is not just made of all-natural and ecologically sustainable materials; its very design, composition, and location all facilitate a kind of communion with nature that is thought to revitalize the spirit.

A number of other farms and ecology centers in the Midwest also make use of straw-bale construction on their properties. Heartland Farm in Pawnee Rock, Kansas, for instance, which is an intentional ecumenical spiritual community sponsored by the Dominican Sisters of Great Bend, features a straw-bale hermitage, a composting toilet, and a solar greenhouse. Michaela Farm in Oldenburg, Indiana, does not use its straw-bale house for contemplation and retreat; instead it houses its head farmer. In raising the straw-bale house, however, the farm invited the community to participate in a straw-bale building workshop so that friends and neighbors might learn how to build their own structures. Again, the Franciscan Sisters at Michaela Farm demonstrate green sisters' commitment to sharing their own experiences in cultivating greener habits so that others can more easily follow suit.

Sisters on the West Coast have also committed to ecologically sustainable building construction. Santa Sabina, a retreat center sponsored by the Dominican Sisters of San Rafael, California, has a straw-bale hermitage on its property, as do a number of other retreat centers where sisters offer ecologically related programming. Tierra Madre in Sunland Park, New Mexico, likely makes the largest scale use of straw-bale construction of any green sister center or ministry. A housing and medical mission of the Sisters of Charity, Tierra Madre is a straw-bale ecovillage providing affordable housing for low-income families in the borderlands. Five families have built their own energy-efficient, passive solar, straw-bale homes at Tierra Madre, and nine more families will do the same before the community is complete. Begun in 1995, the community's focus is on sustainable development, and so the inhabitants make use of solar, wind, and water harvesting to meet their energy needs. The land of the ecovillage is held communally and includes a community garden and a community center for daycare. Solar and gray-water systems are part of the community's commitment to living "lightly on the land" and to building sustainable community infrastructure. In keeping with the tenets of Catholic social justice teaching, Sister of Charity Jean Miller, president of Tierra Madre, describes the ecovillage as providing "an option for the economically poor and for the earth."[32]

Miller's inclusion of the earth in the social justice language of "a preferential option for the poor" sends the message that earth concerns and social justice concerns are inextricably linked. Green sisters commonly make this connection in their written and spoken work, as they make the case for the critical path from social justice action to ecojustice action. Tierra Madre has also been recognized by both the United Nations and the U.S. Department of Housing and Urban Development for its vanguard work creating long-term and sustainable solutions to the problems of poverty and the lack of affordable housing. Creative alternatives being pioneered at Tierra Madre have now become models for sustainable community development in both the United States and abroad, furthering the influence that green sisters are having both locally and globally.[33]

Land as Legacy

At the time of their founding, many religious community properties were purposefully located "away from the world," often in rural areas, in order to create barriers between sisters and secular influences.[34] Traditionally, Christian monasticism has been associated with liminality (living at the threshold) and withdrawal to "empty landscapes."[35] In the twentieth century, especially after the Second Vatican Council in the mid-1960s, much of this marginality shifted for women's religious communities, which now observe a more open form of life and follow a model of "engagement" in the world, particularly concerning the plight of the poor. After decades of selling off rural land holdings to channel resources toward the needs of urban populations, green sisters are now working to take what is left of community lands and put them into trusts that will prevent the land from being sold for future development. Genesis Farm's Miriam MacGillis and Crystal Spring Center's Chris Loughlin have been particularly active in counseling religious communities on ways to preserve their farmland and open space. Both Dominican sisters in affiliation, although from different communities, MacGillis and Loughlin have been involved with forging the Dominican Alliance Land Ethic, which states in part, "We, the Dominican Sisters of the Alliance, proclaim that the gifts of the Earth entrusted to our various congregations are indeed sacred because the Judeo-Christian tradition informs us that God created the human family to be part of the sacred web of life, [and] the land is the primary sustainer of all life, therefore, the Earth and all her parts, are sacred."[36]

Loughlin also educates congregations about land trusts and serves as a steering committee member for "Who Shall Inherit the Land?" a task force Loughlin describes as "a grassroots effort of Dominicans to create a new vision for the sacred lands held in common." Of the historical push to sell off community lands and transfer resources into urban centers, Loughlin observes, "Thank goodness that there were some sisters who had the vision to fight against that."[37] Green sisters are now seeking ways to conserve and sustainably reinhabit communal land that has been considered to be extraneous or a financial burden. Crystal Spring Earth Learning Center, in conjunction with the Massachusetts Coalition of Land Trusts, has now formed the Religious Lands Conservancy Project, whose purpose is to bring religious communities and land conservationists together "to preserve common and complementary values on the land." According to the conservancy project's literature, which is largely aimed at bringing religious communities into conservancy, congregation lands "may well hold an essential key to the recovery of our selves, our mission, and the healing of deep alienation in our culture. If religious congregations could explore a radically different context for making decisions about their land, we might well participate in a deep spiritual, ecological, social and economic healing of the regions in which our lands exist."[38]

Although once located at "the margins," sisters' communities that are still surrounded by acres of undeveloped land have ironically become some of the last outposts of open space amid rapidly encroaching suburban sprawl. At Crystal Spring, the surrounding area has become increasingly suburbanized. Crown Point, a 130-acre stretch in Ohio that the Sisters of St. Dominic converted into an ecology learning center and community-supported organic farm thirteen years ago, is faced with increasing area road congestion and nearby housing developments. During my visit to Michaela Farm in Indiana, Franciscan Sister Claire Whalen pointed out to me the housing development occupying the slope just south of the farm. That land had once belonged to her community but was sold off to developers a few decades ago. Now new development is on its way. Michaela Farm in southern Indiana is still in a fairly rural area, but sisters there (as in many other communities) are feeling the pressures of suburban encroachment and the loss of farmland.

When I first drove out to Genesis Farm in 1994, the area in western New Jersey surrounding the farm was unquestionably rural; locals boasted to me how until recently the town had more cows than people. Since then, a string of upscale "McMansions" have been constructed, devouring open space and farmland. Responding to the region's rapidly shrinking wildlife habitat, in 1998 the educational nonprofit center at Genesis Farm, a ministry of the Dominican Sisters of Caldwell, New Jersey, placed the farm's acreage in trust with the New Jersey Farmland Preservation Program, protecting the land from development in perpetuity. Other communities have taken similar measures. The Sisters of the Order of St. Benedict in St. Joseph, Minnesota, for instance, sold their eighty acres of surrounding wetland to the Sand Prairie Wildlife Management Area. On their farmland, they set up a community supported garden, which in 1999 they placed into a perpetual conservation easement through the Minnesota Land Trust. This easement protects the land from any kind of future development.

It is critical to stress that these decisions to put properties into trust and to sign away development rights to the land are not easy. In many cases, sisters are forced to decide between ensuring a secure retirement for community members and protecting vital habitats. Green sisters have made tough choices and have chosen to protect the land over which they see themselves as stewards in perpetuity. Again and again, they vote to secure the land as their lasting legacy to future generations, even when doing so risks making their own futures uncertain.

When Santuario Sisterfarm's cofounders, the Dominican sister Carol Coston and Adrian Dominican novice Elise D. García, introduced me to the land they now "caretake" in the Texas hill country, they made sure to point out the area of the farm that is respectfully off-limits to humans. As with the specially designated area of the property at Genesis Farm, a concerted effort is made at Sisterfarm to impose limits on the habitat that humans occupy. As I interviewed Coston and García, they grieved over the rapid expansion of megamalls, sprawling housing developments, and costly golf courses into this fragile hill-country habitat. For García, the ultimate insult has been the bulldozing of open space to make way for long-term storage facilities. "We have so much junk," she remarks incredulously, "we can't even keep it all in our houses. We need to take up more and more land just to store our *stuff* some place."[39] Located in the "borderlands" of the United States and Mexico, Santuario Sisterfarm provides safe haven for the "cultivation of diversity"— both biodiversity and cultural diversity. This focus is at the heart of the three major efforts the community is currently undertaking, which include a model site for "living lightly on Earth," a woman's publishing house, and what Coston and García term an "eco-ethno-spiritual journey with Latinas from the Borderlands."[40]

In reinhabiting the ecological, cultural, and religious landscape on a variety of levels, the community at Sisterfarm also provides a model illustration of what sociologist Wade Clark Roof has identified as key developments in religion and culture. In mapping the "terrain" of American religion, Roof has observed, "the images and symbols of religion have undergone a quiet transformation. Popular discourses about 'religion' and 'spirituality,' about the 'self' and 'experience,' about 'god' and 'faith' all point to subtle—but crucially important—shifts in the meaning of religious life." Roof has spoken about the creation of new "religious borderlands"—the increasingly expanding areas where the edges of multiple cultures, ethnicities, and religious signs and symbols all meet and defy the rigid categorizations of the past.[41] Arguably, the "greening" of religion (that is, the integration of religion, ecological consciousness, and green culture) has become one of these borderland areas where subtle but significant symbolic shifts are taking place.

Practicing Green Habits in Everyday Life

From diet and dress to modes of shelter, to the use of nontoxic cleaning products, low-impact composting toilets, energy-efficient light bulbs, and other conservation measures, "green habits"—ecologically sustainable practices and mindful consumption of resources—have become part and parcel of green sisters' vowed life. Such a life demands more, not less, from religious women. In her books on earth spirituality, Sister of Loretto Elaine Prevallet makes the case for the sacred dimension of these daily practices, commenting that, for sisters, "practical disciplines such as recycling, being sparing in our use of water or paper or electricity, being attentive to choices we make in our buildings and our purchases (how things are packaged, whether or not they are 'environmentally friendly'), eating low on the food chain—these need to be recognized as spiritual practices."[42]

A full 95 percent of the sixty-five sisters who were interviewed for this book electronically (as opposed to those interviewed in person or by telephone) identified as part of their spiritual practice such activities as conserving water, paper, and electricity.[43] Sister Diane Roche, a religious sister of the Sacred Heart and former director of the Old North St. Louis Restoration Group in Missouri, calls such practices "social sacraments" and explains that such ecologically mindful behaviors are, in her view, "external signs of an inner awareness of connectedness."[44] In her own community, Roche explains,

> Recycling is a regular part of life.
> No herbicides, no pesticides are used.
> No toxic cleaning agents are purchased.
> No petroleum based detergents are purchased.
> Nothing with ammonia.
> Organic food products are purchased as much as possible.
> Recycled paper goods and plastics are reused.
> Composting is part of our daily routine.[45]

Roche has since moved from St. Louis to Haiti, where her experience with conservation issues and ecojustice concerns, along with her awareness of connectedness, will be put to the test in a country with some of the world's most daunting ecological challenges.

In *The Practice of Everyday Life*, French sociologist Michel de Certeau has argued that everyday practices—"dwelling, moving about, speaking, reading, shopping, and cooking"—far from being insignificant, can be effective "tactical" practices. That is, they can be "clever tricks of the 'weak' within the order established by the 'strong.'" For De Certeau, it is the seemingly insignificant or inconsequential practices of everyday life that, surprisingly, most embody tactics of resistance to the status quo by skillfully "diverting" a system without actually leaving it.[46] Similarly, sisters' reinhabiting the "small details" of everyday life constitutes a strategy for transforming the status quo of religion and culture by modeling workable, greener alternatives.

Connectedness to creation and daily mindfulness of the life community that sustains all beings are themes that pervade a variety of earth literacy centers run by green sisters. During my stay with the Dominican sisters at Crystal Spring Earth Learning Center in Plainville, Massachusetts, for instance, I encountered daily reminders in my immediate living space that evoked conscious conservation of the earth's resources. Quotes or sayings posted near light switches, bathtubs, and sinks reminded me of the precious nature and sacred dimensions of water and energy, their cosmic context, and their spiritual relevance. Each time I washed my hands, I read a sign next to the sink that explained: "The Earth is one planet and its water is one water, flowing on, over and through the Earth and all of its living creatures. In its flow, the water joins each one of us to the other." I also read the following message before taking a shower each morning: "One World. One Water. One Life. Of all Earth's water, 97% is salt water. Of the 3% fresh water, 2% is frozen in polar ice caps."

I confess that these little posted signs achieved their desired effect. As my daily consciousness grew that I was using some of the meager one percent of fresh water available on the planet (and an even smaller percentage that was actually potable) to clean my body, I became filled with profound gratitude for the luxury of a daily hot shower—and tried to make my showering as brief as possible. When I washed my hands or brushed my teeth, I found that I could not help but imagine the water that I was using connecting me to every other creature on the planet, and I remembered to turn the faucet off while soaping up or brushing my teeth. The sisters at Crystal Spring had created an environment where each one of these moments of resource-using personal care and hygiene became moments for contemplation and spiritual reflection. In this way, the sisters incorporated an ecological spiritual dimension into the simplest daily tasks. They made the most of a "captive audience" (the hand washer, the tooth brusher, the bather) as they sought to cultivate awareness about sustainability and conservation.

While at Crystal Spring, one of the sisters told me a story about her early days in the Dominican novitiate. At one point, she had used black indelible marker to write in big letters "STRIVE" on the white forehead band that secured her novice head covering. As she put the white band on each day, seeing the message reminded her to work extra hard in all of her efforts, be they physical, prayer-related, charitable, and so forth. (On very hot days, the marker, softened by perspiration, would brand a faded outline of "STRIVE" on her forehead.) The little notes and signs I encountered around the Earth Literacy center may have been gentler, somewhat less insistent than the black-markered "STRIVE," but they captured my attention no less indelibly. They made it impossible to go about the daily routines of life without contemplating a larger existence and the effect of my actions on it.

Perhaps the most "earthy" example of seamlessly blending everyday mundane activity with contemplative opportunity I experienced was at Genesis Farm in New Jersey, where guests who use the farmhouse composting toilet find themselves a captive audience for information on the fascinating process of water-free human waste recycling. Posted signs in the bathroom instruct guests how to aerate their compost deposits with dry leaves or wood shavings and then invite them to follow the composting process from start to finish via a special illustrated booklet entitled "Goodbye to the Flush Toilet."

The keynote speaker at the 1998 Sisters of Earth conference, bioregional activist and author Stephanie Mills, identifies the ecological practice of bioregionalism as being both "vow" and "devotion." Mills explains that bioregionalism is more than "fifty simple things" people can do to save the planet;

"Off the grid": Genesis Farm solar panels installed and designed by Sun Farm Network™.
(Photo courtesy of Sun Farm Network™.)

it is instead about "growing a lifeway."[47] It is, she says, "a clear morality" that shapes every aspect of life, "from how you shit to how you pray."[48] The daily practices of green sisters exemplify Mills's point. Whether it is driving, washing, or even engaging in bodily elimination, green sisters' ecologically sustainable lifestyles demonstrate that each of these activities can be performed mindfully, consciously, and with deep awareness of the interconnected life community.

In cultivating and modeling ecologically sustainable living, sisters have begun to cultivate habits or disciplines that include much more than simply mindful consumption of water and energy. Cleaning, cooking, clothing oneself, caring for one's body, sheltering (or "sacred homemaking"), and so forth, each takes on an ecological spiritual dimension. I first learned how to make nontoxic window cleaner using vinegar, for instance, when cleaning the Genesis Farm Learning Center's large wildlife-viewing window. I subsequently encountered other homemade brews at other centers and learned that many green sisters take the time to mix their own nontoxic cleaning supplies so as not to pour chemicals down their drains that add to groundwater contamination.

In fact, the sisters at Crystal Spring in Plainville, Massachusetts, hold workshops in which they specifically teach ways to make not only nontoxic household cleaners but all-natural, nontoxic personal care products as well. The sisters identify these "Do No Harm" workshops as part of a larger program series directed at taking "small steps" toward a healthier relationship with the planet. "Like all animals," explain the sisters, "our trails reveal us. Even cleaning products that wipe up spotless leave our mark. Are we becoming a less toxic, more compassionate presence? Can we create products that tell the story of our lives as an inventive, deeply respectful species making new combinations that reveal our capacity for taking other species into account?"[49] Here the sisters' language of "spotlessness" evokes a kind of ecologically mindful consciousness of what it is to be "immaculata"—literally without stain. Consumer culture may market heavy-duty detergents and chemical cleaners as products capable of removing all stains, but the sisters point out that ironically these very products that promise to cleanse and purify our bodies and our environment end up only staining our conscience, our health, and the planet. Significantly, the sisters also acknowledge that like any animal, we all leave trails of some sort. Green sisters' antitoxic programs like the one at Crystal Spring are aimed at softening and lightening those trails in the name of compassion.

When I interviewed sisters about the "spiritual dimension of their ecological lifestyle choices," some of them immediately took issue with my framing of this question. For Diane Roche, the wording of my question seemed to be premised on the assumption that "spirit" and "matter" are different or separate. "The doing of it [daily ecological practices] is the spiritual dimension," she explains. "The doing of it generates the spiritual dimension that claims its own expression . . . spirit and matter co-exist never to be separated. Working for harmony with Earth is both a spiritual and material path."[50]

Sister of Charity Maureen Wild, at the time a resident of a small island off Vancouver Island in Canada, expressed a similar corrective to my question about the spiritual dimensions of things such as consumer choices and other practical daily activities. For Wild, as with Roche, the framing of my question asserted a dichotomy between "matter" and "spirit" that completely missed the point and misunderstood the approach and mindset of ecologically concerned sisters such as herself. Here again, I am grateful that the open-ended format of interviews allowed for sisters to "talk back" to my questions and critique their conceptual framing. In Wild's critique of my question, I discovered a great deal more than I otherwise would have from a standardized limited response. Like Roche, Wild enumerates her daily observance of "practical green disciplines."

I don't use the car unless necessary . . . I "save up" my trips if I can.

I try to buy locally grown organic food.

My diet is primarily vegetarian . . . eating low on the food chain.

I distill my own water and use this for drinking and cooking.

All my bathroom products are eco-friendly (toothpaste, shampoo, soap, health supplements, toilet paper, etc.).

Many of the clothes I wear are recycled from others.

I go for walks in nature.

I listen to the birds while I work at my desk . . . and look out many times to the outdoors, to the trees, the plants, the water (a bay between Vancouver Island and where I live on Salt Spring Island).

I read a lot of earth-related news/thoughts each day.

I bring earth's beauty into my living space with flowers, stones, seeds, shells . . . an ever constant reminder before me.

In moments of prayer, I generally use beeswax candles that purify the air as they burn (i.e., paraffin-based candles add toxins to the air).

I listen to recorded music that helps me to connect with earth.

I do Tai Chi Chih that helps me connect body, mind and Spirit of earth that is me.

I rarely watch TV.[51]

When I ask about the "spiritual dimension" of these disciplines, however, Wild lets me know in no uncertain terms that I am not "getting it." She walks me through the vital difference between the way I have constructed my question and her own holistic understanding of things:

> To practice the discipline of discerning what's "enough" at any one moment . . . the discipline of purchasing products out of a growing ecological sensitivity and responsibly dealing with discarded paper, metal, glass, plastic . . . the discipline of reducing the use of a car . . . the discipline of choosing and using eco-sensitive washing products . . . the discipline of reducing electricity and moderating one's use of fossil fuels . . . ALL OF THIS AFFECTS MY SPIRIT . . . and therefore is a practice of my SPIRIT. Are they "practical disciplines"? Yes. Are they "spiritual practices"? Yes . . . It's all connected to my Spirit dimension. We cannot be separated out—body from Spirit, mind from body, mind from Spirit . . . practical from spiritual . . . consumer products from prayer . . . it's all of a piece for me. So everything becomes a "spiritual dimension" in all my choices. Consumer choices are integral to this. Dichotomies are not helpful to me.[52]

Rose Mary Meyer, a Sister of Charity from Illinois, echoes both Wild's and Roche's critiques of my question and how it was framed. Using Sister of Loretto Elaine Pravellet's language, I had asked sisters whether they regarded ecofriendly lifestyle choices such as recycling, purchasing ecofriendly products, conserving resources, and so forth to be "spiritual practices." Meyer responded, "I must say that I have difficulty [with] the dualistic thinking of separating out practical disciplines and spiritual practices." Later on, she added, "Again, I am having a bit of trouble with the dualistic separation of spiritual dimension and consumer choices. I understand us as spiritual beings, so all our actions have a spiritual dimension."[53] Sister of St. Joseph Mary Southard, cofounder of Allium, an ecospirituality center based in her congregation in La Grange, Illinois, articulates a similarly unified vision of the spiritual and the material, the sacred and the mundane, identifying daily activities such as starting one's automobile, turning on the faucet, and turning on lights—or even daily practices such as yoga and other types of embodied awareness—as "bells of mindfulness" that she says help her to remember "the reality beneath the surface." Such practices, adds Southard, "can call us to 'remember' the presence of the Holy, in whom we live and move and have our being!"[54]

A vital and common critique emerged from Roche, Wild, Meyer, Southard and others in strong favor of holism and interconnection and strongly against what sisters identified as false (and even harmful) dichotomies or dualisms. The point was impressed on me in interview after interview (in person, by telephone, or electronic), a feedback process that helped me as a researcher and as someone outside the community to identify what was truly important to sisters and where my framing of discussion was not speaking to their perspective or experience.

Wearing Green Habits

All of the green sisters I interviewed had, in some way, reinhabited the traditional habits of dress, either by making a commitment to wear used or recycled clothing (so as not to consume any new resources) or, when affordable, making a commitment to support sustainable agriculture by wearing organically produced clothing. Having mostly set aside traditional garments in the 1960s and 1970s to adopt the dress of the day, green sisters' clothing choices constitute yet another area of daily earth mindfulness. Dress, often the physical marker of identity within a religious community, is but one aspect of vowed life that sisters are rethinking through a new ecological context. The "habit," of course, has been a traditional marker that, in recent history at least, has set Roman Catholic nuns apart from the rest of society. (When many women's religious orders were first founded, members simply wore the customary dress of the day.) To a large degree, the wearing of the habit changed among American nuns following the Second Vatican Council.[55] Starting in the late 1960s, many nuns chose to wear the "dress of the day" as their founders had, opting to don the habit only for special occasions. In *Midwives of the Future,* a collection of stories from American sisters about their experiences of the Vatican-initiated investigation of religious life, a 1970 excerpt from Patricia Lucas's diary describes the shift in thinking during this time. She boldly declares: "I don't need a habit if what I am speaks louder than what I wear."[56]

In a new and greener twist on orthodoxy, the Green Mountain Monastery sisters in Vermont have chosen a distinctive religious garment for their community. An attractive but modest brushed cotton blue denim dress (short sleeves in the summer, long sleeves in the winter), has become the Green Mountain sisters' community dress. The dress itself, which is tea length and practical for light physical work, is easily washed and maintained, yet feminine. The sisters do not wear their official religious dress all the time, especially when gardening, cooking, or doing other jobs that call for work clothes, but they do wear the matching dresses publicly while attending Mass or other community events. Their distinctive garb makes them easily identifiable by friends and neighbors, and the simple, economical, and comfortable dress was chosen, according to the Green Mountain Monastery's Rule of Life, in a conscious "act of resistance against the dominant culture of advertising and its large-scale manipulation of women." The Rule of Life goes on to proclaim, "We oppose the unrealistic demands of the fashion world on women both physically and financially."[57]

Whereas the Green Mountain Sisters were the only sisters I encountered who had decided to return to a regularly worn common (albeit updated and modified) religious garment for their community, all of the green sisters I interviewed have, to some degree, reinhabited the traditional habit or religious garment within an ecological context. Sister of Charity Maureen Wild shared with me her "green" clothing habits, explaining,

> I do the following:
> - Buy used and some new clothes . . . made of natural fibres (often cotton or wool) . . . and generally made in Canada.
> - Buy locally made wool socks (wool is an abundant product on an island [Salt Spring Island] with many sheep).
> - Recycle clothing that I have not worn for a while . . . giving items to local thrift stores (like the Salvation Army or Hospital Auxiliary used clothing stores).
> - I generally cannot afford clothes made of organic cotton . . . but do own one or two tee-shirts!
> - I like to hang my clothes to dry if the conditions are right.[58]

For ecologically active sisters, there is a certain ethical or spiritual framework that guides their clothing choices. Today, as before Vatican II, their costume speaks of key values and commitments. Some restrict their purchases of any new clothing to garments made of only organic cotton or wool, thus supporting a market for more environmentally friendly clothing manufacture.

Others speak of never buying new clothes and, instead, shopping in thrift stores for used clothing or exchanging clothes with friends. Some wear as their garb "earth awareness clothing"—earth-related T-shirts with environmental messages on them or with depictions of the cycle of seasonal equinoxes and solstices on the front.

Some sisters I spoke with expressed frustration that, despite practicing ecofriendly clothing disciplines similar to those that Maureen Wild articulates, their wardrobes seem to expand and complicate their "simple" lifestyle. Some sisters have adopted strategies for dematerializing. One rule that I heard repeatedly from sisters was that any item that had not been worn for a year should be given away.[59]

Significantly, in our conversations about contemporary dress and strategies for simplification, a sentiment that repeatedly emerged was respect for the traditional habit. Although none of the sisters I spoke with wished to return to compulsory habit-wearing, contrary to stereotypes about post–Vatican II "new nuns," none of the women with whom I spoke expressed bitterness or resentment about the habit. Instead, sisters often spoke in affectionate terms about the beauty of their community's traditional garb (and its efficacy in limiting clothing consumption). In particular, sisters have told me how incredibly offensive it is for them when, from time to time, they receive calls at their motherhouse from people who ask to "borrow a habit for Halloween" or for theatrical productions.[60] Although almost all of the green sisters I have met do not choose to wear their community garb, they do express a deep respect for this traditional garment and its significance. It is important to note that the sisters of the Green Mountain Monastery who have specifically chosen a community garb have chosen something contemporary to the times, something economical, comfortable, and practical. The fact that the sisters themselves choose to wear this garb frames its wearing according to their own ascribed meaning and significance; that this rule is not externally imposed on them casts a much different light on this practice than was the case in previous generations.

Fasting from Consumer Culture

In the post–Vatican II updating and renewal of religious life, one of the markers of the "new nun" was that she engaged in modern behaviors that connected her to the wider world. Keeping abreast of world events through the nightly news was common practice for the "new nun," who rather than remaining sheltered was instead well informed and active in and among the world.[61] This awareness became especially important in the 1960s as sisters involved themselves in civil rights work and anti–Vietnam War protests. In the 1970s, sisters continued to stay informed about the culture, not simply through their increased contacts with laypeople, but also via various media. By tuning in to a variety of television programs that addressed edgy social issues (for example, racism and bigotry, as represented in *All in the Family;* women's liberation, as shown on *Maude;* and antiwar sentiments in *M*A*S*H*), sisters found themselves better able to relate to and interact with those outside the community. Although in two women's religious communities I visited (one on the East Coast and one in the Midwest) I noticed that a major evening activity for sisters (especially the elderly) was watching television programs, among green sisters who run or staff ecological centers and earth ministries, a countertrend proved to be the norm. Green sisters were concerned about an overabundance of television watching in their motherhouses and among their elderly and expressed a desire to return to evenings of prayer, conversation, instrument playing, or anything that would discourage members from becoming "couch potatoes."

   In contrast to the modern television-watching nun, then, green sisters have swung in the opposite direction, largely "fasting" from television and what they identify as the dehumanizing bombardment of media images and the messages they supply. The sisters of the Green Mountain Monastery, for instance, listen to the BBC radio news, a milieu they prefer as being less frenzied and more substantive than television news. Others listen to National Public Radio, subscribe to weekly magazines like *Time* and *Newsweek,* or share subscriptions to a major newspaper. Still others subscribe to "treeless" news services via the Internet, where they can control what news topics they spend their time on and the medium through which that news is delivered. Diane Roche, a sister of the Religious of the Sacred Heart and the executive director of an ecological restoration group in St. Louis, continues to watch television news but limits her general viewing. Roche says, "I have almost stopped watching television, except for the news and occasional programs on Public Television, because I found it to be addictive and spiritually numbing."[62] Note that Roche's language of addiction sounds very much like Sister of Loretto Elaine Pravallet's warnings about a culture of "collective narcoticization" and Josephite sister Toni Nash's call for practices such as "fasting from that which anesthetizes us . . . noise . . . over-eating and drinking, TV, acquiring, overworking."[63] Sister of St. Francis Marya Grathwohl, who works in a ministry that serves Native American women in Montana, says that she chooses not to watch television because it is "full of messages that define humans as consumers. I don't want to be around that energy. I use the TV almost solely for videos."[64] In my visit to sisters' ecological centers and other earth ministries, television sets were also used almost exclusively for educational program series or films and not for watching reruns of *Matlock*. The evenings I spent at Genesis Farm, for instance, were spent storytelling, stargazing, conversing, or singing. At the Green Mountain Monastery, the sisters brought out musical instruments and played and sang in the evenings before engaging in final evening prayers and subsequently entering into silence until morning. At Santuario Sisterfarm, after supper we went up to the roof of the santuario retreat tower, where a kind of solar calendar has been inscribed into the roof railing, marking the seasonal celestial movements. We conversed and watched the stars, pointing out various constellations and discussing them. Simply modeling a lifestyle alternative (one without television) and introducing it to others constitutes an activist move on the part of green sisters. There also seemed to be a conscious effort to balance serious engagement with the issues of the world with the need to place limitations or barriers on what and how much sisters expose themselves to, so as to prevent a kind of sensory flooding that leads to numbness, despair, and ultimately paralysis. Instead, green sisters seem to prefer replenishing their spirits at the end of the day with things such as music, wonder at the stars, or even simply silence.

What Would Jesus Drive?

On November 20, 2002, the Monroe, Michigan, IHM sisters formed a high-fuel-efficiency hybrid convoy, piling visiting clergy from around the country into their fleet of hybrid vehicles and delivering them to meetings with U.S. auto manufacturers in Detroit. The clergy were members of the National Religious Partnership for the Environment and leaders of other religious organizations that had banded together in an interfaith effort to lobby for more fuel-efficient alternatives to conventional fossil-fuel burning cars. IHM sister Nancy Sylvester drove a Toyota hybrid Prius with a sticker on the back asking, "What Would Jesus Drive?"—a clever variation of the quintessential nineteenth-century Christian morality test question, "What would Jesus do?"[65]

As a growing number of women's religious communities have done, the IHMs have made the conscious choice of replacing their aging vehicles with a fleet of hybrid gas-electric vehicles. With skyrocketing world oil prices in 2005 and 2006, the purchasing of such highly fuel-efficient vehicles became more than simply an ethical answer to "What would Jesus drive?" As it turns out, sisters' communities that purchased hybrids before the 2005–2006 oil crunch had been prescient. Sister Catherine Coyne, ecology director for the Sisters of St. Joseph in Springfield, Massachusetts, recalls that when the Toyota Prius hybrid purchase proposal went before her community's car committee in 2004, gasoline prices were at $1.39 a gallon. Because hybrid vehicles are more costly to purchase, there was some initial skepticism in the community about purchasing a Prius in lieu of a lower-priced vehicle. Two years later in 2006, when I spoke with Coyne, gasoline prices had risen well over the $2.00 a gallon mark. "People have begun asking, 'Why aren't we buying more?'" says Coyne, pointing out how the Prius has suddenly become very easy to make a case for on fiscal grounds. "We originally thought it would take about four and a half years to make the price of the vehicle pay off in terms of gas savings. Now with gas prices as high as they are, it's gone down to about three years."[66] Coyne also made the point that, even though it had been more expensive to buy a hybrid, her community had taken into consideration long-term costs both to the community and to the environment. "You have to look at the real life-cycle cost of any product you are buying," advises Coyne, who likens the community's purchase of the hybrid to their decision to replace 1,500 light bulbs at the Mont Marie Center with energy-saving compact florescent bulbs. The Sisters of St. Joseph's hybrid has also functioned as an important teaching tool. "It's a great conversation piece," says Coyne, whether she's at the gas pump or at a church, a school, or various community events. "People first ask about the car, and then it becomes a lead-in to discussing deeper topics—the oil crisis, patterns of consumption, the war in Iraq. It brings up all sorts of things, and curiosity about the hybrid is the perfect way to move into discussing some difficult issues." She adds that, as fuel-efficient and useful for teaching as the Prius has been, "It's merely an interim step. The next step will be purchasing fuel cell cars." Coyne's comment demonstrates once again how green sisters, as "bioneers" of ecological alternatives, are continually looking to the future. In fact, in our conversation, Coyne pointed out that the word "Prius" itself is a Latin term that means "to go before." In the areas of green building, hybrids, and ecologically sustainable living, sisters are indeed "going before" and creating new paths for others to follow.[67]

The hybrid gospel is spreading quickly. The Sisters of St. Joseph of Springfield's neighbors, the Sisters of Providence, have purchased hybrid vehicles, as have the Sisters of St. Joseph in Cleveland, Ohio, a community that plans to add twenty more hybrids to their fleet of one hundred cars. The Dominican Sisters of Sinsinawa, Wisconsin, have purchased hybrid vehicles and so have the Sisters of the Holy Cross at St. Mary's College in South Bend, Indiana. In 2004, the Sisters of Mercy in Burlingame, California, bought eight hybrid cars for their community, and the Sisters of St. Joseph of Orange (California) had purchased three. The same holds true for the Sisters of Mercy of the Americas, the Missionary Sisters of the Immaculate Conception, The Sisters of St. Francis, and the Benedictine Sisters. The list of hybrid-owning women's religious communities is both long and diverse.

While visiting the Green Mountain Monastery in Vermont, I had the opportunity to take a ride in the hybrid car used by Miriam Devlin and Nancy Earle, Missionary Sisters of the Immaculate Conception who were visiting from their home in Maine. While driving the Toyota Prius, watching the gauge showing how many miles we were getting to the gallon at any one time became a travel game to see how high we could get the miles-per-gallon score. Both sisters spoke thoughtfully about their concerns about global warming and about how this purchase was in keeping with their values and with their commitment to living lightly on the earth. Later, in an interview with Nancy Earle, she spoke with me about how the sisters had begun to think and act in terms of "whole systems." She explained that the vow of poverty goes beyond "monetary poverty" and for her is linked "to being simple and gentle with the Earth." Driving a hybrid vehicle (which she shares) is part of her commitment to being "more respectful of the surrounding ecosystem" and indicative of the "overall life stance" the sisters are trying to develop.[68]

Committing to a hybrid vehicle in Maine, where public transportation is extremely limited and automobile driving a practical necessity, was part of a larger project the sisters began more than a decade ago: reexamining their lives and their effect on creation. In 1980, Devlin and Earle designed the passive solar house they now share, which is extremely well insulated and fuel efficient. The sisters also either grow their own vegetables organically or buy organic produce. Like the Prius, says Earle, organic food is "not cheap," but the sisters have adjusted their thinking to encompass larger concerns and overall costs. She spoke with me about how she and Devlin save on medical bills because they lead a healthy lifestyle and are almost never sick, and by eating organically they are helping to support healthier and more socially just systems of agriculture. In the same way, purchasing a hybrid vehicle may be initially more expensive than purchasing a much "cheaper" conventional fossil-fuel car, but the long-term costs on the health and well-being of the planet make the hybrid the more economical choice overall for the larger community. For these sisters, "cheap" cars, like "cheap" food, are an illusion, and the sisters willingly trade immediate, short-sighted "gains" for holistic approaches and long-term planning.[69]

As with the Monroe IHMs' ecorenovated motherhouse, the fact that green sisters drive hybrids becomes a wonderful metaphor for sisters' own hybridity. Drawing on heterogeneous sources, sisters are composing a "hybrid culture" formed from elements of past religious heritage and current religious transformation, environmental thought and social justice thought, tenets of feminism and principles of the "New Science," communitarian experiment, food ethics, and much more. This complex heterogeneity gives birth to a new religious culture—one that is a product of its elements of origin and new additions but clearly more than a sum of its parts. Sisters drive hybrids, in part, in an effort to implement lower-impact alternatives that mitigate human contributions to the earth's environmental problems. That is, the combination of different categories (in the case of hybrid vehicles, "gasoline-powered" versus "battery-powered") produces a third option. This option might not be an ultimate solution to pollution problems and to the need to reduce greenhouse gases, but sisters consider it to be a better alternative to present behaviors and practices. In committing to this third way and making it part of a larger ethical and spiritual way of life, sisters are themselves giving birth to a new composite entity—a kind of hybridized "greening of faith" that drives the renewal of religious life.[70]

Costliness and "Success Stories"

The daily rigors of adhering to ecologically sustainable ways of life point to a unifying and powerful dynamic: It isn't easy being green. And from a sociological perspective, this bodes well for the future vitality and longevity of the green sisters movement. In 2001, an article in the conservative-leaning *National Catholic Register* posed the question "What attracts vocations?" Among the responses included was a comment from Father Glen Sudano, a superior of the Franciscan Friars of Renewal. His recipe for success was plain: "living a countercultural life that's authentic and fulfilling an evident need in society and the Church." The chief operating officer of the Chicago-based Institute on Religious Life, Michael Wick, similarly weighed in, providing an even more succinct response: "More orthodox communities."[71] In North America, no women's religious community has been championed more by conservative

Catholics as a model for the successful return to orthodoxy than the Dominican Sisters of St. Cecelia in Nashville, Tennessee. These Dominican sisters wear the traditional habit, chant or sing the Divine Office three times daily, observe meals in silence, and require that novices keep contact with outside family members or friends to a minimum. The lines of authority are drawn much more sharply at St. Cecelia's, where the democratic reforms in Dominican women's leadership since the 1960s seem to hold less appeal. Sisters pray the rosary daily, enthusiastically perform devotions to the Blessed Mother, and sing the "Salve" (Hail Holy Queen) after Compline (evening prayers) and before returning to their modest cells. Once in their cells, they have "physical refreshment" each night before rising again at five o'clock in the morning.

Rather than alienating young women with the return to pre–Vatican II norms of religious life, this approach has vocations at St. Cecelia's booming. In fact, novices have had to sleep in sleeping bags on the floor of the novitiate while new facilities are under construction because the sisters have run out of space to house them. The sisters admit anywhere from fifteen to twenty young women per year into their novitiate, culling these from about 100 to 150 applicants. While other communities of religious women have been discussing ways for their communities to "die gracefully," St. Cecelia's is not only moving forward and gaining momentum, but its membership numbers are at a 142-year all-time high. A picture of the 2005 year class shows freshly scrubbed and smiling postulants, some of whom look barely old enough to attend college. The median age of nuns at St. Cecelia's is thirty-six, whereas the median age of sisters nationally is sixty-nine. With statistics like this in mind, it seems that St. Cecelia's has found the secret to reviving vocations and revitalizing religious life. Rather than being viewed as outdated or irrelevant, the return to tradition, greater distinctiveness, and rigor at St. Cecelia's constitutes the community's greatest draw.

A considerable body of sociological research theorizes an explanation for this dynamic. Ask more and not less of community members, make religious life more demanding and difficult, and that life becomes more attractive to recruits and more satisfying to current members. It may seem paradoxical, but "the rewards of costly faith" make members value religious life more. Sociologists of religion Roger Finke and Rodney Stark argue that opening up religious traditions to allow the interjection of broader cultural influences and liberalization of doctrines generates institutional defections and decline. As their case in point, Finke and Stark point to Vatican Council II and its loosening of demands on Roman Catholic religious and laity that effectively eliminated distinctive sacrifices and stigmas (without replacing them), as the cause for the defection from and drop in religious vocations within the Church.[72] Laurence Iannaccone, also a sociologist of religion, has similarly argued that "the Catholic Church has managed to arrive at a remarkable, 'worst of both worlds' position—disregarding cherished distinctiveness in the areas of liturgy, theology, and life-style, while at the same time maintaining the demands that its members and clergy are least willing to accept."[73] Based on his sociological survey data, which look at the success of "costly" religious denominations, Iannaccone concludes that "strict churches make strong churches."[74]

Finke and Stark further cite sociological survey data that suggest "people tend to value religion on the basis of how costly it is to belong—the more one must sacrifice in order to be in good standing, the more valuable the religion." Finke, Stark, and Iannaccone all point the finger at the process of *aggiornamento,* or the "updating" of the Catholic Church with new ideas and influences, as being responsible for weaker institutional commitment among the flock. In Finke and Stark's model, strict, uncompromising religious institutions that impose high costs on their members are successfully competitive players within the "religious market," whereas institutions open to change are the "losers" of the "religious economy."[75]

Finke and Stark fail to address, however, the different fusions of "orthodoxy" and liberalization that are possible in religious communities and how they might also generate a reinvigorating dynamic that defies conventional conservative versus liberal categorizations. The green sisters movement suggests that religious traditionalism in practice, combined with liberalized interpretations of doctrine, can produce a kind of "best of both worlds," in which cherished traditions are still conserved but infused with unconventional content. So-called green neo-orthodoxies challenge the conventional genres of conservative and liberal by embracing salient aspects of both ends of the religiopolitical spectrum, refusing wholesale identification with either. At earth literacy centers across the country, green sisters are blending in various ways what Finke and Stark have set up as binary oppositions. The "Ecozoic monastery" in Vermont, for instance, combines the traditions and strictures of medieval monasticism with a contemporary environmental consciousness that is intrinsically demanding and rigorous. Sisters who are not living within monastic communities have also embraced a kind of neotraditionalist ecospiritual fusion of religious life that simultaneously demonstrates distinctiveness, structure, rigor, and commitment, while still embracing progressive politics, activist ministries, and in many cases a strong feminist consciousness.

One might ask whether having nuns or sisters live the "green" vowed life in daily spiritual practice, consumption of food and other goods, dress, prayer, and labor generates just the kind of "costly investment" that Finke and Stark, in their market-based model, link to statistics of higher levels of commitment and satisfaction among strict religious adherents. In *Reweaving Religious Life* (1991), Sister Mary Jo Leddy makes the case for not throwing the baby out with the bathwater when effecting reform in religious life. She lobbies instead for "loosening the bonds of liberalism" over religious life, arguing that having all community members "comfortable" with the tenets of religious life is not the same as having them challenged.[76] Leddy finds something distinctly satisfying and meaningful about the sacrifice of individual commitments in the service of common commitments, a tenet that is also championed by the environmental movement. Interestingly, by observing a challenging daily ecological practice in purposeful service to the whole earth community, green sisters creatively reclaim some of the traditional elements that have made conservative religious communities so attractive in recent years.

Sociologist of religion and Sister of Notre Dame de Namur Mary Johnson points to "pockets of spiritual resurgence," as evidenced by her research, even as the institutional "decline" of Catholic vowed religious life remains well documented.[77] Green sisters' earth ministries and ecological centers constitute just such pockets of spiritual resurgence. Challenging the conventional wisdom that has dismissed the "doom" of religious orders in America as a fait accompli and unidirectional phenomenon, the green sisters movement demonstrates that ecological practices and commitments can function as a rigorous and reinvigorating force in the lives of religious women. For green sisters, the process of reinhabiting both religious traditions and physical landscapes is not merely philosophized but rather worked out on a daily basis. Through contemplative labor, prayer, art, meditation, worship, and local and international activism, the aim of these religious women has been to move discussion into practice. In their work of reinhabiting, green sisters affirm Albert Camus' observation that "sense of place is not just something that people know and feel, it is something people do."[78]

Are Green Lifestyles the New Asceticism?

Is the practice of ecologically sustainable lifestyles, with its composting toilets, aerated showers, recycled clothing, fasting from television, and return to the basics of nontoxic homemaking, a return to ascetic practices among communities of women religious? Yes and no. It is important to understand that sisters' ecological disciplines and green habits do not constitute a revived culture of women's self-negation, masochism, and self-effacement. Historian Paula Kane has studied the culture of victimhood among religious sisters and found that

> cultivation of victimhood was ubiquitous in convent training prior to Vatican II, often directing a nun or sister to "offer herself up as a victim" in order to relieve a particular priest from physical or mental anguish. Sisters cultivated the victim spirit through prostrate prayer, making Sacred Heart novenas, and keeping the Holy Hour on Thursday night from eleven P.M. to midnight . . . Daily penance might take the form of "fasting and abstinence," such things as kneeling with extended arms when alone, not warming oneself when cold, scourging oneself with a discipline, wearing rough iron chains and hairshirts, etc.[79]

Robert Orsi has also considered the romanticized Catholic culture of suffering. His recent work highlights the early and middle years of the twentieth century, when glorified pain and physical distress were considered a "ladder to heaven." Pain, says Orsi, "purged and disciplined the ego, stripping it of pride and self-love."[80]

Although practicing "green habits" certainly involves self-discipline, lifestyle limitations, and abstention from certain behaviors and consumption patterns, the intent and the end result of environmentally sustainable life disciplines among green sisters depart considerably from the history of victimhood, self-inflicted pain, and self-flagellation among Catholic religious women. For one thing, in the culture of green sisters there is a strong affirmation of the body (especially women's bodies) and of its legitimacy as a material entity, an affirmation that comes from the feminist underpinnings of the movement. Ecological learning and retreat centers like the Allium Center in Illinois have sisters on staff who are professionally certified in massage therapy and various forms of bodywork, helping to nurture sisters' bodies and spirits, keeping them in good physical and emotional health.

Santuario Sisterfarm, too, has a hot tub with a beautiful view of the Texas hill country, where after a hard day's work at cutting back a high-water-consuming invasive species of cedar on the land, we all soaked our muscles and restored our bodies for the next day's physically demanding challenges. This hot tub, which clearly soothes the flesh instead of mortifying it, is a far cry from sisters' wearing hairshirts and doing daily penance. Indeed, it would be a mistake to read sisters' ecodisciplines as a return to a "romantic" culture of suffering and self-victimization among women religious. In keeping with the post–Vatican II culture that renounced an ongoing spiritual war with the body and mortification of the flesh, sisters' ecological learning centers and earth ministries reflect the body-positive aspects of living in an ecofriendly environment. The body, itself an extension of the sacred earth, deserves the same respect and celebration as does the rest of creation, and so it is not uncommon for green sisters to have a daily practice of tai-chi-chuan, yoga, or some kind of body prayer that affirms the sacredness of the body.

Far from leading lives that are pinched, dour, and repressed, green sisters demonstrate the pleasures of ecologically mindful living—a practice of daily meditative nature walks; natural foods cooking; freedom from the din and overstimulation of televisions, cell phones, and other extraneous electronics; the soft feeling of organic cotton; the quiet ride and low operating expenses of a hybrid vehicle; the truly "fresh" scent of a home cleaned with lemon juice and white vinegar instead of polluted with synthetic chemicals; and the comfort of "real" furnishings (albeit modest and recycled ones) made of natural materials instead of polymers, polyester, and particle board.

What is for some "denial" is for others the luxury of respite from the many stressors and the fast pace of modernity—a world that is all too much with us. At one Sisters of Earth meeting, a sister was remarking on a high-end resort in the Caribbean she had read about where guests pay seven hundred to a thousand dollars a night for rooms in which they are guaranteed no phone, no television, no Internet hookup, and no other means by which their offices might communicate with them. She laughed and said, "And to think, we offer all that and *less* and only ask for a $30 donation!"[81] It may not be easy being green, but sisters make a serious case for greener lifestyle habits that provide valuable, deeper, and more fulfilling life experiences—even as they reduce the human "ecological footprint" on the habitats of other-than-human communities.[82]

4. "CHANGELESS AND CHANGING"

Engaged Monasticism in the Ecozoic Era

It is a cool June morning, and just as the sun begins to peek over the Green Mountains, Sister Gail Worcelo, Sister Bernadette Bostwick, and I file out of the sisters' modest farmhouse toward their compact Ford Tempo. The car, fairly long in the tooth but neat and clean with its rust spots carefully patched by Bernadette, brings to mind the environmental adage "recycle, reuse, and repair." Once the three of us are arranged inside the car, Gail takes up a small wooden mallet and strikes a meditation chime located on the dashboard. The chime rings throughout the interior of the car, and all of us fall silent and bow our heads. The chime begins a period of silence in which we reflect on the earth's resources that will be used in the course of operating this vehicle. We take time to be mindful of the effects of driving on all of creation and to be mindful that this practice must be used sparingly. Finally, we pray that no harm will come to other beings as a result of our driving and that no harm comes to us. After a minute or so, Gail raises her head, brightly starts the car, and off we go on a quest for land—scouting possible locations for the first "Ecozoic" monastery. This new foundation will be the first women's religious community explicitly devoted to healing the earth.[1]

Monastic communities in the Western tradition have ideally modeled themselves on the "Kingdom of God." While the Green Mountain Monastery's references to the creation of an "Ecozoic" monastery and to bringing about the "Ecozoic era" do not literally invoke this Kingdom of God image, the community's day-to-day modeling of "earth healing" through greater ecological sustainability does tap into its spirit. A concept derived from the Green Mountain Sisters' mentor, Passionist priest Thomas Berry, "Ecozoic" means "house of life" and refers to what Berry envisions as ideally the next geological

Monastery founders Gail Worcelo and Bernadette Bostwick with Thomas Berry.

stage in evolution, to follow our current "Cenozoic era."[2] In the Ecozoic era, explains Berry, the "distorted dream of an industrial technological paradise [is replaced] by the more viable dream of a mutually enhancing human presence within an ever-renewing organic-based Earth community." He continues, "The dream drives the action. In the larger cultural context the dream becomes the myth that both guides and drives the action."[3]

The sisters of the Green Mountain Monastery consciously embody this dream. By modeling stability, earth literacy, commitment to the land, self-sufficiency, ecologically conscious voluntary simplicity, and even liturgical forms that include scientific evolutionary narrative, they are actively defining what it means to be an Ecozoic monastery. Living as much as they can as if the Ecozoic era has already arrived, the sisters strive to do their part to help bring it about. This connection is explicitly expressed in the design heading the monastery's 2005–2006 stationery, which reads: "Green Mountain Monastery / An *Ecozoic Monastery for the 21st Century / Where the Catholic Monastic Tradition Interfaces With the Unfolding Story of the Universe."[4] Below the heading, an asterisk explains that Ecozoic means "house of life." The choice of the word "interface" here is interesting because it evokes both a modern high-tech electronically based context (as in the interfacing of different computer parts or software systems) as well as a low-tech mending context. For instance, one sews an "interface" that unites the inner and outer fabric of a collar, lapel, or other part of a garment in order to lend it greater strength and stretchiness, an image in keeping with the sisters' mission to mend and strengthen our world.

Much has transpired in the lives of the sisters since I first visited them in Vermont during the summer of 2000 and experienced their "mindful driving" ritual. At the time, the vision of a monastery, as Worcelo describes it, "rooted in a cosmological context and inspired by the thought and spirit of Thomas Berry," was still in its germination phase.[5] The sisters were then observing morning and evening prayers with the Benedictine monks at nearby Weston Priory while developing their own unique rhythm of daily prayer life at their temporary lodging in a simple farmhouse. By the time I returned for a third visit to the sisters in the fall of 2003, the sisters had purchased a beautiful passive solar structure and barn on a 160-acre property in the small rural town of Greensboro, Vermont. This location holds special providential significance for the sisters because Thomas Berry grew up in and has now returned to the town of Greensboro, North Carolina. The sisters now refer to "Greensboro north and south" as being linked by the "great spine" of the Appalachian Mountains, which continues to connect the sisters back to the body of Berry's charism.

The sisters have now raised funds to begin on their new land capital projects and renovation of the existing structures. One such project is a library that will hold many volumes given to the sisters by Thomas Berry from his own collection. The sisters have also attracted over one hundred "companions"—those with whom they engage in daily prayer, study, and spiritual exploration. In 2003, cofounder Bernadette Bostwick (previously a lay associate) took private vows within the new community and officially became a sister of the new monastery. The sisters have composed their Rule of Life (a community's set of guiding principles), guided by an evolutionary consciousness or, as Gail Worcelo puts it, "shaped from the understanding of an unfolding universe."[6] Locally, the sisters have been active in organizing a dynamic series of outreach workshops, fireside chats, and "monastery cafes," addressing a variety of ecological and spiritual topics. Sisters from other communities have partnered with them on a number of projects, including the purchase of the Greensboro property, made possible by many donations and a loan from the Sisters of Loretto based in Nerinx, Kentucky (now officially called the Loretto Community).[7]

By June 2005, the sisters had begun to invite women into a "discernment process" for joining the new community. At the time, the sisters had just modified the main monastery building by adding sixteen rooftop solar panels to serve all of their electricity needs. At the completion of the project, Worcelo exclaimed: "Our monastery has become a mini-generator!"[8] And so it has. The community has become a generator not simply of electrical energy but also of prophetic ideas and energy for exploring both new and old paths of religious life. In environmental terms, the monastery's achievement of self-generated energy is referred to as "going off the grid." In Benedictine terms, the sisters' commitment to using self-generating renewable resources fulfills St. Benedict's insistence on community self-sufficiency. What's more, the monastery's organic garden currently provides much of the community's produce. A greenhouse enables the growth of winter and early spring crops, thus making the community even more self-sufficient.

Like their counterparts in apostolic communities, the Green Mountain Sisters put into practice a number of "green habits" or ecodisciplines. They consume few resources, wear simple denim dresses (their official community garb), observe the traditional monastic prayer times of dawn and dusk, and engage in contemplative labor such as gardening, cooking, bead-making, and religious-icon painting. Reinventing and renewing the Catholic monastic tradition in the context of what they identify as a new evolutionary cosmological consciousness, the Sisters of the Green Mountain Monastery (like apostolic green sisters) seek to reinhabit the traditional vows and live them in more ecologically conscious ways. Under the guidance of Thomas Berry and inspired by the beauty and simplicity of the Rule of St. Benedict, the sisters seek to cultivate a community that is ideally a "seamless garment" of "ora et labora" (words [prayer] and work).

The Green Mountain Sisters' way of life challenges conventional dualisms that oppose monastic retreat and worldly engagement. The sisters instead create a third way: a path of "engaged green monasticism." Their fusion of contemplative and activist inclinations, Western monasticism and contemporary cosmological physics, and Catholicism and environmentalism, affords further demonstrations of green sisters' skillful bridging of conventional "liberal" and "conservative" designations, as they bring together old and new perspectives on religious life. In 1998, sociologist of religion Mary Johnson wrote: "I predict that the twenty-first century will be marked by a Catholic reclamation of spiritualities, prayer forms, traditions, practices, and artifacts from previous centuries, which will be woven into existing institutions and which will become foundational for new institutions . . . The old symbols will be imbued with new meanings in response to the fundamental need to find paths to contemplation in new [contexts]."[9] The Green Mountain Sisters provide a model example of religious women who seem bound and determined to prove Johnson's prediction correct.

Upon This Rock . . .

The preamble to the *Rule and Constitutions of the Sisters of the Green Mountain Monastery* reads:

> In this particular historical period, we come into existence at a time when the total range of life systems of the planet are endangered. The geological, biological and chemical balance of Earth, so necessary for life and the very basis of our continuity as a species, is undergoing irreversible damage and disruption. This loss is bringing with it a corresponding diminishment of soul. In destroying the Earth, the matrix of Mystery and locus of encountering God, we are bringing harm both to our outer world and inner spirit. This devastation is being brought about by an industrial mindset that sees the Earth as devoid of spiritual meaning or Divine presence. In response to the magnitude of the crisis we acknowledge the need for reorientation of Christian thought and action from a primary preoccupation with humans to a primary concern for the total Earth Community. In considering the enormity of what is happening and the consequences for every living being on the planet we are convinced, in light of the Gospel, that this assault on the natural world is sinful and contrary to the teachings of our faith. It is within this urgency that we are founding Sisters of the Green Mountain Monastery.[10]

In settling into their permanent monastery home, one of the first things the sisters did was prepare the monastery's main building (not originally well heated) for Vermont's cold winters. In keeping with their mission and stated "primary concern for the total Earth Community," the sisters researched environmentally low-impact and sustainable heating options appropriate to their bioregion and built two fuel-efficient, clean-burning masonry woodstoves. In the construction of the central stove, the sisters embedded a variety of rocks sent to them from friends and supporters from all over North America and beyond. The sisters note that not only does this stove now provide them heat, but it also tells the geological history of Vermont, the Green Mountain bioregion, and even points to the evolutionary history of the planet.

> As we [the sisters] sit upon the soapstone bench [surrounding the stove]," remarks Worcelo, "we recall the intense heat which forged it and the journey of so many stones through molten magma, lava flow, pressure and intense condi-

tions. As we walk around the stove and place our hands on its solid body we touch vast eras of time. Pre-Cambrian, Cambrian, Ordovician, Devonian, Jurassic, Cretaceous . . . Like a litany, we recite the name of the ancient ones upon whom we lay our hands—granite, marble, slate, quartzite, shale, schist, gneiss, greenstone, serpentine, limestone. Each touch takes us back in time and we experience awe in the presence of this council of elders.[11]

Reaching back through geologic eras of time effectively to the "rock of ages," the Green Mountain Sisters reach back to the bedrock of monastic tradition even as they forge that rock into this, its newest configuration. Worcelo describes the community as "rooted in the monastic tradition of the early Desert Mothers and Fathers of the East and then later St. Benedict in the West."[12] (St. Benedict of Norcia [480–543] is the founder of Western monasticism.) Benedict created a set of rules to organize and provide spiritual guidance to those who would embark on a cenobitic "life in common." In contrast to the eremitic (hermit-based) tradition of monasticism, Benedict's focus was on community life and not on personal contemplative withdrawal from community. "Interfacing" both these traditions, the Green Mountain Sisters balance the importance of dedicated participation within the human order of the monastic community and opportunities for solitary contemplation in close companionship with the natural world. The monastery rule of life, for instance, allows and encourages designated "hermit days" each month, during which sisters may set themselves apart from the human community in order to commune more deeply with the larger biotic community. At her previous monastery in rural Pennsylvania, Worcelo had co-constructed a straw-bale hermitage in the forest for this purpose. (During my solitary visit to this hermitage, I encountered a black bear at close range, which gave me more communion with the larger biotic community than I had bargained for.) As of spring 2006, the building of a timber-frame straw-bale hermitage was under way at the new monastery in Vermont. As prioress, Worcelo was also exploring the inclusion of a wilderness solo component to the novitiate training (similar to solo experiences included in Outward Bound trips) that would provide the novice the benefit of three days of intensive solitary contemplation in the natural world.

Although monastery cofounders Worcelo and Bostwick were originally members of a Passionist monastery (the same order to which their mentor, Thomas Berry, belongs), the sisters have gravitated toward models of both Celtic and Benedictine monasticism for a variety of reasons. One draw in particular has been the ecological aspects of the special relationship Benedictines have historically cultivated with the land. While acknowledging the negative influences of Christian thought and practice on Western attitudes toward nature, the sisters' mentor, Thomas Berry, points to five ecologically positive models that developed through Christian history: "1) the animate model of the Celtic period, 2) the custodial model of the Benedictine period, 3) the fraternal model of St. Francis, 4) the fertility model of Hildegard of Bingen, and 5) the integral model brought to us by Teilhard de Chardin." In discussing the Benedictine custodial model developed between the sixth and thirteenth centuries, Berry makes the case for the Benedictines as important forerunners to the caring stewardship approach now advocated by some "green" Christians. "One of the great things the Benedictines developed," says Berry, "was the idea that intellectual activity was associated with physical work, particularly work with the land . . . There was an emphasis on the cultivation of the soil as well as the learning about it." It was primarily through growing food, explains Berry, that the Benedictines developed an intimate sense of the earth and a spiritual connection to the land.[13]

Advancing these connections, the Green Mountain Monastery's literature identifies several sources from which the sisters draw direction and spiritual nourishment: "This community has its foundation in the Benedictine Monastic Tradition, seeks guidance from its roots in the Passionist charism and draws upon the ancient wisdom of the Desert Fathers and Mothers, those Christian monks and nuns of the East who sought God in the uncompromising silence and solitude of open spaces."[14] Benedictine traditions such as the monastic vow of *stabilitas,* for instance, harmonize particularly well with the ecological value placed on rootedness in community and commitment to place. A vow of stability meant that monastics, like today's bioregionalists, bonded themselves to a particular place, community, and people. For St. Benedict, "stability of place" was significantly linked to "stability of heart." In essence, *stabilitas* meant a lifelong profession to "staying with things"—both community life and the monastic practices of St. Benedict's rule—because "giving up and moving on" was not an option.[15] Similarly, staying at home and cultivating a detailed literacy in a particular ecosystem, watershed, or bioregion, according to contemporary environmental philosophers, is one of the most radical acts one can commit to the welfare of the planet.[16] Buddhist environmental philosopher and poet Gary Snyder, for instance, is famous for urging Americans to stay home and not move. Advocating a profound commitment to embeddedness within a local biotic community and a commitment to the kind of local sustainability that supports the long-term well-being of that community, Snyder comments that "the actual demands of a life committed to a place, and living somewhat by the sunshine green-plant energy that is concentrated in that spot, are so physically and intellectually intense that it is a moral and spiritual choice as well." Although Snyder was trained as a lay Zen Buddhist monk in Japan, there are pronounced affinities between his environmental thought and traditional Western Benedictine monastic values.[17] For bioregionalists, the depth of accountability, continuity, and place memory fostered by a profound rootedness in the local biotic community is an environmental activist's most powerful asset. Truly "to dwell" and to be embedded in place creates a kind of common cause between the landscape and its human inhabitants that bonds their mutual interests. This bioregional consciousness of "home" and the importance of continuity, commitment, and emplacement provide an interesting ecological twist to the habits or conventions of Western monasticism.[18]

At one point in our discussions, Worcelo felt that I was construing too narrowly the historical significance of the founding of the Green Mountain Monastery. She wanted me to understand that the formation of this new community was about something much larger than women's religious creativity and ecological sustainability, as important as those things are. For Worcelo, the founding of the monastery itself represents a major shift in the evolutionary trajectory of monasticism in the West. While focusing on "the trees" in my analysis, I had classically missed "the forest," and she provided the following corrective:

> Just as in the story of the Universe with its major transformational moments, those one time moments of grace that gave shape to everything that was to follow, so too religious life has gone through its own sequence of transformational moments from the time of the Desert Mothers and Fathers to the present. We see the founding of Green Mountain Monastery in this line of transformations. We have been reflecting on 5 great moments in the history of religious life:
>
> 1. In the 6th century, St. Benedict saw wandering men and women dedicated to the God Quest and gathered them together to establish a sustainable way of life.
> 2. St. Francis and St. Dominic in the 13th century founded groups of men and women in a new cultural context. Their founding was a new invention. The mendicant orders arose into being. The new city world needed a new religious identity different from the monasteries Benedict founded.

3. The 16th century called for another new leap in religious creativity. Ignatius of Loyola ignited the intellectual dimension of the tradition in a time of cultural creativity.

4. [Also in the sixteenth century], St Vincent de Paul took women out of the cloister and established activist women religious for the work of social justice in every arena of the human community.

5. [In the twenty-first century], we see ourselves and the founding of Green Mountain Monastery as part of a new phase in the history of the great transformational moments in religious life. This new phase is the cosmological. We consider this the greatest single challenge religious life has yet to face which has to do with the survival of Earth and an understanding of ourselves as both cosmological and planetary beings.

Our founding impulse is to contribute to the evolution of religious life and the Catholic tradition as it enters into its cosmological phase.[19]

One of the key points that Worcelo's explanation underscored for me was just how critically important it is to this community that members situate and root themselves within an honored Catholic heritage. The Green Mountain Sisters genuinely see themselves not as a departure from or a protest against their tradition, but as "caretakers" of its deepest and most powerful essence as it has evolved over time. According to the trajectory Worcelo provides, the sisters are ushering in the latest "great moment" (a major cognitive and practical shift) in the tradition's developmental essence. Not insignificantly, this shift is cast as being far from minor or incidental but on a par with the historically great moments brought about by the "Big Boys" (my phrase, not hers): Benedict, Francis, Dominic, Ignatius, and Vincent. Worcelo's vision further communicates a radically prophetic role that the sisters and their Ecozoic monastic way of life are poised to play in the interrelated evolution of monasticism, earth, and cosmos.

The monastery's Rule of Life, for example, systematically outlines the historic and prophetic dimensions of the monastery's founding. At one point, it declares, "We seek to reinhabit the spiritual landscape of our Catholic Monastic Tradition by understanding ourselves within the comprehensive context of the unfolding universe." Referring to one of "religion's" suggested etymological roots (*religare*—Latin for "to bind"), Worcelo elaborates that "as a new monastery for the 21st century, we 'bind ourselves back to origin' so as to understand our place in this vast, unfolding cosmic drama and guide the process forward."[20] This "binding back" both to Catholic tradition and to a common origin of life in the universe is rhetorically central to the work of green sisters.

The Green Mountain Monastery Rule of Life also suggests a kind of hybrid of traditional monastic principles with Thomas Berry's emphasis on cosmic evolution as the guiding sacred story of our time. According to the Rule, the sisters "are committed to the praise of the Divine through prayer work and scholarship, sustainable farming, and the cultivation of the arts. Our particular focus is to teach, by word and practice, our spiritual relationship with the earth through these various and professional disciplines."[21] This last point about teaching through word and practice raises an important question of which the sisters themselves are acutely aware. That is, if an Ecozoic monastery is founded in the woods (of Vermont) and no one knows it, does it really make a difference? Ecozoic monastic life then necessarily goes hand-in-hand with actively bringing the "good news" to others and with enacting justice in the world in keeping with the implications of that "new story." Fusing both an activist and contemplative life calls on sisters to maintain a delicate balance— to be rooted in and attentive to their immediate home community while carefully eschewing insularity from larger world concerns that affect the fate of the planet.

Engaged Green Monasticism

As Gail Worcelo explains in "An Ecozoic Monastery: Shaping a Transforming Vision for the Future,"

> In these early beginnings we imagine ourselves as missionaries to the bioregion and its life systems of water, air, and soil which must remain healthy if we are to survive. We imagine our monastery as a place of sanctuary for seeds, the new refugees of our time who need to be safeguarded from the fate of genetic manipulation. We imagine activating deep inner capacities still latent in our contemplative depths. We cherish the ability to open ourselves to a comprehensive compassion that is concerned for species thousands of years into the future in order to feel their vulnerability based on our actions now.[22]

For green monastics, figuring out the appropriate ratio of engagement in the broader culture to distance from that same culture is a complex calculation. Like many environmentalists, sisters struggle with whether it is more radical to withdraw from the "toxicity" of a destructive consumer-driven world run amok than it is to remain in the thick of active struggle—protesting, bearing witness to, and ultimately trying to heal the destruction.[23] Green nuns in particular (as opposed to sisters in "active" communities) struggle with these two paths. The first path is clearly radical in its adoption of and modeling of an intensely countercultural lifestyle. The second is also radical in that it adopts the kind of social engagement that not only puts both ethics and prayer into action but also, as we saw in Chapter 2, sometimes even puts nuns in jail.

A similar struggle between action and withdrawal has been faced by "green" Buddhist monks, who have developed a kind of engaged Buddhism that parallels the ecologically conscious approaches of green nuns. The path to engaged Buddhism sheds light on the ongoing development of green nuns' own variety of engaged monasticism. In reaction to the Vietnam War and geopolitical violence in Southeast Asia in the twentieth century, Vietnamese monks found themselves forced to wrestle between an ethical imperative for publicly visible protest against the war and a constant spiritual commitment to Buddhist ideals of nonattachment, meditative withdrawal, and the avoidance of karma-producing action. As Vietnamese monks took increasingly active roles in antiwar protest actions (with some monks famously self-immolating to draw attention to the brutality suffered by victims of the war), a socially engaged contemporary Buddhist monastic practice began to emerge. The Vietnamese Buddhist monk Thich Nhat Hanh and the Dalai Lama (the spiritual leader of Chinese-occupied Tibet) are two figures most widely recognized for their theorizing and practice of engaged Buddhism.[24] Both Thich Nhat Hanh and the Dalai Lama seek to bridge the conventional duality between meditative withdrawal and social or political engagement by offering a third path of "practice in action," which combines mindfulness and meditation with action to reduce the suffering of others.

Buddhist deep ecologist Stephanie Kaza uses the term "ecosattvas" to refer to those engaged Buddhists involved in environmental activism. Kaza says ecosattvas sacrifice their own progress toward release from karmic cycles by dedicating their lives to "saving all souls" through a combined meditative practice and active, nonviolent civil disobedience.[25] In particular, Kaza draws attention to the Buddhist principle of the "web of interdependence" (that which Thich Nhat Hanh terms "interbeing") as a core concept for healing the violence between humans and the natural world.

It is no coincidence, then, that Thich Nhat Hanh's work has significantly touched the life of Green Mountain monastery cofounder Gail Worcelo, one who is also dedicated to "healing" the violence she sees perpetuated by humans on the more-than-human world. In the 1980s, Worcelo read an influential article by Thich Nhat Hanh entitled "Nonviolence Practicing Awareness." It began with Thich Nhat Hanh's poem "Please Call Me By My True Names."[26] The poem tells the story of a twelve-year-old girl who is raped by sea pirates. The speaker of the poem identifies as both the raped girl and the sea pirates who rape her, acknowledging the ways in which each one of us both perpetuates and is victimized by violence. Thich Nhat Hanh's message in the poem is about opening the door of compassion via the realization that we all participate in violence in some form and that all violent acts (and their consequential pain) touch us through a web of interconnectedness. Worcelo says that Thich Nhat Hanh's message of nonviolence resonated deeply with her. After contemplating the poem many times over several years, she reflects, "As a human being who is part of a wider community, as a consumer of limited resources and as one whose nature is marked by sin and greed, I am one with the destructive action of the sea pirate."[27] This realization is echoed in Worcelo's public talks and smaller discussions, in which she discourages the conventional distancing of environmentalists from demonized corporate polluters, forest clear-cutters, corrupt politicians, and so forth. Instead she encourages greater recognition of collective responsibility for perpetuating the earth's problems.[28] In short, no one is *immaculada* ("without stain"), because we all contribute to some extent to environmental pollution and exploitation of the planet's resources.

Worcelo recounts that as a twelve-year-old girl growing up on the streets of Brooklyn in 1968, she encountered her own versions of "sea pirates." Like Thich Nhat Hanh, she speaks of a web of violence, connecting the bullying tactics of mob members toward shop owners in her Brooklyn neighborhood to the larger violence that shaped her young life—the assassinations of Martin Luther King, Jr., and the Kennedys; race riots; and the war in Vietnam. Through her formative study with Thomas Berry since her novitiate in 1984, Worcelo's understanding of this web of violence has broadened to include "the severe degradation of the planet."[29] Her founding of a new religious monastic community stems in part from her discernment that "community is the best arena to struggle toward a nonviolent way of being" and that "healing and protection of the earth from further devastation" begins with modeling new ways and patterns of being present to the larger planetary community. Much as Thich Nhat Hanh called for a new kind of engaged Buddhism in response to the crisis of war, Worcelo now explores a new kind of engaged monasticism or what she terms "sacred activism" in response to the crisis of "ecological violence."[30]

In this regard, Worcelo has been shaped by her American intellectual pred-ecessors in the Catholic monastic tradition, especially those who found com-mon ground between Eastern and Western monasticism. In the "Day Three" entry of a diary Worcelo kept during an Ecozoic spiritual retreat in the sum-mer of 2001, she calls in prayer for guidance from both her mentor Thomas Berry and the American Trappist monk Thomas Merton. She identifies both men as "modern-day Desert Fathers." During a period of meditation, she asks: "Abba [Father] Merton, Have you seen into the nature of reality? . . . Abba Berry, Where can one find God?"[31] The words of Merton, who built bridges between the Western and Eastern traditions, offer Worcelo strength and re-solve. Like Thich Nhat Hanh, whom Merton met at Gethsemani Trappist Monastery in 1966 and referred to as "his brother," Merton lived simulta-neously as monk and antiwar activist. Biographer Robert King defines the common approach of both these men as "engaged spirituality," defined as a wedding of contemplative practice, social action, and interreligious dia-logue.[32] In keeping with the spirit of Merton and Thich Nhat Hanh, Worcelo's work exemplifies King's criteria for engaged spirituality. In fact, as Worcelo's diary of her Ecozoic retreat unfolds over eight days, her ruminations clearly point to a kind of engaged monasticism that now infuses the new Green Mountain Monastery.

In her contemplative dialogue with her mentor, Thomas Berry (both a Passionist and a retired professor of Asian religions), Worcelo explores the challenge and rigor of faithfulness to multiple simultaneous commitments. Drawing from her own experience, she reflects on her final vows ceremony in 1991 when Thomas Berry gave her the ring of final profession. Worcelo recounts that this symbol "not only sealed [her] commitment as a vowed woman in the church but also wedded [her] to a passionate love affair with the Divine as revealed in the universe story."[33] Worcelo's own delicate balance of diverse commitments is reflected in the integration of seemingly opposi-tional elements within the structure and life of the monastery.

Undeniably, the monastery and its grounds, situated in beautiful rural Ver-mont, provide community members and visitors an increasingly rare oppor-tunity—a place to slow down and to reconnect to the natural world, a place of serenity in which one can actually hear oneself think and pray. In *The Solace of Fierce Landscapes*, Belden Lane explores the impulse to construct monastic life in wild places "on the edge" (mountains, deserts, remote islands, and so on). Lane finds that these liminal landscapes "provoke the identification and reordering of boundaries," ultimately confronting people with their own "edges."[34] Much of the impetus to locate the Green Mountain Monastery in a remote rural locale stemmed from the concerted aim to create a sanctuary or haven of renewal and rest from the hectic pace and clamor of contemporary society. "In our time of planetary genocide and biocide," states the monastery's literature, "as we witness the killing of life systems of the planet and the corresponding loss of revelatory presence of God, we are moved to respond."[35] The sisters' Rule of Life develops this theme, stating: "As a monastic community we situate ourselves in a place of *voluntary marginality* rather than *total absorption* in relationship to the culture. We do this in an effort to maintain critical perspective and prophetic witness."[36] Worcelo has spoken more specifically about the important role of healers or shamans who traditionally occupied positions of liminality at "the edge of the village," situating themselves at the threshold between everyday community life and encounters with the numinous that give rise to prophecy.[37]

Consciously locating oneself "on the edge" affords one a fundamentally different and countercultural perspective. The serenity of the Green Mountain Monastery, the sisters' ecologically sustainable (and thus countercultural) lifestyle, the quiet rhythms of daily prayer life, and the observance of seasonal and cosmological celebrations all provide a rare retreat from the frenzy of modernity. Ideally constituting a kind of "house of life," the rurally situated monastery facilitates a stepping back from the dominant culture in order to contemplate and begin manifesting humanity's role in the coming Ecozoic era.[38] But even the idyllically situated Green Mountain monastery is embedded in the struggles of community—local and global, human and nonhuman. Green sisters who have chosen to occupy the countercultural edge do so not to retreat from the tribulations of the planet but to gain a certain amount of prophetic perspective in dealing with these problems. Their use of Ecozoic language and imagery highlights this prophetic focus.

At various points while I was visiting the sisters, they observed silence as part of their day. From morning vigil (beginning at 5:00 A.M.) through breakfast (8:00 to 8:30), there was silence. After the last evening prayers, there was silence as well. And when we took our supper together, we often kept silent while listening to educational lectures on audiotape—a modern version of having the abbess read to the community during meals. But when it comes to peace, social justice, and environmental justice concerns, these sisters are hardly "quiet as nuns." The Green Mountain Sisters actively participate in conferences throughout New England (and as far away as India) that are geared toward working for peace and environmental justice. Although unable themselves to attend the 2003 anti–Iraq War demonstration rallies in Washington, D.C., the sisters participated in a local rally in support of the protesters and saw the Washington-bound buses off "in style." Positioned next to their sign, which read "Sisters of the Green Mountain Monastery—Arm in Arm for Peace," they held vigil candles and fortified demonstrators boarding the buses with hot tea and homemade muffins. They also brought their papier-mâché Peace Geese, which Sister Bernadette crafted after seeing similar puppet forms used by Vermont's political Bread and Puppet Theater. (This is the same theatrical group that helped to hide Vietnam War protestor and priest Daniel Berrigan when he was wanted by authorities for destroying draft records.)[39] As the protesters pulled away in buses, the sisters' Peace Geese gracefully flapped their wings up and down and sent them on their journey.

The Green Mountain Monastery was also one of the cosigners of the open protest letter to President Bush published as a full-page advertisement in the *New York Times* on December 4, 2002. In this letter, Gail Worcelo as monastery prioress, along with others identified as "Religious Leaders for Sensible Priorities," beseeched the U.S. President to turn back from the brink of war with Iraq.

In addition to antiwar work, the sisters have been publicly involved in activism for stricter organic food labeling and grassfed livestock labeling standards, farmland and open space conservation, and a number of other environmental causes. They have written letters to legislators and corporate executives, e-mailed, signed petitions, and worked their network of sister activists. Perhaps their most embodied form of activism, however, is tangibly modeling for others an ecologically sustainable way of life. Through workshops, lectures, and symposia, Worcelo shares with other communities (religious and nonreligious) her own community's efforts to, as she says, "understand themselves as part of a planetary community, a single sacred community of life."[40]

Again, there are identifiable parallels here to the traditional monastic charge to model the Kingdom of God. Of course not everyone can live in a solar-generated rural monastery, but as emissary of the monastery, Worcelo shares things that vowed religious and ordinary laypeople can do to live less wasteful and less ecologically destructive lives, such as using renewable resources, practicing voluntary simplicity, changing consumption patterns, and so forth. Articulating her prophetic vision for creating truly Ecozoic communities, Worcelo (like other women activists) is something of an "edge-walker"— as both a monastic at the margins and an earth activist at the center of struggle.[41]

Like most religious communities in North America today, the Green Mountain Monastery has its own web site that can be found on all major search engines. This web site and an e-mail network list keep sisters tapped in to a larger community and broader exchange of intertwining environmental and religious discourse. The sisters periodically send out newsletters by electronic mail or by conventional mail to keep supporters and friends abreast of their progress. Worcelo also spreads her vision of the Ecozoic monastery, teaching others about ecologically mindful living and spreading Berry's ideas as well as her own, through numerous speaking engagements. Monastery life is thus countercultural but not "out of it," and the community itself provides retreat while also staying very well connected through interlocking webs of correspondence, media, and personal contacts. All of these activities challenge the conventional norms of monastic isolation, while also enabling the community to maintain some degree of distance from the bustle of mainstream American culture.

As they develop a kind of hybrid form of "engaged monasticism," the Green Mountain Sisters respond to Benedict's call for moderation and balance.[42] In the process, sisters effectively intertwine the needs of the monastic community, the immediate surrounding community, and the larger global community. In fact, the very notion of religious community expands as Worcelo considers the entire community of life that encompasses the sisters themselves. Referring to the mountain that defines their landscape, she says, "The mountain is the monastery."[43] Even beyond this, she writes, "The monastery I am is the vastness of the universe itself . . . Bringing the full universe into Christian experience is still a novel and minority movement within my Catholic tradition. But for those of us who have awakened to this possibility, it is a wondrous opportunity."[44] This statement suggests an interface between the Western mystical ideal of "supreme union" and Eastern perspectives on "webs of interconnection" or "interbeingness." Worcelo once told me that there were times early in her journey toward planting the new monastic community when she felt very alone, sensing a call to a new mission but not yet sure what form it would take or how it would play out. During those times, she would pray in her garden, behold the life around her, and remind herself that wherever she was, she was always "in community." In the image of the cosmic monastery of which she is seamlessly a part, she again unites diverse components—the Benedictine emphasis on community, the cosmological science mysticism of Thomas Berry, the holistic cosmic visions of medieval mystics such as Hildegard of Bingen, and even homegrown Transcendentalist conceptions of an interconnected universe in which "the many are as one" in the "Oversoul."[45] It is perhaps the commitment to the cosmic monastery that gives rise to the Green Mountain Sisters' unique form of engaged monasticism—an energy-efficient hybrid, as it were, of monastic contemplation and sociopolitical outreach. Once again, interfacing disparate edges, sisters continuously find new ways to observe a kind of monastic *stabilitas* while answering the call to take tangible action to heal and mend the earth.

Observing the Liturgy of the Cosmos

"Welcome to our evening vespers in the monastery that is the universe itself," says Worcelo as she begins a retreat for a group of Loretto Sisters.[46] Over the course of the retreat, the sisters celebrate the "Liturgy of the Cosmos," a prayerful observance of unfolding cosmic events. The concept of the Liturgy of the Cosmos is borrowed from Worcelo's mentor, Thomas Berry, who believes that "we have lost touch with the cosmological order. The precise hour of the day is more important to us than the diurnal cycles. We're so busy worrying—Will I get to work on time? Will I avoid rush-hour traffic? Will I get to watch my favorite television program?—that we have forgotten the spiritual impact of the daily moments of transition."[47] Worcelo has taken Berry's abstract concept of forging a deeper intimacy and closeness with the cosmological order and translated it into embodied practice. Beginning with what she terms the "Feast of Elements," Worcelo gives each sister a copy of the periodic table of elements. Worcelo explains: "Together we would be doing a kind of *Lectio Divina* or sacred reading of our origins . . . There is no realization more profound than knowing that the elements of the periodic chart were forged in the stars whose dust has become our flesh."[48] Later in the retreat, Worcelo hosts a "cosmological seder supper" in which each table is covered in elements (stardust, salt water, stone, seeds, fruit, salt, herbs, bread, and wine) symbolizing the transformative events of the cosmos that emerged from what she calls "the Great Radiance, when the Fire within the Fire of all things entered the world" (in astrophysical terms, the big bang).

One might reasonably ask what is Christian about this celebration of the Liturgy of the Cosmos, but the premise of that question misses Worcelo's deft fusion of the story of Jesus, the story of the earth, and the story of the cosmos. Part of one vast intertwined evolutionary epic, Christ is embodied in cosmos and thus never separate from it. In fact, Worcelo begins the Liturgy of the Cosmos with the moment of "Great Radiance" (big bang), moves on to celebrate the birth of galaxies and stars and other evolutionary events, and then culminates, as she puts it, "in an Agape, a love feast in remembrance of the birth of Christ. A transformational moment in the history of the story when the universe, through the Christ, realized its complete oneness with itself and its Source."[49] Worcelo also conceives of Christ as "suffering his present Passion" in the wasting of the planet—a theme that is explored more in depth in Chapter 5.[50]

Sociologist Gene Burns would likely not lift an eyebrow at Worcelo's description of the Liturgy of the Cosmos. For Burns, this kind of variation and diversity within the faith is simply indicative of the genius of Catholicism's plasticity. In his research on the broad spectrum of experience and practice encompassed within the "frontiers of Catholicism," Burns observes, "It is clear that the Catholicism of American sisters is quite different from that of the Vatican." Burns explains, however, that "dissenting sisters see themselves as very faithful to the true spirit of Catholicism and certainly not simply as a peripheral faction."[51] In my own research, as I have gone over the transcripts of interviews and combed through the details of my interactions with sisters in the field, Meredith McGuire's caveat to scholars of religion has become a litany in my head. She writes: "We must drop the assumption that traditional institutional religious symbols, language, rituals, and practices are used for the reasons an institution once intended them. We cannot assume continuity between functions served by certain religious expressions in another time and place and the meanings of the same expressions today."[52]

The word "liturgy" itself technically refers to the public and official worship of the Church, but Catholics have a strong tradition of paraliturgical or quasiliturgical traditions: praying the rosary, walking the way (or stations) of the cross, making devotions to Mary and the saints, performing novenas (special prayers that are made nine days in a row), and so forth. It is in these more personal, less authoritatively controlled practices and spaces that historically there has been considerable room for creativity and experimentation. In the academic study of religion, this kind of creativity and experimentation has too often been dismissed as anomalous but interesting (or even quaint) folk practice.[53]

Within hierarchical structures of religious institutions themselves, creative experimentation might be looked on more negatively in terms of error, transgression, or even (in its most extreme varieties) heresy. The tensions over readings of tradition that are new, old, and both new and old are hotly debated among Catholic scholars themselves. In *Inventing Catholic Tradition*, Terrence Tilley cautions scholars of religion to remember that traditions are always "neither made nor found, yet both constructed and given." Tilley finds that scholars of and participants in religious traditions alike often mistakenly "presume that if those who live in a tradition in some way make up that tradition, it cannot be authentic." On the contrary, argues Tilley, "traditions are not fixed but fluid. If we neglect the shifts of tradition or canonize one form as normative . . . we can misread earlier traditions by taking them merely as parts of definable historical trajectories that issue a 'finished product' that is the 'right' tradition. We misread differences in traditions as 'deviations,' as 'errors,' or as 'private interpretations.'"[54] Andrew Greeley similarly argues for the importance of creativity to the vitality of a living faith, advocating a middle ground between the changeless and changing nature of Roman Catholicism. For Greeley, as both sociologist and priest, the creative spirit is essential to the continued vitality and well-being of the faith. He warns that the "high tradition" of the Church, whether theological or magisterial, must "listen carefully to the stories that the popular tradition tells or it will find itself cut off from the origins and the raw power of religion."[55] It bears consideration whether this kind of "raw power" is in fact what is being served for dinner at green sisters' cosmological seders.

During Gail Worcelo's eight-day silent retreat in 2000 to contemplate what form a new Ecozoic monastery might take, the fifth day of her retreat diary begins with her chanting the words of St. Elizabeth of the Trinity: "Changeless and calm Deep Mystery Ever more deeply Rooted in Thee."[56] As she chants this, she contemplates a photograph of the Andromeda Galaxy and reflects:

> I can almost see this, our closest neighbor, swirling within the cosmos that is ever becoming, expanding, and changing. And so, I become the meeting place of ancient Christian tradition and modern scientific discovery. The integration of both forms the matrix of my prayer. Each contemplation is needed: the view inward that the Christian tradition in its sustained contemplation and sacred text offers, and the view outward—the telescopic revelation into Mystery that science articulates . . . The compassionate curve of cosmic spacetime is sufficiently closed to maintain coherence and at the same time sufficiently open to allow for continued creativity. There is something of the holy embrace of God in the very structure of the universe, *changeless and changing*.[57]

Embracing both the changeless and the changing, Worcelo's new community affirms many of the aspects of monastic life that were at one time viewed as antiquated by the modern nun—wearing communal garb, observing the traditional monastic hours of prayer and reflection, making use of hermitage, taking at least some meals in silence, and engaging in *lectio divina* (sacred reading), agricultural self-sufficiency, and contemplative labor. Rather than merely representing a throwback to a bygone era, however, Worcelo has done something radically different with the reclamation and revisioning of her tradition. Her diary entry speaks as much to science mysticism as it does to Christian mysticism—as much to evolution and cosmological physics as to the wisdom of St. Elizabeth. The Benedictine Rule of Life, which informs the Green Mountain Sisters' own Rule of Life, divides the day into periods of sleep, prayer, sacred reading, rest, and physical labor, in which ideally prayer and work *(ora et labora)* become one. As with other aspects of religious life, Worcelo opens up the tradition of the Liturgy of Hours to new meanings. The Liturgy of Hours, says Worcelo, "which emerged from the monastic impulse, was fashioned *within the ever renewing seasonal and diurnal cycles of life.* In this context people gathered together and created their worship according to the rhythms of daily time." She juxtaposes this regular daily observance to the Liturgy of the Cosmos, which "invites participants into a new context of prayer . . . A context in which we enter in the mystery of an emergent universe with singular moments of absolute significance never to be repeated again in the total history of the universe."[58] Thus the liturgy of the cosmos marks and celebrates as holy both one-time cosmological events and seasonal and diurnal cycles.

In the book they are writing on living the vows in the twenty-first century, monastery cofounders Worcelo and Bostwick cast their own spiritually engaged, ecologically mindful practice as stemming not from environmental ethics per se but from what they identify as a more broadly encompassing cosmological evolutionary ethics that is informed by the story of the universe as revealed through modern science. The passion and poetry of this cosmic evolutionary ethic is reflected in Worcelo's diary as she greets the dawn (one of the traditional monastic times of prayer) on the eighth and final day of her Ecozoic retreat:

Every morning when we gather to pray here in our monastery, whether or not we are on retreat, each of us wraps a colored shawl over our shoulders to connect us to a particular moment of grace in the universe story. The color one chooses may change from time to time, depending on what aspect of the cosmic drama we find personally engaging. The shawl I have chosen is red. To me, red depicts the fireball at the beginning of time . . . During this final day of retreat, I drape myself with the cosmic red shawl and feel the stupendous activity of the fireball alive within me. I am moved to write a prayer of intention for my re-entry into the world and to recite each day in our new religious community . . .

O Divine Wisdom, you were present in the Holy Fire at the beginning of time—
Give us Light and Guidance.

You who introduced the first partnership of hydrogen and helium—
Teach us how to combine our energies to give birth to the Ecozoic Era.

You who seeded the dark space with galaxies and stars—
Gift us with abundance.

You who hold all things together in the Holy Embrace of the curvature of
    space—
Keep us grounded and expansive.

You who were there at the sacrifice of Tiamat, our grandmother star—
Teach us to give Everything to the will of the Divine.

In the moment of grace, Earth learned to capture sunlight—
Help us to photosynthesize the Light of Christ and to become food for the
    future.

With awe and reverence we step into the flow of thirteen billion years of
    universe unfolding.

We are a further phase change in the original fireball.
We claim that heritage and say YES to the evolutionary potential that is
    calling us forward and demanding that we reinvent ourselves as a species.

May we shape a monastic life coherent with our place in the universe.
May we come to understand the implications of this. May we advance
    consciousness for the sake of the whole.
May we become expressions of wholeness in this deeply divided world.

We place our highest gifts at the service of this call,
    at the service of Divine Love itself.

As Sisters of the Earth community, we turn to you Mary,
  in your manifestation as the Black Madonna.
We ask you to awaken us to the sacredness of matter
  in our own bodies, in all of life, and in the Earth itself.

We call out to the voices of our ancestors—
Give us Guidance.

We call out to the unborn children of the species—
What do you ask of us?

Rich in its integration of diverse themes and elements, this prayer does important religious "work." It brings together, for instance, concerns for the "unborn" and the "ancestors," spirit and matter, caring for all life species, "reinventing" the human, and shaping a new kind of monastery that is conscious of its place within the universe. In reading it, we are able to see Worcelo's cosmological mysticism and her seamless integration of concepts from both science and Christianity (for example, "photosynthesize the Light of Christ"). In the spirit of the medieval mystic and monastic Hildegard of Bingen, who was a cosmologist, mystic, philosopher, astronomer, and botanist all rolled in one, Worcelo interweaves evolutionary principles with key Christian concepts such as sacrifice, rebirth, redemption, and Eucharist ("Help us to . . . become food for the future").[59]

The prayer also invokes Mary as a figure of immense spiritual power, strength, and guidance. She is cast as both ancient matrix and source of contemporary ecological wisdom (that is, Mary shows us the sacredness in all matter, presumably by herself embodying sacred matter). How is it, though, that all of these diverse elements somehow fit together in the Weltanschauung (worldview) of this new religious community? Terrence Tilley's work offers a possible explanation for the rationale behind this complex thematic simultaneity. Tilley writes: "In a sacramental universe, 'truth is one,' and God has given humanity the ability to understand that truth . . . The Catholic Intellectual has confidence in [both] faith and reason."[60] Interestingly, more than any other image, it is the image of Mary that has come to signify most strongly for green sisters the unification of old and new, faith and reason, matter and spirit, external authority and internal conviction, and other seemingly dualistic disparate parts and competing elements. It is Mary, as cosmic mother, who holds all things together in her universal, or catholic, embrace.

Something about Mary

The icon "Mary of the Cosmos" enjoyed her first public viewing at the 2002 Sisters of Earth Conference in Holyoke, Massachusetts, when sisters integrated the icon into daily prayers: it adorned an altar dedicated to the epic of the unfolding universe. Handpainted on Russian white birch, the icon depicts Mary with planet earth, the moon, and the entire universe contained within her womb. The halo or divine light that surrounds her appears to be the primordial fireball itself, emanating energy throughout the universe. In the language of icons, blue signifies divinity, and it just so happens that Mary of the Cosmos carries a blue planet earth inside her womb. Cast as Holy Mother of the cosmos and cloaked in both the blue undergarment of divinity and the red outer robes of humanity, Mary's eyes appear serene, strong, and filled with compassion.

I asked Mary of the Cosmos creator Sister Bernadette Bostwick what had been her inspiration for the icon, and she related to me a conversation she had had about Mary with her mentor Thomas Berry. Berry had commented, "The Universe is more in Mary than Mary is in the Universe." Bernadette meditated on this image of the "Universe in Mary" and ultimately was moved to write an icon of Mary with the cosmos visible in her womb. Ideally, an icon "writer" does not so much create an icon as become the tool through which God brings a particular image forth into the world. It is customary for icons not to be signed at all, or if they are, with a brief, simple identification on the back. The real author is considered to be divine and the artist a mere instrument. In keeping with this tradition, original icons of Mary of the Cosmos bear a small, modest identification label on the back that reads, "To the Glory of God, by the hand of Bernadette Bostwick." Before Sister Bernadette begins her work, she fasts and prays. The prayer she most often repeats is "Thy will, not my will." She explains, "I want to take myself out of it as much as possible. I don't even like to sell them. It's not artwork; it's a prayer. How do you price that?"[61] As I watched Bernadette put some finishing touches on the icon before the 2002 Sisters of Earth Conference, I looked at the fresh paint and reflected on what an apt image this was for green sisters' reclaiming of Mary—the Holy Matrix as ancient as the cosmos but newly conceived and not yet dry.

Bernadette had been working diligently to finish the icon so that she could present it to that year's conference keynote speaker, Charlene Spretnak.

"Mary of the Cosmos" by Bernadette Bostwick.

Spretnak, author of *The Spirituality of Green Politics* and other works related to women, ecology, and the divine feminine, had just completed her book *Missing Mary: The Queen of Heaven and Her Re-Emergence in the Modern Church.* The title of her keynote address was "Recovering the Maternal Matrix: Mary as Premodern and Postmodern Cosmology." Spretnak's audience of more than a hundred Sisters of Earth was (judging by later comments and questions) a mixture of those quite open and attentive to Spretnak's position as a "Pro-Mary Progressive," and those more wary of the ways in which the figure of Mary has historically been used against women. Like the views of green sisters themselves, Spretnak's own perspectives on Mary and related matters within the church are complex, complicating conventional left- and right-wing designations. For instance, she clearly favors women's ordination but qualifies this statement by proclaiming, "I don't want women priests who don't care about Mary!"[62] In her speech to the Sisters of Earth, she lamented the deposition of Mary from her rightful position of power as a result of decisions that had been made during the Vatican II Council. Still, Spretnak is careful to articulate her praise for Vatican II reforms, enumerating her strong support for these more fully in her book.

> Because Vatican II accomplished numerous positive changes in the Church, most Catholics—and nearly all liberal Catholics, myself included—hold its work in high regard. It established a greatly expanded role of the laity in the spiritual life of Catholic parishes, announced the beginning of a more respectful attitude toward other religions, allowed the mass to be celebrated in vernacular languages, and freed nuns' communities to self-govern (which resulted in many communities eventually sloughing off the hierarchical structure that had been forced on them and devising more democratic alternatives). These are but a few of the scores of liberating results of the great Vatican Council.[63]

Spretnak's support of Vatican II reforms stops, however, when it comes to "throwing out Mary with the bathwater." In her keynote address, Spretnak spoke to the Sisters of Earth about Mary's decline from her powerful cosmic form (as she had been depicted throughout the iconography of the Middle Ages). Spretnak was distressed that Mary had been stripped of her majesty and ignobly reduced to "a mere Nazarene housewife." Furthermore, in the face of Protestant distaste for and discomfort with Mary, and amid anxieties about Mary overshadowing Jesus, the embarrassing but powerful medieval vestiges of Mary as queen and cosmic matrix all but faded and disappeared, only to be revived in the last two decades by ultraconservative Catholics. (Marian devotionalism has never disappeared, of course, from certain ethnic immigrant populations and sectors of society, in which her reign and status as "Holy Queen" is alive and well.) Spretnak, a self-identified feminist, member of the Green Party, and political progressive, regretted that feminist scholars had cast off Mary as an anachronistic oppressive image for women—an "Uncle Tom" whose image enforces female passivity and measures women against an unattainable feminine ideal.[64] When feminists and other "progressives" turned their back on Mary, argued Spretnak, Mary was surrendered to ideological conservatives. In stripping Mary of her import and regal status, feminist theologians (albeit well-meaning ones, Spretnak pointed out) and other feminist critics had ironically discarded their own "birthright" to the "grace embodied in Mary" as Mother of God and symbol of "the sacred whole."[65] The Cosmic Mary of the Middle Ages, recounted Spretnak, disappeared only to be replaced by a censored, sanitized, and disempowered version of her former self.[66]

American Catholic historian Robert Orsi points more specifically to the problem posed by Mary's elevated position in devotional practice during the 1960s, when Catholic leaders were concerned that "the Virgin's place in devotional imaginations of ordinary people had come to overshadow her son." Liturgical reformers did not like this dynamic because they saw Marian devotionalism as "distract[ing] people from the encounter with Jesus in the sacrament of Eucharist." Ecumenicists in dialogue with Protestants during the same period also discouraged Marian devotionalism because they saw it as "the most formidable obstacle to Christian unity." The response to these fears of a Virgin Mary who had stepped out of her appropriate place, says Orsi, was to recast Mary as "the model of Christian obedience, humility, and service" and "to wean Catholics from Marian devotional practices." Orsi examines the traumatic effect of these changes on many ordinary Catholics, especially, as he says, because so little was done to prepare them for these changes.[67]

In her keynote to the Sisters of Earth, Spretnak spoke more broadly to the larger traumatic effect on the planet of Mary "going missing" and more personally to her own longing and mourning for the "whole Mary" she grew up with in her Eastern European immigrant family, as opposed to the "minimalist Mary" that emerged after Vatican II. Yet even as Mary's more powerful personage was deemphasized, folk cultures around the world retained her divine qualities and conserved her cosmic aspects. For example, Our Lady of Guadalupe in Mexico is depicted with sun rays emanating from her head, surrounded by stars, and with planets at her feet. "We need Her," said Spretnak of this powerful cosmic image. "We need conduits to our larger context." As Spretnak called out Mary's many honorific titles to her audience, the list of commanding sobriquets resounded throughout the Le Puy room at Mont Marie Conference Center and took on the quality of an invocation.

Matrix of Being
Mother of Mercy
Star of the Sea
Queen of Heaven and Earth

Mirror of Justice
Mother of Compassion
Seat of Wisdom
Mystical Rose

Just as Spretnak reached a crescendo in her keynote address and called for the return of Mary to our time and consciousness, a woman in the audience began to sway and moan and finally to shriek. Her body jerked and convulsed and she shrieked again, repeating "No, no, no, no, no" many times, and then "Yes, yes, yes, yes, yes" and then alternating combinations of "no, yes, no, yes." She seemed to be fighting something. The sisters around the woman supported her, coming to her aid, supposing that she was ill. From where I was seated, it did indeed look like she was experiencing some sort of seizure. The woman's body then became very quiet and she began to speak slowly. Her voice was loud and seemed much larger—more powerful—than the diminutive woman from which it emanated. She said,

I am Mary.
I am pleased.
I am *very* pleased.
You all are my daughters.
You *understand*.
You are in the presence of Grace.

The sisters looked a bit stunned and the room fell silent. Charlene Spretnak quietly stepped to the side of the podium. Time itself seemed to stop as no one said anything for what seemed to me to be a long time. Finally, someone toward the front of the room, closer to the woman, slowly and in a clear voice began to sing "Salve Regina" (Hail Holy Queen). The other sisters in the room joined her until most of the room was singing in unison:

Salve Regina, Mater Misericordiae:
vita, dulcedo, et spes nostra, salve . . .
(Hail, Holy Queen, Mother of Mercy:
our life, our sweetness, and our hope . . .)

Some of the sisters surrounding me had tears rolling down their faces, and my own eyes filled with tears at the emotion of the moment. The sisters concluded, singing "Clemens, pia, dulcis Virgo Maria. Amen" (Clement, love, sweet Virgin Mary. Amen). When the singing ended, I wrote in my field notes: "I feel a palpable sadness in this room—a kind of mourning and vulnerability that I am not used to experiencing with these women."[68] I had also never experienced anything like this woman's "locution" (verbal manifestation) of Mary. I would like to say that as a researcher I handled this situation calmly and professionally and with total composure, but in truth as it unfolded I felt frightened and unsettled. In my field journal, just after my quickly jotted notes taken during the locution, I find a much more wobbly note to myself written in a shaky hand: "Whoa—we're not in Kansas anymore." At the time, I did not even realize that I was shaking until a sister behind me touched my shoulder to steady me.

Later that night, I spoke with one of the conference organizers about the episode. She related that the woman was not a religious sister but was a woman from the surrounding area who read about Spretnak's lecture, had a keen interest in Mary, and had decided to attend the keynote address. She reiterated that the woman who "received the message" from Mary was not a member of Sisters of Earth nor associated with the group. Apparently, the woman was also not mentally ill, as far as anyone could tell, but she had had previous experiences of receiving "locutions" (verbal messages) from Mary. On a more personal level, I shared with the sister who was one of the conference organizers that I wept as all the sisters sang "Salve Regina" and that I still felt a bit shaky and confused, not altogether sure why it had affected me in this way. She told me that she also wept, and I asked her why she thought that was. "I thought about it for a while after it happened," she told me, "and then it hit me. *I miss my mother.* When they took away Mary and she disappeared and was no longer central to our lives—could no longer be there *for* us and *with* us—it was as if they took away my mother. I miss her and want her back. At a very basic level, *I want my mother.*"[69] I noted that the message from the woman who had "spoken for" Mary seemed to be reciprocal—that Mary misses her "daughters," too, and is pleased to be invoked and rediscovered by them.

In an informal discussion-group session with Spretnak later on in the conference, several sisters raised the problems that Mary poses for women–her virgin status, her desexualized nature, and her passivity and meekness as they have been read through a patriarchal lens and used for misogynist ends. On the first point, Spretnak responded that many powerful divine goddesses are either the product of virgin births or are somehow involved in a virgin birth that demonstrates the kind of self-directed power of "sacred parthenogenesis." She argued that this is precisely what gives them their divine quality, their mysteriousness, and contributes to their special powers—they need no male counterpart to bring forth life and to create, but are instead self-generators of life. As for the use of Mary by patriarchal interests in order to idealize and enforce women's passivity and submission to authority, Spretnak countered that these are largely characteristics of the domesticated, dethroned, postcosmic Mary. According to Spretnak, early iconography of Mary demonstrates her powerful divine qualities and communicates a very different image from contemporary conceptions of Mary as a mere "Nazarene housewife." She further develops this argument in her book, addressing what she calls "the goddess problem" posed by Mary to the Church.[70]

Some participating in the discussion with Spretnak nodded in agreement and seemed to support her arguments, although a few were still wary of the misuse of Mary as a tool to dominate women, and they continued to voice this concern. We continued the discussion at the next mealtime, when one sister floated the possibility that even if the woman who had the Mary episode did have a mental condition and was hallucinating, that something still must have drawn her to this particular gathering, and that her presence at the Sisters of Earth conference and her message were no coincidence. I asked the sister who made the comment about the incident being no coincidence if she thought that Mary had in some way used the woman as a human vehicle for her message. The sister responded, "All I am saying is that she must have been here with us for a reason, and she certainly *did* get us all talking about it, didn't she?" She was right; we were all reviewing what had happened at the keynote address and pondering it from a number of different angles. The sisters at the table were certainly well aware of the presence of ecstatic experiences in the context of Marian devotionalism, and we spoke about this. But (like me) they had not personally witnessed such an intense example of it.

Whether or not Marian apparitions and manifestations have proportionally increased in the past two decades or more or whether greater media attention has simply made it seem so is a matter of scholarly debate. In her book *Encountering Mary: From La Salette to Medjugorje*, Sandra Zimdars-Swartz tracks Marian apparitions in Europe from the mid-nineteenth century to the present. She cites increased numbers of pilgrims to Marian shrines in the 1980s and 1990s, and a 10 percent jump in attendance at Lourdes between 1989 and 1990.[71] In the United States, she finds a real increase and flourishing of Marian centers. Her 1993 survey of 175 of these centers reveals that some had mailing lists of up to 150,000 people. She concludes that even though the Marian revival has not affected the majority of American Catholics, it is still "certainly a force to be reckoned with."[72] She also notes that, depending on the location of the apparition, Mary's messages tend to be driven by a somewhat regional agenda. In the United States, for instance, Mary's messages tend to address "family values," a nationally popular political catchphrase among ideological conservatives. Mary's messages also call for the abolition of abortion and the reintroduction of prayer into the schools, "warning about the punishments that await those who oppose her agenda and the persons who speak for it."[73] In Western Europe and in Eastern Europe, messages address other issues of local interest and debate. Kristy Nabhan-Warren's ethnography of Marian apparitions at a shrine in Arizona provides further evidence of the local specificity of Marian locutions and other manifestations.[74] Nabhan-Warren's informant, for instance, receives messages from the Blessed Mother that address particular aspects of urban social welfare in the Mexican-American community of South Phoenix, where her shrine is located.

Given this kind of adaptability to region and audience, it makes sense, especially considering Mary's associations with nature and the fullness of creation, that a message to the Sisters of Earth conference would address Sisters of Earth as Mary's daughters, express the Holy Mother's pleasure at their environmental work, and affirm their depth of understanding. Robert Orsi writes:

> Mary is a cultural figure not simply in the sense that she "reflects" cultural idioms or social dynamics (although she does) or that idioms or lineaments of Marian piety are inherently generational (which they are). She is a cultural figure in that she enters the intricacies of a culture, becomes part of its webs and meanings, limitations, structures, and possibilities. She contributes to making and sustaining culture, and reinventing it, at the same time that she herself is made and sustained by culture, in dynamic exchanges with her devout.[75]

It thus seems natural that green sisters would seek to reclaim Mary within an ecological context, as both changeless and changing, drawing on the richness of her traditional legacy and her protean quality to those who engage her in the present. Sociologist Andrew Greeley, for instance, analyzes Mary as a powerful feminine image of the "Mother Love of God, the life-giving power of God, and the tenderness of God." Through these qualities and through her powerful connections to the fertility of nature and the fertility of God, as Greeley points out, Mary performs a "similar, though not identical, function to that of the womanly deities of nature religions."[76]

In the discussion session after her conference address, Spretnak observed a fitting connection between the locution from Mary delivered in the Le Puy room of the Mont Marie Conference Center and the history of the Black Madonna of Le Puy. In the eighteenth century, the townspeople of Le Puy, France, risked their lives attempting to rescue their local black Madonna statue from being guillotined and then burned by an anti-Marian mob.[77] Since the 2002 conference and its focus on Mary, the artist, Josephite sister, and Sisters of Earth cofounder Mary Southard has introduced a handpainted statue of the Virgin of Le Puy that is now sold through the Ministry of the Arts catalog produced by the Sisters of St. Joseph of La Grange, Illinois. The catalog copy advertising the statue draws out the Virgin's sacred connections both to nature and the cosmos, while also meaningfully linking the Madonna to the community's European origins and heritage.

> Black Madonna, The Black Virgin of Le Puy: Many traditions and cultures reveal the presence of a "Dark Mother," "Black Madonna" or "Holy Wisdom." Symbol of the sacred feminine, the feminine face of God, here darkness evokes strength and protective power as she presents the divine Child to the world. As the blackness of space is fertile, as black contains all colors, so the Black Madonna embraces all: Wisdom, Compassion, Forgiveness, and Suffering. She brings to light all that we hide from and fear, what is Mystery; she watches over our whole Earth.
>
> Mary [Southard] has modeled our Black Madonna on the Black Virgin of Le Puy, which has been the destination of pilgrims for many centuries and is the city in France where the Sisters of St. Joseph originated in 1650. The rich hand-painted garment covers the child seated on the Mother's lap; the cosmos—sun, moon and stars—radiate on her back. Retired sisters here in the Motherhouse do the actual hand-painting—a labor of love.

Another Madonna who has taken on a significant role for green sisters is Our Lady of Czestochowa (OLC), the black Madonna of Poland. It is no coincidence that this is the same Madonna that watches over the Green Mountain Monastery. Gail Worcelo, whose ethnic origin is Polish, has long held a special relationship with this black Madonna. In her retreat diary from August 2001, she writes:

> It is late evening and I am reflecting on a recent phone conversation with Thomas Berry in which he told me, "We are opening into a new age of Mary." I recall, too, a dream I had: the Black Madonna appeared to me in a field in her Christian manifestation as Our Lady of Czestachowa . . . This image of Mary resides deep in my Polish roots. I have loved Our Lady of Czestachowa,

the Black Madonna, all my life. For me, she announces the Mystery manifesting its radiance in flesh. She is Christ-Bearer, matter impregnated with Spirit. She is woman of grace, accepting her own body as the chalice of the Spirit . . . I find serenity in the Black Madonna and kneel before her now as I have done hundreds of times before in a receptive gesture of prayer. My back is bowed and my hands are open. This Madonna is deeply mysterious. I cannot penetrate the secret of her face. She embodies the divine calm, a concentrated self awareness. I am hungry for her guidance and wisdom; my eyes are teeth, and I receive her as a wafer in communion . . . Praying before her in the stillness of this night I hear her say, "All matter is holy. Divinity is revealed in every being."[78]

The Green Mountain Sisters travel with a small icon of OLC in their car, where she is both prayer companion and a watchful eye over their journeys. In the fall of 2003, I pointed to the icon of OLC in the sisters' car and asked why they were so drawn to her. Worcelo recounted several stories of Polish lore associated with the Virgin. For example, when Czestochowa was besieged by the Tartars, OLC reportedly helped repel them, incurring an arrow wound in the throat in the process. At one point a vandal is said to have struck two blows on her, wounding her cheeks with a sword. Before he could deal the third blow, he was struck down and writhed on the ground in agony until his death. In 1655, the Virgin is said to have driven off Swedish invaders, even though the three hundred Poles guarding her faced twelve thousand Swedes. In 1920, as Russian troops prepared to invade Warsaw, the Poles prayed to Our Lady, and her image appeared in the clouds above Warsaw, at which point the Russian troops turned around and went home. Of course Warsaw eventually was invaded and occupied by the Nazis in World War II, but Poles again prayed to Our Lady for their liberation and again, it is pointed out, she "came through" and the Germans were driven out. One of the things that also drew Worcelo to OLC is that, like the Virgin of Le Puy, she is one of the so-called Black Madonnas of Europe. The significance of dark-pigmented Madonna statues or images in Europe is the subject of intense debate. Some scholars argue that the darkened physiognomy of the Madonnas is merely caused by the soot from centuries of candles, pollution, and exposure to fires. Others contend that there is a connection between these Madonnas and the indigenous agricultural goddesses of the Mediterranean. Like the skin of these goddesses, the Black Madonna's skin is dark like the fertile black soil, suggesting her true identity as "Earth Mother."[79]

At her previous monastery in Pennsylvania, Worcelo had spearheaded the building of an ecologically friendly straw-bale hermitage that she dedicated to OLC. An inscribed dedication within the hermitage reads: "May she teach you about the sacredness of matter, the mystery of Incarnation, the reality that God is All in All. May her gentle grace, and the grace of her Christ, permeate your stay."[80] In the Black Madonna's affirmation of the oneness of matter and spirit, her confirmation of the universal pervasiveness of the divine, and her embodiment of Grace, it is not surprising that OLC shares salient qualities with "Mary of the Cosmos," whose icon and presence are also honored in the Green Mountain Monastery. The sisters and their companions pray the Litany to Mary of the Cosmos, which Worcelo adapted from the Akathist Hymn to Mary. In the original service in which the hymn appears, the priest sings the part of an archangel sent forth from heaven to greet the Mother of God. When he sees her, he is rapt with amazement and cries out to her.

> Hail, O you, through whom Joy will shine forth!
> Hail, O you, through whom the curse will disappear!
> Hail, O Restoration of the Fallen Adam!
> Hail, O Redemption of the Tears of Eve!
> Hail, O Peak above the reach of human thought!
> Hail, O Depth even beyond the sight of angels!
> Hail, O you who have become a Kingly Throne!
> Hail, O you who carry Him Who Carries All!
> Hail, O Star who manifests the Sun!
> Hail, O Womb of the Divine Incarnation!
> Hail, O you through whom creation is renewed!
> Hail, O you through whom the Creator becomes a Babe!
> Hail, O Bride and Maiden ever-pure!

Worcelo has retained the sense of majesty, praise, and awe at the Mother of God but reconceives the litany so that it tells the story of the universe and points to Mary as Cosmic Mother. Note in the new version that the vision of the coming Ecozoic era is included, and Mary is cast as the one who will show the way there:

> Hymn of the Universe . . . Pray for us
> Matter impregnated with Spirit
> Fire of the galaxies
> Dust of the stars
> Music of the spheres
> Mother of the Cosmos

Bearer of the silence unfolding
Hidden sense of the ineffable plan
Energy of the Supernovas
Space of the spaceless God
Depth beyond imaging

Shelter of Earth . . . Pray for us
Refuge of Animals
Protector of our Garden Planet
Table full-laden with gifts
Soil whose fruit brings healing
Guide into the Ecozoic

Rock of Constancy . . . Pray for us
Robe of freedom for the naked
Spring that refreshes those thirsting for life
Pillar of Fire guiding those in darkness
Shield of the Oppressed
Ark of the desolate
Remedy in Perplexity
Mirror in Patience
Calmer of Tempests
Seat of Wisdom
Christ Bearer
Healer of Body and Soul
You who expose the fraud of idols

Mary Divine Mother, be our guide

When asked what Mary meant to the Catholic imagination in the late Middle Ages, Andrew Greeley responds, "Go to Paris or Chartres or Amiens and learn what it meant: life and superabundant life. We have not seen anything like it, not really, ever since."[81] But as Sister Bernadette fills more orders for original icons and prints of Mary of the Cosmos, as Christmas cards of Mary of the Cosmos continue to do a brisk business over the Internet, and as the Litany to Mary of the Cosmos is chanted among green nuns, green sisters, and their supporters and friends, perhaps we shall yet see something like it.

The Earth Rosary

A group of the community's affiliated "companions" gather together at the Green Mountain Monastery kitchen table to volunteer their time in support of one of the monastery's self-sustaining projects. The companions fast and pray while they roll bits of clay into beads for the sisters' Earth Prayer Beads, a kind of planetary rosary for our times. The beads are fired in the monastery kitchen, allowed to cool, strung together, and then each set is placed into a handmade hemp fabric bag complete with a suggested prayer insert. The sisters then make the beads available either for mail order or for purchase through a variety of religious community gift shops.

Each of the beads is a miniature planet earth crafted of blue, green, white and brown clay that has been swirled together and formed into a tiny sphere. Accompanying instructions reflect the sisters' efforts to cultivate a greater "cosmic evolutionary consciousness" in the prayer beads' users. Each little planet earth, the insert explains, "represents a billion years in the unfolding story of the universe. There are 15 beads which reflect the 15-billion-year-old universe of which we are a part." In the center of these fifteen beads lies one brown rectangular bead with a simple fish emblem carved into it. Worcelo identifies this fish as not only the well-recognized ancient symbol of Christ and a reminder of the "urgency to become higher expressions of Christ consciousness in this world for the sake of all life," but as also a tangible reminder of "the depletion of the fisheries of our planet."[82] As with the image of the Cosmic Mary, the image of the Cosmic Christ takes on a multiplicity of meanings both abstract and concrete, some of which are related to environmental concerns and evolutionary contexts.

The suggested prayer enclosed in the bead pouch communicates a clear conception of a God that is distinctly alive and organic. The Divine is addressed using personifications of nature and the planet's four basic elements—fire, water, air, and earth.

Fire of Love . . . purify my heart.
Burning Bush . . . consume me.
Living Waters . . . wash over me.
Deep Well . . . draw me to you.
Spirit of Life . . . enliven me.
Breath of All Breath . . . breathe me forth.
Ground of all Being . . . root me in you.
Womb of All Life . . . birth me anew.

Acknowledging the ancient practice found in a variety of religious traditions of counting or marking repetitive prayers with knots, beads, pebbles, stones, or seeds, the Green Mountain Sisters conserve the profound value of this ancient prayer-focusing tool while opening up its use to include the ecological dimensions of spirituality and prayer work.[83] For sisters such as Mary Ann Garisto, a Sister of Charity of St. Vincent de Paul who directs Sisters Hill Organic Farm in New York, the Earth Prayer Beads are simply a very good visual reminder of her relationship to the rest of the earth community. "I keep the Earth Beads on my desk at work," says Garisto, "as a reminder that all I do is connected to everything else on the planet."[84]

The Green Mountain Sisters are not the only ones crafting a new kind of rosary. At a workshop I attended at Genesis Farm in Blairstown, New Jersey, visiting artist Marion Honors, a sister of St. Joseph of Carondelet, led our group through the process of making Universe Story Beads or Great Story Beads, shaping beads out of clay that would mark "one-time" cosmic evolutionary events along a string of yarn. Honors's own string of beads included at one end a bright orange starburst made of yarn, representing the "cosmic fireball" from which the universe emerged. Other beads represented the death and birth of stars; the formation of our own planet; the evolution of flowers, trees, fish, animals, birds, and humans; and so forth. Although these beads could be used for praying and meditating on the miraculous unfolding of life, they were intended primarily as an aid for evolutionary storytelling.[85] As stories go, a 13.7 billion to 15-billion-year-long story (depending on which timing one favors) is a fairly long narrative with many twists and turns in the plotline. Universe Story Beads are thus designed to assist the storyteller in recounting the epic of evolution by providing tangible promptings. The very special selection or crafting process of these beads reflects the sacred dimension of this story for those who employ them. Like rosary beads, the scapular, the saint's icon, and so many other prayer-focusing tools or devotional objects in Catholic tradition, Universe Story Beads have in effect become a new kind of sacramental.

In her work on Christian material culture, Colleen McDannell points to the nearly indivisible historical association between women and sacramentals, particularly the rosary. In religious articles and in popular literature, the rosary, she says, "like L'art Saint-Sulpice, was presented as a symbol of the inward-looking devotionalism of an old, ethnic, feminized Catholicism."[86] In Protestant critiques, the rosary has been considered backward and even embarrassing—the suspect fingerings of superstitious old women. In Catholic critiques aimed at modernizing Catholicism, particularly from the 1960s, says Catholic historian Robert Orsi, "Old devotions were derided as infantile, childish, or as exotic imports from Catholic Europe, alien and inappropriate in the American context." Orsi points to one Catholic writer who asked in response to the postconciliar climate of 1965 (in which Catholics were discouraged from saying the rosary during Mass), "Is Mary to be exiled from the sanctuary . . . like a senile grandmother hidden in the back bedroom when company comes?"[87] This evocation of images of both the aged and the feminine is no coincidence and speaks to the rosary being cast in terms of a devalued and disposable femininity—a threat to a mature and respectable Catholicism.

McDannell examines efforts from the 1950s to the 1980s to rehabilitate the rosary by "disassociating its roots [from] a feminine devotionalism while simultaneously clothing it in appropriate male symbols."[88] One of her examples comes from an article in *U.S. Catholic* in the 1980s, in which a male author writes about allowing the string of rosary beads to hang down between his legs much in the way the anchor from his fishing boat "plunges" into "secret kingdoms" of deep waters.[89] This language and imagery of this "manly" rosary plunging into the deep waters of prayer while sport fishing is reminiscent of a kind of "muscular Christianity," a nineteenth-century movement (with some renewal in the twentieth century) that sought to rescue Christianity from the devaluating influence of feminine associations.[90] More recent efforts to "market" the rosary more broadly to the interests of men have included Pope John Paul II's 2002 "Year of the Rosary" with its addition of five new mysteries to the rosary, all of them focused specifically on events from Jesus' life, none of which directly concern or highlight Mary.[91]

Environmental historian Annette Kolodny makes a similar argument about the devaluation and objectification of landscape through its identification with the feminine in popular narrative, visual art, and poetic imagination.[92] Her argument is akin to feminist economic analysis that considers the historical reduction in real wages as women move into previously predominantly male professions (which are subsequently labeled "pink collar" work). Both the rosary itself and the work of praying the rosary have been devalued through associations with women. In Kolodny's sense, the rosary as material object has been diminished by being "feminized." Consequently, the work itself of praying the rosary—religious work primarily and traditionally performed by women—has been cast as "pink collar" work.[93]

It is striking then that instead of denying or downplaying the link between women and this prayer-focusing tool, green sisters celebrate and embrace its feminine connections. The Green Mountain Sisters' planetary rosary embraces unapologetically both the feminine and "earthy" aspects of the rosary while reinterpreting the genre of "prayer beads" from sisters' own ecospiritual perspective. The design of the beads contains symbols identified with both genders, but it consists of fifteen feminine earthy orbs that surround one rectangular representation of the fish—much like a convent of sister earths surrounding one Christ. The beads are also called Earth Prayer Beads and not Fish Prayer Beads, so the symbolic emphasis is on earth beads and yet the Christ bead is still central. The sisters' conservation of the rosary as a traditional prayer form, combined with their new creation of the Earth Prayer Beads, further demonstrates an understanding of tradition as something both steady and evolving, changeless and changing.

Guardians of Faith and Fungi

The Green Mountain Monastery is not the only monastic community that has rediscovered the connections between the Benedictine way of life and ecofriendly practice. A very different community, the Abbey of Regina Laudis, also practices ecological sustainability and dedicated land stewardship as informed by Benedictine values and traditions. Conservative Catholic pundits have championed the abbey, a community of cloistered nuns in Connecticut, for its members' strict adherence to "orthodoxy." Much like the Dominican Sisters of St. Cecelia's in Tennessee, the Abbey of Regina Laudis ("Queen of Praise") is frequently cited as an example of what is "Right with Catholicism" or what is "Right with the Church" (double entendre intended).[94]

The nuns at Regina Laudis sing or chant the Divine Office in Latin seven times a day, they wear full traditional habit, they still maintain a cloister grille, and they observe the Latin Mass of Novus Ordo each day. The nuns themselves forgo the self-governance, self-determination, and democratic reforms to community authority that have been hard-won and from which most contemporary religious sisters benefit. For instance, the abbey's nuns favor a traditional centralized and nondemocratic hierarchy in which their abbess receives a life-long appointment from the local bishop, without a vote from the nuns. In most contemporary North American communities of women religious, this kind of outside interference by the bishop would smack of paternalism and would be viewed as an egregious violation of the community's ability to self-govern. For the Regina Laudis community, however, it is as if the post–Vatican II reforms on dress, governance, community, and religious life never occurred.[95]

Because the Abbey of Regina Laudis is so clearly and solidly labeled a "conservative" or "orthodox" community, its members' commitment to environmental action challenges stereotypical notions of "treehugging liberals" in intriguing ways. Like the Green Mountain Sisters, they invoke the special relationship that Benedictine orders have historically had with the land. The abbey's literature proclaims: "The degree of reverence for creation mandated by St. Benedict sets a standard that has made Benedictines environmentally conscious from the beginning of their history. Some areas of the abbey land are especially designated Environmental-Historical Preserve, which means these areas are reserved as part of the monastic enclosure, but also that they hold significant historical landmarks or contain fragile environments, such as wetlands or wildlife habitats that need to be protected."[96] In fact, in August 2000, the abbey was awarded a river restoration grant by the Connecticut Department of Environmental Protection for its work in watershed restoration and protection.

Other projects ongoing at the abbey include forest management, erosion control, recycling, waste management, and water quality initiatives. For more than a decade, the nuns have directed attention toward safeguarding the headwaters located on their property. The abbey's water sources affect both the Housatonic and Pomperaug watersheds, and the nuns explain that "the maintenance of healthy streams and ponds plays a critical role in the local ecology." In practicing careful, mindful stewardship of their land, the nuns are also careful to point out that they approach all aspects of the land as interdependent and fundamentally connected to their agricultural work, to the environment of their neighbors, and to the larger bioregion.[97]

What has inspired the community to take an active role in environmental protection and conservation of land and water? The nuns largely credit the Rule of St. Benedict for their inspiration. Chapter 31 of the rule reads, "Let him look upon all the utensils of the monastery and its whole property as upon the sacred vessels of the altar." They also cite the ecological ethic implicit in the vow of *stabilitas* that bonds Benedictines to a particular community and particular place. As with the Green Mountain Monastery, the abbey literature explains that it is this commitment to stability and belonging to place that enables the nuns "the opportunity to develop a long-term relationship with a region and its people." What's more, the continuity of *stabilitas* enables the community to cultivate an "intimate knowledge of [their] environment and concern for the land future generations will inherit."[98] This kind of belonging to place enables the development of an in-depth "earth literacy" that not only informs one's ability to live in harmony with the local biotic community but also invests one personally in that place's well-being and survival.

What's more, the abbey's celebrated Mother Noella Marcellino has gained international renown as the "Cheese Nun" for her defense of heritage cheeses, rare mold strains, and biodiversity. Marcellino, a trained microbiologist, travels to family farms in France with her sterile scalpel and scrapes mold samples off the ceilings of cheese caves in order to study the mold's microbiology. She also oversees cheese making at the abbey, in which raw-milk fungi are used. Passionate about her calling to both religious life and to fragrant molten cheeses, Marcellino maintains that it is just as important to have "different strains of fungi saved as it is to have rare breeds of animals [saved]."[99] Recognized by France's National Institute of Agricultural Research for her scientific work on the biodiversity of raw-milk fungi, Marcellioni serves now as a much sought-after judge in cheese competitions, where she is known to have a soft side for heritage cheeses made with organic ingredients.

Combining a spiritual connection to the land, responsibility for stewardship, and a commitment to protecting their local watershed and wildlife (from vegetation and creatures to cheese mold), the abbey continues to balance ecological consciousness, sustainability, and religious orthodoxy. Founded in 1947 by a French-raised American surgeon named Vera Duss, the abbey developed in less than a century from a fledgling community to a vibrant, energetic abbey of about forty nuns. Will Green Mountain Monastery cofounders Gail Worcelo and Bernadette Bostwick leave a similar legacy for generations to come? Time will tell. With their denim habits, earth prayer beads, religious icons, ecospiritual liturgical practice, cosmic Liturgy of Hours, solar panels, and less-hierarchical community structure, the Green Mountain Sisters' strain of "green orthodoxy" differs substantially from the variety cultivated by the Regina Laudis nuns. The communities do share some intriguing commonalities, however: (1) a passionate conservation of medieval heritage and Benedictine values, (2) a love of faith and a passion for science (in Marcellino's case, microbiology), (3) a great love and devotion to Mary as Mother of God and Holy Queen, (4) a rigorous lifestyle in which sisters strive to live lightly on the earth and to care for creation, and (5) a combined contemplative and activist orientation. Each of these common elements makes for an interesting comparative study in religiocultural biodiversity. Both communities also defy easy left versus right or liberal versus conservative characterizations that conventionally pit environmental consciousness and activism against orthodoxy. In other words, green sisters come in all varieties, even (or perhaps especially) the "Cheese Nun."

The Future of Green Habits

What potential is there for the green sisters movement to capture and hold the attention of a new generation of young women? My journal notes from one visit to the Green Mountain Monastery provide a glimpse of an answer:

We have just finished the eight-o'clock silent meditation and will now observe silence for the rest of the evening until we rise again for vigil at five-o'clock A.M. I have set my alarm extra early during my visit to the Monastery since I am not used to rising early like the sisters and I'm worried about oversleeping. Earlier today, the sisters and I attended Mass at the barn chapel at Weston Priory, where the Benedictine monks hold common prayer services and where they celebrate the Eucharist during the summer months. There was a visiting high school youth group, and it was so interesting to watch the young girls sneaking curious glimpses at the sisters and examining their matching tea-length "jean-dresses." I noticed that some of the girls themselves were wearing stylish bluejeans or jean-skirts in various states of distress and with various stylish detailing. I wondered what these girls were thinking as they watched the sisters. Were they trying to make sense of the sisters' unconventional garb? The sisters' dresses seem to share the same family of clothing that the visiting girls were wearing, and yet the sisters' garb bears a certain distinctiveness as a marker of something more formal and collective. While I was visiting, neighbors who attend prayers at the Priory repeatedly remarked positively on how the Green Mountain Sisters consistently present themselves very professionally. The way the sisters carry themselves with dignity in this modest but attractive contemporary garb, they might well be wearing traditional garb, and yet they most clearly have concertedly chosen something current. The girls' eyes closely followed the sisters as they went up to receive the Eucharist and then carefully followed the sisters again back to their seats. A few minutes of the girls' smiling and whispering back and forth followed. Did they think the sisters were cool? Odd? I tried to read the girls' faces to see what they were making of these women who had clearly captured their attention.

After the service when Gail and Bernadette were outside the barn greeting friends and neighbors (supporters of the new monastery), I stepped away from them to join a group of people visiting with some of the Priory's farm animals over a pasture fence. One of the girls from the youth group turned to me and shyly asked, "Are you with the eco-nuns?" Her tone sounded like she had just asked, "Are you with the rock stars?" I told her that I was in fact with them but clarified that I was just visiting and not an "eco-nun" myself. I then asked her what she thought of the sisters. She shrugged her shoulders. Her friend then offered as a way of explanation, "We like their outfits."[100]

Girls' early encounters with religious sisters often shape their favorable receptivity later in life to religious vocation. One of the three major reasons cited for the reduction in women's vocations is the shifting composition of parochial school teachers in the later part of the twentieth century, which resulted in ever fewer religious sisters being responsible for the day-to-day education of Catholic children. For many years, Catholic sisters provided "cheap labor" for these parochial schools, but as sisters' communities focused their missions on other needs, ongoing interactions between young Catholic girls and religious sisters greatly decreased.[101] (The other two major factors in the reduction of vocations cited are the increase in other job opportunities for women and the change in age requirements for recruits.) When sisters are visible to girls and recognizable as vowed members of religious communities, girls are more likely to pursue vocations. Conversely, as sociologist Roger Finke has found in cross-referencing data from a number of religious community studies, "when religious orders blend in, they fade away."[102]

When I have asked sisters what first attracted them to the particular order they joined, the most frequent answers were that they had been taught by the nuns of the order they ultimately chose or that they had had a favorite aunt or other relative who had been a member of that order. Not insignificantly, however, several sisters recounted that as young women they had seen sisters whose garb caught their attention and provoked their curiosity or that they had looked through a special guidebook that showed photographic examples of each community's official garb. The beauty or gracefulness of a particular habit, a dramatic headdress, or appealing veil had prompted them to explore that community further. The garb itself may have not been the reason sisters ultimately decided on a specific community, but as indicated by the Catholic high school girls I spoke with at the priory fence, the visible identity and aesthetics communicated by religious dress should not be trivialized.

The full appeal for those discerning a vocation with the new Green Mountain Monastery, with the rigorous demands of its ecologically sustainable lifestyle, Benedictine prayer life, and engaged monasticism, remains to be seen. Unlike St. Cecelia's century-and-a-half of history or even Regina Laudis's more than half-century of history, the Green Mountain Monastery community has only just recently begun its journey, locating land in 2004 and officially opening its doors to inquiring women in June 2005.

Women who have expressed interest in the new community may not be the early "twentysomethings" that St. Cecelia's attracts, but they are thus far women in their early thirties, which is younger than the forty- and fifty-year-old applicants that many religious communities currently receive. Even if the community does end up attracting "second-career" women at midlife—women who have often already raised a family and then discovered a calling to religious life—the physically active and health-conscious lifestyles of green sisters put them in good stead for making energetic and productive contributions to the community for many years to come. In an era when it is said that "forty is the new twenty" for everyone, then green sisters—with their vigorous life of gardening, ecobuilding construction, landscape maintenance, body prayer, liturgical dance, yoga, labyrinth walking, natural-foods cooking, intellectually stimulating study, and active prayer life—should feel energetic well into their later decades.[103] Sisters who commit to a discipline of walking or biking whenever possible, instead of burning fossil fuel by riding in automobiles, boost their activity levels even more.

In fact, sociologist Mary Johnson has been notably critical of the ageism and sexism that she identifies as pervading evaluations of women's religious communities and the well-being of religious life. Johnson finds that studies that focus almost exclusively on median ages and numbers of entrants largely ignore "the quality of ministry and the people performing it." These studies, she argues, are premised on the very ageist assumption that "sisters over sixty have nothing to contribute."[104]

My own research experiences among green sisters support the legitimacy of Johnson's critique. As a fit woman in my thirties, I have experienced being exhausted (and sore) trying to keep up with sixty-some-year-old Dominican Carol Coston and her chainsaw as she eradicated invasive species and hauled brambles over Sisterfarm's rough Texas terrain. I have had a seventy-four-year-old green nun from Ireland wait patiently and politely for me on the Appalachian Trail as I hiked up a ravine to catch up to her. There are many more examples of sisters several decades more senior than I out-digging me in vegetable beds, out-weeding me, out-swimming me, out-hiking me, and generally outlasting me. If physician David Snowdon, the conductor of the so-called "Nun Study," is correct, better-educated sisters who maintain physically active lifestyles and active prayer lives, and continue to be lifelong self-educators as they age, are likely to live productive lives well into their nineties without the need for nursing care and without loss of their mental faculties to the risk of Alzheimer's disease.[105]

Green sisters fit this profile, except that they add an element that no one has yet studied. Instead of consuming the highly processed institutional food of most conventional motherhouses, green sisters who run the more than fifty identifiable ecology centers or related earth ministries are consciously eating diets that are primarily vegetarian (organic when possible), feature few processed foods, and are rich in whole grains and all-natural foods. How eating patterns may or may not affect the health and longevity of green sisters would make a compelling research study.

Whether fueled by ecofriendly diets or by their delight in the earth and its creatures, the sheer energy and passion of green sisters also provide ideal points of interface for what has been called Generation Green—"young rebels with a cause, taking to the streets, the parks, and the treetops to fight for the planet."[106] These are young people who very much want to make sacrifices for the planet and who are willing to risk their lives to do so. Forest activist and tree sitter Julia "Butterfly" Hill, for instance, who withstood frostbite and the worst El Niño storms in California's recent history during her two-year vigil atop a fifteen-story-high old-growth redwood tree, is a prime example of a young person ignoring danger in service of environmental protection. Forest activist and "green martyr" David Chain, who was crushed by a falling tree while engaging in civil disobedience to stop the ongoing logging of old-growth forest, is another oft-cited example of the kind of ardent commitment and selfless sacrifice among Generation Green activists. Arguably, these two qualities (ardent commitment and selfless sacrifice) also make one an excellent candidate for religious life, especially for a religious community that combines the rigor of an intense daily lifestyle with engaged activist ministries.

As discussed earlier, sociologists Roger Finke and Rodney Stark write about the post–Vatican II liberalizing of the Church as having achieved the "worst of both worlds" by diminishing the distinctiveness and difficulty of practicing Catholicism. By contrast, could the Ecozoic monastery and apostolic sisters' greening communities be cultivating the best of both worlds? That is, might they attract Generation Green with the demands of costly but meaningful personal commitments and embodied investments, offering young activists the rich traditions of Western monasticism infused with an appealing mix of contemplation and activist engagement? By doing so, new green religious communities could offer opportunities for both service to and sanctuary from the modern world.

The Green Mountain Monastery is just one such community that holds promise for attracting Generation Green into its midst. Through sisters' inter-actions with laypeople and their surrounding communities, one can already see a cross-fertilization of ecological ideals and lifestyle disciplines put into practice not simply among lay Catholics but among those of other faiths as well. As apostolic communities integrate the rigors of ecologically sustainable living as daily ecospiritual discipline—as it gets tougher and yet more reward-ing to be mindfully "green"—we see vowed religious women reinventing themselves yet again within a tradition that is ever "changeless and changing."

This dynamic was impressed upon me as early as June 2000, when I made my first visit to the Sisters of the Green Mountain Monastery. A passage from my field journal reflects this recognition.

As a summer rain falls on the farmhouse roof, I am indoors participating in the sisters' period of time designated for contemplative labor. Sister Berna-dette is sitting at the kitchen table and is engrossed in the delicate work of icon writing. She makes a few tiny marks with one of her small, thin paint-brushes on the slab of Russian white birch, then pulls back in her seat to ex-amine it from a distance. In the other room, Sister Gail's fingertips generate a constant tap-tap-tap on the keyboard of the computer in concert with the tap-tap-tap of the rain on the roof. She is returning e-mails via the Internet and working on a talk that she will soon give to another religious community. I am sitting on the couch reading, somewhat equidistant from both of these scenes. The other day, I came upon a copy of Eugene Kennedy's *Tomorrow's Catholics, Yesterday's Church* in a local Vermont used-book store, and now I begin to read it. Inside the cover, there is an inscription dated July 1995 from someone named "Alicia" to her brother. She writes, "My darling bro—What a world that was—we were blessed, yes? But today is here! I rejoice and am glad in it—and this work helped—and you always do. Your loving sister, Alicia." I look up from this inscription that presumably has something to do with its author's and recipient's experience and understanding of a Catholic past ("worlds" no longer) and the present ("But today is here!"), and I watch Sister Bernadette still intent on her icon writing. I return to reading, and Sister Gail's printer now chugs into high gear; I can hear it churning out labor of a very different kind. I find myself wondering who "Alicia" is, whether her brother read the book I now hold in my hands before passing it on to the used-book store, and what her brother's and her impressions might be if they were sitting at my current vantage point, between a monastic practice that is at once centuries old and now also linked instantaneously via computer to a wider and ever-changing world.[107]

5. NOURISHING THE EARTHBODY

Sacramental Foodways and Culinary Eucharist

The subject of food—its mindful production and conscious consumption—is central to the literature, learning programs, liturgy, prayer, and daily spiritual practice of green sisters. At Sisters of Earth conferences, food has consistently been a topic of major importance and common interest for discussion. In consultation with one another, sisters explore foodways (the eating habits and culinary practices of a particular community, culture, people, region, or historical period) as an entry point for developing more peaceful relations between the human and the more-than-human world.[1] For instance, for some green sisters, the religious practice of abstinence from eating flesh has reemerged in a new context. Instead of being associated with penance, the choice of vegetarian diets has become a devotional act, inspired by a desire to live "lightly" on creation by eating low on the food chain. Sisters such as Miriam MacGillis speak about each meal as being a blessed sacrament by which humans enter into communion with the whole of the life community.[2]

> It has become clear to me that the concept of food itself is key to the transformation of our ecological crisis. Unless our human species can open itself to the contemplation of food as a holy mystery through which we eat ourselves into existence, then the meaning of existence will continue to elude us. Our present cultural experience of food has degenerated into food as *fuel*, for supplying the energy of our insatiable search for what will fill the hungers of our soul. When we understand that food is not a metaphor for spiritual nourishment, but is itself spiritual, then we eat food with a spiritual attitude and taste and are nourished by the Divine *directly*.[3]

Through organic farming and land restoration projects, "earth literacy" programs, natural foods cooking workshops, earth activism, as well as hunger and ecojustice programs, green sisters pursue the transformation of foodways as a powerful means to healing an ecological crisis that affects the world's poor most adversely.[4]

Historically, Roman Catholic vowed religious women have had a complex relationship with food. In Caroline Walker Bynum's study of the food-related suffering self-inflicted by "saintly women" of the Middle Ages, many of them contemplatives, she explains that "to religious women, food was a way of controlling as well as renouncing both self and environment. But it was more. Food was flesh, and flesh was suffering and fertility."[5] Patricia Curran, in her study of pre–Vatican II convent food culture in the United States, similarly describes a constant tension for religious women between valuing food as a gift from God and fearing it as a potential source of sensate pleasure. Fasting and abstinence in the Christian monastic tradition, explains Curran, "fostered detachment from the things of the world."[6]

In contrast, the ecospiritual foodways that green sisters are currently developing are based on a simultaneous nurturing and healing of women's bodies and the earth's body. In this context, some sisters have recast the act of growing food unadulterated by chemicals or genetic engineering in terms of "priestly practice," the sacred act of cooking in terms of a daily Eucharistic ritual, and the sensate experience of eating as a sacramental communion that affirms the human body as an extension of the sacred "earthbody."[7] Drawing from the work of Thomas Berry, Sallie McFague, and other ecological thinkers, sisters' approaches to food and earth ministry embrace a kind of sacramental earth body, human body, and cosmic body continuum.[8] The foodways of contemporary environmentally activist religious sisters reveal a complex religiocultural fusion in which sisters' practices actively reclaim elements of mindful consumption, spiritual fasting, and abstinence reminiscent of traditional convent food culture while powerfully transforming those same elements within the context of what I argue is an affirming ecological feminist body politic.

Throughout my research with green sisters and throughout my fieldwork in diverse regions of North America, the role of food has repeatedly functioned as a common starting point for sisters' earth activism. Food as symbol, metaphor, and literal life-sustaining substance serves as an entryway into a matrix of issues to which green sisters have become attentive: the health of ecosystems and the effects of toxins on the well-being of creation, world hunger, ecoracism, environmental injustice, spiritual renewal, "simple living," reinterpretations of religious tradition, cultural transformation, and new ways of defining religious community.

In the foodways of green sisters, three major factors emerge as being particularly significant: (1) ecospiritual and ethical considerations in food choices based on the purity or "integrity" of the food, (2) mindful, sustainable modes of food cultivation and delivery, and (3) gratitude and celebration expressed in the sacramental rituals of meal preparation and consumption.[9] In each of these three areas, sisters I interviewed seemed to regard food and spirit (and, more generally, matter and spirit) as a unified, sacred whole. The embrace of this sacred whole characterizes the emergence of a new "food culture" of spiritual ecology among religious sisters who conserve resonant traditions of religious devotion and vowed religious life while transforming and remaking these traditions within a "greener" context. Closer examination of how sisters are working to create this new "food culture" of spiritual ecology provides a powerful demonstration of the role that religious women play as active producers and shapers of religious culture even in (or perhaps especially within) a religious institution that continues to deny women full official participation at all levels of leadership and governance.

What's more, in the food culture of green sisters, we discover still more salient support for Mary Farrell Bednarowski's observation that women are innovating "more subtle ways to stay in and out [of religious institutions] than had previously been supposed."[10] In fact, green sisters are creating alternatives beyond the polarizing choice of being either "in or out" of both kitchen and church. Food, in all of its complex dimensions, is making a way for sisters to generate those critical alternatives.[11]

Eating and Fasting to Heal the Earthbody

Earlier I described how the Sisters of the Green Mountain Monastery have reinhabited the traditions of Western monasticism even as they recycle those traditions through newer interpretations. The same may be said about sisters' reinterpretations of spiritual practices regarding food. For example, for twenty-four hours, from sundown Thursday to sundown Friday, the Green Mountain Sisters fast for the "healing of the earth."[12] During this period, which ends with the singing of Vespers, the sisters fast on water and herbal tea. Some one hundred "companions" (or supporters of the monastery and its mission) fast along with the sisters to varying degrees. The community's Rule of Life explains that members fast in part to "feel the hunger of the planet."[13] Monastery cofounder Gail Worcelo explained at the 2002 Sisters of Earth conference that this fasting is an act of "prayer and healing" for both the individual and the planet, a practice in which one cleanses environmental toxins from one's own body while also "holding a 'prayer vigil in the body' for the healing of the planet."[14]

Friday is the day that Roman Catholics have traditionally fasted (usually in the form of meat abstinence) in observance of Christ's Passion. In founding the new Ecozoic monastery, Worcelo says she has come to see the Passion of the gospels and the Passion of the human as extending to the "Passion of the Earth." According to Worcelo, "The pathos of our times has manifested itself in the severe degradation of the earth . . . It became clear to me that this was the place where Christ was suffering his present Passion."[15] In this way, fasting for the healing of the earth's body, like suffering with body of Christ, becomes a devotional act but one that also involves a complex ecospiritual body politic—one that unites the earthbody, the human body, and the Christ body into a holistic continuum.

In her history of Christian fitness and diet culture, R. Marie Griffith observes that "prescriptions and practices of nutritive abstinence" have fluctuated throughout history and that although examples of "intense food refusal" have not exclusively involved women, women have most certainly been the primary participants in devotional food abstinence. During various periods, food abstinence has also served multiple functions—"as a means of baptismal preparation, a means of purification, a sign of grief, a work of charity, or an expression of penitence and the desire for God's mercy."[16] In the food culture of green sisters, fasting also serves complex and intertwined purposes. Fasting can be a means to get one's attention and to focus mindfulness on the needs of the planet. Fasting can also be an intensive way to place the body into prayer—in the case of the Green Mountain Sisters, healing prayer for the planet.

It may seem obvious to characterize the act of fasting among green sisters as yet another example of women victimizing their own bodies. Wioleta Polinska, for instance, has written about the history of women's bodies as "bodies under siege" from a variety of social and cultural forces that contribute to their being fattened, starved, slashed, burned, surgically mutilated, and corseted.[17] In the context of both green sisters' mindful eating as well as mindful fasting, however, bodies (human and nonhuman) are recognized to be under siege from the hostile forces of environmental pollution and industrial toxic chemical assault. Green sisters' fasting practices thus add a "green" dimension to what Polinska characterizes as the "battleground" for a protracted war on the flesh.[18] By cleansing or "detoxing" the body of environmental pollutants and industrial poisons, fasting can be a nurturing practice of caring for the body that ideally defends it from catastrophic illnesses (such as breast cancer and reproductive cancers) that the sisters recognize as having environmental components.

Green Mountain Monastery prioress Gail Worcelo asserts that one of the "most radical things women can do is to slow down, take time for life, and not to be so exhausted all the time."[19] The weekly fasting at the monastery is thus set in a context in which women make time to slow down, rest their bodies, nurture themselves, and "go within." This period of rest even extends to resting the digestive system from its normal vigorous work. This fasting period also vividly highlights a general atmosphere at the Green Mountain Monastery that celebrates the pleasures of food preparation and consumption. During my visits in the summer of 2000 and again in the summer and fall of 2002 and 2003, Green Mountain sister Bernadette Bostwick spent considerable time working with fresh organic ingredients to create gourmet meals to nourish the community and its guests. Sisters' summer picnics were simple but rich and flavorful—featuring succulent heirloom tomatoes, local organic Vermont cheeses, old-fashioned juicy organic white peaches, hard-boiled eggs laid by free-range hens, and fresh local bread baked with organic whole grains. Despite their organic contents, because ingredients were local and meals contained no meat or purchased processed foods (packaged cookies, crackers, and so forth), the cost of these meals remained relatively low while still supporting more sustainable food production.

Although the sisters consumed organic dairy products during my visits, they refrained from eating animal flesh. The Green Mountain Monastery Rule of Life specifies that unless the sisters raise their own animals (which they currently do not do), they "do not eat the meat of animals, especially those who are raised in cruel and unnatural conditions or who are forced to produce in ways that violate the integrity of their being. We avoid complicity with companies and industries that seek profit over right relationship."[20]

The sisters do not support industries whose products cause major health problems and suffering. To this end, the sisters refrain from consuming substances such as nicotine, alcohol, sugar, and caffeine. Their Rule of Life casts the choice to commit to more ecologically conscious food choices as simultaneously an ethical commitment to take care of the earth's body by not consuming food that poisons the soil or violates other beings in the life community and a commitment to nourish the physical and spiritual well-being of sisters' own bodies.[21]

Rather than using food or absence of food as a means of "renouncing both self and environment," as Caroline Walker Bynum's work demonstrates in the cases of religious women in the Middle Ages, green sisters' foodways in many ways concertedly affirm both. For medieval religious women, argues Bynum, women's bodies became a locus for "discipline and control" that was, in part, influenced by the desire to escape an imprisoned materiality in favor of celestial joys.[22] Patricia Curran specifically points to the influence of Augustinian theories of the body on the history of food culture in women's religious congregations, especially St. Augustine's formulation of the body as being in competition with the soul. "Why, therefore, is it of benefit to us to abstain somewhat from food and carnal pleasure? The flesh draws one to the earth. The mind tends upwards; it is caught up by love, but it is slowed down by weight," concludes Augustine (354–430).[23] Curran points to the various ways in which Augustine's positive images of rising spirit and negative images of earthbound weight fault the materiality of both earth and body. In contrast, green sisters strongly affirm their ties with the earth, its creatures, and its life systems, as they work to heal both the assault on women's bodies (cancers, environmental illness, and so on) and the earth's body. The most immediate sphere most contemporary Westerners have direct control over is what they put or do not put in their bodies, and so ecological spiritual practice for green sisters begins in that area, in the most immediate "bioregion"—the body.

In many ways, sisters' green adaptations and renewal of religious life actually put into practice on a grassroots level what ecotheologian Sallie McFague articulates as a theology of "the earth as God's body." McFague argues that Christianity has historically placed too much emphasis on transcendence and has consequently neglected the material and organic. Christian notions of the bodilessness of spirit and the ideal of the perfection of nonmateriality as the ultimate ontological goal, according to McFague, have done harm not only to humanity's self-conception, but to the earth's material condition as well. And yet, paradoxically, because of its doctrine of incarnation (the Word made flesh), Christianity is the quintessential "religion of the body," says McFague. If this is truly so, posits McFague, then "what if we did not distance ourselves from and despise our own bodies or the bodies of other human beings or the bodies of other life-forms, but took the positive evaluation of bodies from Christianity, feminism, and ecology seriously?" She continues, "What if we dared to think of our planet and indeed the entire universe as the body of God?"[24] As religious sisters create new green liturgies, cultivate a daily ecospiritual practice, and implement environmentally conscious modes of religious life, they effectively explore McFague's question in everyday practice.

Ecological Purity and Danger

Since the inception of Sisters of Earth conferences in the mid-1990s, religious sisters have repeatedly spoken at these conferences about food as a medium for addressing the world's gravest environmental problems.[25] In addressing the 1996 annual conference of Sisters of Earth, Sister Miriam MacGillis stated that while all humans have the responsibility to make changes in their diets, Roman Catholic religious women and men have a "special moral obligation to do so" because they have made sacred vows to engage in discipline and restraint.[26] Not surprisingly, much of this restraint concerns the eating of animal flesh, which has historically been suspect within Roman Catholic religious orders. Even after 1335, when Pope Benedict XII gave permission for the consumption of meat in monasteries three or four times a week, a separate refectory was often set up where monks ate in relays to counteract the meat's supposed laxity-producing energies, which made monks more lethargic and less obedient.[27]

MacGillis's concerns about flesh eating are somewhat different but no less vigilant. "Seventy-eight percent of America's farmland is used to grow food for animals. We [vowed religious Catholics] cannot be a part of that," entreats MacGillis. "It's based on a totally inhumane, sacrilegious, dysfunctional, unsacred treatment of animal beings in the community of life who are our companions."[28] In this statement about the moral obligations of vowed religious persons, MacGillis parallels the sentiments expressed by ecofeminists such as Carol Adams, who argue that feminists have a special moral obligation to be vegetarian.[29]

Jeannine Gramick, a member of the Sisters of Loretto, has been one of the more outspoken green sisters about her commitment to vegetarianism and about the connection of that commitment to Catholic social justice teaching and the principles of nonviolence she identifies as being "at the heart of Jesus' gospel." Gramick relates the powerful story of her conversion to vegetarianism during a 2002 course she took on nonviolence that was taught by former Trappist monk Colman McCarthy.[30] She reports on her personal transformation during this course and the shift in the way she began to view creation and its interrelationship of creatures:

> I no longer believe in the old cosmology I had been taught—the hierarchical pyramid of creation in which human animals, near the top of the pyramid, are assigned more worth than non-human animals and other beings toward the bottom. I am beginning to accept a new worldview in which all creation

has inherent worth and beauty—a moral order in which all created beings are moving to a stage of harmony, equality, and respect for each other . . . I no longer believe that non-humans are inferior to humans in God's scheme of creation.[31]

Here Gramick articulates the philosophical basis for "biocentric" philosophy—that all beings have intrinsic worth and should not be hierarchically subordinated one to the other. Biocentrism is generally identified with the environmental philosophy of "deep ecology" and differs significantly from the "stewardship" model, a more anthropocentric model favored by the institutional Church and promoted in Vatican documents on the environment.[32] Gramick's model eschews a top-down schema of humans as the crown of creation, especially if such a model justifies humans' right to exploit, enslave, and inflict pain on nonhuman animals based on humans' needs taking precedence over those of other creatures. "We need to pause," she cautions, "and be reminded that two hundred years ago human beings in the United States raised other human beings for the purposes of enslaving them for their economic gain. This was not morally justifiable. Neither is it justified to raise non-human animals to be born and raised for the purpose of killing them for our own use."[33]

For a variety of reasons that range from "eating low on the food chain" to animal rights and humane concerns, 64 percent of the sixty-five environmentally active religious sisters with whom I conducted electronic interviews described themselves as mostly, almost always, or always vegetarian. Many added that it was "a process" and remarked that they "periodically slipped" but returned repeatedly to the goal of eating a diet that would contribute to a healthier and more just planet. Those who did report eating meat and poultry said they made an effort to do so only if the animals were organically fed, free-range, and preferably locally raised. Others reported that they consumed flesh from time to time but stuck to fish and fowl instead of consuming meat from quadrupeds (cows, pigs, sheep, goats, and so forth); they chose species lower on the food chain that require fewer of the earth's resources.[34] The Franciscan sisters at Michaela Farm in southern Indiana raise free-range organic beefalo (part North American bison and part domestic cow), but they do so as part of the farm's comprehensive prairie restoration program, in which the beefalo play an integral and critical role in restoring the health of the larger prairie ecosystem via their mutually symbiotic relationship with native grasses.

In addition to moral considerations, spiritual considerations in food choice are also very important to green sisters. At the 1998 Sisters of Earth conference, Gail Worcelo asked the attending women: "Are we getting the kind of food we need to bring us into the Ecozoic era?"[35] In Worcelo's 1998 comments, she expresses concern that if everything we eat has had "the life force processed out of it," then that is what we become—deadened and lacking the creative energy to make real and necessary change in the world.[36] In an interview in 2002, she similarly posed the question, "What kind of creativity comes out of saturated fat and depleted processed foods?" and answered, "None or very little!"[37] Worcelo stresses that food that abounds with vitality gives those who consume it the strength, creativity, and spirit to make the kinds of changes needed to create a mutually enhancing earth-human relationship.[38] "It has to do with the quality and the consciousness in which food is raised," explains Worcelo. "Tomatoes grown biodynamically and factory-farmed tomatoes are as different as the living are from the dead! Matter and Spirit are One!"[39] Dominican sister Sharon Zayac of Springfield, Illinois, sounds a similar note, saying, "Factory farm tomatoes are as violated as are our factory animals. They, too, are force-fed, constrained, and objectified. We become what we eat."[40]

Sister of Charity Maureen Wild echoes these sentiments about food overprocessing, food vitality conservation, a critical recognition of the unity of matter and spirit, and the transmission of the spirit of the food into the flesh of the consumer. Wild, who inhabits a small cottage in the Gulf Islands of British Columbia, offers ecospirituality workshops and retreat programs to religious communities and other groups. Wild says,

> Food choices are ethical choices. We prioritize our spending and choose what we value. We become what we value. We are what we eat. I can't "stomach" factory-farmed anything . . . monocultures . . . overly processed, preserved, and packaged. The earth can give us vital foods only when the conditions for its growth and care model health and vitality . . . of soils, seed, water. Spirit courses through everything. I go for quality of Spirit in my food. It is a daily communion for me . . . a "eucharist" with the body of the earth and sun.[41]

Miriam MacGillis is even more emphatic, proclaiming, "If we truly saw the Divine in a potato, we could not turn potatoes into *Pringles!* It would be sacrilege to do so."[42]

Eighty-one percent of the sisters who were interviewed as part of my research reported eating organic food "mostly," "almost always," or "all of the time." But a handful of the green sisters interviewed questioned the appropriateness of those who have taken a vow of poverty to be paying more for organic food. Environmentalist and futurist Sister of Charity Paula González of Cincinnati, Ohio, for example, suggested that since organically grown food is too expensive for the world's poor, those religious communities who want to maintain an organic diet should make the commitment to grow or raise their own food, otherwise "[eating organically] is rather luxurious."[43]

The majority of respondents to the electronic interviews, however, reported making organic choices in part to create a much-needed market for organic food and to support less-toxic growing methods so that eventually this type of food would become more affordable and available to all socioeconomic sectors. Even sisters on a strict budget spoke of making the "sacrifice" to buy organic food whenever they could afford it because of the truly devastating "hidden costs" in conventional produce—the poisoning of water supplies by toxic agricultural runoff (from which the poor suffer most acutely), the birth defects caused in the children of migrant workers from repeated exposures to pesticides, and the cancer clusters concentrated most heavily in impoverished minority populations where such chemicals are manufactured—not to mention the severe toxic effects on wildlife and the general health of ecosystems. With this kind of costliness, sisters who consciously "kept organic" did not regard conventionally grown produce as being "cheap" or as being in accordance with their vow of poverty. Sisters also spoke of things such as turning down the heat, forgoing air-conditioning, biking instead of operating a car, and opting not to buy household convenience items such as microwaves or dishwashers, preferring to prioritize the money saved for use toward higher-priced but more earth-friendly food.

Missionary Sister of the Immaculate Conception Nancy Earle has found that in her small community in Maine they have saved money on medical bills by committing to a diet of organically grown, nutrient-rich fruits and vegetables. "We buy only organic and grow our own vegetables," says Earle, who reports being much healthier since making this switch several years ago. She asks, "What is the cost of buying organic versus the cost of being sick?"[44] Earle also spoke about making the cognitive shift to "whole systems thinking," which takes into account the effect of seemingly minor actions (like individual food choices) on larger planetary systems. In this context, buying "cheap" pesticide-laden food truly is "penny-wise and pound-foolish." In short, green sisters overwhelmingly viewed food choices that support more sustainable earth practices not as "luxuries" but as a practical, moral, and spiritual imperative. Miriam MacGillis underscores this point in her "Food as Spirit" workshop, emphasizing that by eating foods grown with conventional industrial chemical practice, "We are eating the suffering. We are eating the toxicity."[45]

Anthropologist Mary Douglas argues in her now-classic book *Purity and Danger* (1966) that notions of purity and pollution in a variety of cultural contexts are often less about "dirt" per se and more about the violation of categories—matter in the wrong place.[46] Deciding what is and is not "pollution," according to Douglas, is more about defining the relationship among things rather than about the nature of the things themselves. In the sacramental foodways of environmentally concerned religious sisters, however, there is a strong practical dimension to these women's food choices that goes beyond mere symbolic "pollution." Although it has become fashionable for postmodern cultural theorists to talk about "nature" as merely a fictive term—an invented sign within the larger signification of cultural discourse—the dismissing of environmental pollution and toxicity as merely invented products of culturally defined signifying systems leaves little room for the acknowledgment of the real biophysical consequences of environmental toxins on communities (exposure to chemical spills, radiation, PCBs, dioxins, and so on).[47]

While there is clearly a strong spiritual and ethical component to sisters' concerns about environmental pollution, and there is a metaphysic of unified matter and spirit that is knit up with green sisters' food choices and lifestyle practices, it is critical to recognize that sisters are also responding to real, quantifiable environmental health hazards to humans and other species. The fact that some sisters refrain from consuming food or water that is contained in plastics, for example, is a response to a variety of books that occupy sisters' bookshelves, bookstores, and book groups—works such as Theo Colborne's *Our Stolen Future* (1997), Sandra Steingraber's *Living Downstream* (1997), and John Wargo's *Our Children's Toxic Legacy* (1998)—all of which cite research studies pointing to the leaching of chemicals from plastic containers into the foods they "protect."[48]

Mary Douglas's thesis of "purity and danger" is further complicated by sisters' complex reasons for eschewing produce grown with chemical pesticides, fertilizers, and fungicides. Responsive to the "danger" and "impurity" of conventionally produced fruits and vegetables, sisters cite scientific reports on such things as the gross mutations of amphibians exposed to high levels of agricultural pesticide runoff, developmental problems in children exposed to mercury in the womb, PCB levels in human breast milk that exceed a child's lifetime allowance for exposure to those chemicals, and the links between consumption of freshwater fish and serious degenerative diseases, especially in women occupying rural agricultural areas.[49] In the food choices made at green sisters' ecological centers, ministries, and motherhouses, questions of purity of content and preparation involve a consciousness of very real physical danger. Serious questions about the moral complicity of participating in a system that perpetuates that danger and the consequences for the physical and spiritual health of the whole life community factor into the choices made for each meal, but sisters also point to published scientific research from the fields of medicine and environmental sciences as their sources for determining practices that will either contribute to or undermine the planet's well-being.[50]

Less directly influential than commitments to vegetarian and organic food consumption, but no less important, is the consideration of "food miles" that have gone into a particular food item. At Genesis Farm, for example, the community-supported garden produces shares of organically produced vegetables and fruit fifty-two weeks a year, but some of the food for the farm's Earth Literacy Center programs must be supplemented at times with external produce. A pervasive bioregional ethic at the farm prompts the community to take into account that food consumed in the United States travels an average of 1,300 miles before it reaches the consumer's table.[51] In other words, the issue of "food miles" raises the question of just how "unpolluting" an organic apple is if after it has been produced under sustainable earth-friendly conditions in Brazil, it has used a thousand miles' worth of fossil fuel to be delivered. Content, mode of cultivation, and proximity of location thus all figure into the ethical and spiritual dimensions of food decisions.

Historian Patricia Curran observes that one of the things that distinguished Christianity from Judaism was its break with dietary rules. As an example, Curran cites Jesus's teaching in Matthew 15:11: "Listen and understand. What goes into the mouth does not make one unclean, it is what comes out of the mouth that makes one unclean."[52] In green sisters' commitments to practice vegetarianism, eat locally, and "keep organic," however, there is the recognition that toxic pesticide residues, PCBs, antibiotics and bovine growth hormones, chemical preservatives, and synthetic fillers do indeed simultaneously make one physically unclean (through the ingestion of disease-causing environmental toxins) and spiritually unclean via the complicity in supporting a system that poisons the life community.[53]

As Caroline Walker Bynum has noted, the rejection of dietary law in early Christianity was replaced surprisingly quickly by ascetic food practices among the zealously devout.[54] For instance, fasting and abstinence from certain foods, especially abstinence from flesh eating, have traditionally characterized spiritual discipline in convent settings and have accompanied the cultivation of mystical experience. For contemporary green sisters, "conscious eating"—being mindful of natural resource consumption, animal welfare, and the general health of ecosystems—has become a daily spiritual practice that acknowledges the limits of desire while aiming to listen to and abide by the needs and well-being of the contiguous human-earth body. Sister of Charity Maureen Wild gives voice to this kind of daily practice and its rationale particularly well: "An important dimension of my daily living is 'conscious eating' . . . and it has been, in every intentional way, for at least a decade. Conscious eating choices have come with deepening consciousness of earth and universe, earth as self-nourishing, earth as self-healing, sustainable food systems, affects of globalization, the value of supporting local economies, [and] community supported agriculture."[55]

Whereas consciously consuming organically and bioregionally grown food clearly presents a challenge and at times a financial burden, forgoing commercially grown produce that has been raised for "shelf life" rather than taste can also be more pleasure than ascetic hardship. Thus "ascetic" is not an accurately nuanced adjective to characterize the daily discipline of conscious eating. The kind of fresh and rare heirloom organic fruits and vegetables consumed at green sisters' organic farms are fare that one would gladly pay steep prices for at a four-star restaurant.[56] Because bioregionally consumed produce does not have to travel long distances and is often eaten the same day it is picked, sisters are also able to plant more delicate, sweeter, and more perishable varieties of food that would normally never make it to a conventional supermarket. Moreover, presiding over the cooking of these delicacies that have been mindfully grown with spiritual intent becomes itself a thoroughly sensual and sacred process. As with other green practices, conscious eating demands rigor and commitment, but its rewards also affirm rather than denigrate the pleasures of the earthly realm.

Conscious Eating and Culinary Eucharist

"I prefer to relate directly, sensually with my food. It is a spirit-nourishing experience for me . . . through the engagement of my senses . . . I just like to prepare things mindfully, sensually. Everything becomes the meditation. I don't impose words on the experience."[57] Following her articulation of conscious eating, this is Maureen Wild's description of her own mindful approach to cooking. The sensuality of her cooking experience is not unusual; in fact, many sisters reported to me that they say prayers of thanksgiving while cooking or sing simple chants that affirm the connections among food, earth, and spirit. Several describe this preparation as a "holy time" in their day, a time when they meditatively preside over a blessed communion. This forms a striking contrast to Patricia Curran's history of convent culture, in which she observes, "Religious congregations, in particular, held the idea that sensations of pleasure were suspect, that satisfaction and delight of eating distracted the member from being concerned with God alone, and opened the gates to sexual disorders."[58]

Along with Maureen Wild, Miriam MacGillis speaks about the cooking process itself as being, in essence, "eucharistic" and asks, "Do we know how to cook? . . . to be a priest in the midst of this transubstantiation of food into the community?" Within a religious institution that denies women the official priestly roles that would enable them to preside over an official Eucharistic meal, religious sisters have brought the essence of that ritual into a daily mindful practice available to all. "Transubstantiation," Sister Miriam MacGillis explains, "is a very sacred word referring to Jesus Christ speaking over the bread in which the outer form didn't change but the bread itself transformed on the inner plane where God was present. This has been going on all along. This is not an act confined to specially designated human beings . . . The entire universe is a giveaway that is ultimately transubstantiated and transformed." The act of eating, says MacGillis, is therefore the ultimate act of breaking down boundaries—a radical and literal assimilation. She reminds her earth literacy students that "the Eucharist is not 'hocus pocus.' It is not abstract."[59]

In the Genesis Farm newsletter, MacGillis further describes her mystical experience of recognizing "eucharist" (note the small "e") in a sacramental bowl of organic vegetarian chili:

> It occurred to me that this bowl really held rock and soil, minerals and water, and the energy and heat of the stars. All the ingredients—the beans, onions, garlic, carrots, tomatoes, basil, pepper and oregano—had once been seeds that I inserted into the soil . . . Now they were providing me with delight and nourishment. And they would soon become my blood, my bones, my sight, my movement, my thoughts, my prayers. I was overwhelmed by the limitless generosity of the universe and its Creator. It was *gospel* and *eucharist* in a sacrament so simple, so holy, my heart brimmed with gratitude.[60]

In this moment, MacGillis's reflection suggests no boundary between human and earth in the act of eating. Instead, eating is an act in which earth, water, and sun become human flesh and are transformed. The conversion of food into love and prayer, thought and deed is, for MacGillis, truly a holy mystery.[61]

Cooking classes offered by green sisters similarly emphasize that mindful preparation of food is integral to the spirit that food transmits into the body. Sisters provide instruction in slower, microwave-free cooking methods and the "lost technologies" of basic food preparation (that is, "cooking from scratch"), as well as traditional preservation methods like canning and drying. The food preparation process itself is key to eating consciously. It makes a difference, for instance, whether corn on the cob has been wrapped in plastic and carelessly "nuked" in the microwave for five minutes, or if it has been tended to and mindfully "presided over" in a solar oven. An important aspect of green sisters' commitment to "voluntary simplicity" includes cooking with whole foods instead of purchasing refined, additive-laden, and expensive packaged foods. The more challenging change in lifestyle and the pace necessitated by slow, contemplative meal preparation is precisely the point for green sisters.

With this in mind, it is important to note that religious sisters have consciously chosen lifestyles in which they are not bound by the cultural obligations often attached to being wives and mothers. Making time to ceremonialize the cooking and eating process is just one aspect of the larger countercultural choices and commitments they have made as vowed persons within religious communities. This is not to say sisters do not understand other women (and men) making less mindful choices about eating, or that they do not acknowledge the economic stresses and time pressures on working families. Embracing the value of conscious eating does not translate into holier-than-thou attitudes, as Dominican sister Carol Coston demonstrates. Coston, cofounder of Santuario Sisterfarm in Texas, speaks of the importance of "good food grown carefully and prepared with joy and sensitivity." She qualifies this statement, however, by saying, "The idea of fast food is never one I've liked, and yet I understand from my high school friends that if you had four kids you'd be glad for McDonald's."[62] She stresses that the point is not to make people feel guilty about eating fast food or taking shortcuts but to support the accessibility and economic feasibility of more sustainable and healthier alternatives for everybody. A meal, according to Coston, can be "an act of thanksgiving or prayer . . . instead of something that you gulp down to get through the day. [You can] make it a moment of connecting with all life."[63]

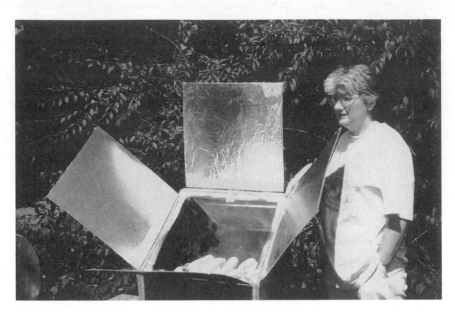

Sister of Charity Maureen Wild steams organic corn in a solar oven.

In the cooking classes I have taken with green sisters, the sacramental power of presiding over a meal (cooking as a sacred act of working with the life force) was communicated both implicitly and explicitly. The Dominican sisters who founded and now operate Crystal Spring Earth Learning Center in Massachusetts, for instance, express a mystical understanding of the life force in food and cultivate a spiritual dimension to its reverent preparation. In an essay called "Bread Is Alive!" the sisters draw readers into the mysteries of "sacred bread baking," clearly communicating a sense of the "living body" of the dough and the baker as its spiritual attendant.

> What we once knew as hunger for bread, we now understand as hunger for what is alive. Bread is alive. Wheat berries holding earth and sun, crushed by heat and pressure, sift through your fingers into a bowl of water. Bidden by work of your hands, these ancient living tools, gluten strands like muscle and tissue, mysteriously emerge into being. Protein is released to nourish; peculiar features give way to form; a rise is anticipated.
>
> Wild yeasts appear from everywhere; from within the dough, some surrounding the bowl, on your counter, the ones that thrive in the kitchen . . . Your hands mixing create more tension, resistance, change. Starch begins its conversion, its breakdown into various sugars. Now for the wait. Time and

space and spiritual patience, a long slow fermentation. You are looking forward to the texture and flavor rising in the loaf. Bread incubating in your
kitchen. Finally oven heat urges the loaf into food.[64]

In the bread-baking course I took at Crystal Spring, each time the group
fed the dough's yeast starter, it was a ritual process involving mindfulness and
meditation. The dough would be brought into our circle and then fed the
starter by a designated person as we all directed our thought to what we
would like to make manifest and grow with the bread—justice for the poor,
compassion, unconditional love for all of God's creatures, and so on. Later,
each participant silently took a turn kneading the dough, contributing the salt
of her palms into its composition and then inviting the local wild yeasts to
take part in this co-creative ritual. When we finally placed the dough into
baking molds, they were spiral shaped, imprinting the symbol of an unfolding
universe into the bread. The sacred bread-baking process at Crystal Spring,
which spanned an entire weekend, evoked both the context and the imagery
of Thomas Berry's unfolding "universe story" and Sallie McFague's mystical
understandings of "the earth as God's body," while affirming a shamanic or
priestly understanding of cooking as a powerful act that works transforma-
tively with spirit and matter.[65]

Various countercultural movements in American Catholic religious history
have played a direct role in shaping the green sisters movement. The legacy of
Catholic Worker farms, the Catholic back-to-the-land movement, and the
American Grail movement can be seen throughout sisters' earth ministries
and greening motherhouses. As sisters engage in rediscovering and reincorpo-
rating "heirloom" mystical traditions of Catholic contemplative life, there are
also indirect connections between sisters' ecospiritual foodways and countercultural movements in America's history. For instance, the value placed by
green sisters on the importance of whole foods, particularly whole grains;
their respect for the spirit and vitality of food; and their concerns about the
spiritual and physical health consequences of having "all the life processed"
out of the food most Americans consume echo a variety of spiritual and cultural reform movements. In the nineteenth century, followers of whole-grain
advocate Sylvester Graham "witnessed to" the powerful transformative effects
resulting from their "conversion" from refined flour products to subsisting on
"coarse bread," a fundamental lifestyle change many felt greatly improved
them not only physically, but morally and spiritually as well.[66]

Similarities in food culture can also be drawn between nineteenth-century

Shaker communities and sisters' ecological centers founded from 1980 to the present. Shaker food culture that praised the spiritual benefits of "simple foods" and unprocessed grains has found new appreciation in the simple whole-foods diets embraced and promoted at sisters' ecological centers and within their earth ministries. For instance, a recipe sent in the nineteenth century from one Shaker elder to another insists that the flour used in the bread contain the kind of spirit it will transmit to its consumer: "home-grown and coarse-ground." Other types of flour, the author warns, when ingested will transmit the wrong kind of spirit.

> You might as well go to [Dwight] Moody and [Ira] Sankey [the popular revivalist preacher and hymnist] for pure Christianity as to go to a worldly miller with our wheat to grind . . . I want to inherit something solid and substantial. I want to inherit substance—I want to see the redemption of the Stomach, redemption of the land; and the redemption of the creative forces of man or woman. The first step in the work of human redemption is to make and eat good bread.[67]

Another Shaker manuscript, this one describing "Spiritual Cake," similarly talks about the spirit that is baked right into food and again reminds us of the "gospel" slow-cooked into Miriam MacGillis's vegetarian chili. The Shaker description reads: "This cake is raised with gospel leven / In which we taist the joys of heaven / Tis also baken with gospel fire / Of burning truth and pure desire."[68]

There are also intriguing parallels between green sisters' food culture of today and the "feminist food culture" created in alternative women's communities and collectives in the United States. One of these, the Bloodroot Collective founded in 1977 in Connecticut, claimed in its first cookbook, *The Political Palate*, "Feminist food is seasonal. We use what is close at hand, what is fresh and local and therefore least expensive and least 'preserved.'"[69] In their second cookbook, the feminist authors cite Kim Chernin's work on healing women's body image and Carol Adams's perspectives on vegetarianism, which link the objectification and oppression of women's bodies, animal bodies, and the suffering of the earth.[70] Again, green sisters make similar connections in their earthbody-cosmic body-human body continuum, drawing attention also to the environmental illnesses made manifest both in women's bodies and in the earth's more encompassing body.

Food preparation, Arlene Voski Avakian tells us, much like housework (or what Michaela di Leonardo refers to as "kin work"), "is part of the invisible labor of women. Though absolutely central to our survival, it is what is taken for granted." In her exploration of women's meaning of food and cooking, Avakian says that although the aims of the women's movement have at various times sought to liberate women from the kitchen, freely reclaiming the act of cooking can indeed be an empowering act: "If we delve into the relationship between women and food we will discover the ways in which women have forged spaces within that oppression. Cooking becomes a vehicle for artistic expression, a source of sensual pleasure, an opportunity for resistance and even power. By reclaiming cooking we ensure that we are not throwing the spaghetti out with the boiling water."[71]

I would similarly argue that sisters' conscious reclaiming of the realm of food is not a mere retreat back into domestic roles stereotypically expected of women. It is critical to keep in mind that while sisters reclaim the sacredness in food preparation, they are also balancing center budgets and managing finances, running complex ministries, managing retreat facilities and directing programs, teaching earth literacy courses, performing leadership in their community, and engaging in political activism (from blocking the construction of incinerators to disrupting corporate shareholder meetings, or even sabotaging nuclear missile silos).

When I visited Santuario Sisterfarm, for instance, each meal we shared was made up of natural foods, much of it locally grown on the farm, and all of it mindfully prepared and consumed. But the community also manages and operates an active feminist publishing company (Sor Juana Press), an organic garden, and a women's retreat space; runs programs that engage Latinas in the borderlands in dialogue about the earth and spirituality; and sponsors educational programs addressing the need to preserve heirloom seeds amid the dangers of genetic engineering.[72] As with their relationship to the Church, within the lives of green sisters the dualism of being either "out of the kitchen" (and thus liberated) or "in the kitchen" (and thus confined to a regressive gender-defined sphere) is fundamentally a false one. Once again, green sisters have created a third way.

As religious sisters, who are denied the official authority to administer the sacraments, preside over the "transubstantiation" of earth into the life of the community through the nourishment of food, their mindful cooking and eating practices in effect open up the sacramental act of meal consumption beyond the jurisdiction of a special class of people (priests) and broaden its reach. In this way, Arlene Voski Avakian is correct that reclaiming cooking can be a source of resistance and even power. For sisters, it can also be a source of healing and reconciliation. Through the sacred acts of food cultivation, preparation, and consumption, Miriam MacGillis reminds her earth literacy students, "We *are* the earth nourishing itself."[73]

Communion and Consumption

Mindful meal preparation can lead to culinary delight, as sisters consume what has been spiritually cultivated and then prayerfully cooked. Josephite sister Mary Southard of LaGrange, Illinois, describes her own experience of cooking and consumption, saying, "I love to cook as a spiritual exercise, eat in silence, having set two places (one for me and one for the Beloved), have candlelight, eat mindfully, grateful for the beings who give their lives to be food . . . Praying that my life (our lives) may be good food for one another."[74] Southard's description of consumption, much like Maureen Wild's description of cooking, is again sensual, embodied, and affirming of food and body as sacred matter. Unlike Wioleta Polinska's "bodies under siege," green sisters' responses suggest that, rather than being considered indulgent, sinful, or full of false satisfaction, experiencing the "pleasures of the palate" through food that has been grown and lovingly cooked with spiritual intention constitutes a "sacred communion" with the divine that "celebrates the gifts of the universe."[75]

Understanding food within a fundamentally sacramental context, green sisters often specifically do not bless the food before a meal, considering the food "already blessed" because it is a manifestation of the Divine. (In fact, at some Catholic ecological centers I have visited, the sisters actually ask the food to bless them.)[76] Barbara O'Donnell, a sister of the Humility of Mary and director of Evergreen ecological center in Pennsylvania, reasons that we should "allow earth to bless us rather than humans blessing what is already sacred."[77]

The serving table at green sisters' meals frequently becomes, in effect, an altar around which prayers are offered to honor the fruits of creation and the service of the cooks. There is often a special time set aside in which all those who have made the meal possible, including the sun, the rain, the growers, and even the microbes in the soil, are ritually thanked.[78] Then everyone is silent while the person or persons who have cooked the meal step forward to introduce each dish and identify the source of the ingredients ("the squash is from the garden, the apples are from the farm down the road"). The cooks are subsequently praised and thanked, and only then does the meal begin.

Maureen Wild describes a similar but simpler individual practice: "When alone, I often look at my food for a moment before I begin to eat . . . and give thanks to the beings who have given their lives for my nourishment."[79]

The menu content at a variety of sisters' ecological centers is eclectic and incorporates a wide variety of native, ethnic, and cultural traditions, embracing a kind of "culinary ecumenism." The recipes in *The Genesis Farm Cookbook,* for instance, have an Italian, Mexican, Chinese, Japanese, Indian, African American, Creole, or Middle Eastern flair, at times combining more than one genre in the same dish. The recipes developed and used at Genesis Farm also retain many traditional culinary forms easily recognizable as middle-American "comfort food," such as stroganoff, shepherd's pie, lasagna, gravy, and hamburgers. Yet as with MacGillis's explanation of the bread that transforms on the inner plane but retains the same external form, the outer form of these familiar dishes remains the same while the content has been transformed, giving them lower-fat, vegetarian face-lifts. (One example of a modified recipe that I learned to make while at the farm was vegetarian "Mexican lasagna" made with organic tofu and whole wheat tortillas.) The combination of traditional familiar forms infused with innovative content eases students into new cooking and eating habits, much in the way that sisters infuse familiar and traditional frameworks of Catholic religious life with ecumenical influences and ecospiritual content.

Recipes for Greening Religious Life

Environmental activists have long stressed the importance of personal consumption patterns, life choices, and dietary modifications for lessening humans' negative influence on the earth. Feminism has similarly embraced the ethic that "the personal is the political," a core tenet of feminist philosophy and practicum. In making decisions about ecologically appropriate food choices, appropriate preparation, and appropriate honoring of that food through ritual and ceremony, green sisters are reinventing a new culture of religious life—one that embraces ecologically sustainable living as daily spiritual practice. Since women have traditionally been the preparers of food, perhaps it is appropriate that religious women have made food the starting point for this shift. Caroline Walker Bynum argues that food "is not merely *a* resource women control; it is *the* resource women control." That may be so, but contemporary green sisters possess far more freedom and autonomy than their forebears did in their finances, education, political participation, mobility, dress, and vocation. If, like Bynum's religious women, today's green sisters are using food as a "means of resistance and control," it is to cause tangible institutional, cultural, political, and environmental change on earth while also effecting a less-tangible spiritual deepening of religious life.[80]

In doing so, sisters have begun with food as the great universal—food as the sacred communion of all life, and food as both a symbolic and physical means for healing and rapprochement between human bodies (especially women's bodies) and the earth's body. By retaining traditional forms of religious devotion, yet adapting the content and contextual meaning of those forms, green sisters are devising strategies for achieving the kinds of change they hope will bring organic renewal to both the living systems of the planet and to the living and lived practices of religious life. Despite women's exclusion from official positions of leadership within the hierarchical Church, these women demonstrate their efficacy as active producers and shapers of religious culture at the grassroots level. Again, much like Miriam MacGillis's image of the bread that retains the same external form but transforms on an inner plane, green sisters may be working within traditional structures of the Church, but they are nonetheless engaged in a powerful internal metamorphosis. Drawing ingredients from cultural movements in American environmentalism, feminism, and social reform; from the heritage of Catholic vowed religious life; and from their own creative theological imaginations, green sisters are experimenting with various recipes of what they hope will constitute a more ecologically and spiritually "nourishing" religious culture.

6. "THE TRACTOR IS MY PULPIT"

Sacred Agriculture as Priestly Practice

 In the early 1940s, Irish Dominican father Vincent McNabb wrote: "If there is one truth more than any other, which life and thought have made us admit, against our prejudices, and even against our will, it is that there is little hope of saving civilization or religion except by the return of contemplatives to the land."[1] At the time, McNabb, who championed the cause of the small farmer, almost certainly would have been surprised to learn that more than a half a century later his words would take on deep prophetic significance for a dynamic movement of organic-farming religious sisters. True, most green sisters are not "contemplatives" as such, but they have approached their "return to the land" in a contemplative manner—combining prayer and planting, contemplation and cultivation. Medieval historian Lowrie Daly writes that by the ninth century in some monasteries in Europe, agricultural fieldwork had become more formal and ceremonial. Monks would actually process out to the fields singing or reciting psalms on their way to perform this sacred work.[2]

For today's green sisters, working with the land can be, among many other things, devotion, worship, contemplation, prayer, sacred service, and mystical experience. In many cases, religious community lands have become the last outpost of open space amid encroaching "sprawl" (ever-expanding development that consumes parks, farmland, and open space and increases dependency on driving). Where once communities of family farms surrounded sisters' lands, now housing developments, condominiums, and strip malls encase fertile topsoil under concrete and macadam. By planting community-supported organic gardens on their properties, sisters hope to sustain their religious communities with organically grown food, while in many cases also providing the surrounding community, especially those most in need, with food that is fresh, locally grown, and pesticide-free.

Social justice and ecojustice concerns are central to green sisters' agricultural ministries, but so are the spiritual experiences of sisters who sink their hands down into the earth to bring forth new life. "The process of gardening," says Genesis Farm's cofounder, Dominican sister Miriam MacGillis, "is an invitation into the journey of the cosmos as it unfolds and reveals itself in a cauliflower."[3] Sister of St. Joseph Marilyn Rudy says of being in the garden and working with the soil, "I realize that we are all of one piece. I become at one with the soil, I am at peace, and know the soil. The plants, the animals, and the bugs find me irresistible. This experience is totally connected with the New Cosmology. I am like a new person and I love it and am joyous."[4] Rudy is former codirector with Maureen Murray, a Sister of the Sacred Heart of Mary, of an earth ministry in California originally named Eartheart. During the 1990s, the sisters ran "Contemplative Gardening" retreats together at La Casa de Maria in Santa Barbara, California, and began an on-site garden to provide pesticide-free produce to the retreat center kitchen. The sisters have since renamed their ministry Earth Harmony and now travel to religious communities, retreat centers, and schools (Rudy says, "We travel just about anywhere someone will listen to us"), offering programs on how to live "in harmony" through more sustainable choices and a broadened ecospiritual consciousness.[5]

Maureen Wild, Sister of Charity of St. Vincent de Paul of Halifax, Nova Scotia, also speaks of the spiritual nourishment she receives from gardening, saying, "My hands in the soil connect my soul to the soil. I love to start seed, and see the new sprouts. It feeds my Spirit."[6] Michaela Farm, a Franciscan-sponsored organic farm, invites farm guests to "connect with the 'sacred acres' at Oldenburg [Indiana] to nurture both body and soul . . . Renew your spirit; deepen your connection with the Universe." The theme continues as the farm's invitational literature enthusiastically proclaims, "The Spirit of St. Francis is alive at Michaela Farm where rolling hills, meadows, woods, fresh air, water, plants, animals and gardens call out to the human spirit to seek a deeper connection with creation and with the Creator of all. Spiritual renewal here is as important as organic food production, ecological education and community building."[7]

In surveying a "bumper crop" of sisters' organic farming ministries since 1980 (a full listing is provided in the Appendix), three important qualities emerge that are key to the cultivation of a new culture of "sacred agriculture."

1. Nature as Teacher and Cocreator   Sisters stress the importance of working with nature and not against it, studying the earth's ways of growing living things and ways of self-nourishing, and making human approaches to agriculture mimic this "earth wisdom" as much as possible. Toward this end, the sisters most frequently use a "permacultural" or "whole systems" approach to gardening and landscape design that integrates organic gardening with the surrounding ecology, creating mutually enhancing relationships that closely imitate the design of naturally evolved ecosystems. Developed by Australian biogeographer Bill Mollison, permaculture harmonizes particularly well for those who, as I describe later, view creation as "revelatory."

2. Putting Sustainable Alternatives into Action   Green sisters get their hands dirty, taking the conceptual philosophies of environmental sustainability and turning them into compost, carrots, and community. By growing their own food on-site, sisters reduce their "ecological footprint" (the sum of their effects on natural resources). Many of these organic farms also provide surrounding families and individuals with food, as well as supply area foodbanks and feeding centers with fresh, locally grown organic produce.

In the process of forming community-supported gardens (in which community members agree to "share" the costs of growing food and in return share the harvest), sisters not only have come to know their neighbors better but have encouraged connections among neighbors. These community-supported gardens have provided a means to organize area families and individuals along issues of food security and safety; farmland conservation; environmental sustainability; habitat protection; clean water, soil, and air; and other ecological concerns. In many cases, the community-supported gardens and ecology centers run by sisters have also become community meeting places where people come together to celebrate Earth Day and participate in seasonal festivals and other community-building events.

It is important to note that green sisters' organic farming ministries are not relegated only to rural areas, although certainly most are located where sisters' communities have historically owned farmland. Instead, there are a growing number of organic farms and gardens in which green sisters have reinhabited urban cityscapes, providing inner-city communities with fresh produce and an opportunity to interact in an embodied way with earth, seeds, water, and sun. In these urban gardening ministries, sisters talk about making use of the "healing gifts" of the earth when working with marginalized (often wounded) populations such as homeless people, those with addictions, or women and children who have survived domestic violence.

3. Fieldwork as Prayerwork   Whether their farms are located in rural, suburban, or urban settings, there is an overwhelming sense among green sisters of the profoundly sacred nature of this work. To work in the garden is to engage prayerfully with the land; to serve others through its gifts; to create gentler ways to work with the land to meet human needs; and to be deepened, delighted, and spiritually renewed in the process. Genesis Farm cofounder Miriam MacGillis understands farming to be a profoundly sacramental act. She declares, "We need to see farmers as entering the sanctuary of the soil and engaging the mysterious forces of creation in order to bless and nourish the inner and outer life of the community they serve." MacGillis goes on to characterize farming not as it has conventionally been conceived of, as trivial and "menial" labor, but as a kind of priestly practice. She says, "If we were to accept the Earth on the terms and under the exquisite conditions in which it continues to evolve, the role of the farmer would be raised to a most honorable and sacred human profession. Relieved of the illusions that they are manufacturing food, or that they are worthy of success to the degree that they are also economists, cosmeticists, and managers, farmers might understand themselves as acting in something akin to a prophetic and priestly role."[8]

Gail Worcelo of the Green Mountain Monastery offers another powerful image of this kind of sacred role when she proclaims, "The tractor is my pulpit!"[9] As sisters become farmers engaging in sacred agriculture, they not only transform our very basic models of agriculture, but also challenge conventional gender norms in the realm of the traditionally male-dominated fields of both agriculture and religion. In working cocreatively with the earth, sisters simultaneously cultivate new sources of nourishment for the community while cultivating a new kind of spiritual ecology.

Working with Nature

Founded in 1994, the Franciscan Earth Literacy Center is an environmental education center situated on a five-hundred-acre property owned by the Sisters of Saint Francis of Tiffin, Ohio. The sisters have chosen permacultural principles to guide the agricultural and landscape design of the property. To create the Earth Literacy Center, the Franciscan sisters remodeled an old dairy barn using ecodesign and permacultural techniques. The sisters cite several key reasons for their choosing permaculture over other organizing approaches: permaculture designs tend to result in diverse and stable ecosystems; permacultural systems are ecologically sound and self-sustaining; and permaculture is based on a philosophy of "working *with*, rather than against nature, and of living in harmony with the natural world."[10]

Sister Rita Wienken, director of the Earth Literacy Center and co-coordinator of the Franciscan sisters' Seeds of Hope Farm, holds a master's degree in pastoral ministry with a special emphasis in earth literacy and sacred agriculture. In her book *Patterns of Wholeness,* she discusses how nature's "patterns of wholeness" were successfully applied to the "greening" of the Brown County Ursulines' Motherhouse in St. Martin, Ohio, thus creating a "healing relationship" among the earth, the human community, and the divine.[11] Coming into harmony with nature's "patterns of wholeness" has been integral to the creation of the Franciscan sisters' Seeds of Hope Farm, which grows produce for the religious community and supplies organic produce to the Ecumenical Sharing Kitchen and the Salvation Army. As of spring 2005, the Seeds of Hope Farm Market, an offshoot of the garden, began supplying area restaurants with organic ingredients and selling to those who visit the sisters' produce cart on the St. Francis campus. Like so many other green sisters involved in farming ministries, Wienken has also expanded the garden to include community-supported agriculture (CSA), by which area families buy shares of produce that they pick up each week. The farm also provides a community service option for troubled youths sentenced through the juvenile court system. "What we give to them," says Wienken, "besides work experience, is a positive attitude." Wienken says she sees the healing effects of the land on eleven- and twelve-year-olds who have already led "a tough life," especially when they stay with the farm long enough to harvest what they have planted.[12]

Like nearly all of green sisters' earth ministries, Seeds of Hope Farm and the Franciscan Earth Literacy Center are small, localized projects, but the effects are more far-reaching than one might expect. For instance, participating in an organic CSA both protects the local environment (including ground water and wildlife) from the polluting effects of conventional industrial agriculture and reduces the demand for the petrochemicals used in conventional agriculture and for the petroleum used to truck or ship produce long distances to stores and consumers. Indirectly then, the CSA also reduces dependence on oil reserves and the burning of fossil fuels that produce greenhouse gases and contribute to global warming. Green sisters, who drive hybrid vehicles or choose to walk or bicycle instead of operating conventional automobiles, make very real connections between oil consumption, war, food, and the degradation of the planet's life systems. Local organic community supported gardens embody the faith that peace and justice can begin with food—table by table.[13] As Missionary Sisters of the Immaculate Conception Nancy Earle explained to me, speaking about her decision years ago to start growing organic vegetables, "A butterfly flaps its wings and who knows what can happen? . . . It's all about whole systems. It's all connected. So we need to take a different look at how we live. We need to be simple and walk gently on the Earth."[14]

After serving as parochial schoolteachers for forty years, School Sisters of Notre Dame Kathlene and Annette Fernholz (who are also biological sisters) returned to their family's aging 240-acre conventional farm in Minnesota to convert it to organically based agriculture and resurrect it as a community-supported organic farm called EarthRise. The sisters were committed to working with nature and to finding kinder and gentler ways to cultivate the land than those offered by industrial agricultural techniques. They explain: "We humans, the youngest species to arrive in a bioregion, must make its rhythms our patterns, its laws our guide, its fruit our bounty."[15]

Here the sisters' call to harmonize with the earth's rhythms and patterns echoes the ecodesign or biomimicry principles imbedded in building strawbale houses and other ecosustainable living structures—an ethic that says humans must learn from the earth's ways of sheltering, growing food, and sustaining life. Commenting on the Fernholz sisters' decision to embark on the EarthRise project, Sister of Loretto Mary Ann Coyle, writing for the *Loretto Earth Network Newsletter,* observed, "One might say that the words of [feminist poet and novelist] Marge Piercy were ringing in their ears and they could not help but respond: "Because you can die from overwork, because you can die from a fire that melts rocks, because you can die of the poison that kills the beetle and the slug, we must come again to worship you on our knees, the common living dirt."[16]

One of my favorite stories about sisters harmonizing with the earth and concertedly working with nature comes from Medical Mission sisters Jane Pellowski and Estelle Demers of Pennsylvania. The sisters recount their ongoing struggles to protect their garden produce from being consumed by competing wildlife and told how their own attitudes graciously shifted in the process of dealing with this problem. They report: "We have done plenty of research on ways of protecting vegetation from deer. P.S., none of them work. We have even invited people who do cross-species communication to come and help us. It has helped us, but did not change the deer patterns."[17]

Being myself native to suburban New Jersey, which is overrun by deer, I could not help but feel the sisters' pain as well as smile at their "solution." Their account brought to mind the story of St. Francis intervening when a wolf kept terrorizing the small Italian town of Gubbio. The story ends with St.

Francis ultimately negotiating a truce between the townspeople and the wolf, in which the people recognize the wolf's hunger and agree to feed him, and the wolf agrees to behave himself. In the deer saga faced by Pellowski and Demens, I imagine the cross-species communicator negotiating a similar truce, in which the sisters humbly agree to accept and adapt to the deer's nature, and the deer simply continue to eat their share of organic delicacies from the garden.[18] No one said working with nature was easy.

Sharing the Harvest

Since 1996, the Sisters of Charity of St. Vincent De Paul of New York have turned a property willed to them in 1916 into a thriving community-supported organic garden. Sisters Hill Farm enables families in Stanfordville (in the Hudson River Valley area of New York) and New York City to purchase high-quality organic food at affordable prices. In fact, the garden's shareholders would actually pay more to purchase conventional produce from local stores; that is, by purchasing through the organic garden, they effectively save 35 to 50 percent over nonorganic local store prices.

Making fresh, locally grown, pesticide-free produce affordable and accessible is integral to the sisters' mission. A section on health in one of Sisters Hill Farm's pamphlets articulates a holistic vision and approach: "As an expression of our reverence for creation, the mission of Sisters Hill Farm is to grow healthy food, which nurtures bodies, spirits, communities, and the earth." The very production of this healthy food is itself a spiritual process. Sister Mary Ann Garisto, a former biology teacher with a keen sense of humor and an extraordinary amount of energy, directs Sisters Hill Farm. Speaking of energy, she says, "I am conscious of the wonderful energy of the food grown on small organic farms ever since we started one, and I have met wonderful 'spiritual farmers' including our own."[19] In her community's commitment to organic growing standards and in their commitment to share the harvest, the sisters also intertwine care and concern for creation with their mission to serve those most in need. Advocates for the poor for more than 180 years, the sisters identify the community-supported organic farm as a natural extension of their commitment to society's most vulnerable members. The sisters share a portion of the harvest with those in need in the local community, either directly with low-income families or via soup kitchens and food pantries. Each week, the sisters also deliver food to the Bronx for New York City shareholders and for urban organizations to which they donate part of the harvest.[20] Shareholders are also encouraged to select certain weeks, especially when they plan to be out of town, when they will donate their produce to the poor. To reduce their "ecological footprint" even further, in the summer of 2006 the sisters added solar panels to provide energy for the operation of the barns, greenhouse, and living quarters. Garisto says that the decision to "go solar" is "in keeping with [the sisters'] desire to model sustainable practices."[21]

Providing affordable organically grown food to their surrounding communities, as well as serving the urban poor and providing them with the same high-quality organic food, are common endeavors among green sisters' community-supported farms and gardens. When I visited Crown Point Ecology Center in Bath, Ohio, the sister who gave me my tour pointed out the considerable section of the cultivated land that is donated to feed poor people in the city of Akron, Ohio, via the Akron-Canton Regional Foodbank. Purchased by the Sisters of St. Dominic of Akron in 1967 and converted from a school into an ecology center in 1989, the farm at Crown Point defies the conventional wisdom once preached in women's religious communities that ministries needed to be located in urban centers in order to serve needy populations. Crown Point is one of the many examples of green sisters' ministries that maintain vital connections to urban centers—even as the sisters use farmland conservation, sustainability, and production of low-cost, locally grown fresh food as a means of addressing systemic problems such as hunger, food safety, soil and water toxins, and ecological injustices.

Seeds of Hope Farm, Michaela Farm, EarthRise, Sisters Hill Farm, and Crown Point Ecology Center are among many such projects that have sprung up since the 1980s. Crown Point, along with Sophia Garden in Amityville, New York; Shepherd's Corner in Blacklick, Ohio; Heartland Farm in Pawnee Rock, Kansas; Jubilee Farm in Springfield, Illinois; and Crystal Spring in Plainville, Massachusetts, all feature organic agriculture projects run by Dominican sisters and together form ecological ministries of the Dominican Alliance, a network of nine Dominican congregations that support one another in their efforts to "live out Catholic social teachings on the care of creation."[22]

In Canada, the Sisters of Saint Ann operate an earth ministry called Providence Farm in Saint Joseph's Province, British Columbia. The Sisters of Charity of Halifax also operate an organic farm, as do the Sisters of Providence of St. Vincent de Paul in Kingston, Ontario.[23] Most of sisters' organic farming projects are located in rural or suburban areas, and in these places, sisters' ministries involve intense farmland conservation efforts.

Sister Miriam Brown, a member of the Dominican Sisters of Sinsinawa,

Wisconsin, relates that until recently, her community was able to manage its own land and do much of the farming themselves. Now the sisters hire help on the farm but continue their commitment to organic gardening and environmentally sustainable practices. Their decision to keep the farm despite financial challenges was made not only to conserve farmland but also as an act of solidarity with struggling small family farms in their region. "In these days of low prices for all commodities," says Brown, "we have looked anew at the question of keeping the farm and feel it is one very real way we can share with our neighbors the challenge of good stewardship in the face of difficult times."[24]

Why do sisters regard farmland conservation to be such a critical issue? Cornell University Division of Nutritional Sciences Food and Society Policy research fellow Jennifer Wilkins reports that "From 1993 to 2000, 33,000 farms with annual sales of less than $100,000 disappeared. Meanwhile, very large farms play a larger role in the United States: farms generating more than $500,000 a year are only 3.3 percent of all farms but use 20.3 percent of America's farmland and account for 61.9 percent of all sales. The 10 largest food companies account for more than half of all products on supermarket shelves."[25] Green sisters' rural farmland ministries directly address issues of economic justice, food security, and the threatened extinction of the small family farm, particularly as the growth of agribusiness squeezes small growers and results in the paving over of hundreds of thousands of farmland acres each year.[26] The work of "sacred agriculture" and small farm "salvation," however, is not simply confined to rural contexts. Green sisters are also actively involved in urban community gardens and the greening of cityscapes.

Urban Sacred Agriculture

After a crack house burned down in 1995 and left yet another nondescript addition to Detroit's more than sixty thousand abandoned city lots, Sister Elizabeth Walters says that "hope took root"—literally. The mission of the Hope Takes Root community garden, sponsored by the Monroe, Michigan, IHM sisters, is manifold. Walters says, "We teach each other how to grow healthy, nutritious food in an urban setting. We sponsor soil testing and encourage community and yard gardens. We are part of a movement to stop hunger in Detroit. We create safe, welcoming, beautiful green spaces where folks can connect with Earth. We try to build a sense of community, love and peace in our neighborhood and beyond."[27]

Hope Takes Root pays homeless people to plant, weed, and harvest—as Walters calls it, "God's good urban Earth." Neighbors also work in the garden, sharing in its yields. When neighbors are unable to work in the garden but still wish to be involved, Hope Takes Root comes to them, helping the elderly, for instance, to create and maintain planters or space-efficient "square foot gardening."[28] Hope Takes Root also partners with the Hunger Action Coalition to provide any extra food from the garden to area soup kitchens. Mostly, though, the garden serves its immediate neighbors. Walters says, "[The harvest] happens every evening. Folks come with plastic bags to take the food they need."[29] Those who do not live in neighborhoods like the one served by Hope Takes Root often do not realize the utter lack of fresh vegetables and fruit in some inner-city neighborhoods. In the mid-1990s, when I volunteered with a group at Food from the Hood, an organic community garden operated by high-school students in South Central Los Angeles, it was startling for me to realize that there were almost no fresh fruits and vegetables in the area. The nearest grocery store was a considerable drive away, and the only other food available in the immediate area came from fast food restaurants or overpriced convenience stores. Simply getting a few fruits and vegetables a week into the diet of the neighbors had a huge positive effect on community health.

Since 1995, Hope Takes Root has expanded to include over six abandoned city lots and serves more than thirty-five area families. Walter's formula is simple: "If we look out for the Earth, we're looking out for each other."[30] As an inner-city gardening ministry, Hope Takes Root has had special challenges. At one point, a crack addict stole all of their hoses and there was no way to water the crops. But because the garden had strong community ties, the hoses were promptly recognized and returned by two neighbors. In short, the garden has gained ground where many other programs have fallen short. In her work with Hope Takes Root, Walters has found that "gardens have a miraculous, life-giving power, and they create community in the face of insurmountable obstacles."[31] In May 2006, as Walters and fifty other gardeners, including the homeless "neighbors" of the garden, were preparing the earth for the new growing season, she reported, "Hope Takes Root flourishes and participation has grown. May Hope Takes Root bring revived hope to many, many communities!"[32]

In Denver, EarthLinks codirectors Cathy Mueller, a Sister of Loretto, and Bette Ann Jaster, a Dominican Sister of Hope, also work to build community and to link the city's marginalized and most vulnerable populations to "the

Sisters Cathy Mueller and Bette Ann Jaster in EarthLinks'
organic garden for the urban homeless.

healing benefits of nature." Mueller says that EarthLinks (begun in 1996) provides "opportunities for folks to develop and nurture a heart for the earth and
to experience their place in the diverse web of life."[33] In their program "Spirit
Journeys," which the directors describe as "a practical form of Earth Literacy
with the poor and marginalized," EarthLinks provides field trips to nearby nature areas in Colorado. "We offer time to walk and soak in the majesty of nature, and we also provide snacks and a meal, since most of our participants
are hungry . . . people look out for one another, share their stories, and enjoy a
nutritious meal," explains Mueller. "Our goal is to enable people to experience
Earth, her mystery and awe, her diversity and marvelous generosity, and her
invitation to be part of a wider community, a web of life."[34] In essence,
EarthLinks programs are at once educational, spiritual, and practical, effectively offering those it serves both "bread and roses."[35]

The EarthLinks literature describes the ministry's unique approach:

We use the Earth that is around us as the teacher, the textbook, the classroom,
and the nurturer of life. We provide new opportunities for our participants,

who are living with homelessness, violence, addictions, mental health issues or poverty. Through day trips into nature, garden projects, education workshops and bioregional study, these women, men and children have a chance to experience new learning, the welcome of community and enjoy the peacefulness of the natural world. The experiences are simple and yet profound. People's lives are touched, spirits renewed, their bodies relaxed. Awareness of the natural world increases, which serves them well as they return to difficult situations where they attempt to make life-giving choices.[36]

In their "Seeds of Sustainability" garden projects, EarthLinks works with at-risk populations in Denver to create community gardens. The goal of this work is to have "the external activities of the garden mirror the transformation happening within participants' inner lives."[37] When I visited one such community garden for the homeless with EarthLinks codirector Bette Ann Jaster, I encountered a very thin elderly man from Mexico in soiled clothes. He had two filthy rags bound as bandages around wounds on each wrist. He had wandered into the garden that morning, discovering it for the first time. His walk was frail and his face was deeply creased, but it lit up when he encountered certain plants. He spoke to me in Spanish and showed me the mint, pointing to his stomach and instructing me that this was good medicine for stomach pain. Then he showed me the garlic, saying it too was good medicine and helped to fight infection. He found his way to other herbs and gently ran them through his fingers, talking to them softly and nodding with a smile of recognition. He turned to me and told me that these were his "amigos" from home and that he knew them well. What I got from this moving encounter was the sense of a man who was very lonely, far from home, now homeless, and unable to care for himself. Somehow, however, in the life community of the garden he had found the unexpected blessing of company and friendship in the plants he knew from home.

Later, Sister Bette Ann told me similar stories about how homeless people had found comfort and sanctuary in the garden. Since the garden was located across from a day shelter for the homeless, the homeless guests would sometimes work in the garden planting or harvesting their own food. Afterward, they would get to eat what they had helped to produce in the form of salad or vegetarian chili, cooked in the garden on a camp stove or in a solar oven. This gave them the sense of accomplishment of having helped bring the food to the table. She also spoke about the calming affects that nature experiences have had on the homeless who are mentally ill. Since my visit in August 2001, the lot where the community garden I visited had once stood has unfortunately been sold by its owner for condominium development, and the community garden has been moved elsewhere (not an uncommon occurrence as the urban homeless are edged out of areas undergoing gentrification). EarthLinks has created more gardens, however, and in 2005 opened its GreenFingers Peace Garden.

Besides providing the spiritual and nutritive benefits of these urban community gardens to low-income and homeless people, EarthLinks has also created very practical microeconomic development programs connected to the yields of these gardens. For instance, in the GreenFingers program, homeless and low-income people are able to earn an income by selling products created from what they have grown in the garden. For example, they might grow flowers in the garden and then harvest them to make pressed-flower bookmarks, candles, cards, or even vases. Or they might cultivate gourds, make them into attractive birdhouses, and sell them at craft fairs, festivals, church events, or at specially organized GreenFingers "house parties." Although GreenFingers products only generate a modest income for their makers, crafting these items from start to finish boosts participants' feelings of self-respect. The GreenFingers project and other microeconomic development programs operate along a "teach a man to fish" sustainability principle, providing more than charity by offering job skills, social networks, and a sense of real accomplishment—critical steps toward rebuilding a life.[38]

Mueller's and Jaster's approach is significant in part because the ministry operates from a foundational premise unlike that which undergirds much of the Church-produced literature on the environment. EarthLinks programs are built on the premise that earth concerns and the plight of the poor are fundamentally and inextricably intertwined. In other words, environmental violence and injustice and economic violence and injustice are part and parcel of one another. In describing what is unique about EarthLinks, board of directors member Patricia Sablatura, who holds a doctorate in clinical psychology and is a former member of the Sisters of St. Francis of Rochester, Minnesota, summarizes the holistic approach of EarthLinks. She says that EarthLinks "continues to demonstrate its innovative and life-inspiring mission—that caring for the most vulnerable persons and caring for the earth are intrinsically connected. A unique model of community development, EarthLinks is empowering people at all economic levels to be affected by the beauty and wonder of creation."[39] In their ministry, Mueller and Jaster have, in effect, created a common ground in which both solidarity with the earth and solidarity with the earth's poor take root together and nourish the urban community they serve.

In Oakland, California, in the 1990s, Patricia Nagel, a Sister, Servant of the

Immaculate Heart of Mary, along with Notre Dame De Namur Sister Sharon Joyer, took "sacred agriculture" to the inner city. In a neighborhood infested with drugs and plagued by gang-related shoot-outs and turf wars, Nagel and Joyer founded Earth Home, an earth-based learning center that does neighborhood gardening outreach through a community-supported garden. Once their Oakland neighborhood garden was established, they created another garden in the city that now serves low-income seniors. Part of the sisters' vision for these gardens was that they would serve their immediate communities and supply food to area food banks, thus doing something tangible to address the problems of hunger and malnutrition in the city. Both sisters are graduates of John F. Kennedy University's School of Holistic Studies. Nagel and Joyer, who had previously worked in Guatemala and rural Appalachia, respectively, originally had searched for land in a rural area where they could situate Earth Home and begin their agricultural projects. Now the sisters are committed instead to earth ministry in urban landscapes. Having successfully established community gardens in Oakland, the sisters have now begun similar projects to reinhabit inner-city areas of Portland, focusing on healing and restoring city neighborhoods through green initiatives.[40]

The stories of both EarthLinks and Earth Home speak to the multidimensional ways that green sisters are ministering to the earth and its life communities. Green sisters in rural areas are practicing farmland conservation and small sustainable farming methods. They eschew the use of high-tech agricultural chemicals, preferring more labor-intensive techniques that they consider to be gentler on the earth and less toxic to water, soil, plants, and animals. Green sisters in suburban areas are preserving open space and vital habitat while helping surrounding communities to resist sprawl and to become more locally self-sufficient. Green sisters in urban settings, meanwhile, are discovering the creative ways that urban earth ministries can provide ecologically just solutions to problems of poverty, hunger, and homelessness.

The composition and dynamics of ministries such as EarthLinks and Earth Home also exemplify two prominent features of the green sisters movement. One is the importance of the Sisters of Earth network for providing support and opportunities for sisters to compare notes and learn from each others' experiences. Mueller, Jaster, Nagle, and Joyer are all Sisters of Earth, and information about their ministries has been shared at Sisters of Earth conferences, either through presentations or through their participating in the conferences' open discussion periods. EarthLinks and Earth Home also model what is referred to as "intercommunity collaboration," that is, they reflect a movement-wide proclivity for sisters from different religious orders to work together in planting and tending new earth ministries.

Green sisters' urban earth ministries in Detroit, Denver, Oakland, and now Portland are just some of the agricultural projects with which sisters are involved. A community organic garden project headed by Dominican sisters in Houston, for instance, has supplied over four tons of fruits and vegetables to area food pantries over the past decade.[41] The regional diversity of these projects once again points to the broad geographic scope of this movement. Each of these projects may be relatively small and localized, but the large task of re-inhabiting the earth in more sustainable ways begins first with one's own backyard.[42] Remarkably, sisters are reinhabiting urban cityscapes even when there is no backyard.

Biodynamics as Sacred Agriculture

Gardening at Genesis Farm in New Jersey does not simply mean working with the soil; it means working with the energies of the land and the creative forces of the universe. The farm's mission statement reads: "Believing in the spiritual dimension of farming, Genesis Farm promotes the concept of sacred agriculture in both its biodynamic approach and in its educational outreach." A ministry of the Dominican sisters of Caldwell, New Jersey, and based in Blairstown, New Jersey, Genesis Farm comprises both an Earth Literacy Center and a community-supported organic, biodynamic garden. The community-supported garden, which produces weekly shares for two hundred local families year-round, is cultivated according to the principles of biodynamics, which (as mentioned in an earlier chapter) is an agricultural approach founded in 1924 by Austrian metaphysician Rudolf Steiner.[43] Only a very few of the sisters' organic farms are based on and operated according to biodynamic principles. (Franciscan-sponsored Michaela Farm in Indiana and Dominican-sponsored Hope Sprouts Farm in Shepherd's Corner, Ohio, are two such biodynamic farms.)

The biodynamic approach is labor intensive; requires many years of intensive, specialized training to implement correctly; involves a complicated planting calendar; and often necessitates the hiring of a professional biodynamic farmer. Most green sisters who garden organically choose not to go this route. Nearly all the earth ministries I have mentioned have had some connection to Genesis Farm; either they have sent a sister to receive "earth literacy" training in one of the farm's programs, had their founder do an internship at the farm, or invited Miriam MacGillis to speak with or lead a workshop for the group. MacGillis is also a Sister of Earth and was a keynote speaker at one of the network's early conferences, so she is often consulted by other Sisters of Earth for advice, especially regarding farming projects. Essentially then, Genesis Farm has served as a highly influential "seed community" that has led to the development of many other earth ministries. Even sisters who have chosen to design and cultivate their gardens according to different agricultural approaches are still likely to have some familiarity with Genesis Farm, biodynamics, and MacGillis's articles, audiotapes, or videotapes.

The *Genesis Farm Community Supported Garden Handbook* identifies these key aspects of biodynamics:

Broad Perspective: Since plants are utterly open to and formed by influences from the depths of the earth to the heights of the heavens, our considerations in agriculture must incorporate a broad perspective.

Reading the Book of Nature: Everything in nature reveals something of its essential character in its form and gesture, revealed through careful observation.

Cosmic Rhythms: The light of the sun, moon, planets and stars reaches the plants in regular rhythms and contributes to the growth of the plant. Ground preparation, sowing, cultivating, and harvesting can be timed to take advantage of these rhythms.

The Life of the Soil: Biodynamics recognizes that the soil itself can be alive, and this vitality supports and affects the quality and health of the plants that grow in it. Composting and cover-cropping are crucial elements of biodynamic agriculture.

A New View of Nutrition: Since we gain our physical strength from the process of breaking down the food we eat, the more vital our food, the more it stimulates our own activity. Biodynamic gardeners aim for quality, and not only quantity.[44]

The farm handbook further explains that biodynamics is not just an assemblage of methods and techniques but is, in fact, a "unique worldview . . . an on-going path of knowledge . . . grounded in the belief that the Earth is a living being." Planting times are governed by the astrological positioning of the sun, moon, stars, and planets. In the principles outlined by the garden handbook, a doctrine of correspondences is reflected at several points, particularly in the "as above so below" reasoning that identifies plants as "utterly open to and formed by influences from the depths of the earth to the heights of the heavens."[45]

The farm handbook also describes the importance of harvesting in accordance with the "cosmic rhythms." To facilitate this method, the Biodynamic Farming and Gardening Association publishes *Stella Natura,* a yearly calendar that guides biodynamic farmers in ongoing astronomical movements, which in turn inform farmers about the best days to work with certain kinds of plants.[46] Depending on phases of the moon, conjunctions, oppositions, and other celestial events, some days are considered good days astrologically for working with leafy plants but not necessarily for working with roots. Other days are seen as good for working with roots but not flowers. Still other days are marked as being good for working with fruit but only in the morning and good for working with leafy plants, but only between six in the evening and midnight. When Saturn is in "retrograde" (moving in an orbital direction opposite to the earth's journey around the sun), the biodynamic calendar advises that this condition makes things "dramatically more difficult or opposite to expectations" and is particularly not a good time to work with flowering plants.[47]

This conviction that a "retrograde Saturn" makes new projects or current actions more difficult is a basic principle in Western astrology. Much of this emphasis on the cosmic forces in the soils and plants in biodynamics is also reminiscent of "vitalism," a philosophy popular in the seventeenth and eighteenth centuries that held that plants and animals "act according to an indwelling, mysterious power that physics or chemistry cannot analyze."[48] Biodynamicists make a point of distancing themselves from vitalism, however, emphasizing that while they do acknowledge a vital force within the plant and mineral world, they also recognize that the laws of physics and chemistry apply to living systems; they enthusiastically embrace science.[49]

It makes sense that MacGillis would find affinities in the philosophy of biodynamic farming and its methods. The broad perspective embraced by biodynamics that takes into account the relationship of the plants to influences from "the depths of the earth to the heights of the heavens" is essentially a means to garden within the context of a "cosmological consciousness." That is, practices in the garden take into account not just what is going on in the immediate ecology of the garden, but also the position of the sun, moon, planets, and stars. This approach harmonizes well with Thomas Berry's holistic perspective on the cosmos and his three guiding principles of "differentiation, communion, and interiority." That is, from Berry's perspective, the universe is a spiritual union (a "communion") of many different parts ("differentiated subjects") in relation to one another, and all share a common sacred essence ("interiority") that makes everything in the universe both physically and metaphysically "one."[50] As a disciple of Berry, MacGillis chose to create a garden in which cosmic rhythms are taken into account, and the timing of the preparation, sowing, and cultivation of the earth is in keeping with the spiritual framework of her mentor's teachings.

The biodynamic principle of "reading the book of nature" also harmonizes well with Dominican perspectives. In her book *Earth Spirituality: In the Catholic and Dominican Traditions,* Dominican sister Sharon Zayac makes these connections explicit: "Thomas Aquinas [also a Dominican, although trained as a child by Benedictines] tells us that 'Sacred writings are bound in two volumes, that of creation and that of holy scripture.' He speaks of creation first because creation is the primary revelation. We came to know God in creation long before we met God in scripture."[51] The language of "reading the book of nature" is also connected to rationalist philosophy and early modern science, which held that the "Book of Nature" should be held up alongside the Book of Revelations as an equally valid epistemology and path to knowing God. In the North American context, extensions of this philosophy run through both the deist movement and, later, the discourse of the Transcendentalists who, with Romantic resonances, were said to see "books in running brooks and sermons in stones."[52] The writings of Ralph Waldo Emerson, who saw nature as teacher and the study of nature as a spiritual path, are in some ways strikingly similar to Berry's more contemporary cosmic ruminations.[53] In his journal from 1841, Emerson wrote:

> Yet the whole code of nature's laws may be written on the thumbnail, or the signet of a ring. The whirling bubble on the surface of a brook admits us to the secret of the mechanics of the sky. Every shell on the beach is a key to it . . . from the beginning to the end of the universe she has but one stuff—but one stuff with its two ends, to serve up all her dream-like variety. Compound it how she will, star, sand, fire, water, tree, man, it is still one stuff, and betrays the same properties to the anointed eye.[54]

Miriam MacGillis also highlights connections between biodynamics' founder Rudolf Steiner and the "New Cosmology":

> Steiner lived in Austria at the turn of the [last] century, and while he did not have available the insight drawn from quantum physics, or from Gaia theory, or the observations of our space explorers, his knowledge of the spiritual

world pervading the world of matter resulted in an approach to farming and to the nourishing function of food that is extraordinary. Since 1987 the fields and gardens of Genesis Farm have been cultivated in this biodynamic approach. The food from this garden is literally a manifestation of Spirit.[55]

Founded in 1938, the Biodynamic Farming and Gardening Association (BFGA) holds that biodynamics is the oldest nonchemical agricultural movement of the twentieth century, predating the "organic farming" movement by twenty years.[56] More than simply advocating chemical-free agriculture, biodynamics is geared toward working with the "health-giving forces of nature" by increasing the vitality of the soil as living matter. As with regular organic farming, biodynamics places heavy emphasis on composting and building up the vitality of the soil through applied organic matter. This is also one of the biodynamic farmer's main defenses against disease and pests.[57] Similar to the tenets of homeopathic and naturopathic medicine, biodynamics is based on the premise that disease and pestilence only find openings in a weak or compromised body. Like human bodies, plant bodies that are not vital and strong become easy prey. Composting and soil vitality are therefore part of a comprehensive approach to strengthen soil and plants so that disease can find no purchase. Part of this plan includes the application of herbal homeopathic preparations to the agricultural compost. The BFGA refers to these preparations as "medicine for the earth," deriving them from Steiner's "science of cosmic influences."[58] Some preparations may include, for example, solutions of horsetail or nettles. Other preparations are considerably more complex, such as the infamous "Preparation 500," which entails gathering manure from a pregnant cow while she is standing in the field (preferably during a rain), packing the manure into the horn of a bull, and burying the horn in the ground or at the bottom of a lake bed for one winter. In the spring, the farmer (or preparation supplier) digs the horn up, adds the decayed matter to water (preferably rainwater), and then stirs the preparation a certain number of strokes in one direction before application.[59]

Such intricate recipes reflect Steiner's fascination with and explorations of the traditions of alchemy that became so central to the Rosicrucian path.[60] Clearly, however, these methods are somewhat unconventional within the context of modern farming techniques, even for more low-tech organic farmers. They can also be a challenge for some green sisters who find Steiner's approach to be problematic on a number of levels. Josephite sister Marilyn Rudy, for instance, says matter-of-factly, "I want to practice them [biodynamic approaches], but so far I cannot get started. Perhaps they are too much like a religion and I already have one of 'those.'"[61] Green Mountain Monastery prioress Gail Worcelo simply found Steiner's philosophies and methods too inaccessible: "I completed a nine-month course in biodynamic agriculture a year ago. I found it very helpful, expanding and educative. I also found the teachings of Steiner too esoteric and not within my practical reach."[62] Dominican sister Sharon Zayac of Springfield, Illinois, finds Steiner's philosophies and methods "very appealing," but adds that her community cannot implement them because "they are way too labor intensive for us."[63]

Sister of Charity Maureen Wild, who spent many years living at Genesis Farm and served as its director before returning to her native Canada, witnessed biodynamic farming in action over the course of several years. While she appreciates aspects of the approach, she also finds Steiner problematic, and for reasons other than those offered by Rudy and Worcelo:

> I appreciate the philosophy that honors the living earth, Gaia, and has developed an agricultural approach that is so in tune with the subtle forces and energies of earth and cosmos. I have had direct experience of this form of agriculture at Genesis Farm and could literally "taste" the wonder of this relationship [of farmer with soil/plant and the earth, moon, cosmic rhythms]. The vegetables, herbs, and fruit were the best I've ever eaten. However, I do find Steiner's cosmology quite limiting. It still smatters of human dominion . . . the human as crown of creation . . . as ultimately responsible for everything in nature. I believe it is rooted in inadequate theological grounding of biblical interpretation . . . a kind of human-centered, fundamentalist interpretation.[64]

Steiner, who founded and was at one time president of the German section of the Theosophical Society, eventually precipitated an ideological split within the Theosophical community and founded a new Anthroposophical movement. In part, his move was a reaction against the increasing "Orientalism" of the Theosophical movement; furthermore, it was a reaction to the sensationalism surrounding Theosophy at that time. Ultimately, however, Steiner created a movement that retained Theosophical principles but remained more focused on the Western esoteric tradition, Rosicrucian thought, and mystical Christianity. Steiner was still very interested in "Oriental philosophy" and used concepts from Eastern religions throughout his work, but he was fascinated by Christian mysticism and scientific theories of "the cosmos, man and planetary evolution."[65] In fact, reflecting these interests, one of Steiner's most notable students, Max Heindel, became an acclaimed leader in the American Rosicrucian movement and produced works such as *The Rosicrucian Cosmo-Conception* (1909) and *Mystic Christianity* (1911).[66] The combination of mystical interest in cosmology, Christian mysticism, and the spiritual dimension of science is clearly also of interest to Thomas Berry and those at Genesis Farm.

Interestingly, Steiner derived much of his insight about matter and spirit not just from his original encounter with Theosophy but also from Catholic sacramentalism. Steiner was a student of Catholic mysticism and, like a number of contemporary Catholics, became especially drawn to the work of Meister Eckhart.[67] What is perhaps appealing to devotees of Thomas Berry about Steiner's work is his blending of scientific and mystical epistemologies, a theme repeated within the work of both Berry and Teilhard de Chardin. The mystical elements of biodynamic philosophy thus complement and are mutually supportive of the existing ecotheological frameworks of an embodied cosmos, a living creation process, and a sacramental universe that are already embedded in Genesis Farm's earth literacy programs.

The seemingly "magical" alchemical practices of biodynamics, such as those found in "Preparation 500"; biodynamics' use of astrology in planting and harvesting cycles (a suspect practice for some green sisters because of astrology's associations with Western occultism); questions about what kind of scientific foundation this agricultural approach could have; and the highly specialized training involved all make it unlikely that biodynamics will receive wide adoption by organic-farming sisters. In addition, as Sister Marilyn Rudy put it, biodynamics can seem too much like a "religion." (This may be one reason that permaculture, which features a less-controversial ideology and more accessible methods, is largely preferred.) Other areas of discomfort with biodynamics stem from Steiner's relationship to both Theosophy and Anthroposophy, two nineteenth-century metaphysical movements that are seen as foundational to contemporary New Age philosophies (which are also suspect for some sisters). Indeed, sisters who choose to go biodynamic with their farms do so delicately because such associations can be contentious and divisive both within religious communities and in relation to institutional Church authority. How green sisters negotiate these sorts of conflicts will be taken up more fully later.

A relationship between Roman Catholicism and metaphysical movements such as Anthroposophy, however, is certainly not unique or confined to Genesis Farm or similar Catholic-sponsored biodynamic ministries. American religious historians Catherine Albanese and Mary Farrell Bednarowski both document strong affinities between American Catholics and the American metaphysical tradition. Revealing yet another cultural "companion-planting," Albanese and Bednarowski point out close links between Roman Catholic spirituality and the meaning of spirituality for metaphysics, a tradition that Albanese says draws heavily on the Western esoteric tradition, including Neo-platonism, Gnosticism, Kabbalah, and alchemy.[68]

According to Albanese, the origins of metaphysics "in Roman Catholic intellectual neighborhoods are not inappropriate for the metaphysical tradition with its almost crypto-Catholic nuances of mysticism and its self-conscious searches for unity with the One."[69] Bednarowski similarly asserts that the key concepts of immanence in "New Age thought" stem largely from esoteric Christianity, Eastern esotericism, occult orientation, and Roman Catholicism's sacramental worldview. She explains that it is the closely related concept of the "interconnectedness of all things" that, according to metaphysical philosophy, holds the "possibility of healing the fragmentation, the individualism, the purposelessness and the exploitation of the earth's resources."[70]

With respect to affinities between contemporary Roman Catholic spirituality and the American metaphysical tradition, there is in some cases a double or even triple feedback loop of various themes and currents. Contemporary Roman Catholics borrow some elements and insights from the metaphysical tradition, but many of these tend to be the very same elements that metaphysical traditions had initially borrowed from Christian mysticism and Roman Catholic sacramentalism. These elements, such as mysticism and divine immanence, filtered as they are through an American metaphysical lens, are particularly resonant for American Roman Catholics and correspond to frameworks with which they are already comfortable. Albanese makes the argument that the metaphysical tradition is as "American as apple pie" and has been greatly overlooked as "a major player in the evolution of a certain type of religiosity in the nation."[71] She traces a "broad strand" of metaphysics that emerged from nineteenth-century movements such as Theosophy, Anthroposophy, and New Thought, and shows how they continue to shape American religious culture today. Metaphysics, argues Albanese, "is as normal a feature of the American spiritual landscape as the proverbial God and motherhood."[72] This may be so, but for the time being at least, except for a few exceptions, green sisters' apple pies are more likely to be simply organic rather than biodynamic.

Spiritual Ecologies and Edge Effects

In supporting and facilitating many different kinds of habitat on their lands, through regenerating wetlands; maintaining forests; allowing native field, meadow, and prairie grasses to return; or even regreening polluted urban cityscapes, green sisters' approach to caring for their lands encourages what permaculture founder Bill Mollison calls "edge effects." Edge effects concern the dynamics of the connecting edges or border areas of any given landscape. Edge is defined, in biogeographic terms, as "an interface between two mediums," such as the area between forest and grassland, the shoreline between land and water, or the borders between desert and less-arid ecologies. Fostering such areas of intersection in the landscape produces places of intense and "varied ecology" that cannot be defined as being part of one medium or another but have blended features of both. One so-called edge effect is that "productivity increases at the boundary between two ecologies . . . because the resources from both systems can be used."[73] That increased productivity at the intersection of two or more ecologies creates another edge effect; it is found to generate species that are particular to that combination.[74] A particular landscape or portion of landscape can be characterized by yet another edge effect—a dynamic in which its edge or boundary "acts as a net or sieve" in which materials drift or get trapped at the edges, much as leaves collect at the side of the road or silt accumulates within a marsh.

In the spiritual ecology of green sisters, where Roman Catholicism, environmental activism, nature mysticism, social justice, feminism, and in some cases, even aspects of the metaphysical tradition come into relationship with one another, there is a similar presence of edge effects. That is, there is an interface between two or more media that creates a varied spiritual "ecology." In this ecology, we see a reshaping of religious culture, born of a system that draws simultaneously on a plurality of resources. We can also identify a net or sieve effect, by which a plurality of "religious and cultural objects" end up collected together and recombined with one another, producing some religious forms that are perhaps regional to that particular, localized area of intersection.[75]

Although religious forms, spiritual expressions, cultural systems, and the like cannot be reduced to biogeographical principles, the landscape design framework is valuable in this case because it originates from a definitional premise that religion and faith are, in fact, organic, changing processes, rather than static entities with fixed borders. The design component also makes room for human agency in the creation and cultivation of new religiocultural designs. It is, in fact, a way of talking about religion, culture, and modernity that replaces the imagery of "fracture," "fragmentation," and "rupture" (all of which connote a rigid "shattering" of a fixed entity) with an imagery that reflects the protean nature of living systems.

Permacultural approaches also focus on the cultivation of diversity and pluraculture, a practice that often blurs borders and categories. In contrast to the "ordered, linear, segmented thinking of Europeans," says Mollison, with permaculture it is "no longer clear where orchard, field, house and garden have their boundaries, where annuals and perennials belong, or indeed where cultivation gives way to naturally evolved systems."[76] In the pluraculture of sister's organic farms, as in the ecology of the green sisters movement, there is a certain ease with complexity, combination, and flexible boundaries.

In her book on the spiritual dimensions of permaculture and its relationship to Santuario Sisterfarm, Dominican sister Carol Coston talks about her process of unlearning to garden like a neatnik. Since studying permacultural principles, she describes her "transformation of consciousness about 'order' and 'disorder.'" In learning more about the ways that nature plants and configures things, she came to the recognition that "nature doesn't create a forest or a meadow in straight lines and out of a single species the way agribusiness grows most of our food crops. Nature loves a diversity of plants and trees, the crawling creatures and the flying ones. There is, in short, a 'useful connection' between the vine and the fig tree and us."[77] Coston's observation is perhaps particularly a propos for Santuario Sisterfarm, which is located along the edges of the United States and Mexico.

Although different in philosophy from biodynamics, permaculture also ties in well to Thomas Berry's work on the "new cosmology" or "universe story," which has been key to the germination of the green sisters movement. Bill Mollison's emphasis on finding the underlying connections between seemingly disparate elements, for instance, bears affinity to Berry's assertion that the world must not be viewed as "a collection of objects," but instead as a "community of subjects," all divinely related to one another.[78]

Berry, like Mollison, sees an integral and inseparable relationship among elements that emerge from a unified cosmos. The ethic of diversity or multiplicity in permaculture corresponds to Berry's principle of differentiation in the universe, and the implementation of pluraculture fits well with his discussions of the ways in which life is biased toward greater variation.[79] In her book on permaculture, Carol Coston makes these connections explicit, writing, "Permaculture's Earth-care ethic has special resonance with me because it embodies much of what I hold as spiritual truth—particularly its inherent call for us to live in consideration of the common good of all creation. It also resonates with me because it offers practical ways . . . to respond to the imperatives of the 'new story of the universe.'"[80]

In analyzing diverse and pluracultural landscape designs in which apparently divergent biotic elements function together cooperatively, Bill Mollison notes: "To the observer, this may seem like a very unordered and untidy system; however, we should not confuse order and tidiness . . . Creativity is seldom tidy." Those of us who study the phenomenon of religion in its various forms and permutations have no doubt noticed this about our own subject. Permaculturalists, like scholars of religion, must allow for an organic "messiness." Yet Mollison observes that, rather than being haphazard, a creative order integrates diverse species and elements that are compatible, resulting in a permaculture characterized by a deceptive stability. From a permacultural perspective, seemingly disparate connections and combinations are not viewed as a liability or devolution ("syncretism"), but as a strength ("diversity, stability, resilience"). In fact, for Mollison, there is a danger to the rigidity of monoculture that stems from the way in which such a culture can both ignore or even work against the characteristics of the landscape and be ill-prepared and resistant to deal with change, whether environmental or social. It is interesting that even though Mollison's book is about biogeography, he chooses to name religion first on his list of potentially dangerous monocultures. He warns: "Beware the monoculturalist, in religion, health, farm or factory."[81]

Accordingly, in sisters' organic gardens planted along permacultural principles, vegetables, fruits, and flowers grow together, and mutually symbiotic plants grow in close relationship to one another, each putting back into the soil that which the other takes out.[82] Sisters' gardens display a profuse mix of different heights, colors, and varieties, all intensively grown together. Santuario Sisterfarm's Spiral Garden, for instance, features the "Three Sisters"—corn, beans, and squash—all planted together to form a "guild." To these organic "sisters," a Texas native perennial called "Gregg's Mistflower" has been added. Carol Coston reveals the permacultural symbiosis embodied in this combination: "[Gregg's Mistflower] strengthened the guild's interactions because the bees and the butterflies that are attracted to it help pollinate. The beans fix the nitrogen used by the corn and squash. The corn provides a place for the beans to climb up and around, and the squash takes up the ground level."[83] Louise Riotte, as discussed earlier, talks about this technique of coplanting mutually beneficial species in terms of "companion planting." Much as "carrots love tomatoes" and beans love squash, so green sisters love pluracultures. For organic-farming sisters, cultivating the land and cultivating a new culture of vowed religious life both entail a valuing of diversity, flexibility, and mutually enhancing combinations. In the actual nitty-gritty cultivation of the soil and in the cultivation of garden as sanctuary, fieldwork as prayer, and sacred agriculture as social justice ministry, the principles of permaculture are indeed at work.

Sister Farmers and Male-Dominated "Fields"

One last note on Catholic religious sisters and farming: there is a pattern of cultural "cultivation" within the green sisters movement in which "fields"—areas of expertise—traditionally dominated by males have been replanted to be more gender-inclusive. In her study of farm women, ethnographer Nettie Wiebe notes that "the agricultural sector, from the family farm to the corporate agribusiness domain, remains a deeply patriarchal system." Wiebe points out that the word "farmer," like "priest," although it is gender-neutral, "has almost exclusively male connotations in the English language." In the institutions of farming, such as agricultural supply companies, or in educational publications on agriculture, this image is reinforced by referring to the farmer almost exclusively as "he" or by speaking of the "farmer and his sons." In reviewing representations of farmers in material culture (including children's books), Wiebe finds that "the images that come to mind when farmers are referred to are most often images of men in overalls and/or on tractors. Reading articles on farming or watching farm advertisements on television serves to reinforce the predominant impression that farming is a male profession."[84] Such frameworks cast women either as invisible or as invaders—"weeds."

In analyzing the culture of wilderness and the colonization of the American West, environmental historian Frieda Knobloch has further drawn parallels between attitudes toward weeds as "invaders" and "enemies," and cultural repudiation of difference and multiplicity.[85] In the hostile rhetoric of "anti-weed" legislation passed in many U.S. states, outlawing such plants as thistles, or in frontier documents speaking to the "agricultural war on weeds," Knobloch discovers distinct parallels between the language used for irradicating weeds and narratives of cultural purity.[86] As green sisters cultivate new forms of religious life and in effect a new spiritual ecology, will they in some sense be seen as "weeds" in the church and face attempted eradication? Of course, from a permacultural perspective, each so-called weed has a valuable story to tell about the land. Some weeds, for example, give off significant amounts of nitrogen and specifically migrate to soils that are nitrogen poor in order to "serve" them. Mollison points out that these plants, rather than being a nuisance, work as both soil test kits, indicating what the soil is lacking, and as on-site soil reconditioners. Even unwanted tubers or nuisance rhizomes, such as couch grass, often function as vital "reclaimers," loosening hardened areas and transforming them into soil that is aerated, looser, and more prepared for diverse plant growth. In working with nature, permacultural approaches value weeds and regard them as important contributors to a given ecology. No doubt green sisters themselves would echo Bill Mollison's warning to "Beware the monoculturalist, in religion, health, farm, or factory."[87]

7. SAVING SEEDS

Heirloom Conservation and Genetic Sanctuaries

Heirloom Tomato Tasting Day has become an annual ritual at Heathfield, the appropriately earthy-sounding motherhouse and grounds of the Sisters of Providence of St. Vincent De Paul in Kingston, Ontario. Each August, the sisters open Heathfield to visitors who feast òn more than eighty varieties of "heritage" or "heirloom" tomatoes. Many of the varieties conserved at the Heirloom Seed Sanctuary at Heathfield are more than a hundred years old; many are no longer available in seed catalogs or from distributors. More familiar tomato heirlooms such as Brandywine (1885) and Beauty (1886) grace the sisters' tasting tables, as do rarer varieties such as Honor Bright (1897), Perfection (1880), and Yellow Pear (1805). Rare tomatoes are not the only species that are provided sanctuary at Heathfield. The Sisters of Providence Heirloom Seed Sanctuary provides haven for the seeds of some four hundred varieties of herbs, flowers, and vegetables (for example, "Swedish Brown" beans [1830], "Monk" peas [1500s], "Sweet Bullnose" peppers [1759], and "Deertongue" lettuce [1740]) that have been grown for generations in "open pollinated" (nonhybrid) forms.

Heirloom conservation is an important component of the green sisters movement. In fact, there are key resonances between sisters' commitment to conserve botanical heritage through sustainable agriculture and their commitment to conserve heritage traditions of vowed religious life—simultaneously cultivating a kind of greater spiritual "biodiversity" in both fields. Horticulturally, the designation "heirloom" generally means that seeds are public-domain (nonpatented), nonengineered, nonhybrid plants that have passed through generations of cultivation. Unlike most hybrid plants, heirloom varieties can reproduce themselves, making it possible to save and re-plant seeds from year to year instead of having to repurchase seeds with each planting. (Through what is called "terminator technology," agricultural suppliers can genetically engineer any seed to be sterile after a plant ripens, so that farmers must buy seeds from the commercial supplier again each year.) Heirlooms are also usually adapted for particular bioregional, climatic, water, disease, and pest conditions, making them naturally more resistant to threats such as blight and drought.

Because many heirloom varieties predate the mass transportation of produce across lengthy distances, these fruits and vegetables tend to be bred for taste more than for shelf life. They are also often more nutritious than commercial varieties. Kara Ferguson, a special guest speaker at the 2006 conference of Sisters of Earth, works with an organization called Dream of Wild Health that saves and propagates heritage seeds passed on to them by Native American families. In independent testing, the heritage lima beans given to the organization by a Native American elder were found to have twenty thousand times the levels of antioxidants as commercial lima beans. As she read these results, I could see sister farmers around the room nodding their heads.[1]

The Sisters of Providence are concerned about the extinction of heirloom varieties as heirloom seeds are driven out of the marketplace and supplanted by mass-produced and bioengineered sterile seeds, a process that also narrows species biodiversity and compromises food security. For an example of the kind of havoc that can be wreaked by the imprudent narrowing of species diversity, cofounders of the Heirloom Seed Sanctuary Carol and Robert Mouck are quick to point to the great Irish potato famine of the mid-nineteenth century.[2] In just five years, the famine killed more than a million people through starvation and forced at least that number to flee Ireland. Although the famine itself was largely caused by economic and political forces that prohibited the Irish from retaining the bulk of their own domestic supply of grains (oats, wheat, barley, and so on), which were instead exported to England, the potato blight was made more devastating by the genetically limited and uniform nature of the "lumper" potatoes to which the Irish had access. In the literature about the Sisters of Providence Heirloom Seed Sanctuary, the potato famine functions as a cautionary tale about the dangers of genetic uniformity—putting "all of one's genes in one basket," as it were. Furthermore, the sisters are concerned about the long-term effects of genetically engineered and patented seeds not just on community health and food security, but also on the viability of small sustainable farmers. The Sisters of Providence's director of ecology and earth literacy, Sister Shirley Morris, says, "We are called to live sustainably, simply, in a balanced relationship with all of creation. That means making choices about the food we grow and eat."[3]

Constitution 20 of the Sisters of Providence of St. Vincent de Paul reads: "Our respectful use of the environment witnesses to the values of all creation." And Directional Statement 5 from the congregation's 1994 chapter reads: "We promote rediscovery of our spiritual relationship with each other and with the earth, through ongoing education and action in the areas of: ecology and health, ecology and the work environment, ecofeminism, and ecospirituality."[4] Like Catholic women's sisterhoods in the United States, between 1990 and the present, Catholic sisterhoods in Canada have adopted ecological language into their constitutions and chapter statements with great enthusiasm and then set about putting these statements into action, in a practice commonly referred to as "walking their talk."[5]

A major step toward the Sisters of Providence's living their directional statement on ecology came in 1998, when they teamed up with Robert and Carol Mouck, organic farmers and the guardians of an impressive rare heirloom seed collection that they had spent thirty years acquiring. After selling their farm in 1997, the Moucks were looking for a safe haven for this unique genetic legacy, and the Sisters of Providence were glad to provide sanctuary. Together, the sisters and the Moucks have created an heirloom seed-savers group that meets at Heathfield once a month. The sanctuary has also sponsored "weed walks," botanical Latin classes, and seed-saving workshops. Members of the seed-savers group and friends in the surrounding community also gather at Heathfield several times a year to celebrate the seasonal changes at the equinoxes and solstices—ecumenical festivals that bring together diverse groups of people. The Moucks manage the seed bank and the actual planting and harvesting of the seeds; the sisters provide facilities and help with planting, sorting, harvesting, cataloging, and storing.[6]

The seed sanctuary description reads, "An Heirloom seed is a seed treasured by people who love the names, history, flavour, fragrance and feel what the plants share with them. Saved seeds often become best friends, part of the family."[7] Perhaps this kinship is solidified by the fact that in the twenty-first century, both seeds and religious sisters (or at least their way of life) have been threatened with extinction. More centrally, however, the commitment of the Sisters of Providence to new directions in "creation care" and to seed conservation reflect their own process of renewal and faith in the future.

The sisters first acquired Heathfield in 1930 to use for their new novitiate. From the 1930s well into the 1950s, the gardens at Heathfield produced enough food to sustain the sisters and the orphans for whom they had historically provided.[8] Following the pattern of many women's religious communities in North America, the Sisters of Providence at Heathfield made a transition in the late 1950s to dependence on commercially produced food. The replanting of the grounds in 1998 to host their organic heirloom variety garden began a return to sustainability and self-sufficiency. The garden now provides food to local soup kitchens and food banks, as well as to the sisters and some of the gardeners.

The only Catholic women's religious congregation founded in Kingston, the Sisters of Providence are also acutely aware of their geographical and historical location at what was once the terminus of the "underground railroad" in the nineteenth century.[9] Escaped slaves from southern states in the United States were brought up through Oswego County in western New York, where ships would then take them across Lake Ontario to Kingston or other nearby towns on the Canadian side. Several highly publicized cases of escaped slaves culminated in the ex-slaves' finally reaching sanctuary in Ontario and settling in Kingston.

In 1839, for instance, Harriet Powell's escape was arranged by abolitionists in Syracuse, New York, while her captors (in Syracuse visiting from their home in Mississippi) were distracted by a high-society party. With the help from the Freedom Trail Network and other abolitionist sympathizers, Powell was secreted in a number of safe houses and then transported across the lake to Kingston, where she ultimately sought refuge. Another escaped slave, William "Jerry" Henry, was freed in 1851 from the custody of U.S. marshals (entrusted with returning the fugitive to his owners) by an abolitionist mob in Syracuse. Like Powell, Henry was hidden by local abolitionists until he could be safely transported out of the United States, where he, too, sought sanctuary in Kingston, Ontario. Both of these escape stories were featured prominently in major New York newspapers and were used by abolitionists to illustrate the violence engendered in the system of slavery and the heroics performed by those who subverted it.[10]

A 1998 Canadian television documentary series, *A Scattering of Seeds: The Creation of Canada*, further tells the story of African American refugees as they sought sanctuary from slavery in the relative safety of Kingston and surrounding towns in Ontario, thereby "planting" themselves as "seeds" in the new community. The links between Kingston as a historical place of sanctuary for refugees and the sisters' recent establishment of an heirloom seed-saving sanctuary may seem tangential until one realizes that green sisters do indeed view unadulterated, nonpatented, nonengineered seeds as "refugees" in need of protection from the violence of bioengineering, agribusiness monopoly, and eventual extermination. Prioress Gail Worcelo of the Green Mountain Monastery in Vermont makes this link explicit when she says, "We imagine ourselves as a place of sanctuary for seeds, the new refugees of our time who need to be safeguarded from the fate of genetic manipulation. We imagine activating deep inner capacities still latent in our contemplative depths. We cherish the ability to open ourselves to a comprehensive compassion that is concerned for species thousands of years into the future in order to feel their vulnerability based on our actions now."[11] It is significant that Worcelo used this particular language in a speech addressing a community of religious sisters located in St. Louis, Missouri—home to agribusiness and biotech giant Monsanto Corporation.

Green sisters in both the United States and Canada are creating heirloom seed sanctuaries, participating in aboveground seed-saving networks and in informal underground seed-saving exchanges, protesting the introduction of genetically modified organisms (GMOs) into the food system, and arguing in favor of mandatory GMO labeling. Working from both within and outside the system, sisters are on a mission to safeguard seeds as the genetic heritage of the future. In a variety of contexts, seed-saving sisters have likened their mission of providing "sanctuary" for heritage seeds during the "dark times" of bioengineering to the ways that medieval monasteries in Europe provided safe haven for the great classical texts, ultimately enabling their rediscovery in the Renaissance.

The New Sanctuary Movement

In Chapter 2, I discussed the involvement of North American sisters in the sanctuary movement (1982–1992), when sisters (among some four hundred congregations of various faiths) provided safe houses to those fleeing the political violence and dire economic conditions of Central America, primarily El Salvador and Guatemala. Sisters in religious communities located in regions along the border of the United States and Mexico, such as Arizona, Texas, New Mexico, and California, were particularly active in this movement.[12] In the spring of 1999, I was helping two sisters in one of these bordering states move their belongings into a small cottage located on the campus of a Catholic women's religious community. The sisters were moving into the cottage to be closer to the site where they would begin a new sustainable organic farming and ecological education project. The little cottage was nondescript, run-down, and overgrown with foliage. Before the sisters did some renovation and repair, one could barely see in or out of the windows. In fact, I had driven by the cottage many times and never even knew it existed because it blended so well with the overgrown vegetation.

As workmen from the property helped us unload the sisters' modest amount of furniture from a pickup truck, I remarked to one of the workers that it seemed strange that the religious community, so tidy and orderly in its care of all its other buildings, had left this one apparently totally neglected. It seemed completely uncharacteristic of the other well-kept areas of the property. He told us, "The people don't come anymore, but for a lot of years they did . . . during the night." He said no one said anything about it or drew attention to the cottage, but that in cleaning up here and there, he and some of the other groundskeepers knew there were "folks" in there. "Then, next thing you knew, they'd be gone . . . after a while, new ones would come." As we spoke with him further, it became apparent that this little house had been a stop on the twentieth-century version of the "underground railroad." It had been a safe house where the community had quietly sheltered individuals and families fleeing violence and persecution in their countries of origin and seeking a better and freer life.[13] Now this safe house would be supporting the sheltering of refugees of another sort, as sisters planted and propagated organic seeds— seeds not patented or controlled by agribusiness corporations—seeds that could be freely saved by small subsistence farmers to feed their families. It may seem odd to compare these two forms of "refugees," but in a "whole systems" approach, green sisters draw tangible connections between protecting freely pollinated, nonengineered seed stock and struggling against the root causes of war, violence, injustice, hunger, and poverty.

In 2004, Dominican-sponsored Santuario Sisterfarm organized a San Antonio conference on genetic engineering and "biocolonialism," enlisting the cosponsorship of more than ten communities of Catholic religious women. The conference program focused on the connections between GMOs and ecojustice issues, including a "What Can We Do?" workshop offering action strategies for opposing the spread of GMOs. Once again, the cosponsorship of this conference demonstrated the wide range of cross-community support for seed conservation issues within the green sisters movement. The Benedictine Sisters of Boerne, Texas; the Brigidine Sisters; the Peace and Justice Committee of the Sisters of Incarnate Word in San Antonio; the Peace and Justice Committee of the Sisters of Providence; the Sisters of the Holy Spirit and Mary Immaculate; the Sisters of the Incarnate Word and Blessed Sacrament; and three different congregations of Dominican sisters were all among the cosponsors. The opening and closing blessing at the conference was offered by the Grupo Tradicional de Danza Ceremonial Azteca Xinachtli (a traditional Aztec ceremonial dance group), of which Santuario Sisterfarm staffer Xochitl Codina is a member. Santuario Sisterfarm board president Maria Antonietta Berriozabal and Elise D. García participated in the rituals, which included an honoring of "sacred corn."[14] Dominican sister Sharon Zayac, who has published a book on earth spirituality with Santuario Sisterfarm's Sor Juana Press, spoke on the twenty-first-century food crisis and food as sacrament, outlining the relationship of both to Catholic social teaching.[15]

Inspired in part by South Asian scientist and author Vandana Shiva's work on "biopiracy," Santuario Sisterfarm's codirectors Carol Coston and Elise D. García have placed diversity and justice issues at the center of the group's mission. "At the heart of our major projects," says Coston, "is the cultivation of diversity—biodiversity and cultural diversity. One of these projects, the Rosa y Martín Seed Project [named after Dominican Peruvian saints Rosa de Lima and Martín de Porres], addresses the issue of the dangerous loss of biodiversity and the exploitation of economically impoverished peoples by multinational corporations." Like other ecology centers run by women religious, Santuario Sisterfarm is simultaneously addressing the intertwined issues of environmental genetic pollution and concerns for social and economic justice. "By asserting 'intellectual property rights,'" explains Coston, multinational corporations effectively "[usurp] the seed lines developed over centuries by small farmers and indigenous people around the world." Coston suggests several approaches for struggling against the considerable inroads that GMOs have made into the U.S. marketplace and ways that concerned citizens might prevent their further spread. First, she encourages both women religious and others to begin planting, sharing, and saving heirloom seeds wherever they can. In addition, she advocates activism against GMOs on both grassroots and institutional levels, including shareholder actions to oppose companies' manufacturing of GMOs or their purchase and use of GMO ingredients in their products.[16]

Green sisters have already filed a number of shareholder resolutions along these lines, protesting various companies' policies on GMOs or calling for more research to be conducted on both the biotic and socioeconomic effects of GMOs. In 2005, for instance, the Sisters of St. Francis of Philadelphia, the Sisters of St. Joseph of Springfield (Massachusetts) and the Camilla Madden Charitable Trust (the pension fund for the Adrian Dominican Sisters) conjointly filed a shareholder initiative with McDonald's Corporation requesting that an independent board review the company's use of GMOs in their food products and present the results at the annual shareholders' meeting.[17] As of January 2006, representatives from McDonald's were trying to persuade the sisters to withdraw their shareholder initiative before the annual shareholder meeting so that the issue would not be put to a vote.

Through such negotiations, sisters' communities are able to effect real policy changes within companies that would much prefer not to have public attention drawn to the company's practices related to sensitive issues such as health and the environment. "If the initiative goes forward," explained Roberta Mulcahy, the Sisters of St. Joseph of Springfield's coordinator of the Peace and Justice Committee, "then it goes on to the shareholder proxy statement and the shareholders vote on that. Generally, companies don't want that, so they will instead engage in productive negotiations until the initiative is withdrawn. Last year [2005], we co-filed on four and two were withdrawn."[18]

The Sisters of St. Joseph of Nazareth (Michigan) and the Sisters of Mercy of Detroit co-filed a similar "GMO-Free Initiative" with the Kellogg Company (maker of cereals and other food products). In both these cases, intercommunity collaboration through co-filing is an important strategy since the total sum of the filers' stock holdings tends to lend the initiative more weight. For example, the Michigan Josephite Sisters' eight thousand shares of Kellogg Company common stock as part of their retirement plans, when combined with the Detroit Mercy Sisters' 1,100 shares of common stock, make this sort of shareholder initiative very difficult for a company to ignore.

The Story of the "Seed Martyrs"

Whether it is through shareholder activism, local protest, or providing heirloom sanctuaries, why do green sisters view seed saving as such a critical mission? There are manifold reasons, some of which I have already discussed, but recounting the story of the Russian "seed martyrs" offers further insight. The story of the martyrs, which sisters have shared with me at least a dozen times in various contexts, was first told to me by Sister Constance Kozel, a member of the Dallas, Pennsylvania, Sisters of Mercy of the Americas. Kozel, a freelance writer on environmental issues, is one of the "founding mothers" of the Mercy Earth Harmony Network. Similar to the Loretto Community's Loretto Earth Network, the Mercy Earth Harmony Network is a group of Mercy sisters who work together on environmental issues.[19]

Kozel focused on seed saving and biotech issues for several years and facilitated a number of educational workshops dealing with biodiversity and the threats posed by genetic engineering and agribusiness monopolies. After providing a summary of the story of the seed martyrs in one of her seed talks, Kozel referred me to the account in Cary Fowler's and Pat Mooney's *Shattering: Food, Politics, and the Loss of Genetic Diversity*.[20]

In 1985, the Swedish Parliament awarded Fowler and Mooney the Right Livelihood Award (the alternative Nobel Prize) for their work on the loss of plant genetic diversity. Fowler and Mooney have chronicled, crop by crop, the narrowing of plant varieties in the twentieth century as agribusinesses have come to dominate the seed market. For instance, in 1903, there were 578 different varieties of garden beans in cultivation in the United States. By 1983, U.S. seed banks had only saved stock for thirty-two varieties of garden bean, with less than a handful of those varieties still in cultivation. The rest of the garden bean stock has been bought up by seed companies and taken off the market in order to streamline production to a few varieties. Similarly, there were approximately 789 varieties of corn in cultivation less than a century ago, and now the world relies on fewer than ten (mostly transgenic) varieties. To be profitable, seed companies are interested in eliminating competition from noncorporately controlled varieties and then producing narrow seed lines engineered to prevent independent propagation.[21]

In the same year they received the award from Sweden, Fowler (who is from the United States) and Mooney (who is from Canada) teamed up to visit the Vavilov Institute in Leningrad. While there, they interviewed the scientists and archivists about the institute's history. Embedded in their account of the seed-saving martyrs in Russia during World War II are powerful images of sanctuary, sacrifice, mission, and salvation that clearly strike a chord among seed-saving sisters.

The Russian seed martyrs were the scientists who worked at the Vavilov Institute, the first major seed bank of its kind to acquire and store large-scale seed collections of different agricultural varieties. Before the war, institute founder Nikolai Vavilov developed a devoted following of biologists committed to his gospel of species diversity and the vital preservation of genetic variety. Traveling the world, Vavilov and his cadre of students compiled a unique and extensive collection of seeds for rare crops and disease-resistant varieties. In 1942, however, Nazis surrounded Leningrad in a siege that lasted nine hundred days, cutting the city off from food, water, and basic supplies. As spring came, the institute's valuable blight-resistant potato collection began to sprout, prompting the scientists to risk planting them in a field in front of the institute in order to preserve the potato samples through propagation. When the fields later came under German bombardment, the scientists dashed out of the institute and madly began to dig up the samples, risking their lives to salvage the potatoes amid falling mortar shells. Those who were evacuated from the institute smuggled the potato samples out with them, carefully sewing them into their clothes close to their warm bodies so that the potatoes would not freeze. During the Nazis' nine-hundred-day stranglehold on Leningrad, 600,000 people starved to death in the city, including almost half of the institute's remaining scientists, some of whom died at their desks surrounded by bags of rice and seeds they might have eaten in order to save their lives. Such sacrifice and commitment came at a time when, according to the story, it seemed to the scientists that humans were destroying the world. As they endured starvation and bombardment to protect the collection of unique genetic stock, the scientists were said to have reassured one another: "When all the world is in the flames of war, we will keep this collection for the future of the people."[22]

And so, too, green sisters set about protecting at all costs the sacred genetic "scriptures" evolved over generations of propagation and saving contained in heritage seeds. The Leningrad siege and the stranglehold of biotechnology have become powerfully and prophetically linked for sisters dedicated to preserving an embattled heritage for future generations. Green sisters explain why they view this current siege as ominous. Dominican sister Carol Coston, for instance, characterizes the current situation this way:

> Over the course of its nearly five-billion-year life, our planet has unfolded and evolved in astounding fecundity—a blue-green jewel in space [that has] become habitat to giraffes, crickets, dolphins, humans, rainforests, oceans, nematodes, elephants, orchids, and countless other forms of magnificently differentiated life . . . Astonishingly, in just the last 100 years of this evolving plentitude, we humans have begun to reverse the divine course, precipitating a dangerous loss of biodiversity on Earth through our destruction of habitats and species, on one hand, and development of mass monocultures of crops, on the other.[23]

As part of the larger effort by green sisters to struggle against this "reversal of divine course," Genesis Farm in New Jersey puts out a seed-saving kit called Sowing Seeds of Hope. The kit provides practical information on seed saving and connects its users to a variety of "living gene banks," such as Canada's

Seeds of Diversity (an heirloom or "heritage" seed-saving network) and its U.S. counterpart, Seed Savers Exchange.[24] The development of informal seed-saving exchanges among households and communities is also encouraged. Amid the specter of bioengineering and seed patenting, efforts such as these to keep plant varieties from becoming extinct have taken on an element of sacred mission, with nonpatented seeds circulating to network members through a kind of "underground railroad." These seeds, passed independently from hand to hand, have symbolically become seeds of rebellion against transnational genetic supply corporations.

The Sowing Seeds of Hope kit also refers its users to the work of Kenneth Ausubel, one of the founders of Seeds of Change, a one-time small alternative company (now bought out by Mars Inc.) that continues to sell organically grown heirloom seed varieties. Ausubel writes about the gardens at Seeds of Change, located in New Mexico, in somewhat biblical terms, as collectively a "botanical ark" that has provided a kind of "genetic shelterbelt against an eroding future."[25] Ausubel sounds the warning that the ongoing narrowing of biodiversity places world food security in a precarious position: "The loss of genetic diversity in the food supply directly imperils the safety of crops, because their ability to adapt to resist blights, pests, and disease depends on variation."[26] This lack of diversity, says Ausubel, also leaves the world vulnerable to a major food crisis.

Following the terrorist attacks within the United States in 2001, food policy experts such as Jennifer Wilkins at Cornell University have further pointed to the extreme vulnerability to the threat of bioterrorism caused by narrowing species diversity and to the subsequent risks of potentially devastating global consequences.[27] Much like the seed martyrs in Russia, many of those involved in seed saving see themselves as guarding the legacy of life through a potentially catastrophic period in world history.

Seeds of Social Justice

Articles on biotechnology in green sisters' earth ministry newsletters expressly appeal to the strong tradition of social justice concerns among vowed religious Catholics. These articles explain to readers that by legally patenting bioengineered life forms, seed companies now hold licenses that forbid farmers from harvesting even the most readily available seed, such as corn and peas, and thus essentially make farmers "renters" of germ plasm.[28] In many cases, seeds are shipped to the farmer already pelleted in a clay "chemicals package" of the agricultural company's fertilizer, fungicide, or pesticide products. Not only is private propagation of these seeds illegal, but farmers are obliged to sign contracts to repurchase seeds from the same company each year or to return any saved seeds to the company to have their chemical products injected into the seed coating prior to planting.[29] As a means of maintaining corporate monopoly and control over this process, companies offer farmers rewards for informing on one another, and company inspectors are permitted to make surprise farm inspections for five years following the purchase of their seed. "We call it bioserfdom," says Hope Shand, research director for the Rural Advancement Foundation International (now called the ETC Group).[30]

The specter of bioserfdom raises concerns about social, economic, and environmental justice that are already central to green sisters' work. Sister Marilyn Rudy of Earth Harmony in California, for instance, spent decades working on behalf of the homeless in Los Angeles, and then later on behalf of people infected with HIV/AIDS. Now her peace and social justice concerns have turned to the earth. Why? Rudy says that previously she had been dealing with symptoms of our gravest problems but she felt that she never really approached their underlying causes. Poverty, hunger, homelessness, social injustice, war, an extractive economics that exploits the poor and less fortunate—all of these things, she says, stem from a worldview or cosmology that objectifies creation. "All my life I have been moving toward this call and did not know it until I arrived," says Rudy. "The earth has been calling and only after long preparation and gradual realization have I come to Earth Ministry and interest. While working with the poor, I came to realize that as we treat the earth so we treat people, especially those in need and those outcast by our society. We see creation as object not subject and hence we see people the same way."[31]

Other sisters talk about having been radicalized by the Vietnam War, themselves engaging in protest or being moved by courageous acts of civil disobedience by activists such as the "Catonsville Nine"—a group of Catholic clergy who took direct action in 1968 by breaking into the draft board in Catonsville, Maryland, removing draft records, and setting them on fire. Such drastic efforts were seen as justified by the need to subvert continued death, destruction, and human suffering in Southeast Asia. And what of the death and destruction that sisters warn can be precipitated by the release of GMOs into the ecosystem, where they can freely cross with nearby unadulterated species to create irreversible "genetic pollution"? I do not know specifically of any cases of crop sabotage by green sisters. But I do know that the practice it-self, as a purely nonviolent action, garners some degree of sympathy and sup-port from those who view such efforts as acts in defense of unique species that, like the natural world itself, constitute an irreplaceable source of divine revelation.

Members of the Loretto Earth Network in St. Louis, Missouri—home to biogenetically engineered food manufacturer Monsanto Corporation—have been particularly active in the struggle against GMOs. Their efforts have in-cluded participating in local actions to support labeling initiatives as well as meeting with Monsanto employees to discuss their concerns about genetic engineering.[32] Sister of Loretto Gabriel Mary Hoare speaks out against the bioengineering of so-called Frankenfoods that create patented seeds by com-bining genes from animals and vegetation or by inserting pharmaceuticals into crops like corn. "What should alarm us," says Hoare, "is that it ["bio-pharming"] is an experiment that cannot be taken back. Once the altered genes are out there they will continue to propagate. It is seriously estimated that outside of seed trusts, it is almost impossible to guarantee that a seed source is free of genetically engineered properties."[33]

The Loretto Community's "Biotechnology Statement" protests the release of GMOs into the environment and calls for a moratorium on any further spread of GMOs. The statement also takes a strong social-justice stance, pro-claiming: "The genetic inheritance of flora and fauna is a common resource. We, therefore, challenge the right of individuals or corporations to patent life forms and claim ownership based on the rearrangement of genetic material. Such commercial exploitation and domination of nature is reducing life-forms to mere commodities and violates the sacredness of life." The statement further draws attention to the effects of "terminator technologies" on subsis-tence farmers, explaining: "This technology which renders seeds sterile is a threat to global food security and to the one billion families in the developing world who are subsistence farmers and who are unable to buy new seed each year."[34] Here, once again, green sisters make the case that economic justice, peace, and environmental concerns are inseparable.

An analogy to current struggles over bioserfdom can be made to struggles over cottage handmilling rights in the fourteenth century. As environmental historian Carolyn Merchant describes in her book *The Death of Nature,* when feudal lords built large central watermills, they ordered all of the peasants' handmills to be destroyed, creating further economic dependence by denying peasants the means to process their own grain. Peasants were then beholden for their survival to a centralized means of food processing, thus precipitating handmill rebellions. Merchant says that such rebellions were testimony "not to the resistance of peasants to technological innovation, but to their economic need to retain control over their own technology." Owning one's own handmill, according to Merchant, became a subversive act against monopolistic control over the means of food production.[35] Within the corporatized seed patent system, seed saving, too, becomes a subversive act. "No one person or group of persons," declares a section of Genesis Farm's Sowing Seeds of Hope seed-saving kit, "should have the right to claim exclusive ownership of this integral part of the entire Earth community."

By contrast, the Vatican's position on the issue of GMOs has fluctuated from cautious to supportive to agnostic to relatively silent on the topic of bioengineering and plant species. Vatican positions opposing bioengineering in human beings, especially as it relates to reproductive technologies, have been much more definitive. After years of cautious statements by John Paul II, Pontifical Council for Justice and Peace president Archbishop Renato Martino made a statement on the Vatican radio station in August 2003 that seemed to indicate the Vatican would support the implementation of GMO technology in agriculture as a way to feed the world's hungry.[36] The statement elicited protest from environmentalists around the world, including Catholic orders working in missions in Africa and Asia. Prior to Martino's comments, Jesuit priests in Zambia had been key to that country's 2002 decision to reject famine relief offered by the United States in the form of genetically modified foods.[37]

Zambia's decision shocked the world as the Zambian people struggled to feed themselves, and the U.S. government criticized those who had counseled Zambia's refusal as "revolting and despicable." In September 2002, the British magazine *The Economist* covered the story under the incendiary headline, "Better Off Dead Than GMO-Fed." But Zambia's reasons for the refusal were much more complicated than simply health concerns; instead they tie into many of the same economic and social concerns for long-term sustainability that green sisters themselves have raised with regard to GMOs. The Zambian minister, with the support of the Jesuits, justified the refusal of GMO aid on a number of grounds, but one was that Zambia would "rather starve one year than the next twenty years." Dependence on GMO maize that could not be saved by its own farmers, or dependence on "Roundup Ready" corn (or other so-called junkie crops), would make Zambia extremely dependent on U.S. agricultural products and markets for its continued survival.[38] Additionally, if

GMO relief corn were actually planted in Zambia and contaminated other crops, the country would risk losing its GMO-free status and subsequently its access to European markets, where consumers have vehemently opposed the introduction of GMOs into their food supply. (Subsequent offers of GMO relief food to Africa have been accepted on the condition that GMO maize be thoroughly ground into flour, rendering it impossible to cultivate.)

In November of 2003, the Vatican held a conference called "GMO: Threat or Hope," which was organized by Archbishop Martino. The outcome of the conference was generally positive toward the use of GMOs, and Martino in his closing comments spoke again about the promises that GMOs hold for addressing world hunger. His statements were read by many as a Vatican endorsement of GMO food, and yet no official statement on the Vatican's position on GMOs was issued.[39] On the Sisters of Mercy Earth Harmony Network web site, the Mercy sisters feature the debate among Catholics over GMOs, calling attention not only to Martino's pro-GMO comments but offering counterpoints and opposition to GMO use from other sources of authority, such as Filipino bishops who have been wary of GMOs.[40] Green sisters also cite the work of Columbian missionary priest Father Seán McDonagh, the author of *Patenting Life? Stop!* and other publications arguing against GMO food.[41]

In terms of agribusiness promises to "feed the world" and end starvation with GMOs, green sisters are quick to point out the history of failed promises by agricultural companies that their products (chemical pesticides, herbicides, fertilizers, and fungicides) would "feed the world" and end hunger once and for all. Instead, sisters explain, these products created greater resistance from "superpests" and "superweeds," and, especially in the poorest countries, further polluted fragile water sources while creating economic dependence on chemical products among poor farmers who can least afford to purchase them.[42] Sister of Loretto Gabriel Mary Hoare writes:

> In the late 1960s, a movement called "The Green Revolution" promised that food production could be maximized for farmers by following a prescription designed by multinational corporations: 1. New crop cultivars, 2. Irrigation, 3. Fertilizers, 4. Pesticides, 5. Mechanization. What's *new* is that the "new crop cultivars" are derived by a process called genetic engineering, the fertilizers are developed by chemical companies that already produce pesticides which have been genetically introduced into the seeds. The farmer must use only seeds

provided by contract with the chemical company which has managed to buy up a large percentage of seed companies. It [has become] a crime to save seed from year to year. This is a perfect recipe for a monoculture; insuring the eventual destruction of diversity of seed production developed over centuries by farmers who know the land and what it's capable of producing . . . [Indian scientist and activist] Vandana Shiva watched with dismay as the Green Revolution resulted in the enforcement of chemical farming and the introduction of a monoculture, which did more to impoverish third world countries, including her own country of India.[43]

Sisters who have worked closely with foreign aid nongovernmental organizations (NGOs) or who have worked in foreign missions dealing on the ground with hunger and poverty are especially skeptical of both the motives and outcomes promised by large GMO-producing corporations. After a sister got up at the 2002 Sisters of Earth conference "open microphone" period and urged all the conference participants to read Vandana Shiva's book on biopiracy, I visited the conference bookselling booth to take a look at Shiva's book. As I flipped through the book with another sister in the booth, she likened the current situation with GMOs to the aggressive marketing of Western baby formula to mothers in the third world. Such marketing policies have now been largely reversed because of international outcry, but the sister (who had spent time working in Africa) made the point that companies would convince mothers that their children would receive "superior nutrition" through their products, at which point mothers would stop producing their own milk and switch to formula. These same mothers' babies would then starve when there was no money to purchase formula or when water sources to mix with the formula became contaminated. The sister's point was that GMOs promise the same sort of salvific nutritive benefits but instead only deliver dire economic consequences that further exploit the world's poor.[44]

As of July 2006, the Vatican had not issued a definitive statement sanctioning or denouncing the genetic modification of organisms for agricultural use. Sustainable agriculture advocates, ecojustice proponents, and heirloom conservationists (Catholic and otherwise) are crossing their fingers, hoping for a negative statement, especially considering these groups' fears that a ringing endorsement would have a detrimental effect on policies implemented in poorer Catholic countries. As they await Pope Benedict XVI's clarification of this issue, green sisters continue to "dig in" and move ahead with the practical work of cultivating, saving, and sharing heirloom seeds, filing shareholder resolutions, and heading grassroots efforts to stop or at least contain GMO production.

The Power of Seed in Mystery and Metaphor

Seeds appear in myriad contexts in sisters' earth ministries, not simply in the rows of their organic gardens. Sisters draw distinct connections between the biophysical and spiritual nature of seeds. In essence, the seed provides a transformative and empowering metaphor in the lives of green sisters—one that provides guiding inspiration for their works. Cellular biologist and Sister of St. Joseph Mary Louise Dolan, director of the Earth Literacy Master's Degree Program of Saint-Mary-of-the-Woods College in Terra Haute, Indiana, demonstrates this perspective in her work. "We influence and generate future life," writes Dolan. "So the seed image 'works' biologically for us. It also 'works' for the psycho-spiritual aspects of our biology." During a seed-planting ritual in a workshop Dolan participated in, she reports that a powerful realization struck her. "My teachers had sown seeds which had taken root in me. Seeds planted years ago were continuing to unfold; new seeds were being planted. Moreover, the planting and growing were mutual. It was a splendid mix of past and present, an example of 'wild discontent with any final expression of itself' [a reference to Thomas Berry] that characterizes the universe, and, with luck and grace, characterizes us."[45] In another column for the *Spiritearth Newsletter*, Dolan writes of how, as she unseals a pod of moonflower seeds and holds them in her hands, they teach her not to fear "the death of our way of living" and not to fear "the death of that which seems to give meaning to our Western culture."[46] She says that the seeds remind her of the power of transformation within the cosmos, the human, and the dominant culture.

In writing for the *Loretto Earth Network Newsletter*, Sister of Loretto Mary Rhodes "Rhodie" Buckler, like Dolan, contemplates the power of seeds. She writes, "Seeds! A seed of hope. A seed of progress. 'A seed of freedom' illuminated in my Vernal Equinox meditation. Then I open my current *Yes Magazine* to find a young girl wearing the words 'Seeds' on her T-shirt in the midst of sprouting gardens in the toxic atmosphere of Watts, south central Los Angeles. Take 'Seed' literally or metaphorically, seed carries a promise."[47]

This radical image of potentiality was incorporated in a celebration called an "At-one-ment Ritual" (a play on the word "atonement") I attended at one of Genesis Farm's summer programs. In one portion of the celebration, the words to the song "Edelweiss" were changed to "Seeds of Life." In the "Seeds of Life" version, the original "Edelweiss" verses, expressive of Austrian homeland nationalism, had been transformed into expressions of earthly devotion, honoring cycles of growth, death, and rebirth:

> Seeds of life; Seeds of Life—
>   Millions of years in the making
> Seeds of Life; Seeds of Life—
>   Each spring we see you awak'ning!
>
> Wonder of Wonders! You die and grow;
>   Die and grow each springtime.
> Seeds of Life; Seeds of Life;
>   Nourish our Earth home forever.

Greeting cards bearing wildlife scenes of Genesis Farm and made available to students and guests in the farm bookstore also invoke images of seeds from a variety of cultural contexts. One such card draws on the mystical and female-identified nature imagery generated by twelfth-century German nun and accomplished naturalist Hildegard of Bingen, a heroine for many green sisters. The Hildegard quotation reads: "The earth is at the same time mother; she is mother of all that is natural, mother of all that is human. She is mother of all, for contained in her are the seeds of all." Another card just as easily draws on the *Chandogya Upanishad's* wisdom about the real and mystical potential of seeds. It reads: "Even if you cannot see with your eyes that subtle something in the seed which produces this mighty form, it is present nonetheless. That is the power, that is the spirit unseen, which pervades everywhere, and is in all things."[48]

At a winter solstice celebration I attended at Genesis Farm, a tree at the center of the celebration bore cards with brief meditations or affirmations. On one side of the card was a picture of a nautilus (often used in green sisters' liturgies as a symbol of the unfolding universe), and on the other side were thoughts on which to meditate in the new solar year. In the course of the ritual, I randomly picked two cards from the tree. The first read: "Sowing the seed, my hand is one with the Earth. Eating the fruit, my body is one with the Earth." The second asked: "What are the future beings asking of you? You are a seed. Everything you need is within you." Afterward, in seeing some other cards, I saw that they were not all seed-themed, but many of them were, invoking the seed as a metaphor of new beginnings especially appropriate for the winter solstice—the marker of the new solar year.

Certainly the seed has been the perfect metaphor for the new beginnings of the Green Mountain Monastery in Vermont. In the nuns' prayer space sits a jar of mustard seeds. The jar is there, says Worcelo, to remind the community each day that the monastery is like a mustard seed. Referring to the biblical parable of the mustard seed and comparing the reign of God to "a pungent shrub with dangerous take-over properties," Worcelo, as does Sister Mary Rhodes Buckler, finds strength and inspiration in the "vast potentialities" contained in a tiny seed. To Worcelo, "Once it [the mustard seed] becomes a plant it tends to take over, grows out of control and refuses to be domesticated. The Reign of God, Jesus says, is much like a mustard seed, as pungent and as fiery and wild and impossible to contain as the unfolding universe . . . Where can *Wisdom* be found? Enter the Mustard Seed. A revolution in evolution! An unstoppable force pointing to the wild original freedom of the Divine in this world."[49]

Although they come from different "varieties" of Christianity, Worcelo and Methodist pastor Brian Bauknight share some common ground when it comes to seed language and metaphor. Bauknight actually takes the metaphor one step further. Coeditor with David Mosser of *First Fruits: Fourteen Sermons on Stewardship,* Bauknight boldly proclaims, "Jesus is the heirloom seed of God." Commenting on the more "flavorful" nature of heirloom varieties, Bauknight observes that once we recognize Jesus as an heirloom seed of God, "We can truly say with the Psalmist, 'O taste and see that the Lord is good.'"[50]

Worcelo's own conception of seeds transmutes and evolves, taking many forms. In addition to speaking of the mustard seed and the reign of God, she also envisages seeds as prayer tools and conceives of the first germination of the new Ecozoic monastery in terms of a seed.

> I have been reflecting on the image of the seed, that unassuming, modest powerhouse of potential which reaches through the ages. My fingers have touched hundreds of seeds and they have become my prayer beads. Kneeling in my garden every Spring I have softly whispered a prayer for the world with each seed being placed in the ground. The inner dynamism of the seed captures my attention, inviting me into its mystery and metaphor. Seeds are living guarantees of continuity between generations, carrying within their cells the genetic memory which reaches deep into the past and far into the future. It is within this dynamic that I want to tell you about the seed of our future monastery.[51]

The "Story" in the Seed

From both a prophetic and scientific vantage point, green sisters speak about the importance of saving the "story in the seed."[52] Dominican Sister Miriam MacGillis, in particular, has framed the issue of seed saving and the threat of GMOs from the perspective of the "universe story"—the holistic view of on-going cosmogenesis taught by her spiritual mentor, Father Thomas Berry. MacGillis describes the genetic coding found inside the seed as its "internal guidance system" that is part of the larger internal guidance system of the planet and, ultimately, the universe. From this perspective, to disrupt the evolutionary wisdom (what Carol Coston calls "the divine course") of this story is not only ecologically disastrous but also, in the context of a worldview that conceives of an alive, intelligent, divinely embodied, or sacramental universe, desecration. MacGillis says, "Every aspect of a living organism, of the living organism of the planet, carries within it the physical and inner psychic story of the journey it has come through." According to MacGillis, technologies such as bioengineering and hybridization short-circuit the divine wisdom of that story and disrupt the integrity of the internal guidance system of both plant and planet.[53]

Moreover, the disappearance of certain varieties of seeds cuts off humans from the particular revelation of the divine contained within the interior dimension of those seeds. Again, in the context of green sisters' seed activism, we see Thomas Berry's principles of "differentiation" (diversity), "interiority" (subjectivity), and "communion" (sacred unity of all) infuse discussions of biodiversity, integrated wholeness, and care for creation. These concepts have resonated with the seed-saving efforts of sisters who speak of the loss of local, nonengineered seed varieties not just in terms of a threat to food security and a danger to the biodiversity of ecosystems, but also in terms of grave spiritual loss. Carol Coston writes: "Now, as my sense of the common good has expanded to embrace all of creation, my heart indeed does grieve for all that has been destroyed—and for all that will be destroyed if we don't change our ways."[54]

Green sisters are saving heirloom seed stock and promoting diversity not only in their gardens, but, metaphorically, in their spiritual traditions as well. In fact, Miriam MacGillis has said that she thinks of herself as a kind of "seed keeper" for the mystical tradition of Catholicism.[55] By reinhabiting traditions of vowed religious life and various customs of monastic culture, and by infusing a variety of devotional practices with new life, green sisters in effect conserve the "seeds" of the past while inserting them into newly prepared soil. Rather than narrowing the range of possibility, sisters, as both farmers and as vowed members of religious communities, promote conservation as a means to greater diversity. By cultivating a "pluraculture" of past and present, green sisters seek to cultivate a stronger and more sustainable culture—both agricultural and religious.

8. STATIONS OF THE EARTH

Body Prayer, Labyrinths, and Other Peripatetic Rituals

 It is early in the morning before breakfast at the Dominican motherhouse located atop Sinsinawa Mound, a natural outcropping of dolomite stone that rises up from surrounding lowlands where the Mississippi River flows through the southwest corner of Wisconsin. The Lakota name for the mound, "Manitoumie," means "where the Great Spirit dwells." The Dominican Sisters of Sinsinawa have lived on this mound since their founding in 1847. A little more than 150 years later, the community has become host to the third international Sisters of Earth Conference. On this morning, a gathering of religious sisters from the conference is assembled on the grass outside the motherhouse. The group faces the rising sun in the east and moves silently in unison. The gestures are slow, synchronized, meditative, and resemble those of tai chi chuan, with movements flowing easily and naturally. The group seems to sense the beginning of the next move without needing to look at one another, making the collective shift of weight from one leg to the other smooth and subtle. Having learned this meditative sequence three years earlier, I (and two other laywomen who also know it) enter into the prayer with the sisters and move through the forms with them. Each morning of the conference, we gather to offer this same prayer, starting in the east with the rising sun and moving clockwise ("sunwise"), repeating the same sequence of movements to the south, the west, and the north. We bodily trace the form of the cross while simultaneously honoring the four cardinal directions of the earth. The sisters engaging in the morning prayer come from different religious communities and bioregions; different ethnic backgrounds, experiences, and life stages; and yet together perform this exercise as one body.[1]

Referred to variously as the "morning body prayer," the "earth body prayer," and the "morning prayer to the four directions," this prayer is a mainstay at green sisters' retreat centers and in their earth literacy programs. I first learned it simply as the "morning body prayer" in an earth literacy program I attended at Genesis Farm in New Jersey. Each morning of the two-week program we greeted the sun in this way. A small, informal pamphlet that explains the significance of each movement was given to our group. The body prayer begins by opening the left arm toward the east. This movement is followed by opening the whole of the body in the same direction as the arm. The guide explains that the first movement made with the left arm "opens your heart to the blessings of the natural world." The right arm then repeats the movement of the left arm and opens the heart "to the blessings of the world of human traditions."[2]

The next movement of the prayer involves reaching down to the ground with both hands "to gather the blessings of the Earth." For those who are familiar with the practice of tai chi chuan, this movement looks very much like a move called "embracing the tiger." In the morning body prayer, however, instead of "setting the tiger on the mountain" (a move in tai chi chuan that looks just like it sounds), the hands continue up above the head. Here, the arms are open and the hands are open and rotated out, as the guide says, "to give the blessings of Earth to the heavens." This movement is then repeated in reverse to offer the blessings of the heavens back to the earth. Then, the left foot is extended in front as both hands reach out to gather and embrace the blessings of the east. The body prayer guide advises: "Holding the blessings to your body, twist around to the right to face the opposite direction. Keeping the flow of the motion, give out the blessings to the universe by simply opening your hands and moving them out away from you in a sweeping motion." The same movements are repeated to the other three cardinal directions (south, west, and north). When the sequence has been completed four times, the group takes one collective "step into the day" and a second step into the "Great Mystery."[3]

Despite the body prayer's similarity to a variety of Asian forms of moving meditation, the body prayer guide makes a point of saying, "Many people from many traditions have created these movements. They are deliberately described in general terms. Feel free to modify and/or extend them." In fact, I have asked sisters from a variety of communities in the United States and Canada what the origin of this prayer is and who first began it. Some reported having learned it at Genesis Farm, but others had learned it at other retreat centers (Catholic, Episcopal, or interfaith), environmental conferences, or prayer and movement workshops given by guest facilitators within their communities. As an exercise in contemplative gesture, the body prayer has been passed on from friend to friend, through colleagues as well as spiritual retreat and earth literacy workshop participants, and has "cross-pollinated" through religious communities via sisters' intercommunity collaborative ecological projects.

Modified by different green sisters in different locations, the morning body prayer readily adapts to varied environments and takes on multiple layers of meaning. In one sense, it is a daily mindful orientation of the body in space and time that responds to Thomas Berry's critique that in modernity humans have developed a kind of "Earth autism."[4] Part of humans' modern-day earth autism, says Berry, comes from our not knowing how to locate ourselves within the universe and within the earth community. The body prayer does just that, orienting the individual in relation to the four cardinal directions of the earth and within the context of the "cosmic liturgy" of the sun's rise in the east. In the guide I received to the prayer, the four directions of the earth are identified with four corresponding elements: earth, air, water, and fire. This obviously corresponds to the Native American practice of praying to the four cardinal directions, which in many Native American sacred systems correspond in some way to the four basic elements of the earth. When I have asked about the connections of this prayer to Native American traditions, the similarities are acknowledged but sisters also point out that many cultures regard the cardinal directions of the planet to be sacred, and indeed Christianity identifies itself symbolically with the four directions via the sacred iconography of the cross.

The guide to the prayer in fact shows how each of the four directions also corresponds to different aspects of biblical tradition. The north, for instance, corresponds to the theme of transformation and includes the figures of Abraham and Sarah, Elizabeth and Zachary, Mary, and "Christ in the Tomb." The east is the direction of incarnation or resurrection and is associated with the infant Moses, the child Miriam, the infant Christ, and the resurrected Christ. The south is the direction of vision and prophecy and thus of the young David, Tobias, Sara, and the boy Jesus. And finally, the west is identified as the direction of "maturity and inner strength" as embodied by Solomon, Judith, Esther, and Christ in the desert.

There are strong Jungian overtones in this directional quadrant schema and its corresponding identifications. The prayer itself seems to function as a kind of performative prayer mandala of archetypes.[5] Each cardinal direction also corresponds to a different archangel. The north is identified as the direction of "regeneration and Mystery" and corresponds to Archangel Gabriel.

The east is the direction of "healing and regeneration" and corresponds to Archangel Raphael. The south is the realm of Archangel Uriel, who is identified as the "Guardian of the Secret Songs of Humanity." And the west is the direction of Archangel Michael, who is the "Defender of the Light." Beyond the guide I received to the prayer, there are a number of variations in different contexts as sisters have added further interpretations. Some sisters, for instance, pray the directions as "the sign of the cross" with the corresponding four directional dedications made to "Father"; "Son"; "Holy Spirit"; "One God, Mother of us all." This variation conserves a Trinitarian framework but creatively finds a way to infuse that framework with greater theological gender balance.[6]

Beyond the biblical and angelical references, each direction and corresponding element (earth, air, fire, and water) also corresponds to a different season (winter, spring, summer, and fall), as well as to a category or genre of earth community. So, for instance, the north is the realm of the "animal community," the east is the realm of the "human community," the south is the realm of the "plant community," and the west is the realm of the "mineral community." As the guide encourages, sisters do modify and extend these associations. In some variations, the second step at the end is "into the Great Mystery," in others it is a "step into the Universe," and in still others, it is a "step into the 'Great Work.'" These last two additions clearly make reference to Thomas Berry, his "universe story" paradigm, and his call for humans to set about the "Great Work" of becoming an enhancing instead of disruptive presence to the planetary community.[7]

When I first learned the morning body prayer and learned of its many meanings and correspondences, I asked a naive question about the prayer to a sister participating in the same earth literacy program. She was already familiar with and practicing the body prayer. I asked, "When you pray to each direction, how do you keep straight which aspects you're including and what sort of prayer you're saying?" With a quizzical look on her face, the sister replied, "Your body *is* the prayer. You don't 'say' anything, Sarah. Your body does all the 'talking.' That's the point."[8] Comparative religions scholar David Chidester echoes this explanation but phrases it in a more technical way when he observes, "In the kinesthetic movements of the body, tactile information is acquired. For the study of religion, kinesthesia calls attention to embodied movements—kneeling, standing, prostrating, walking, climbing, dancing, and so on—not only as types of ritual performance, but also as paths of knowledge."[9]

In the case of the green sisters, the body prayer provides just such a path of knowledge. The movements tracing each of the four directions (which form both a circle and a cross) reflect the full path of the sun around the earth. Performing the prayer enables sisters to experience the sun's path and progress and to "know" this path in an embodied way. The body prayer as a path to knowledge also communicates "cosmic location" (within the diurnal rhythms of the sun) and situates the individual in relationship both to the basic elements of earth and to other subjects within the natural environment. Furthermore, it is a path that connects all earthly beings to supernatural figures and forces, such as angels, the powers of healing, regeneration, and the "Great Mystery" at the heart of the universe. Finally, the embodied movements function as a path of knowledge into the Christian and Jewish biblical traditions, inviting, for instance, the archetypes of Moses, Mary, Sarah, and Jesus into intimate and cocreative relationships with earth elements and sisters' own imaginative spirits.

When I have contemplated the complex interplay of meanings, elements, and symbols contained within the body prayer, I have repeatedly been reminded of my initial confusion as I looked at the intense interplanting of herbs, flowers, and vegetables in sisters' organic gardens. It took years before my eyes were trained enough to see more than a hodgepodge of plants, and before I could actually recognize patterns and designs in the intentional "pluraculture" of vegetation. Over time, as I have experienced green sisters' prayers and green liturgies, I have come to think of these gestures in terms of the permacultural practice of "stacking," which is also implemented in green sister's gardens and landscapes. Permaculture designer Patrick Whitefield explains that ideally, "trees, vines, shrubs, herbs, and vegetables grow together just as they do in the forest. This structure, called 'stacking' by permaculturalists, enables gardens to be far more productive than either orchards or annual vegetable gardens can be on their own, because several crops are being grown on the same spot at the same time."[10] That is, plants are placed together in such a way that fosters a particularly fertile and productive ecology.

What's more, stacking deliberately mimics nature by fostering a diverse grouping of elements and species that work together in a close area. Permaculture founder Bill Mollison asserts that it is precisely the primacy of relationship that makes such disparate elements function together as a system or what he terms a "guild." One illustration of this phenomenon presents three separate elements: water, a chicken, and a tree. Mollison employs this image to explain what permaculture is and is not about: "It's not water, or a chicken, or the tree. It is how the water, the chicken and the tree are connected. It's the very opposite of what we are taught in school. Education takes everything and pulls it apart . . . Permaculture makes the connection, because as soon as you've got the connection, you can feed the chicken from the tree."[11]

So, too, in the "spiritual ecology" of green sisters, there is an internal logic to how eclectic elements fit together to form a functioning system or "guild." As with natural environments, the connections formed in these guilds are not immediately obvious and require time and patience, allowing for patterns and relationships to emerge organically. What emerges in the ecology of green sisters' earth ministries, everyday ways of life, and ritual practices is a kind of ecospiritual mimetics in which culture mimics the patterns of life and growth in the natural world.

Stations of the Earth

Before environmental artist Sharon Brady began her commissioned work to create the Earth Meditation Trail at Genesis Farm in New Jersey, she spent months living on the land in the area where she thought the trail might "unfold."[12] The horses that used to roam that part of the farm had already created a path through the woods, so Brady decided to follow their lead and work with what they had begun. It was important to her that she take the time to be with the land, learn the land, and to "listen to its voices." After months of observation and meditation she finally began the project, working with the contours of the land, allowing images and places of prayer and reflection to emerge out of the land's own features. What came out of this process was an "environmental art pathway" designed to be a performative meditation into the life journey, into earth-human relations, and into the spiritual dimensions of cosmogenesis.

The Earth Meditation Trail consists of a series of contemplative areas or prayer "stations." The stations, following the stages of life and aging, are also places of prayer and connection with the natural world. Not surprisingly, various sections of the trail consciously incorporate Thomas Berry's influence, invoking his three principles of the universe: differentiation, interiority, and communion. Above all, says its creator Brady, the pathway is intended to "amplify one's connection with self, others, and the Earth."[13]

The first station one encounters on the trail is the "Threshold of Birth," which Brady identifies as symbolic of a rite of initiation into the community of life. Here the pilgrim travels through a womb-like opening that has been created by arching branches overhead, combined with upward sloping slabs of stone sunken into the earth that curve inward to form an oval passageway.

The stones that form the bottom curve of the womb opening are made from the same kind of stone often used for grave markers, and so the portal is symbolically both an entrance into life and a passage into death. In the middle of the path, past the threshold, sits the "heart stone." In her guide to the trail, Brady instructs: "Step over the stone on the ground. This stands for your first heartbeat, the inner beat of all things, and in a cosmic sense, the genesis of all creation."[14]

The pilgrim then reaches down and touches the stones, closes her eyes, and feels her own heartbeat. Many walk the trail on their own with no guidebook, but if Brady is guiding the meditation experience for a particular group, she makes a drum available at this station, which the pilgrim takes up and beats in rhythm with her own heart. In time to the heartbeat, the pilgrim then announces herself to the community of life, repeating three times: "Behold I come. My name is ———. Accept me here. Accept me now."

The next station is called "The Portal of Breath," and the meditation is on the first breath of a human, on the first breath of the cosmos, and on using breath as a way of midwifing life's transitions. Brady suggests: "Go through the Entry Portal which stands for birth, creation, passage from one form of being to another. This is a place to reflect on birth: the birth of the cosmos, the birth of life, the birth of all humans from our early amphibious state, the birth of conscious life." The imagery here is at once evolutionary and evocative of personal spiritual transformation. The breath station is located in a corridor of cedar trees, where the pilgrim is asked to take in a long, slow breath and then to expel it very slowly, while concentrating on giving that breath to the surrounding cedars.

As the trail proceeds, the pilgrim comes upon a series of mirrors hidden among trees. At first, it appears to the lone traveler that she has come upon a community of others in the woods, until the realization is made that she is seeing so many reflections of the self. This section of the trail is called "The Path of the Original Face," and the pilgrim is asked to touch her reflected face in the mirror with one hand and then touch her real face with the other. The image of the many faces of the self is then abstracted to include the many faces of the "Earthself," as Brady guides: "Give thanks for your original face. What do you want to reveal to the community of life? Look at the other 'faces' being reflected back to you: the trees, the other creatures . . . What are they revealing? Touch them. Ask." Here we see not only a visual and interactive engagement in the "Earthself" but also concerted communication and interaction with the faces of the earth.

Next, the pilgrim picks up a river stone from a pile of similar size river stones and holds it in her hands. A slab of slate, decorated with a spiral, reads: "Choose a stone to carry with you on the trail. It holds the spirit of your life journey." Underneath this message, there is a quotation from poet Octavio Paz: "I will speak to you in stone language. Answer in a green symbol." The passage from Paz's *The Labyrinth of Solitude* sets the stage for a performative language of experience, image, and movement that the pilgrim will use to communicate with the life community along the trail.[15] This "prayer stone" will carry the pilgrim's prayers for the earth, specifically her personal commitments to the life community. Brady also suggests that the traveler "listen" to the stone just as the stone will listen to and absorb the prayers, thoughts, and questions of the one who journeys.

Descending a steep slope into the woods, the pilgrim comes upon a stone circle under a grove of tall trees. Designed so that groups can meet in council seated on large stones, this circle is used for various programs and workshops, including a "Council of All Beings"—a ritual in which humans take on the persona of various members of the life community to discuss what is wrong on earth from a nonhuman perspective.[16] This stone circle is marked as the station of the "Threshold of Voices." Brady reminds the pilgrim as she enters the circle that there is already assembled a gathering of the community of life within the circle that the pilgrim honors and joins. Brady says, "This is a place to gather together with them [the community of life], to communicate feelings with them. This is a communal place of stillness in filtered light, a place to praise the voices of the natural world, a place to listen in communion with the trees and insects and birds and other creatures, and to confirm and affirm your oneness with them as a sacred community." For green sisters especially, the resonant themes of "communion" and "sacred community" are key here, in that they extend the idea of living in spiritual community beyond the boundaries of religious order or religious congregations to include the entire life community as spiritual community. It is in this sense that Green Mountain Monastery cofounder Sister Gail Worcelo speaks about the "Cosmic Monastery" as one interdependent spiritual community.[17]

At the "Threshold of Voices" station, once again, communion and meditation are performative. The pilgrim is invited to pick up clay rattles and make sounds—in particular, to hum from deep within her body, placing her hands on her chest to feel the vibration of the sound as it rises and is brought forth. The guide suggests the pilgrim ask for her own "sacred song" and request, too,

Stone station along the Earth Meditation Trail.

that the song be a "deep 'yes' to the call of life, to develop and give away your gifts and blessings to the mystery which your life is unfolding." Sometimes groups are asked to close their eyes and try to identify as many different voices in the forest as they can. Within the stone circle, there is a bowl of oil from which the pilgrim anoints herself to confirm, as the guide says, her "intentions to be for life." Again, this language of "being for life" taps into an already well-established and recognizable Catholic idiom of the "culture of life," "defending life," "protecting life," and so forth; here the power of this language is applied to an ecological context.[18]

From the stone circle, the path continues along the "Narrow Ridge of Searching" (a narrow path that comes at the edge between woods and wetland) and through the "Path of the Great Elders" (a section of the trail that honors the old sugar maple trees). Finally, one reaches "The Place of At-One-Ment." In this place, a stone seat has been fitted into the hillside, facing a gnarled old cherry tree, the "Survival Tree," that has been tangled up in and scarred by a barbed wire fence from an old cow pasture. Through the years, the barbed wire has cut deeper into the tree's flesh, mangling and contorting its branches with barbs. In turn, the cherry tree has oozed large sap scabs with which it has encompassed the metal material, healing right over the wounds inflicted by the barbs by absorbing them into the body of the tree. Tied both to the barbed wire and to the tree's scarred branches are strips of cloth and ribbons with prayers written on them. Brady's guide for the trail says,

> Reflect on the wounds and sufferings and violations that have occurred within Earth's life and your life.
> Reflect on the wounds you have inflicted on others, consciously or unconsciously.
> It is all a learning.
> Observe how nature heals over and renews itself.
> Ask to be reconciled with all those whom you have harmed.
> Ask to be reconciled with your own wounded Self—your memories.
> Reflect on how humans wound and degrade the natural world.
> Ask to be forgiven by this community.

In the "At-One-Ment station," we see elements reminiscent of the Catholic rite of reconciliation (confession), the Jewish "atonement" observance of Yom Kippur, and the Shinto practice of hanging prayer rags—a pluraculture united by the overall Jungian thematic message that the "wounded earth" and "the wounded self" are one.

Among other stations on the trail is a shelter in the woods with a lookout window for wildlife observation. Brady calls this the "Listening Lodge of Midlife."[19] The shelter is crafted of copper shingles and looks somewhat like an armadillo. The metal framework on the inside of the shelter is woven into a spiral formation, symbolic of the unfolding universe, and a portion of the ceiling is left open for stargazing. Inside, there are candles placed on a small stone altar that can be lit. Prayers written on paper may be burned as well, with the smoke traveling up through the sky hole in the roof.

Climbing out of the woods and up a hill, the trail feeds into the "Laughing Fields" at the edge between dark and light, forest and meadow. The Laughing Fields are less a station and more a meander through a playful maze of wildflowers, complete with dead-ends in some places and connecting routes in others. In places, the meadow vegetation grows as high as four or five feet, making it easy to become lost. When the children in the farm's summer program go through this station, they seize on the concept immediately and laugh heartily and unself-consciously at the top of their lungs as they skip and run through, losing themselves in the maze. The mood here is celebratory, and it is encouraged by a quotation from Thomas Berry, printed on a rock at the threshold between forest and meadow, "The flowers are what made it possible for us to live." Berry's meaning here is poetic and aesthetic, but it is also evolutionary, as he speaks of flowers as some of the earliest forms of vegetation that made possible the migration of other life forms onto the land.

Eventually, the wildflower maze connects to the station of "The Four Arches." Each arch is made of twisted vines and is positioned to face one of the four directions of the earth: north, south, east, and west. Each arch also corresponds to a season and is planted with a variety of vines that bloom in that season, so that at any given time, one of the arches has something flowering on it. Other devotional objects have been placed within the woven vines of the arches, corresponding to the elements of earth, air, wind, and fire. The arch that corresponds with air, for example, has feathers woven into it, and the arch that corresponds with water has seashells hanging from it. At the center of the four arches, which also forms a cross, there is a circular fire pit which, as Brady says, "symboliz[es] cleansing, purification, transformation, the culminating experience of old age—a time for wisdom and balance." As with the morning body prayer, the orientation within the four cardinal directions is important to the meditation and interweaves symbolism that is both recognizably Christian and principally "planetary."

Just past the southern arch, the pilgrim comes to the "Gift Station," where she leaves the prayer stone she has carried with her on the trail. At this station, the pilgrim is asked what gift her life will leave the world—what her life's legacy will be. She meditates on what her unique commitment and offering might be and then expresses that gift in words or in symbols by decorating the river stone with colored oil pastels. Each stone is a vow. There are hundreds of brightly decorated gift stones like this placed in the altar area of the "Gift Station," which has become a veritable archive of travelers' sacred commitments and pledges. Some people have also made little gifts and left written notes, bits of pottery, drawings, or designs.

Finally, the trail loops back on itself, having arrived full circle at the initial portal station—the "Station of Life/Death/Transformation." As the pilgrim approaches the portal, this time from the opposite direction, she reviews her life. "Before passing through the portal," suggests Brady, "reflect on your last moments of life in this body, your last breath, your transformation."[20] With that, the pilgrim steps through the portal and arrives simultaneously at the end and the beginning.

The imagery in the Earth Meditation Trail is varied and complex, and in it we see a reinhabiting of traditional Roman Catholic frameworks to reflect "green" content. Made manifest in its design is, again, a kind of ecospiritual mimetics. Like the morning prayer to the four directions, the trail displays an affinity for what poet Phyllis McGinley calls "the planet's holy heterodoxy."[21] The configuration of the trail into stations is evocative of the Catholic paraliturgical activity of walking the "stations of the cross," a devotional act in which Catholics trace fourteen traditional progressive stages that led toward Christ's crucifixion. Originally, pilgrims visited the actual sites in Jerusalem connected with the story of the Passion. As pilgrimage grew too dangerous and costly during the Crusades, symbolic pilgrimages were set up in Europe in the Middle Ages. Later, in the eighteenth century, stations of the cross enthusiast Franciscan Leonard of Port Maurice set up more than five hundred symbolic pilgrimages in Europe, including one in the Roman Coliseum.[22] Now Catholic churches and Catholic religious communities all over the world frequently bear some sort of representation of the stations of the cross.

One of the most striking aspects of the Genesis Earth Meditation Trail is the way that it maintains traditional and resonant (often medieval) mystical traditions within Christian forms, such as pilgrimage, labyrinth, and devotional paraliturgy, as a medium for cultural and spiritual transformation. Once again, reflective of Andrew Greeley's research on Catholics and the communication of narrative through visual culture, the trail is most effective in its creative and artistic performative narrative aspects.[23] Whereas the stations of the cross follow Christ's journey, the Genesis Earth Meditation Trail more broadly follows the stations of the life journey. Rather than the specter of Christ's Passion, the trail at Genesis Farm evokes the notion of the earth's Passion, providing space for confession or reconciliation, as well as atonement for human sins perpetuated against the planet.

The labyrinthine quality to the trail reflects the contemporary spiritual fascination with the use of medieval labyrinth as a tool for spiritual transformation.[24] Minister and author Lauren Artress, who has spurred much of the contemporary interest in labyrinth walking, speaks about the labyrinth as being simultaneously a journey outward and a journey into the self. Both indoor and outdoor labyrinths that replicate the labyrinth on the floor of Chartres Cathedral in France have become wildly popular among green sisters, Catholic religious sisters and brothers in general, and the Catholic and Protestant laity. At the Sinsinawa Mound in Wisconsin, the Sisters of St. Joseph's Mont Marie Center in Massachusetts, Prairiewoods in Iowa, St. Mary's College in

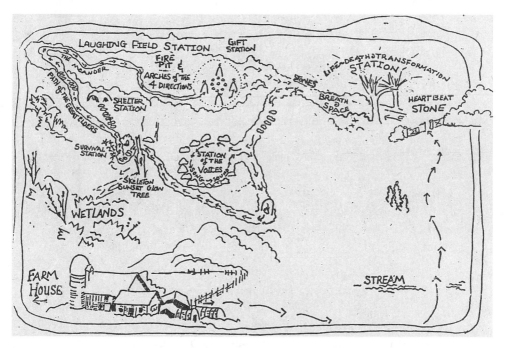

"Stations of the Earth" map by artist Sharon Brady.

Indiana, Carondelet Center in Minneapolis, and many other retreat centers, motherhouses, educational institutions, and ecological learning centers, the use of the labyrinth as a meditation tool has undergone a true renaissance.

The Earth Meditation Trail at Genesis Farm is not a traditional labyrinth, but it does have labyrinthine qualities and it similarly creates a space for peripatetic contemplation of earth, self, and cosmos. It is a journey simultaneously into the center of the self, the center of God, and the center (or "heart") of the cosmos, which the symbolism of the trail suggests are all spiritually "one." The design of the Earth Meditation Trail also embodies the traditional spiritual progression of labyrinth walking, in which one passes through stages of "purgation" (emptying or releasing), "illumination" (meditation, prayer, and receptiveness to insight), and "Union" (communion with God). In the Genesis trail, these three stages are concertedly intertwined with Berry's principles of differentiation, interiority, and communion. In describing the last labyrinth stage of "Union," the guide to the Holy Cross Sisters' St. Mary's Labyrinth in South Bend, Indiana, says that as the individual leaves the center of the labyrinth and travels back out to its edges, "In communion with God you go back to your ordinary life renewed and empowered to act. You bring your gifts to the service of the world."[25] The Genesis Earth Meditation Trail places a similar emphasis on fusing contemplation with service and action in and among the world. The activities to be performed at each station in conjunction with each station's imagery cultivate a kind of "green" mysticism. That is, each progression along the journey of the trail brings the pilgrim into a deeper level of communion with the Divine as experienced through the natural world. The immediacy of Divine presence in the "voices" and "faces" of nature evokes the traditional Christian mystical ideal of union with the Divine through a sacramental universe.[26] The design of the trail, however, goes beyond the more abstract aims of cultivating a meditative or contemplative mindset, to concertedly nudging those who walk the path in the direction of direct action. The meditative experience is not sufficient without the reciprocal and closely attached call to service. Brady's Earth Meditation Trail guide explains:

> When the interconnectedness of all things is *felt,* then it is clear that the Earth is the source of our survival. Studies show that we learn and retain information when our *feelings* are related to our learning. Further, when feelings are present with learning, humans are likely to *act* on those feelings. This work is about creating awareness between people and other living and non-living forms. It offers the real possibility of connecting *nature, feelings,* and *action.*[27]

Here, simply contemplating one's navel, even if it is the cosmic navel (the omphalos, as Mircea Eliade would say), is not sufficient.[28] Much as with green sisters' innovations of different forms of engaged monasticism, or as with the earth charter component of the Sisters of Earth ritual described in Chapter 1, sisters' experiments in new forms of prayer and ritual often include a practical action component. This is in part why the "Gift Station" at the end of the Earth Meditation Trail is so important to the experience and why the prayer rock accompanies the pilgrim throughout her journey along the path. It is the rock, as the guide explains, that carries her "intention." Much of the trail's design is geared toward getting those who walk it to recognize their oneness with the sacredness in all creation, and then getting them invested in making change—that is, enabling them to become more clear about what their particular mission is and then helping them to make a commitment to doing that work. Affective experience and spiritual insight are thereby channeled into activism.

The meditation path also embodies themes central to bioregionalism: decentralism, participation, mutualism, and community.[29] The "pilgrimage" itself is not so much about a particular destination as it is about an embodied performance of perpetual leaving and returning—a decentralized, nonlinear pilgrimage in which one comes to the end only to rediscover the beginning. Bioregionalists Freeman House, Michael McGinnis, and William Jordan all advocate the importance of "performative, community-based activity based on social learning" to the generation of an "ecologically sustainable culture."[30] McGinnis, in particular, makes the case that community and a sense of place are restored most effectively through direct human participation with nature and that participation is achieved not only thoroughly direct nature experiences, but also (and critically so) through cultural mimesis—in the form of dance, art, poetry, theater, and ritual. In its integration of nature experience, ritual, and the arts, the Genesis Earth Meditation Trail closely resembles McGinnis's prescriptions for the performative "restoration of the human ecological relationship," a relationship that he says has been damaged through the ravages of industrialism.[31]

Because the Earth Meditation Trail at Genesis Farm physically changes from year to year with the seasons and weather, so does the ritual experience of walking it. As Brady returns to the trail, again and again, to a work that is always in organic process, she stresses that it is a work of "living art" in which aspects of the trail may be removed by winter storms or added by Brady or the staff at Genesis Farm. Ritual theorist Catherine Bell argues that "despite many popular preconceptions and a number of anthropological models of ritual, ritual is not primarily a matter of unchanging tradition." In fact, she stresses that many analysts have discovered just the opposite, characterizing ritual as "a particularly effective means of mediating tradition and change, that is, a medium for appropriating some changes while maintaining a sense of cultural continuity."[32]

We see just such an interplay between change and cultural continuity imbedded in the journey of the Earth Meditation Trail, with its Christian stations format providing the overall contextual framework. Bell points out that ritual can only play its transformational role "from within the system, that is, as a component of the system that is defined and deployed in ways that interlock with how tradition and change are viewed." Bell contends that not only do rituals change as a community changes but also—and more importantly for the green sisters movement—new ritualized activities "can be taken as traditional within a very short time; they can also be flexibly appropriated; they may be practiced more or less faithfully despite strong reservations about every aspect of them."[33]

Installations of earth meditation trails that use stations to tell the interwoven earth, human, and cosmic story have become popular within the culture of green sisters, especially over the past ten years. Another example is the Passion of the Earth Trail, commissioned by the Benedictine Sisters of the Monastery of St. Gertrude in Cottonwood, Idaho. Like the Genesis Earth Meditation Trail, St. Gertrude's trail evokes a common theme in the green sisters movement—the earth's "Passion" and the relationship of humans to earth's suffering. This is a theme addressed in both the written work and public talks of Sister Gail Worcelo, who has identified the environmental crisis as an extension of "Christ's passion."[34]

The Dominican sisters at Crystal Spring Earth Learning Center in Massachusetts actually offer an "Earth's Passion" retreat in the traditional holy days before Easter. In this retreat, participants "reflect, ponder, and participate in the exodus experience that brings us toward a human-earth healed relationship."[35] In Thomas Berry's poem "Morningside Cathedral," Berry sounds a similar theme, suggesting that the Passion of Jesus be extended to the "Passion of the Earth." This same theme is repeated throughout his work and thus has been passed on to sisters who read his work and subscribe to his perspectives.[36]

A multimedia environmental meditative art project, the Passion of the

Earth experience at St. Gertrude's Monastery in Idaho comprises two parts. The first is an indoor Passion Walk located inside the monastery's spirituality center, which includes seven "narrative stations" of original art. Each station tells the story of the origins of the universe, as well as the earth's story, within the larger cosmic context. These stations take on themes such as "mystery," "flare," "laughter," "balance," "greed," "choice," and "abundance." The "Flare" station, which refers to the "flaring forth" of the universe, includes a narrative that says "Only God knows why, in a paroxysm of energy, in a single moment, the universe exploded into matter until billions of years, atoms, cosmic dust and divine desire collided to form the blue-green jewel of our home." The other stations include similar narrative and contemplative promptings.[37]

The second part of the monastery's Passion of the Earth project is an outdoor walk featuring a second installation of the original seven "narrative stations" as well as seven new "non-narrative" stations. Four of the non-narrative stations represent each of the basic elements of the planet (air, fire, water, and earth). Two stations are dedicated respectively to "plant life" and "animal life." And a final station, called "Take It All In," creates a space for absorbing the experience of the trail and reflecting on its images.[38] Locating these trails in woodlands or other natural settings is important because doing so speaks to those who, as Sister of St. Joseph Joellen Sbrissa of LaGrange, Illinois, phrases it, acquire their "spiritual energy from nature and the earth." "I pray best with nature," explains Sbrissa. If the growing number of outdoor earth meditation walks, labyrinths, and other environmental art installations are any indication, she is not alone.[39]

In locations such as Idaho with cold, inhospitable winters, an "indoor" meditation trail is obviously practical. In commissioning both the complete indoor and outdoor installation of the Passion of the Earth stations, it is perhaps fitting that the Benedictine Sisters of the Monastery of St. Gertrude commissioned textile artist Melanie Weidner to design and complete the work. Weidner weaves together concepts from the fabric of Catholic paraliturgical tradition and Thomas Berry's work on the "universe story" with threads of grace and incarnation evocative of Sallie McFague's theology of the earth as "God's body." Benedictine Sister Teresa Jackson, who has headed the Passion of the Earth project, explains, "The 'Passion of the Earth' is designed to be a spiritual exercise that enables people to see the earth and the cosmos not only as God's creation, but as the most basic expression of God's very self."[40] Stations five through seven of the Passion of the Earth artistically deal with the destruction of earth's resources. Station six is dedicated to reflecting on human choice as it relates to the fate of the planet. A fabric art installment at this station is accompanied by a narrative that reads, "We will decide: a re-creation or continued destruction; a dream of hope or the nightmare of our greed."[41]

Sociologist Andrew Greeley points to "statistically significant" research demonstrating a positive correlation between U.S. Catholics who go to church regularly and higher rates of interest in the fine arts. "Liturgy and the fine arts are linked," says Greeley, "a notion which would have been taken to be obvious and beyond debate from Constantine to the Council of Trent."[42] (Interestingly, Greeley finds that the relationship is inverse among Protestants, who demonstrate less interest in the fine arts as a function of churchgoing and church involvement.) Consistent with Greeley's data are green sisters' enthusiastic commissioning of environmental artists to create "living art" projects to facilitate prayer and ritual within their religious communities, motherhouses, retreat centers, and educational ministries. In addition, sisters who are themselves artists and whose work strongly embodies ecological themes—such as Mary Southard, Nancy Earle, Marion Honors, and Ansgar Holmberg—enjoy strong support for their work in and among the broader community of green sisters.[43] Higher levels of Catholic interest in the fine arts, theorizes Greeley, are a function of a "powerful liturgical imagination" infused by artistic and visual rendering of graceful stories of God that are "at the core of Catholic religious heritage."[44]

Greeley subsequently argues that this distinctive, imaginative, and powerful liturgical spirituality among Catholics "merits further reflection as a resource for, and challenge to, Catholic leaders. More theologically, it is a spirituality that reflects the nearness of the Spirit, a present and not distant Spirit, an analogical and not dialectical Spirit, among the Catholic laity." Greeley qualifies that when he speaks of the "liturgical imagination," he is not speaking of what, as he says, "passes for Liturgy" in many American parishes. "If the liturgical imagination continues to survive," predicts Greeley, "it will do so despite the 'liturgists' and not because of them. Its strength is rooted in the depths of the Catholic psyche with its ability to sense grace lurking everywhere."[45] This is especially true for green sisters who seem to sense "grace lurking" in media as varied as earth meditation trails, earth rosaries, gardens, kitchens, and straw-bale houses, and who sense the Spirit being as near as the prayer rock they hold in their hands.

The Cosmic Walk

Another variation on "walking the stations" is the development of "cosmic walks." When asked about efforts to "green" liturgy in her community, Betty Daugherty, a Franciscan Sister of the Perpetual Adoration, responds, "I love the Cosmic Walk. We tell the Universe Story in many ways at Prairiewoods [a Franciscan spirituality center in Iowa] and have had several workshops and retreats that use this ritual . . . One staff member has used the Cosmic Walk in her college courses. We have developed a Cosmic Walk in our woods . . . we have established eight cosmic stations along our woods trail and provide a re-flection paper for retreatants and others to use as they walk."[46] Like the trail at Genesis Farm, the walk created at Prairiewoods provides a nature-based med-itative experience in which one passes through a sequence of prayer stations; however, the walk at Prairiewoods refers much more directly to the evolution-ary cosmic events that make up what Thomas Berry calls "the universe story."

Living Water Spiritual Center in Maine, a ministry of the Sisters of St. Jo-seph of Lyon, has also installed a cosmic walk on its property. The walk con-sists of twenty-five stations in a pine grove near the center, each of which is identified by an artistically hand-painted slate that depicts a major event in the evolutionary history of the cosmos. The trail unfolds in a chronological progression of these "one-time cosmic events," which retreatants are invited to contemplate as they "walk the story of the universe" and thereby come to know that story in their own bodies.[47] As with earth meditation trails, the design of these cosmic walks speaks to the importance of kinesthetic know-ing through some sort of peripatetic ritual. Green Mountain Monastery co-founder Gail Worcelo refers to this dynamic more personally when she re-counts the first time she "walked the story of the universe" in a cosmic walk. She says, "My experience was one of having an understanding of the Universe Story drop from my head into my body! The experience was one of knowing the Story to be in me . . . in my cells, bones, body . . . literally star stuff!"[48]

Again, we see the considerable influence of Thomas Berry's work on the green sisters movement. According to Berry, "The Universe is a great liturgy," and sisters have set about the work of creating liturgies and prayers that em-body this notion.[49] Despite the growing popularity of cosmic walks created in woodland settings, a portable version is most often utilized by sisters. First created by Sister Miriam MacGillis, who is also an artist, the portable form re-quires relatively few inexpensive components: roughly 100 to 140 feet of rope, twenty-five to thirty index cards, votive candles, and optional meditative music. The rope is arranged (either inside on a large floor space or outside in a natural setting) so that it takes the form of a large spiral with pathways wide enough to allow one or two persons to walk and pass one another. This rope spiral signifies the cosmic unfolding of the universe. Every few steps or so along this spiral path, there is a card marking an event in the universe's cosmic history. One by one, each person (usually as part of a retreat group) journeys to the center of the spiral, holding an unlit candle. As she stops at each station along the path, she symbolically travels farther back in time, making a "pilgrimage" back to the origin of the cosmos. Cards may read something like this:

- 110 million years ago—the first mammals emerge
- 210 million years ago—the continents drift apart, the Atlantic Ocean is formed
- 425 million years ago—the first life forms leave the oceans
- 4.25 billion years ago—the earth cools and forms an atmosphere
- 14 billion years ago—the primal stars and galaxies take shape

In all, participants make their way through some twenty-five or thirty evolutionary events, taking time to reflect on each one. At the very center of the spiral sits a larger, lit candle. Sometimes this larger candle is held in a large bowl of water or a smaller votive candle is used that floats on the water. A card at its side reads "15 billion years ago—The Flaring Forth: the universe was dreamed into being." This "primordial flame" lights the candle of each cosmic pilgrim as she pauses, closes her eyes, meditates on sensing her presence at that first event, and then reflects on the notion that, as part of the universe, she too is 15 billion years old. With a lit candle in hand, the cosmic pilgrim now turns around and spirals forward again in time, finally arriving at the present, emerging from the labyrinth of time. She announces, "Today I know the story of myself," and is greeted with congratulations from the other ritual participants.[50]

The cosmic walk is practiced by a variety of groups in different settings, as a ritual celebration of what Thomas Berry has called, interchangeably, the "New Cosmology," the "New Story," and the "Universe Story."[51] Those who walk the story of the universe learn the history of cosmic evolution as it has been explained through modern science, while they (ideally) experience themselves as a living part of that story—in essence, they become the story participating in its own telling. The cosmic walk is intended to communicate in a participatory and embodied way that there is no finite created world, only an ever-expanding universe constantly changing, and of which humanity is inseparably a part. It is a nonverbal way to get at what Sister Miriam MacGillis calls a "mystery we can't even begin to find language for. The vastness of it and the depth of it are beyond us."[52] The universe, the solar system, and the planet earth, says Thomas Berry, "in themselves and in their evolutionary emergence constitute for the human community the primary revelation of the ultimate mystery whence all things emerge into being."[53] Those who make the cosmic walk thus in some sense dramaturgically experience their own being as the cosmos "made flesh." Furthermore, the ritual itself instills a kind of cosmic "communitas," in which those who walk the cosmos experience themselves not as separate or above creation (the "crown of creation") but as simply another "index card" ("2.6 million years ago—homo habilus, first humans emerge") on the timeline of one-time evolutionary events.

There is both a mood of solemnity and of celebration to the ritual. Sister of St. Francis Marya Grathwohl, for instance, tells of preparing for a retreat in which she would be leading a cosmic walk: "I was playing Pachelbel's Canon as I worked [to set up the cosmic walk]. Then, the spiral completed and the cards and the candles in place, I spontaneously danced the walk to the music, worshipping each event."[54] Others, however, are not as enthralled with the cosmic walk experience. Dominican Sister Miriam Brown (of the Sinsinawa Dominicans), for instance, who has been attuned to the "New Story" since the 1980s when she began reading the work of Thomas Berry and Brian Swimme, finds the experience somewhat lacking. After years of being steeped in the "New Story" consciousness and having experienced the cosmic walk many times, she offers a less ecstatic perspective, saying, "I am finding that I now experience those presentations as overly 'literal.' I need the "Mystery" to be evoked and the sense of divine connection."[55]

To be sure, the cosmic walk is both intensely literal and symbolic. In fact, one of the major aims of the ritual is to (in anthropologist Michael Taussig's terms) "tangibilize" the story of cosmic evolution, taking an otherwise abstract epic of evolutionary process and making it accessible, intimate, real, and relevant to the participant. What is perhaps most striking about this embodied "cosmic liturgy" is the acute and central importance and sacredness of story (or narrative) to its structure. As social scientist, priest, and novelist, Andrew Greeley posits that "Catholics may be especially addicted to fine arts storytelling because their lives have been shaped by so much storytelling since their first conscious moments."[56]

More generally, sociologist of religion Keith Roberts theorizes that one of ritual's central functions is "the enactment of a story or myth" because it "symbolically reminds participants of the mythology of the faith by moving them through a series of moods."[57] We clearly see this dynamic rooted in the cosmic walk as participants symbolically reenact the epic of the birth of the universe and, by extension, the story of their own primordial creation. Anthropologist Clifford Geertz regards ritual as a "cultural performance" that symbolically fuses ethos and worldview, and just such a cultural performance is evident in the cosmic walk. An ethos of unity, interdependence, and reverence for all life is fused with a worldview of a cosmos that is fundamentally alive, all of a piece, and continues to unfold. For Geertz, the performance of ritual is critical to formulating "a broad range of moods and motivations" that "shape the spiritual consciousness of a people" and undergird the efficacy of religion as a cultural system.[58] This is something that green sisters seem to sense naturally and deeply on an intuitive level as they creatively integrate rituals related to evolution and oneness with creation both into special ceremonial contexts and into their everyday lives.

Earth Holy Days

"I can't remember not doing it," says Sisters of Earth cofounder and Sister of St. Joseph Mary Southard of celebrating the seasonal solstices and equinoxes that divide the solar year evenly into quarters. She continues, "I find myself experiencing the changes and rhythms of the seasons in connection with the rest of the earth community—migrations, sounds, sights, dynamics, temperatures, stories, etc. I feel a part of all these."[59] The fact that solstice and equinox celebrations have become so ingrained in Southard's life that she cannot remember a time before their regular observance is consistent with Catherine Bell's conclusion that, despite common associations with rituals as practices and performances that are gradually culturally embedded over many generations, in fact, rituals "can be taken as traditional within a very short time."[60]

This is especially true if new rituals are filling a void left by the absence or withering of other cultural performances. Rosine Sobczak, a professor of biology and Sister of St. Francis (Congregation of Our Lady of Lourdes in Ohio), recalls, "We used to celebrate Rogation days in the Church, but they have since been long gone!" Rogation Days were agriculturally linked days of prayer, fasting, and procession during which crops were ritually blessed and prayers said for a bountiful harvest. Although they have enjoyed a recent and limited revival among Catholic environmentalists, these days are for the most part no longer observed. Sobczak, however, enthuses, "These solstice gatherings are a good replacement!"[61]

Like the morning body prayer and the cosmic walk, celebrations of the seasonal cycles and the positioning of the sun and earth throughout the solar year are ways for sisters to, as Thomas Berry says, relate to "the universe as a great cosmic liturgy."[62] Berry contends that indigenous or land-based peoples have historically done this by acknowledging their place within the cosmological order at transformative moments: "springtime rituals, summer harvest festivals and the winter solstice at the moment of decline." According to Berry, "This is the order of the universe and ritual is the way in which humans establish their basic rapport with the natural world in visible form."[63]

Similarly, Sister Miriam MacGillis speaks about the solstices and the change of seasons on the planet as "universal events" that the entire earth community can come together and celebrate, regardless of religious affiliation or cultural background. This point is of special importance to green sisters, who run ecological learning centers that attract participants of all faiths. It is also important in the administration of green sisters' community-supported gardens, in which shareholders may come from a variety of different religious and ethnic backgrounds. In seeking to "create community" through joint celebrations of friends, neighbors, and garden shareholders, sisters specifically try to come up with celebrations in which everyone may participate. This also reflects a greater post–Vatican II ecumenical consciousness among sisters and their efforts to create possibilities for interfaith worship.

To those who would associate observances of solstices and equinoxes with pagan worship, MacGillis emphasizes that these days "are not pagan events; they are cosmological events," and as such belong to everybody.[64]

MacGillis's conviction that the solstices and equinoxes can be celebrated without their being pagan per se speaks of a broader movement among Roman Catholics to develop ways to observe such events. One example of this movement comes from Edward Hays's *Prayers for a Planetary Pilgrim* (1989). Hays, who has been a Catholic priest for more than thirty years, features prayers for the winter solstice, a blessing for a solstice feast, and a ritual for a winter solstice fire. In terms similar to MacGillis's, he talks about the solstice as being a completely appropriate time to come into "communion with the earth at this sacred moment of changing seasons." Furthermore, he writes that the solstice is also an ideal opportunity for humans, as prisoners of the marvels of technology, to reconnect with "Mother Earth" and cosmic realities, celebrating the promise of the coming light.[65]

In the short talks that MacGillis gives at solstice and equinox events, she speaks about how collectively observing the great seasonal cycles is critical to humans' experiencing themselves as part of the web of life. These celebrations are important to humans' getting to know the seasons of winter, spring, summer, and fall and learning that seasonal changes are not simply happening within the growth cycles of plants or the hibernation patterns of animals, but also biologically within themselves. In other words, just as the solstices and equinoxes are transformative events in the cosmos, so they are physically and spiritually transformative events in humans. "These [seasonal] patterns are absolutely essential for the development of the human," says MacGillis. "Our species cannot be what it is except for what is revealed in these powerful, powerful revelations."[66]

At Genesis Farm's summer solstice celebrations, there is a quite literal demonstration of the use of these solar events as a means to reorient humans to the universe, enabling them to locate themselves within the time and space of cosmic events. During the celebration, a large, festively decorated "sun staff" ritually marks the movement of the earth around the sun. A designated celebrant moves the sun staff into the position of the proper summer solstice trajectory between earth and sun using a cloth streamer that is then anchored with a rock (which symbolizes the earth). For those who are not completely familiar with the physics of where the earth is in relation to the sun at any given time of the year (myself included), this demonstration helps show the movements of the earth and sun over the course of an astronomical year. At one summer solstice, when the earth rock was moved around the sun from its position at the equinox to its new position at the solstice, a child next to me pointed and asked his mother, "What's that?" She responded, "That's *us*. That's where we are *right* now." The child nodded, seemingly satisfied.[67]

As with the Genesis Farm's Earth Meditation Trail, the solstice and equinox rituals celebrate not only earth-human-cosmic mystical oneness but call for political and community action based on that oneness. At the same solstice celebration just described, contact forms were handed out at one point to each participant so that the Genesis Farm staff could match up solstice celebrants with earth activist groups in the area. Participants got the message very quickly that becoming cognizant of one's place in the universe and celebrating the spiritual dimension of the seasons are not just about feel-good celebrations, as important as those are. Clearly, the ritual stressed the responsibilities of service that come with a felt sense of communion with the Divine through creation.

Dominican-sponsored Crystal Spring Earth Learning Center in Massachusetts has a special section dedicated to earth festivals on their yearly program schedule. According to the program, these festivals "are a conversation with the seasons, a reminder of the cycle of life—birth, death, resurrection. We celebrate seasonal festivals to add what comes from the human heart. Join us as we celebrate Earth's kinship."[68]

These festivals take a variety of forms at Crystal Spring, depending on the season. The winter solstice, for instance, is focused around a central ritual. "As a community of friends and cosmic companions," explains the program schedule, "let's celebrate this wondrous festival. In ritual and song we'll enter the mystery of darkness and our collective receptivity to rebirth and recovery." The spring equinox celebration, however, is designed around a worm composting workshop, in which participants also learn how to make "compost tea" for their gardens. "Participate in the promising communion of sun and soil," invites the program, "from worms and waste to healthy gardens and food." The summer solstice celebration involves a mindfulness meditation along the center's considerable woodland trails, and the autumn equinox includes an "earth literacy" section that teaches how to recognize different signs and tracks left by animals so as to be able to identify local wildlife. Most of the earth celebrations at Crystal Spring, as at other similar centers facilitated by green sisters, culminate in some sort of potluck feast. Rituals may be accompanied by music or include some kind of liturgical dance. Rituals can also involve very simple or more complex exemplars of participatory dramaturgy. A winter solstice at Genesis Farm included a solemn night procession along a luminary-lit woodland trail to a pond where a small barge made out of fallen tree limbs and twigs awaited us. We had brought with us, written on flat sticks, the things we had vowed to "leave behind in the passing solar year." These sticks were inserted into the "prayer barge," which was then towed out by canoe to the middle of the pond and set aflame to create a bonfire that lit up the dark solstice sky. We also made prayers for what we would like to bring into our lives and into the world in the coming year, and MacGillis spoke about how symbolically there is a "divine child" ready to be born or reborn in all of us. Later, we feasted on a sampling of natural foods cuisine contributed by solstice participants, as musician shareholders from the community-supported garden offered flute accompaniment.

Gathering as a religious community and as an extended community for prayer and ritual at the quarter days of the year (two solstices and two equinoxes), as well as in some cases at the "cross-quarter days" (the midway points between those solar events), establishes regular and predictable communal earth-based seasonal observances. Why choose these days as "holy days"? In an essay printed in Susan J. Clark's *Celebrating Earth Holy Days: A Resource Guide for Faith Communities,* Thomas Berry encourages the practice: "In our totality we are born out of the Earth. We are Earthlings. The Earth is our origin, our nourishment, our support, our guide. Our spirituality itself is Earth-derived. If there is no spirituality in the Earth, then there is no spirituality in ourselves. The human and the Earth are totally implicated in the other."[69]

The celebration of "earth holy days" varies from community to community. Dominican sister Chris Loughlin, one of the cofounders of Crystal Spring Center, recounts the celebration at the center of the day known as Candlemas, which falls exactly halfway between the winter solstice and the spring equinox: "This year at the time of Candlemas, thirty-eight women gathered to lift their human voices on behalf of the 'great work' of personal, social, and planetary transformation through the power of music and song." In her description, Loughlin includes a chant from the celebration that evokes a mystical sense of unity between participants and the natural world:

Be there Spirit of the wind, breathe in me
Spirit of the Sun, rekindle my flame
Spirit of the Rain, fill my dry and deep recesses
Spirit of the Land, raise me again.[70]

At some centers, such as Michaela Farm in Indiana, in addition to celebrating solstices and equinoxes, Earth Day is a vibrant celebration that attracts immediate neighbors, the surrounding community, and even those who drive considerable distances for the occasion. At other centers such as Waterspirit, an ecology and spirituality ministry sponsored by the Sisters of St. Joseph of Peace and located on the New Jersey shore, staff downplay the importance of Earth Day. Like most centers run by green sisters, Waterspirit, which primarily offers earth literacy programs focused on water issues, hosts solstice and equinox celebrations. "These celebrations bind us all together," explains Director of Waterspirit Sister Suzanne Golas. "This is the common foundation for beings—the earth itself." As at Genesis Farm, Waterspirit's ritual celebrations combine both mystical and very practical, action-related elements. A description of Waterspirit's "Come to the Water Celebration" invites, "Come back to the sea for a weekend of learning, ritual, and reflection on the sacredness and significance of water and how water is key to our interconnectedness with all creation." But the staff at Waterspirit concertedly connects this kind of learning, ritual, and reflection to practical activities like beach cleanups and includes an essential program component in which participants "re-commit to action to protect Earth and her waters."[71] Golas says, "I always had a little problem with Earth Day because it's only one day, you know . . . The day it's not Earth Day, we cease to exist."[72]

Earth holy day celebrations create a kind of newly expanded ecological liturgical calendar. This brings us back to Franciscan sister Rosine Sobczak's comment that solstices and equinoxes were a "good substitute for Rogation days" that for the most part are no longer observed today. Even with the movement currently afoot among Catholic environmentalists to bring back Rogation Days, my sense is that the solstice and equinox earth festivals, which now play a valued role among green sisters, will not be displaced.[73]

Andrew Greeley cites data on high levels of Catholic "sociability" that he

Seasonal ritual celebration at Waterspirit, Stella Maris Center,
Elberon, New Jersey.
(Photo courtesy of Regina O'Connell, CSJP.)

correlates with Catholicism's identity as a "religion of festival." Greeley remarks that the Catholic imagination "revels in stories that are festivals and festivals that are stories."[74] Catholic historian Robert Orsi also details the history of the effervescent "feste" culture among Italian-American immigrant Catholics in New York City. Orsi demonstrates how "feste challenged the authority of official Catholicism over the religious lives of immigrants." Italians, Orsi tells us, "make a rather clear distinction between religion and church, and they often view the latter with critical cynicism. The feste and the festa societies competed successfully with the clergy for the people's loyalty, devotion, and money."[75] In different ways, both Greeley and Orsi point to Catholics' "liking a good party," and Orsi in particular refers to the reluctance of Catholics to give up culturally resonant festivals or to surrender control over them to clerical authority.

Not only does green sisters' inclusion of solstice, equinox, cross-quarter day, and even Earth Day observances within their yearly calendars tap into to the Catholic heritage of vibrant festival culture, but such festivals also do so in a way that is spiritually and ecologically meaningful for sisters. Consider that many green sisters are in some way involved in agricultural ministries, whether organic farming, organic dairying, organic beekeeping, or even sustainable Christmas tree farming. Others are heavily involved in things such as prairie restoration or other wildlife habitat restoration. Sisters who are doing this kind of work are working closely with the land and observing seasonal changes on a daily basis. Having some sort of communal ritual observance of seasonal shifts thus takes on even greater importance.

Yet reinhabiting the "bioregion" of prayer, ritual, and liturgy requires sisters' most delicate arts of diplomacy. The observance of solstices, equinoxes, and cross-quarter days is commonly identified with pagans (the "old" kind) or so-called neo-pagans. It may be that, as sisters identify them, these days are "universal cosmological events that everyone can celebrate," but the public perception on this point is a tough sell.

Sisters may also see themselves as "midwifing" Christianity into a new evolutionary moment, or as ethicist Mary Evelyn Tucker gracefully phrases it, helping Christianity to enter its "ecological phase." Tucker explains that "the environmental crisis calls the religions of the world to respond by finding their voice within the larger earth community. In so doing, the religions are now entering their ecological phase and finding their planetary expression. They are awakening to a renewed appreciation of matter as a vessel for the sacred."[76] Right-wing Catholic critics, however, have seized on examples of solstice rituals and the like as opportunities to portray sisters as being alarmingly misguided, New Age, or even heretical Gaia-worshipping pantheists. How will sisters continue to deal with these sorts of tensions and political pressures, while still managing to continue their work on behalf of the earth? With their labyrinths, earth meditation trails, and cosmic walks, perhaps the practice of peripatetic prayer will prepare green sisters well for the journey ahead. They are sure to encounter more than a few challenging "stations" through which they must pass.

CONCLUSION

Stepping into the Future

Rather than politely ignore the "elephant in the motherhouse," Dominican sister Sharon Zayac has made it her business to address head-on fears that reverence for the earth and earth spirituality may really be nature worship:

It is safe to say that many, if not most, of us Catholics in the Western world struggle with reconciling what we are beginning to learn about the origins of life with both what we have grown up believing about nature and what we think our Church teaches us about creation. We are wary, if not frightened, of dabbling with pantheism and nature worship. A good analogy is to liken the fear of our growing understanding about creation and our role within it to many non-Catholics' assumption that we worship Mary or the saints. We don't worship her or the saints, nor is this growing awakening to Earth a misplaced worship of nature . . . Knowing our history will put our present and growing understanding of creation in the proper context. It should help us see that our emerging understanding is not a new cult and that we ought not to fall into the trap of dismissing it as some kind of "New Age" stuff. The creation story we are newly awakening to is, in fact, a vital part of our Christian heritage.[1]

In her approach, Zayac skillfully touches on a cultural sore spot for many Catholics—that of being dismissed or labeled "primitive" by Protestant misunderstandings of Catholic customs of veneration and a culture of sacramentalism.[2] By comparing Protestant anxieties about Mary worship to current anxieties about nature worship, Zayac finds an analogy that works simultaneously on several levels—cultural, historical, psychological, and iconographic. Zayac's analogy is especially appropriate for green sisters, who have unapologetically reclaimed Mary as "cosmic matrix" even as they have reclaimed the earth as holy scripture and as a source of divine revelation. Zayac goes on to explain (as green sisters have necessarily become increasingly well practiced at doing) the theological difference between "pantheism" and "panentheism" and why the former is heresy and the latter is in keeping with the teachings of the Roman Catholicism.

> In our haste to affirm that God is greater than creation, we have put God above it, outside of it. We have totally separated God from nature. We have convinced ourselves that only "primitive" people believe God resides in nature. And in our minds, we have converted indigenous people's pan*en*theist beliefs to pantheist beliefs. Pantheism is the belief that identifies God with the universe, God and creation are one. So to worship nature is to worship God. Pan*en*theism is the belief that God resides in the world God made, and all creation resides within the God who made it since nothing can exist outside of God. Therefore, creation is reverenced as a worthy gift of a loving and generous God. It is reverenced and respected, not worshipped.[3]

In developing her argument in *Earth Spirituality: In the Catholic and Dominican Traditions,* Zayac draws on a valued collection of Catholic (and especially Dominican) "heirloom seeds" to strengthen her point and lend it generational value. The first heirloom seed is a young Spaniard by the name of Dominic de Guzmán (1170–1221), who in the thirteenth century founded an order of preachers (later known as "the Dominicans") to preach against the Greek-inspired dualistic view of "spirit" and "matter," a belief that conceived of "the world and all created matter as evil and the invisible, spiritual realm as the only good." The second heirloom seed is Benguine mystic Mechthild of Magdeburg (1210–ca. 1280), who saw "all things in God and God in all things." The third heirloom seed is Dominican scientist Albert the Great (ca. 1200–1280), who rejected Plato's dualistic view of matter and spirit and turned instead to Aristotle's more positive view of created matter. The prize heirloom seed in Zayac's collection is Saint Thomas Aquinas (1225–1274), who taught that "God is both transcendent over creation and immanently present in each creature" and that "sacred writings are bound in two volumes, that of creation and that of holy scripture." Zayac emphasizes this last point by writing, "God is present in all creation and if we want to pay tribute to the creator, we must respect the actuality, the concrete reality, the essence of all things."[4] The condensed message of Zayac's book might read something like this: "We're *not* 'New Age,' we're *not* pagans, we're *not* pantheists, we're *not* heretics, and what we believe about God and the reverencing of creation is steeped in the living traditions of the Catholic Church, John Paul II's 1990

'World Day of Peace Message,' and numerous bishop's pastorals. So, for goodness sake, quit calling us all of that!"[5]

Why do Zayac and other green sisters feel a great need to lay out these arguments explicitly and to "clear the air"? As the phenomenon of the "greening of faith" percolates through a variety of religious institutions, debates and tensions have intensified between those who welcome shifts toward infusing religion with a heightened sense of ecological consciousness and those who perceive "greening" trends to be pernicious threats to orthodoxy.[6] The New York State–based Catholic Conservation Center, for instance, takes sharp aim at both the Universe Story approach to Catholic environmental thought (largely embraced by green sisters) and the United Nations' Earth Charter project, which has been officially endorsed by a number of Catholic religious organizations, including more than fifty communities of Catholic women religious. The Earth Charter is an international declaration of fundamental principles for global partnership aimed at creating a "more just, sustainable, and peaceful world."[7] The Catholic Conservation Center devotes much of its web site to unmasking this effort as a kind of New Age conspiracy with which a growing number of Catholics have been complicit.

The attacks on both Thomas Berry and the Earth Charter are part of the center's broader scope of work, in which it monitors Catholic environmental activity and then generates position papers that "expose" Catholic environmentalists who have "stepped over the line" and are no longer, according to center director Bill Jacobs, following the teachings of the Church. Featured on the center's web site is an article entitled "New Age versus Christian Environmental Justice," which argues that Christian environmental justice "has been corrupted by New Age ideology. Proponents of the New Age movement use the defense of nature to advance their beliefs. The Earth Charter is a good example. New Age leads us away from God and His Church, thereby leading us away from the authentic solutions to our environmental problems."[8]

Jacobs further warns Catholics that figures such as Father Thomas Berry are "false prophets" who undermine the "authentic interpretation of God's law" by the Church.[9] Under the bold and alarming subheading "False Teachings," Jacobs refers to Berry as a "dissident Catholic priest" and identifies him as a leading proponent of the "new cosmology and other forms of neopaganism." Berry's views, Jacobs cautions the faithful, "are connected more to the views of animistic or shamanistic faiths than to Christian tradition."[10] In case his readers are at all confused about his discussion of "Creation Spirituality," Thomas Berry, and the "New Cosmology," Jacobs provides a glossary definition of the term neo-pagan at the end of his article: "A wide variety of Earth-based, nature-based, New Age, and goddess beliefs, as opposed to Judeo-Christian religion."[11]

Carrie Tomko (to some, the Ann Coulter of right-wing Catholic commentators) has similarly targeted Miriam MacGillis, Thomas Berry, and an organization with which many women's religious congregations are affiliated called Global Education Associates. (The former name of GEA is Beyond War.) Tomko rails against MacGillis, Berry, and GEA for being out of the mainstream and for promoting an "earth-centered spirituality" that is "more akin to Gaia worship than to the worship of the Triune God."[12] As chief proof of this, she cites the fact that solstice and equinox festivals (traditionally pagan holidays) are celebrated at both Genesis Farm in New Jersey and Michaela Farm in Indiana, both communities that practice forms of "biodynamic agriculture," and both of which are registered affiliates of Global Education Associates. Exasperated, Tomko asks when the bishops will actually "do their job" and "take a critical look at dissenting groups in the Church who enjoy the privilege of calling themselves Roman Catholic while promoting ideas which are not?"[13]

In terms of who gets to be called Catholic and who does not, Tomko (and anyone else) are of course entitled to their opinions, but there are very specific official channels within the Church for determining this sort of status. Historically, these channels have been used relatively sparingly.[14] The Church knows well from experience that once such pronouncements or condemnations of individuals are made, those whom they have disciplined can become exponentially more popular as sympathetic (in some cases, even martyr-like) figures.[15]

Disciplinary channels also tend to be reserved for only the most severe cases of those whose work clearly presents "a danger to the faithful." In this regard, it is important to remember that women religious are not a part of the magisterium (the teaching office and authority of the Catholic Church). Sisters might offer avant-garde workshops and retreats, but sisters themselves are officially classified as laity and possess no hierarchically recognized authority over other laity within the Church; they also, significantly, have no officially recognized power to administer the sacraments. They are thus considered to be much less a concern than would be, say, a renegade priest.

This is not to say that women religious have not been targeted for disciplinary action in the recent past; they have. In 2001, for instance, upon discovering that Sister Joan Chittister (former prioress of Mount Saint Benedict Monastery in Erie, Pennsylvania) was scheduled to speak at the First Annual Conference on Women's Ordination Worldwide (WOW) in Dublin, Ireland, the Holy See's Congregation for the Institutes of Consecrated Life wrote to Chittister's prioress and explicitly instructed that Chittister was to be forbidden to attend the conference or else face "just penalties." The Holy See (a term that refers to the pope together with the Roman Curia who assist in central Church administration) determined that Chittister would be in violation of the decree of "Ordinatio Sacerdotalis," which states that priestly ordination will never be conferred on women and therefore the matter must never be discussed.[16] Chittister's prioress politely declined the Holy See's order, citing obedience to conscience, and said that Chittister would need to make her own decision as to whether or not she should attend the conference. Chittister's sisters in the monastery voted 127 to one in favor of allowing her disobedience to the decree. Other monasteries also wrote the Holy See in support of Chittister's being allowed to make her own decision about attending the conference. Chittister did end up attending the WOW conference in Dublin and, despite the Church's threat of "just penalties," she ultimately retained canonical status.

Upon hearing that Sister Miriam MacGillis had been invited by the major superiors of five religious orders to speak in New Zealand, one retired theologian and seminary professor in that country became so upset that he sent memorandums to each New Zealand bishop, telling them that they were "under a serious obligation to warn the faithful" that MacGillis's views constituted pantheism and that "Catholics attending her lectures could be endangering their faith."[17] (MacGillis, much more than any other green sister, tends to be targeted in these attacks in part because her work is more widely known and available internationally.) It is telling, however, that this theologian's letter of request was largely ignored, the visit was deemed not to be of concern, and apparently MacGillis was judged to be "not teaching controversial doctrine," or at least not controversial enough to merit any kind of warning from the bishops.

Were anyone to receive some kind of censoring or disciplinary action from the Vatican, it would probably be Thomas Berry, because in addition to his considerable influence on former students and his ardent following, he actually possesses the official authority to administer the sacraments. (This is only if Berry's teachings were officially deemed to be objectionable, which thus far they have not.) But Berry is in his eighties now, frail, and living in a care facility. He is a far cry from the "young Turk" that Dominican priest Matthew Fox was in 1984 when he first caught the eye of then-cardinal Joseph Ratzinger (now Pope Benedict XVI), who at the time was in charge of the Congregation of Doctrine and Faith, the Vatican's department for protecting orthodoxy. (Incidentally, this department was called the Office of the Holy Inquisition until 1965.) Fox was officially silenced in 1988 and forbidden to teach, lecture, or publish for a year. When his superiors later recalled him to Chicago from his Institute of Creation-Centered Spirituality in California upon penalty of expulsion from the Dominican order, Fox chose expulsion rather than compliance. In 1994, he removed himself from the jurisdiction of Roman Catholic authority completely by becoming an Episcopalian.

Now that Ratzinger is Pope, it remains unclear if his past position as chief defender of orthodoxy will mean that his papacy will launch more "investigations" or impose harsher standards of "discipline" than have recent papacies. Were such an authoritarian action to be taken against Berry, it might only further energize his following. Such charges would also be extremely hard to prove. Even Matthew Fox was never found guilty of heresy, and Berry's work tends to be on the aggregate more moderate than Fox's. It's important to remember that those who do receive punitive treatment from the Church hierarchy are often later embraced. A relevant example is Pope Benedict XVI's announcement in July 2006 that the founder of the Sisters of Providence at Saint Mary-of-the-Woods (Indiana), the Blessed Mother Theodore Guerin, would be canonized as a saint in the Roman Catholic Church during ceremonies at the Vatican held the following October. This news was exciting and perhaps surprising for green sisters and not simply because American canonizations are relatively rare.[18] In establishing the Sisters of Providence in 1840, Guerin had had a particularly dramatic and complicated interaction with hierarchical authority. A quintessentially resilient "frontier nun," Guerin held a strong vision of an active community for the Sisters of Providence and was steadfastly determined to see its successful realization, despite a number of heated disagreements with the local bishop. When she refused to deny her own conscience (by subverting the vision of religious community that she felt had been sent her by God) in order to comply with the bishop's demands, the bishop proceeded to her lock her up in his house. She was only set free when her sisters came to the bishop's house and demanded her release. Subsequently, the bishop deposed Guerin from her role as superior of the community, "released" her from her vows as a sister, and exiled her from the diocese. Sisters were forbidden to communicate with her, and any sister who chose to leave the diocese and join her was threatened with excommunication. Undaunted, the sisters packed up and left, following their beloved founder and defying the edicts of Church authority in the process. The bishop ultimately resigned and was replaced by a new bishop. Guerin was reinstated and she and her Sisters of Providence went on to build their community at St. Mary-of-the-Woods.[19]

Today, the Sisters of Providence motto is "Breaking boundaries, creating hope."[20] Almost four hundred acres of the sisters' land has been state certified as "organic farmland," and an ecofriendly straw-bale house graces their property, as does a sustainably managed herd of alpacas. In 2003, the sisters converted their congregation's heating system to burn recyclable "biomass" instead of oil. (Biomass includes matter such as husks and straw left in fields after the harvest [plentiful in Indiana] and even truckloads of "imperfect" macaroni sent to them by the Kraft company in Illinois, which Kraft would otherwise have had to deposit in a landfill at its own expense.) Saint Mary-of-the-Woods College, the oldest Catholic liberal arts college in the United States and also founded by Guerin, is now one of a few places in the country to offer a master's degree program in "earth literacy." (The program is directed by Sisters of Earth cofounder Mary Louise Dolan.) The Sisters of Providence also sponsor the White Violet Center for Eco-justice, one of the more active green sisters' earth ministries in North America. The center's programming for summer 2006 included a weeklong immersion program called "Earth Plunge for Women Religious." Program topics included "Sacramentality of Food," "Ethics of Eating," "The Universe Story," "The Cosmic Walk," and "The Vows in an Ecological Age."[21] In keeping with the example set by Saint Theodore Guerin (canonized as of October 15, 2006), the sisters continue to "break boundaries," abiding by a prophetic vision of hope and healing for the earth, even when that vision conflicts with some official sources of institutional authority. As throngs of devotees begin to arrive at the new saint's shrine, they may catch a glimpse of sacred agriculture being practiced, seasonal liturgies being observed, sustainability projects in process, and religious sisters who are consciously living their vows in an "ecological age."

In terms of Thomas Berry's (and consequently many green sisters') focus on the "Universe Story" or "epic of evolution" as the sacred unfolding of creation, it is also important to remember that the Vatican itself has come out with some very strong statements supporting the legitimacy of the science of the evolutionary process. When speaking to the Pontifical Academy of Sciences in 1996, for example, Pope John Paul II pronounced that "new scientific knowledge has led us to the conclusion that the theory of evolution is no longer a mere hypothesis."[22] More recently, in 2006, the director of the Vatican

Observatory, Father George V. Coyne, officially and very publicly criticized what he characterized as the kind of "crude creationism" put forth by proponents of intelligent design, which he warned only "diminishes God." Coyne further emphasized that "evolution is no longer a mere hypothesis" but is instead "a fundamental Church teaching."[23]

Despite recent alliances with Protestant Christian fundamentalists on issues such as abortion, euthanasia, and gay marriage, the Vatican clearly has parted ways with fundamentalists when it comes to the merits of evolutionary science. There are complex reasons for this position, to be sure, but one involves the Church's not wishing to get embarrassingly "left behind" scientifically (as it once was during the Copernican revolution). Another reason for the Church's strong support of evolutionary science is the sheer numbers of highly trained Catholic scientists (many of them religious brothers and sisters) teaching and conducting research at Catholic universities around the world. The loss of prestige to these academic institutions, not to mention the outcry from Catholic university scientists (again, many of them vowed religious) if the Vatican were to side with what is seen to be "junk science," would be formidable. The Vatican itself also employs a considerable number of scientific researchers who work on special projects for the Vatican, including Father Coyne of the Vatican observatory. Research in astronomy in particular has been of great interest to the Church, an area in which abounding evidence points to ours being a vast universe many billions of years older than fundamentalist creationism proponents acknowledge.

It is precisely this kind of astronomical scientific discovery that inspires Sister Gail Worcelo's mystical reflections on the universe. As she says, "The galaxy in which I pray is 100,000 light years wide. A single light year is equal to six trillion miles. Our nearest neighbor, the Andromeda Galaxy, is 2.3 million light years away. This takes some time to absorb. We are located in vastness, in the vast heart of God."[24] These are likely some of the same thoughts that Vatican astronomers themselves have had looking at the night sky through their high-powered telescopes. In this sense, the Vatican itself has embraced the "Universe Story," even if not Thomas Berry's particular take on it. Green sisters' wonderment and reverence for the sacredness of cosmic evolutionary process are likely shared by astronomers who report to the Holy See.

It has been quite interesting to me that when I have presented research material on green sisters in a variety of academic settings, it has always been conservative Protestants in the audience or around seminar tables who have voiced hostile reactions to various aspects of the green sisters movement. Conservative evangelical academics in at least two separate venues have quickly issued attack words such as "heresy," "pagan," and "New Age." By contrast, Catholic academics in these same settings have seemed to take information about the green sisters movement in stride, seemingly more comfortable with a wide spectrum of belief and practice. Although Catholic reactions within the academy have thus far been quite receptive and open to learning about the work of the green sisters, some sectors of the Catholic community are clearly perturbed by the growing links between religious sisters and earth spirituality. There are indeed Catholics who unmistakably side much more closely with sisters' Evangelical Christian critics.

"New Age" Name-Calling

In 1998, Michael Rose, editor of the now-defunct Catholic journal *St. Catherine's Review,* published a scathing report on that year's EarthSpirit Rising conference in Cincinnati. The conference is an environmental gathering that is cosponsored by a number of Catholic women's religious congregations in the Midwest. Rose warned his readers, "From exaggerated environmentalism emerges a kind of spirituality of the cosmos that desires to 'ensoul' the entire universe or to bestow on creation a magical force. The eco-fem [*sic*] movement rejects the Christian notion of a personal God, above creation and outside the history of time, in favor of an impersonal, divine force that is in everything and is everything. This return to naturalistic pantheism finds support in many religious movements coming from the East and in a return to pagan religions." Rose further sounded the alarm that the EarthSpirit Rising conference was confirmation of just how deeply "New Age ideas" had worked their way into the Church.[25] Publishing the names of every community of Catholic women religious that sponsored the event, Rose called for a flurry of protest letters from readers addressed to each of these communities and to each community's overseeing bishop.

What is somewhat ironic about "New Age" accusations such as Rose's is that green sisters themselves are no great defenders of the New Age. That is, they themselves tend to be critical of and eschew New Age things. As I mentioned earlier, some green sisters have shied away from certain astrological or alchemical aspects of the biodynamic farming approach specifically because they perceive these things to be New Age. When I asked green sisters why they had gravitated to a greater degree to the work of Thomas Berry and not to a figure such as Matthew Fox (who also deals with environmental issues from a spiritual perspective), the reasons were manifold and complicated but one prominent reason was that sisters perceived Matthew Fox to be associated with a kind of "New Age spirituality" and this connection made them uncomfortable. (In all fairness, several sisters passionately defended Fox's contributions and said that he had broken important ground for a lot of work being done today.)

Because of her higher visibility as a speaker and writer, Sister Miriam MacGillis seems to receive more New Age labeling than any other green sister. Again, ironically, MacGillis herself has been no friend to the New Age movement. Taking a dim view of the mercenary financial aspects she perceives in the New Age industry and its seeming preference for profit over service to others, MacGillis carefully warns her earth literacy students to be skeptical of New Age "gurus" and always to "watch their wallets." MacGillis, like other sisters I spoke with, was also wary, if not disturbed, by aspects of the New Age movement that she thinks promote a kind of "shallow" spirituality and a self-absorbed "me-ism" that prioritizes self-actualization and personal fulfillment over the needs of others, especially the needs of the poor and marginalized. Green Mountain Monastery Sister Bernadette Bostwick echoed these concerns and cautioned against a kind of power imbalance and "shallowness" that can result from superficially dabbling in others' traditions, rather than re-inhabiting one's own. "What some people don't realize is that you do not have to leave your tradition," she told me in an interview, "you just need to go deep enough into it, and most people just do not go deep enough."[26]

Particularly for green sisters, who have placed a renewed emphasis on living in community, living more ecologically sustainable lifestyles, and thus sharing resources, the degree of self-absorbed individualism they perceive within some New Age spiritualities proves incongruous with their religious training and service sensibilities. MacGillis speaks about how both New Age and neo-pagan spiritualities are too caught up with ego and fall prey to oversimplifications.[27] No doubt this is a point on which MacGillis and Carrie Tomko agree; in fact, MacGillis finds common ground with conservatives generally on this point. When asked about her thoughts on the New Age by *Creation Spirituality,* a magazine with a New-Age bent, MacGillis replied critically, "There's a lot of confusion and fear now, and many people who are in the 'New Age' are not in deep context . . . They are superficial, with quick fixes, a lot of individualism. This waves all kinds of flags to me. So I can't say that New Age people are on the good side and conservatives on the bad side. I see we're all groping for ways to break out of the world because it's not working."[28]

Part of the challenge that green sisters face, then, is the labeling of their movement as "New Age" by those wishing to close off dialogue and to inspire fears about nature worship. Sisters are not alone in struggling with this problem. The hostile use of New Age as an epithet against any kind of religiously based earth activism is a challenge that all mainline "greening" movements (Protestant, Catholic, Jewish, Muslim, and so on) are currently facing and struggling to neutralize. Part of the reason that the New Age is so quick to be associated with "greening" movements is because of the active roles that those holding noninstitutional and alternative spiritual commitments have historically played in the environmental movement. What makes it even trickier for Catholic environmentalists is that many of the "God in everything" philosophies often associated with the New Age found their way there through nineteenth-century founders of metaphysical movements, who were themselves enamored of and captivated by Catholic traditions of mysticism and sacramentalism.[29] This connection has in effect created a "chicken and egg" phenomenon that is difficult to sort out.

In his essay "Whither the New Age?" Gordon Melton speaks to the historical partnership between New Age philosophies and the environmental movement. "Early on," says Melton, "the New Agers made common cause with the older environmental movement. The mixing of New Age and traditional environmental ideas became especially easy after the Gaia Hypothesis, the concept that the earth is best understood as a single living organism."[30] He also addresses, however, the more recent use of the moniker "New Age" as a means of sabotage. In the 1960s, for example, New Age was used to describe those who were said to be "points of light," working to bring about the Aquarian Age—a period when the world would be transformed and birthed into a new, enlightened existence. The Findhorn community in Scotland, according to Melton, was one of the quintessentially New Age twentieth-century communities that sought to cultivate the energies of the incoming spiritually enlightened age. To achieve their goal, those at Findhorn "attuned themselves to the nature spirits" of their land and grew large vegetables that thrived despite rocky soil and harsh climatic conditions. Although the New Age was popularly characterized in the 1960s and 1970s by a distinct optimism and a desire to "heal the planet," Melton observes that, by the early 1990s, "fewer persons than previously would identify themselves as New Agers." By the late 1990s, the New Age had become largely a phantom movement, in which publications and conferences of New Age materials continued to thrive but were often publicized by less pejorative names, such as "whole life." For some in the movement, says Melton, these new names actually better described what they saw as a community of "transformed, spiritually awakened, compassionate, earth loving persons."[31]

As with other mainline religious "greening" movements, green sisters are grappling with the fact that the terms of the current debate over the "greening of faith" are firmly set against them. This quite successfully forces green reformers like the sisters into a defensive posture. Within the discourse of greening movements in religion, terms such as "nature worship," "paganism," and now "New Age" carry powerful and culturally embedded negative responses within biblically based religions. In subway terms, these epithets constitute the "third rail"—the track rail that is electrified to a high and dangerous voltage, the hot rail one must not touch. And yet movements to harmonize religions with themes, images, or patterns of nature almost immediately trigger the use of these terms. Green sisters are thus thrust into the distracting position of having to reassure and deny. Consequently, they rarely get to the point of actually contesting the terms of the debate in a way that would establish a broader cultural, historical, and political context for each of these terms, what they mean, and how they may or may not be relevant today. In the absence of widely circulated treatises such as Zayac's, questions posed to green sisters about "greener" worship and ecospiritual practices tend to be framed from a critical rather than metacritical standpoint. That is to say, challengers ask rhetorical questions such as, "But this is nature worship, isn't it?" rather than asking what it really means to worship nature and how an opposition between Christianity and earth-reverence or earth spirituality developed in the first place.

To the extent that sisters are able—through their earth ministries, their written work, and even their artwork—to shift the framework of these discussions away from a binary opposition between legitimate Christian worship and closeness to nature, they will likely change the tone of some of these exchanges. If they are unable to do so and their opponents are indeed successful in using the New Age label to discredit the movement as flaky, silly, superficial, or self-absorbed, the movement's efficacy may be seriously threatened. It is thus critical that sisters find ways to reframe discussions so that they are not so often placed on the defensive about these issues.

In order to shift the debate away from New Age name-calling, the sisters have instinctively tried to demonstrate systematically that they are historically rooted in traditions of the Church. They return again and again to their Catholic heritage, digging into the soil of their own "backyard" and recovering its "heirloom" seeds to replant and cultivate. Repeatedly, they assert ownership of Roman Catholic traditions and claim this realm as the living "bioregion" to which they are indigenous. This is likely a good strategy, not because such an approach will ever get anyone of Bill Jacobs's or Carrie Tomko's ilk to agree with them, but because it comes from the heart. If green sisters did not value and love the living traditions of the Church (even with their difficulties) and revel in their study, debate, and analysis, which they so clearly do, they would have "pulled up stakes" and "moved on to new ground" long ago. In the case of sisters such as Gail Worcelo and Maureen Wild, who professed final vows in the 1980s and 1990s, or of Elise D. García, who entered a novitiate in 2005, they may never have entered a religious community at all.

What will end the New Age name-calling? Perhaps overuse. If "New Age" is indiscriminately applied to everything that might be considered religiously suspect, then it will lose its power and cease to function as a meaningful descriptive term. Readers and other audiences may tune out this hackneyed epithet instead of heeding it. But this possibility applies equally to right-wing Catholic pundits and to green sisters' own use of that term to describe things that they fear and find most suspect. No matter which end of the political spectrum employs it, the New Age seems to be everybody's favorite whipping boy.

Sustainability of the Movement

The challenges the green sisters movement share with other mainline religious greening movements may not be a great source of solace, but they do further illustrate that collectively, green sisters are by no means a *vox clamantis in deserto* (a voice crying in the wilderness).[32] Cultural observers predicted in the 1970s with the advent of Earth Day that the trend toward the "greening of faith" would burn itself out quickly and simply go away.[33] More than thirty years later, the "greening" movement in religion has taken firm root and is continuing to shape ethics, spirituality, and religious action in ways once never imagined.[34] In the first decade of the twenty-first century, it has in fact become a vital and thriving movement. Unfortunately, one of the things that continue to fuel this movement is the presence of serious and persistent environmental problems. To the degree that green sisters' ministries and other religiously affiliated greening movements are successful, they will work themselves out of a job (and likely happily so). Until then, there is no shortage of grim environmental news—from global warming and ozone depletion to toxic oceans and rapid species extinction.

There are several dynamics present within the movement, cultivated either instinctively or strategically by the sisters, that bode well for its future. First, sisters have conserved rigor, albeit in the form of ecological lifestyle rigor, and have not been afraid to experiment with different combinations and ratios of orthodoxy and innovation. As discussed earlier, the fact that "it isn't easy being green" is actually a positive feature for the movement, because it imposes a kind of "costliness" that sociologists of religion have repeatedly found correlates with a greater appeal to new converts and to higher rates of commitment from existing members.[35]

Second, in living countercultural lifestyles, green sisters also live in a certain amount of tension vis-à-vis the dominant culture in North America. At the same time, green sisters live in a certain amount of tension vis-à-vis the institutional Church. Strangely enough, both loci of tension may be important factors that strengthen the green sisters movement. In new religious movements in general, maintaining discontinuities with the prevailing culture and espousing countercultural values often generate a kind of productive "creative tension" that energizes a religious movement and catalyzes its growth.[36] If tensions in these areas become too intense, as perhaps with a major punitive action taken by the hierarchy, it might tip the scales in the other direction and negatively affect the movement. But a major punitive action could also successfully unify and further invigorate the movement by generating greater feelings of solidarity—from other women religious and from friends and neighbors of diverse religious backgrounds—in response to apparent outside "persecution."[37]

Religious sisters are also in a very different "place" than they once were when many of the changes that accompanied the Second Vatican Council and the process of renewing religious life first arose. The reaction of Sister Joan Chittister's community to the conflict over her participation in the 2001 Women's Ordination Conference is an excellent illustration of this shift. Chittister's community overwhelmingly stood by her in her conflict with the hierarchy. The 127-to-one vote by her community was clearly not the action of infantilized religious women, cowering in the shadow of scary threats from Church patriarchs. Instead, sisters stood their ground, respectfully but firmly. Sisters have also learned a great deal in hindsight about power struggles with the hierarchy. A widely publicized incident in 1970, in which the Sisters of the

Immaculate Heart of Mary in Los Angeles and then Cardinal McIntyre entered into a conflict over the community's internally proposed "updating" of religious life, today might have had a very different outcome. One of the sisters' proposed updates included no longer wearing the habit, a practice that in less than ten years would become accepted and commonplace for the vast majority of Catholic religious sisters in the United States. But the cardinal, then already in his eighties, disallowed these changes, and the conflict ended with 315 of the 380 sisters asking to be released from their vows (at which point they reformed a lay organization called the Immaculate Heart Community). As happens so often in the history of Catholic women religious, it turned out that the Immaculate Heart Sisters were at the forefront of change and the Church would eventually catch up to them.

It is doubtful, however, that the sisters would have chosen the same course in today's climate. That is, instead of asking to be released from their vows and forming a lay community, the sisters may have simply ignored the bishop, teamed up with other women's congregations to continue to appeal his decision, found other ways to implement their changes despite the ruling, and so forth. In the struggle for the ability to define their own communities and for the freedom to pursue the callings they have discerned, sisters have become more practiced in what it means to deal with power and more savvy about how power itself works. Catholic writer Annie Milhaven summarizes this kind of education in power when she observes that power lies not in the control over property and judicial authority, but in "the cultural hegemony to define the meaning of community and its mission."[38] Mother Theodore Guerin and the Sisters of Providence knew this instinctively more than 150 years ago. Through sisters' own communities, organizations such as the Leadership Conference of Women Religious of the USA (LCWR), intercommunity collaborative ministries, and even Sisters of Earth conferences, religious sisters are now much more intensely networked to one another than they have been in the past. These growing webs of connections have generated a greater sense of solidarity and strength.

In the green sisters movement, there is also an important decentralized structural quality to these networks of resources and support that lends the movement a kind of greater "natural" resistance to outside interference. In a small-group discussion at the 1998 Sisters of Earth Conference, conference co-organizer Sister Mary Louise Dolan asked, "Is it time for rhizomes to rise?" Here Dolan employed philosophers Gilles Deleuze's and Félix Guattari's image of the rhizome as a metaphor for the growing network of environmentally active sisters. Deleuze and Guattari use the rhizome to theorize postmodern, nonhierarchical epistemologies, but environmentalists such as Dolores La Chapelle have expanded the rhizome model to apply to social movement and grassroots environmental activism.[39]

Because the root structure of the rhizome is diffuse and horizontal rather than central and vertical, the strength of rhizome networks is their tenaciousness. A section of the network can be removed, and the rhizome will simply send out new shoots and runners from unaffected areas to work around the disruption in the root structure. In fact, attacks on various sections of the rhizome only stimulate new growth and make it stronger. Unlike plants with one centralized root (like a tree), rhizomes are structurally less vulnerable to eradication efforts. Green sisters' networks operate along similar lines, reflecting a preference for decentralization, rotating facilitation of gatherings, having little governance structure, and relatively small, bioregionally based projects over central hierarchical leadership and organization. As these decentralized networks grow and expand, there is also a growing sense of "critical mass," "safety in numbers," and sisterhood that cuts across conventional boundaries. As I mentioned at the beginning of this book, when I began to study green sisters' ecological learning centers back in 1995, I was able to identify only about a dozen. Now, in 2006, I am able to document at least fifty such centers and related ministries, and I am well aware that my list is not complete. (See "Critical Mass," pages 289–292.) If green sisters have garnered notice from critics, it is because they are much more visible now that the movement itself has become more mainstream.

Another factor working in favor of the movement's long-term sustainability is the green sisters' main concern—nature and the environment. As discussed earlier, environmental issues hold special import for members of what demographers are now calling Generation Green, the growing cohort of teenagers and twentysomethings who are eagerly dedicating themselves to environmental causes.[40] This demographic has already led to an infusion of energy from young laypeople who are lending their energy to sisters' ministries. This surge in energy and interest can especially be seen during community "work days" at the Green Mountain Monastery, when young "companions" to the sisters help the sisters build things like yurts (low-cost sustainable housing modeled after Mongolian structures) and ecofriendly outhouses, and work to maintain the monastery property. Whether and to what degree Generation Green energy and enthusiasm will translate into a new, younger cohort of sisters remains to be seen. But for at least the next two decades, age and vitality are not a pressing problem for the movement, because it has already attracted educators, organizers, and facilitators who are in their forties and fifties. With a number of decades ahead of them in which they are able to do "heavy lifting," these are for the most part extremely productive years in sisters' lives. Additionally, with the healthy active lifestyle, intellectual engagement, and rich prayer life fostered by the movement's culture, green sisters in their sixties, seventies, and even eighties continue to be productive in earth ministries.

To a certain extent, I suspect that the success or failure of the Green Mountain Monastery in Vermont to attract new vocations into the movement will be a harbinger of how this movement will affect the revitalization and reinvention of Catholic religious life in the twenty-first century. But another kind of objective merits evaluation: whether the green sisters movement achieves its larger goal of ecological sustainability in human intraplanetary relations. Sociologist of religion Meredith McGuire observes, "Historically, religion has been one of the most important motivations for change because of its particular effectiveness in uniting people's beliefs with their actions, their ideas with their social lives."[41] As sisters model sustainable living within their neighborhoods and bioregions, how much of their ecological consciousness will cross over into the community networks they have built? After all, sisters' ecological learning centers cater to people of all backgrounds, and one need not be a Catholic sister to "keep organic," to practice "mindful driving," or to engage in "sacred agriculture."

Already, schools, summer camps, service projects, bioregional conservation corps, and of course seed-saving networks have grown up alongside green sister's ecological centers. In both rural communities and in the inner city, green sisters' ministries have become centers of learning and culture and are providing loci for community revitalization efforts. Sisters are feeding the poor and homeless, helping to defend minority populations in the city from ecoracism, helping their neighboring family farmers in rural communities keep their farms, providing low-income families with sources of reasonably priced fresh healthy food, and providing community gatherings, book discussion groups, natural foods cooking classes, straw-bale construction workshops, permaculture intensive instruction, and women's support groups. They are helping their surrounding communities to resist the incursion of garbage incinerators, cell phone towers, unrestricted development (sprawl), and mega chain stores that drive out local businesses. Bioregion by bioregion, green sisters in apostolic communities and monastic communities alike are bringing their "good news" of peaceable relations between humans and earth to individuals and families of many different faiths. (This is largely why simply celebrating Christmas or Easter or even Rogation Days as communal festivals would not include all of the diverse coalitions of friends and neighbors that sisters have built over time.)[42] With few exceptions, they have built strong grassroots bonds with immediate and extended neighbors, and this may be another predictor of long-term success for the movement. Amid corruption scandals that have rocked the Church in recent years and spurred cynicism about the integrity of the institution, sisters have instead, on a grassroots level, functioned as goodwill ambassadors of a sort for the faith—accessible, generous, dedicated to serving others, nonauthoritarian, and willing to roll up their sleeves and get their hands dirty, literally. This kind of goodwill, carefully tended and nurtured, makes the movement much more difficult to target. Recognition of sisters' embeddedness in their local communities and the strong alliances they have formed may further encourage the Church to take a hands-off approach to the movement. With the many public relations problems related to scandal and abuse currently occupying a significant portion of the Church's time, personnel, and financial resources, authorities might find it expedient to leave community-building organic-farming nuns alone.

Strategies for Dealing with Conflict

One of the questions I asked of sisters in electronic interviews was how they have responded to hostile reactions to their ecological beliefs and practices. Sisters' overlapping responses suggested eight common strategies for dealing with these sorts of situations:

1. Practice Humility—"You don't know it all."
2. Be Patient—"Everyone's in a different place."
3. Instead of making a statement, use the form of a question—"I wonder what Jesus might think of how we are treating the earth?"
4. Empathize—"This is hard, isn't it?"
5. Do not preach, do not judge.
6. Invite an outsider in to speak—"You are never a prophet in your own land."
7. Tie your comments into something everyone is already comfortable with, such as the community's charism.
8. Be not afraid.

Sister of Charity Maureen Wild offered the most comprehensive response:

Listen deeply to what the person is saying. Affirm aspects of what you recognize to be truth in what they say. Do not meet a negative or hostile response with negativity, hostility or defensiveness. Be positive in your tone. Deflect or disarm the negativity. Be humble, and acknowledge your own limitations, if needed. Make sure to stand strong in the consciousness of what is best for the common good of Earth (i.e., avoid slipping into a human-centered response). This can be done by asking a question rather than giving a command statement . . . Know your material. Be confident. Be creative with diverse forms of presentation (visuals, words, music, experiences, etc.). Engage their participation. Be interesting. Be profound. Be poetic. Be humorous. Be challenging. Ask questions. Connect things with your personal story. Invite listeners to reflect on their story or relatedness to earth/cosmos. Invite them to think about how we've been culturally conditioned by dysfunctional worldviews of our time. Relate implications of the story to religious life . . . the charism of the congregation, the vows, the virtues of Christian life, the golden rule, archetypal themes of exodus and exile. Be up front about how you see God's presence in this new understanding . . . and reflect on the meaning of Jesus in light of this context. Connect something of your presentation to familiar Gospel stories that carry some interesting parallel or connection to these new understandings.

Sister Gail Worcelo of the Green Mountain Monastery is one who has found it helpful to bring in outside speakers. She says, "I would suggest invit[ing] a sister from another community in to do [a talk] . . . it seems to work better. A prophet is not accepted in her own native place!" She adds, "It has worked best to go easy, to not preach, judge, [or] criticize. It has also gone well for me to stand firm, keep the focus, stay consistent, move ahead, and not be afraid."[43]

Sister Mary Southard urged "empathy," providing the following example statement: "This is hard isn't it? It changes so much of the way we thought things were."[44] She, like Maureen Wild, stressed the efficacy of asking questions rather than making rigid pronouncements. Sisters Kathleen Sherman and Marilyn Rudy both advised tying ecological subject matter into a community's own charism. They echoed Maureen Wild's suggestion to begin with something with which the audience is already comfortable and familiar. "In our spirituality as Sisters of St. Joseph," says Sherman, "we talk about uniting neighbor with neighbor, and neighbor with God. 'Neighbor' for me means all of creation."[45] Rudy similarly says, "We try to respond to the 'Dear Neighbor' and what could be better than our earth and all of creation as our 'dear neighbor?'"[46] The overall message that sisters seemed to convey was that when attacked, they should be patient, listen, empathize, but stand firm and root what they are saying in something that is already foundational.

The overall tone of sisters' responses clearly communicates tactics of negotiation, mediation, de-escalation, and other nonviolent forms of communication. Upon further reflection, I suspect that this dynamic, which one sister humorously referred to as "the old nun-jitsu" (gracefully using the force of an attacker's own strength in order to disarm him or her) will serve green sisters well in the long run, in terms of both fostering positive relations within their own communities and being able to continue their work without hierarchical interference.

It is also worth noting that nothing in any of the sisters' responses could be characterized as "strident," "brazen," "shrill," or any of the other common epithets historically used to vilify and effectively silence women who are advocating social or institutional transformation. Green sisters stand firm in their convictions and clearly are not pushovers, but neither do they show disrespect toward the institutional Church or project an in-your-face attitude. Repeatedly, they call for humility in the event of conflict and stress the importance of listening and remaining open and receptive to other points of view. Respectfully but nimbly finding a path between authority of institution and authority of conscience, the sisters, row by row and community by community, simply continue their work of planting "seeds of change."

Persistence and Prophetic Work

No matter the external and internal challenges faced by the movement, green sisters continue to be highly motivated to persevere with their work of tending and healing the planet. Much of this motivation comes from the prophetic dimensions sisters identify in this work. Green sisters are not simply pulled by the vision of helping to midwife humanity into an Ecozoic era of peaceable planetary relations, but also recognize this task as the "Great Work" of their time. Their theorizing and implementation of the Great Work is drawn, not surprisingly, from the writings of Thomas Berry. Berry contends that "history is governed by those overarching movements that give shape and meaning to life by relating the human venture to the larger destinies of the universe. Creating such a movement might be called the Great Work of a people . . . The Great Work now, as we move into a new millennium, is to carry out the transition from a period of human devastation of the Earth to a period when humans would be present to the planet in a mutually beneficial manner."[47] Contributing to the Great Work, then, is a fundamentally "catholic" or universal mission that is larger than any one church, religion, country, or region of the world. It is also a sacred mission to which all people are called, as the sisters stress to their friends and neighbors.

Inspired by this vision, many green sisters have now dedicated their lives to helping to bring about this kind of ecologically positive planetary transformation. In some cases, this has meant sacrificing jobs and comfortable living arrangements to take on primitive living conditions while restoring ecosystems, organically homesteading farms, and building ecological learning centers. In other cases, it has meant serving time in prison for direct protest actions. For urban green sisters, it has meant moving into what are sometimes essentially war zones and working alongside neighbors to provide both "bread and roses" to a wounded community. No matter what the sacrifices or challenges, green sisters stand their ground and remain committed to doing their share of the Great Work.

Dominican sister Sharon Zayac explains that she will continue her work no matter what the challenges because "It is the right thing to do. It makes the ultimate sense to me. It is the first time in my religious life that I feel I am making a significant contribution. I feel connected."[48] Sister of Mercy Corlita Bonnarens communicates a similar sense of feeling renewed and energized to continue her work on behalf of the earth. She writes, "It feels right and harmonious, organic and spiritually connecting. It makes sense to me to do things that are 'natural'—of nature . . . I get nourished when I am in natural surroundings that reflect the beauty and intimacy of life and the Creator, and I get inspired to create, and tend to Earth issues."[49]

Sisters repeatedly articulated the experience of being "spiritually fed" or "spiritually nourished" by this work instead of feeling drained or exhausted, as is the case with many activist efforts. This nourishing dynamic, if it can be sustained, suggests a greater sustainability in the long run for the green sisters movement. Discipline, hard work, and sacrifice are hardly new challenges for sisters, who instead of viewing these things as liabilities, are trained to regard them as opportunities for spiritual growth. As Dominican sister Ardeth Platte remarked after her release from three years in prison for symbolically sabotaging a nuclear missile silo, "Each moment in prison was a precious gift that I cherished. Each moment was an opportunity to serve and minister to the women there."[50]

Green Mountain Monastery sister Gail Worcelo envisions far more difficult times ahead for the planet but has faith in the human capacity to meet the challenges ahead. She says, "In seed language—We are the inner germ life. Our times are the hard shell through which we must pass."[51] Sister of St. Joseph Mary Louise Dolan also uses the metaphor of seeds when contemplating the "Great Work" and possibilities for cultural change. She writes, "We are, I would suggest, seed and earth for seed. We are seed, we are seeded, we are sowers. We constantly constellate new enfleshments, new faces of creation by giving expression to all that has been sown in us. We cast the seeds of these enfleshments about us as we live life."[52] Like Dolan, Franciscan sister Betty Daugherty has found unmistakable "seeds of hope" as she has watched the movement grow over time: "I am encouraged because so many women religious are leading in this area. The issue of our relationship with nature and the issue of just treatment of women and the poor are so closely related."[53]

Dominican sister Carol Coston uses yet another organic metaphor to speak of her hopes for the future and her faith in the human capacity for transformation. She takes Berry's vision of what is entailed in the future of the "Great Work" and puts it into very "earthy" and accessible language:

> In gardening terms, the eggplant is a heavy feeder—that is, it takes so many nutrients from the soil, that, after it is harvested, additional phosphorous and potash must be returned . . . In economic terms, it appears that we in the United States have a long history of being eggplants: relying on the resources of poorer countries to keep us supplied with our own nutrients, and often depleting the ecological foundation as a result. I believe we would go far toward sustaining a "healthy web of life" and creating alternative economic systems if, instead of being global eggplants, we acted more like earthworms. As global earthworms, we would embody a key principle of organic gardening: We would be conscious, in all our activities, personal and institutional, of giving back to the earth as much [as], or more than, we took from it.[54]

As both planetary and Catholic "earthworms," green sisters seek to loosen, aerate, and enrich the very soil that has nourished them and given rise to their being.

"Renaturing" the Category of Religion

Earthworms, eggplants, seeds, rhizomes, gardens, bioregions, ecosystems? With such a rich collection of organic metaphors employed in the movement, my work with the green sisters left me no choice but to reexamine the category of religion and its traditional conceptions. Social anthropologist Anna S. King has said, "The institutionalized understanding of religion has led many Western academics to sterile conclusions about the function and role of religion within society."[55] The fecund ecology of green sisters has led me in the opposite direction, and I believe that insights from the green sisters movement can assist the field of religious studies with the ongoing "renaturing" of the category of religion, much in the way that Eugene Rochberg-Halton and others contributed to the "renaturing" of the category of culture within the humanities and social sciences.

Indeed, the understanding and approach to religion and culture have undergone similar revivification processes. In the mid-1980s, Rochberg-Halton wrote in *Meaning and Modernity* that "to say that culture *lives* is anathema to most contemporary social theory . . . To even suggest that 'culture' lives would mean to some, such as Marshall Sahlins, Anthony Giddens, Jürgen Habermas, Claude Lévi-Strauss, and Umberto Eco, a basic confusion of the culture category with the nature category, a kind of naïve naturalism that would put one in the camp of sociobiologists, those latest avatars of capitalistic social Darwinism."[56] Rochberg-Halton alludes to the historical shifts in conceptions of culture prior to and after the seventeenth century that Raymond Williams had documented.[57] Williams had noted that, prior to the seventeenth century, "culture" had "meant, primarily, the 'tending of natural growth,' and then, by analogy, a process of human training. But this latter use, which had usually been a culture *of* something, was changed, in the nineteenth century, to *culture* as such, a thing in itself."[58] In becoming denatured, argues Rochberg-Halton, culture "became divested in common usage of its quality of human practice in favor of a status label or thing."[59] In renaturing the category of culture, Rochberg-Halton reconceives of culture as itself a process of cultivation.

In the study of religion, scholars have faced similar obstacles upon encountering inherited categories of religion that have divested religion of its organic qualities and generated falsely static, reified concepts. The academic study of religion has been, and still remains to some degree, bound to a lingering framework of doctrinal orthodoxy, institutional focus, and singularity of religious expression. Within this framework, religion was not supposed to take on organic or protean qualities because it was supposed to be revealed. Timothy Fitzgerald thus argues that the idea of studying religion and religions, in effect, "imports a theological agenda into what represents itself (with some justice) as a non-theological academic humanistic inquiry."[60] Much like static conceptions of culture, religion has thus been characterized as: (1) something separate from everyday life, (2) something fragile that can be "lost" or can "vanish," (3) something separate that must be guarded or preserved, and (4) something extraordinary that is to be placed in special institutions (churches, museums, libraries, and so on).[61]

By contrast, scholarship that presumes religion to be preeminently organic sees religious people as active, creative, and embodied meaning-makers, symbol users, storytellers, and dynamic shapers and reshapers of culture. Beginning with an approach to religion as an organic system spurs the researcher to look for religion embedded in stories, everyday practices, foodways, material culture, common sense, humor, practical ways of life, and so forth, in addition to examining specialized knowledge, ideas, beliefs, and, yes, central institutions. Research into the more neglected of these areas demonstrates that religion by nature is a realm of constant change and redefinition, whereby transformation, exchange, combination, and creativity are not anomalous but simply the way things operate.

To the project of renaturing religion as a living category, Rochberg-Halton once again lends assistance. In theorizing "culture as cultivation," he draws on nineteenth-century logician and philosopher Charles Sanders Peirce's notion of religion as something not made up of fixed, a priori concepts, but as "living and open to change."[62] In "The Fixation of Belief," Peirce argues that it is absurd to say religion is mere belief, saying, "You might as well call society a belief, or politics a belief, or civilization a belief. Religion is a life and can be identified with belief provided that belief be a living belief—a thing to be lived rather than said or thought."[63] In Peirce's pragmatism, then, there is a concern for the practicalities of what is actually lived as well as a conception of religion as something that grows and changes with time.

More recently, scholars of religion have taken a definite turn toward conceptions of religion that presume its organic qualities.[64] The increasing interest in religious ethnography has fueled much of this turn since, as Peggy Becker and Nancy Eisland point out, ethnography's focus on religion as it is actually lived makes scholars "aware of the inadequacy of our most frequently used theoretical categories."[65] Drawing from his own field work experiences, Fitzgerald further drives home the point that religious studies has "institutionalized 'religion' in a way which does not reflect the actual research that many of us are doing."[66] Even historians have begun to tap into the constructive theoretical benefits of conducting ethnographic research, as this book shows. American religious historian Catherine L. Albanese pronounced in reviewing Robert Orsi's ethnographic history *Thank You, St. Jude,* that "in Orsi's case and in the cases of many of the other emerging projects, we are looking at a new way of doing religious history."[67]

In my endeavor to identify, articulate, and elucidate the dynamics and relationships at work in the ecology of the green sisters movement, I have used organic metaphors in part because they fit my subject matter so well. As permaculturalists advise, I have done my best to "work with the landscape." As I became more practiced at doing this, it led me to different ways of looking at religion altogether. I began to regard religions themselves as "bioregions" of sorts. As bioregionalist philosophers Peter Berg and Raymond Dasmann write, "The realities of a bioregion are obvious in a gross sense. Nobody would confuse the Mojave desert with the fertile valley of Central California . . . But there are many intergradations. The chaparral-covered foothills of Southern California are not markedly distinct from those of the coast ranges of Northern California. But the attitudes of people and the centers to which they relate (San Francisco versus Los Angeles) are different, and these [differences] can lead to different approaches to living on the land."[68] So then clearly Catholicism is not Buddhism and Buddhism is not Judaism, and one "region" may define itself in relation to one center or another, but in actual practice, there are many "intergradations." Because Berg and Dasmann identify bioregions as both geographic terrains and "terrains of consciousness," they point out that the boundaries of any given bioregion cannot be clearly mapped—because their perceived boundaries depend largely on the attitudes of those actually living in place. As green sisters define and redefine the boundaries of Catholicism, environmental thought and practice, and their intergradations, they demonstrate Berg's and Dasmann's point that bioregions and their edges continually shift over time as the bioregion's own inhabitants change to reflect new environmental and climatic conditions.

"A Feeling for the Organism"

The importance of the organic model extends to a final observation I would like to make about ethnographic relationships. In the fall of 2005, I was participating in a workshop of religion scholars at a university in the Midwest, and after I presented a section of this book a colleague commented, "Clearly, you like these nuns. How do you deal with that?" Yes, I do like them, and I feel for and greatly respect colleagues who spend years of their lives studying groups of "skinheads," neo-Nazis, or other groups with which it might be very emotionally difficult and draining to spend a lot of time. I was fortunate to have found a research project in which I truly enjoyed spending time getting to know the people involved.

What I think my workshop colleague was getting at in his comment about "liking the nuns" was the possibility of my having, as ethnographers say, "gone native." I have thought quite a bit about this expression—"going native"—especially within a cultural context in which "becoming native to place" and "embedding oneself in the landscape" are not simply ideal goals but ethical imperatives. "Becoming native to place" is the antithesis of a kind of superficial tourism in which one merely extracts resources from a particular area and moves on. So yes, much as a naturalist would, I have tried to learn the bioregion not from afar but by being in relationship to it, situating myself within its life community as one of its living members.

Nonetheless, I would never presume to be "native" to the world of green sisters, an extremely rigorous world of total life commitment that I have neither chosen nor earned. Because of my different social location and life commitments, I will never be native, and I respect those boundaries. First and foremost, I have not made the vows or intense sacrifices sisters have, and those are experiences that I cannot know. In contemplating the vast difference between my experiences and green sisters' experiences, I recall iconographer and Green Mountain Monastery sister Bernadette Bostwick's powerful and yet simple prayer, "Thy will, not my will."[69] That kind of total trust and release of oneself into the Divine is something to which green sisters have made a life-long commitment—one that is renewed each day. These are not commitments that I have been so fearless as to make, and again I do not claim to have "insider" knowledge of them.

I am similarly moved by Sister Gail Worcelo's fearlessness and passion when she talks about taking the parable of the mustard seed to heart. She says that to do so "is to throw into the fire all the fears and desires of the false self and to abandon all safeties and securities except those rooted in God. If millions of humans were willing to make such a leap into authentic love then the forces destroying the earth and causing untold suffering for billions of beings would be reversed . . . Here at the Green Mountain Monastery we take this possibility for profound transformation seriously. We give ourselves to the Fire of Love blazing at the heart of the universe so that we can be changed into it and the world can partake more and more in its Truth."[70] I reread this passage by Worcelo just after I had returned from shopping for a child safety seat for my car and could not help but wonder, "How can I throw all fears and desires of the false self into the fire" when I am this anxious about picking out the right car seat? Simply the process of giving birth and becoming a new parent in the course of this project has impressed on me the kind of extraordinary time and degree of service commitment to the planet that sisters exercise in fulfilling their vocation and again how different this is from my own life. The kind of intense time commitment and energy sisters put into earth ministry and direct environmental work is just not possible for women who are raising children (or at least is not possible for this woman raising a child). When Sister of Loretto Elaine Prevallet speaks of sisters' channeling their reproductive energies toward healing the planet, which they then offer as a gift to the life community, my own journey into motherhood has driven home what a generous gift this truly is.[71] Although my life experiences and those of sisters are quite different, we continue to be a part of one another's worlds, and I, like other people in lay communities that surround sisters, have a deep respect and affection for them.

I do not regard the close relationships I have built over time with sisters as being in any way detrimental to the research I have conducted. On the contrary, they have been essential to my being able to develop ways of seeing and understanding the green sisters' world that would otherwise have been off-limits to me. In her biography of biologist Barbara McClintock, Evelyn Fox Keller asks what it is in a scientist's relationship to nature that facilitates the kind of "seeing" that eventually leads to productive discourse. She answers, "Over and over, [Barbara McClintock] tells us one must have the time to look, the patience to 'hear what the material has to say to you,' the openness to 'let it come to you.' Above all, one must have 'a feeling for the organism.'" Keller concludes, "Good science cannot proceed without a deep emotional investment on the part of the scientist. It is that emotional investment that provides the motivating force for the endless hours of intense, often grueling, labor." Not only does it provide motivation, but Keller adds that there are real benefits to the scholarship as well. "For all of us," she says, "it is the need and interest above all that induce the growth of our abilities; a motivated observer develops faculties that a casual spectator may never be aware of."[72]

I am by no means a scientist, but Keller's words resonate deeply with me and speak to my own ethnographic experiences with green sisters. Similarly, my feeling for the "organisms" who are green sisters has provided a compelling and motivating force for me to do this work. The use of "organism" here in the biological context is especially apt for me, since it stresses the living and changing quality of my research. This quality, more than anything, has also made it extremely difficult to choose an arbitrary place to stop and actually publish the results. Clearly, every day the story continues to unfold as green sisters live their lives. I find myself wanting to borrow and apply Sister Miriam MacGillis's caveat about the mutability of narrative to my own work: "But it cannot be freeze-dried!" As a scholar and researcher of those whose lives will continue to unfold and develop, I am acutely aware that even as I publish this book, the ecology of the green sisters movement is adapting to the introduction of new phenomena and to perpetual changes in environmental conditions within each of the sisters' bioregions. As I have shared this manuscript with sisters and asked for their comments, they have expressed their frustration with the necessary limitations of the genre, pointedly reminding me that, as one sister put it, "We continue to *evolve*." Perhaps, then, the best way to conclude this book is not with an ending per se but with a kind of "bell of mindfulness," that audible cue in monastic life that signals a transition or calling to a new hour and new area of attentive focus. One of Sister Gail Worcelo's morning meditations at the Green Mountain Monastery assists with just such a transition.

> The bell rings as the first glimmer of dawn appears in the morning sky. The hour of prayer is over. I blow out the prayer candle, extinguishing the flame. Yet I know full well that the Fire within the fire of all things still burns in every creature, galaxy and star and in every person who hungers for the Holy.[73]

CRITICAL MASS: EARTH MINISTRIES IN THE UNITED STATES AND CANADA

The following is a list of ecological learning centers, ecospiritual retreat centers, organic farms with community supported agriculture groups (CSAs), and other earth ministries run by green sisters in the United States and Canada.

Advocates for the Earth
Sisters of St. Martha of Prince Edward
    Island
Charlottetown, Prince Edward Island,
    Canada

Allium Center/The Well
Sisters of St. Joseph of LaGrange
LaGrange Park, Illinois

Canticle Farm
(organic CSA)
Franciscan Sisters of Allegany
Allegany, New York

Cecilian Center for Earth, Arts, and Spirit
Sisters of St. Joseph
Philadelphia, Pennsylvania

Center for Earth Spirituality and Rural
    Ministry
School Sisters of Notre Dame
Mankato, Minnesota

Clare's Well, a Women's Spirituality Farm
Franciscan Sisters of Little Falls,
    Minnesota
Annandale, Minnesota

Crown Point Ecology Center
Sisters of St. Dominic of Akron
Bath, Ohio

Crystal Spring Earth Learning Center
Dominican Sisters of Kentucky
Plainville, Massachusetts

Earth Harmony
Joint project of a Sister of St. Joseph of
    Carondelet and a Sister of the Sacred
    Heart of Mary
Sherman Oaks, California

Earth Home Ministries
Sisters of the Immaculate Heart of Mary
    and Sisters of Notre Dame de Namur
Oakland, California

EarthLinks
Loretto Community and Dominican
    Sisters of Hope
Denver, Colorado

Earth Partners
Working Group of the Sisters of St. Joseph
    Justice Commission
St. Paul, Minnesota

Earth Rise Farm
(organic CSA)
Sisters of Notre Dame
Louisberg, Minnesota

Ecology Committee and Garden Project
Dominican Sisters Congregation of the
    Sacred Heart
Houston, Texas

EverGreen
Sisters of the Humility of Mary
Villa Maria, Pennsylvania

Franciscan Earth Literacy Center
Sisters of St. Francis
Tiffin, Ohio

Franklin Farm
Sisters of Holy Cross
Manchester, New Hampshire

Genesis Farm
(organic CSA and earth literacy center)
Dominican Sisters of Caldwell, New Jersey
Blairstown, New Jersey

Glenairley Centre for Earth and Spirit
Joint project of the Sisters of St. Ann and
    the Sisters of Charity of Halifax
Sooke, British Columbia, Canada

Heartland Farm and Spirituality Center
Dominican Sisters of Great Bend, Kansas
Pawnee Rock, Kansas

Heirloom Seed Sanctuary
Sisters of Providence of St. Vincent de
    Paul at Heathfield
Kingston, Ontario, Canada

Hope Takes Root
Sisters, Servants of the Immaculate Heart
    of Mary
Detroit, Michigan

Jubilee Farm Ecology Learning Center
Dominican Sisters of Springfield
Springfield, Illinois

Living Water Spiritual Center
Sisters of St. Joseph of Lyon
Winslow, Maine

Loretto Earth Network
Loretto Community
St. Louis, Missouri

Mercy Earth Harmony Network
Sisters of Mercy of the Americas
Silver Spring, Maryland

Mercy Ecology Institute
Sisters of Mercy
Madison, Connecticut

Michaela Farm
Sisters of St. Francis
Oldenburg, Indiana

Nazareth Farm and Nazareth Center for
    Eco-Spirituality
Sisters of St. Joseph of Nazareth
Nazareth, Michigan

Passion of the Earth at Spirit Center
Benedictine Monastery of St. Gertrude
Cottonwood, Idaho

Prairiewoods
(Franciscan spirituality/ecology center)
Franciscan Sisters of Perpetual Adoration
Hiawatha, Iowa

Presentation Center
(straw-bale green welcome center)
Presentation Sisters of the Blessed Virgin
   Mary
Los Gatos, California

Providence Farm
(organic farm and horticultural therapy
   center)
Sisters of St. Ann, St. Joseph's Province
Duncan, British Columbia, Canada

Sacred Earth and Space Plowshares II
(direct action earth ministry)
Adrian Dominican Sisters
Baltimore, Maryland

Santa Sabina Center
Dominican Sisters
San Rafael, California

Santuario Sisterfarm
Adrian Dominican Sisters
Boerne, Texas

SEED (Sharing Earth's Ecological Design)
Sisters of St. Joseph of Springfield
Springfield, Massachusetts

Shepherd's Corner—Eco-Justice/
   Spirituality Center
Dominican Sisters of St. Mary of the
   Springs
Blacklick, Ohio

Sinsinawa Mound Ecospirituality Retreat
   and Conference Center
Sinsinawa Dominican Sisters
Sinsinawa, Wisconsin

Sisters Hill Farm
(organic CSA)
Sisters of Charity of New York
Stanfordville, New York

Sisters of the Green Mountain Monastery
(Ecozoic monastery and Thomas Berry
   sanctuary)
Greensboro, Vermont

Sisters, Servants of the Immaculate Heart
   of Mary
(ecorenovated motherhouse, organic
   farm, and ecovillage project)
Monroe, Michigan

Sophia Garden and Learning Center
(organic CSA)
Sisters of St. Dominic
Amityville, New York

Springbank Center for Eco-Spirituality
   and the Arts
Dominican and Franciscan Sisters
Kingstree, South Carolina

St. Catherine Farm and Dominican Earth
   Education Center
Dominican Sisters of St. Catherine
St. Catherine, Kentucky

St. Joseph Woods Earth Spirituality, Earth
   Care, and Eco-Justice Center
Sisters of St. Joseph of Carondelet
St. Louis Province
Ferguson, Missouri

Tierra Madre Sustainable Community
Sisters of Charity of Cincinnati, Ohio
Sunland Park, New Mexico

Waterspirit at Stella Maris Retreat Center
Sisters of St. Joseph of Peace
Elberon, New Jersey

White Violet Center for Ecojustice
Sisters of Providence at Saint Mary-of-
   the-Woods
Saint Mary-of-the-Woods, Indiana

The Woodlands Retreat and Learning
   Center
Sisters of St. Francis of Assisi
Osseo, Wisconsin

NOTES

Preface

1. There are those who have used the moniker "Sisters of Earth" to denote green sisters in general, but this has created confusion because those who are members of a particular network of green sisters called Sisters of Earth identify themselves that way. In other words, whereas Sisters of Earth are green sisters, not all green sisters are Sisters of Earth. I provide further explanation and background for this terminology in Chapter 1.

2. Linda Archibald and Mary Crnkovich, "Intimate Outsiders: Feminist Research in a Cross-Cultural Environment," in Sandra Burt and Lorraine Code, *Changing Methods: Feminists Transforming Practice* (Peterborough, Ont.: Broadview, 1995), 105–126.

3. Margaret Mies, "Women's Research or Feminist Research? The Debate Surrounding Feminist Science and Methodology," in Mary Margaret Fonow and Judith Cook, eds., *Beyond Methodology: Feminist Scholarship as Lived Research* (Bloomington: University of Indiana Press, 1991), 60–84; Sherna Gluck, "What's So Special about Women? Women's Oral History," in David Dunaway and Willa Baum, eds., *Oral History: An Interdisciplinary Anthology* (London: AltaMira Press, 1996), 215–230; Sherna Gluck and Daphne Patai, eds., *Women's Words: The Feminist Practice of Oral History* (New York: Routledge, 1991).

4. The Loretto Earth Network, for instance, has published a series of books featuring presentations on environmental issues at conferences sponsored by the Loretto Community. See, for example, Elaine Prevallet, *In the Service of Life: Widening and Deepening Religious Commitment* (Nerinx, Ky.: Sisters of Loretto, 2002); Ivone Gebara, *Sacred Universe, Sacred Passion* (Nerinx, Ky.: Sisters of Loretto, 2001). Santuario Sisterfarm in Boerne, Texas, has also established a new and independent publishing house called Sor Juana Press, which publishes works by women authors, especially women of color, on earth-related issues. Sor Juana Inez de la Cruz was a seventeenth-century Mexican-born poet who is sometimes referred to as the "Mexican Hildegard of Bingen" because she is considered to have been a brilliant and creative thinker unrecognized during her lifetime. More recently, she has been rediscovered and celebrated, especially by feminist cultural and literary scholars. See Stephanie Merrim, *Feminist Perspectives on Sor Juana Ines de la Cruz* (Detroit: Wayne State University Press, 1991). Such reclaimed figures in Catholic women's religious history play an important role in the consciousness of today's religious sisters.

5. Danièle Hervieu-Lèger, "'What Scripture Tells Me': Spontaneity and Regulation

within the Catholic Charismatic Renewal," in David Hall, ed., *Lived Religion in America: Toward a History of Practice* (Princeton, N.J.: Princeton University Press, 1997), 22.

6. For further discussion of the shift to a more praxis-oriented research, see Robert Orsi, "Everyday Miracles: The Study of Lived Religion," in Hall, *Lived Religion*, 8.

7. Ann Braude, "Women's Religious History Is American Religious History," in Thomas Tweed, ed., *Retelling U.S. Religious History* (Berkeley: University of California Press, 1997), 87–107; Sarah McFarland Taylor, "From the Left Hand to the Right: Moving Women and Religion to the Radical Center," *Epoche* 21, no. 1 (Fall 1998): 25–30.

8. Robert Orsi, *Thank You, St. Jude* (New Haven: Yale University Press, 1996), xv. The saying about African women and water is an anthropological take on the aphorism "All Indians walk in single file, at least the one I saw did."

9. John Comaroff and Jean Comaroff, *Ethnography and the Historical Imagination* (San Francisco: Westview, 1992), 20.

10. Ibid., xi, 9.

11. For further discussion on ethnographic subjectivity, see James Clifford, "Introduction: Partial Truths," in James Clifford and George E. Marcus, eds., *Writing Culture: The Poetics and Politics of Ethnography* (Berkeley: University of California Press, 1986), 1–26; Carol Stack, "Writing Ethnography: Feminist Critical Practice," *Frontiers* 13, no. 3 (1993): 80; Judith Stacey, "Can There Be a Feminist Ethnography?" *Women's Studies International Forum* 11, no. 23 (1988): 21–27; Michael Jackson, *Minima Ethnographica: Intersubjectivity and the Anthropological Project* (Chicago: University of Chicago Press, 1998); Michaela di Leonardo, *Exotics at Home: Anthropologies, Others, American Modernity* (Chicago: University of Chicago Press, 1998), 55–66.

12. Hildegard of Bingen's music, science, and philosophical observations are featured in the bookstores, gift shops, workshop themes, and artistic expressions of green sisters and their contemporary religious sisters in North America. Hildegard's name is integrated into gardens, prayer groups, and other places that are designated of special value. Historian Barbara Newman has contributed to Hildegard's contemporary following by bringing to light her unique theological, mystical, and scientific contributions. See Newman, *Sister of Wisdom: St. Hildegard's Theology of the Feminine* (Berkeley: University of California Press, 1987).

13. Field journal notes, Sisters of Earth International Conference, Mont Marie Conference Center, Holyoke, Mass., August 3, 2002.

14. Braude, "American Religious History Is Women's History," 87. For further discussion of the absence of women in the study of religion, see Rita Gross, "Where Have All the Women Been? The Challenge of Feminist Study of Religion," in her *Feminism and Religion* (Boston: Beacon, 1996), 65–104; Catherine Wessinger, *Women's Leadership in Marginal Religions* (Chicago: University of Illinois Press, 1993), 1–22; and Mary Farrell Bednarowski, *The Religious Imagination of American Women* (Bloomington: Indiana University Press, 1999), 4–5.

15. Rita Gross, for example, describes the "bad old days" in religious studies when men's religious experience was assumed to be universal. See Gross, *Feminism and Religion*.

16. I have borrowed this phrase from the work of Teresa de Lauretis in order to ap-

ply it to the study of women and religion. See De Lauretis, "Gramsci Notwithstanding; or, The Left Hand of History," in her *Technologies of Gender: Essays on Theory, Film, and Fiction* (Bloomington: Indiana University Press, 1987), 93; and Taylor, "From the Left Hand," 26.

17. Meredith McGuire, *Religion: The Social Context,* 4th ed. (New York: Wadsworth, 1997), 119.

18. Yvonne Chireau, "The Uses of the Supernatural: Toward a History of Black Women's Magical Practices," and Sharla Fett, "It's the Spirit in Me: Spiritual Power and the Healing Work of African American Women in Slavery," in Susan Juster and Lisa MacFarlane, eds., *A Mighty Baptism: Race, Gender, and the Creation of American Protestantism* (Ithaca, N.Y.: Cornell University Press, 1996), 171–209; Jordan Rosen and Susan Kalcik, eds., *Women's Folklore, Women's Culture* (Philadelphia: University of Pennsylvania Press, 1985).

19. McGuire, *Religion,* 118.

20. David Snowdon, *Aging with Grace: What the Nun Study Teaches Us about Leading Longer, Healthier, and More Meaningful Lives* (New York: Bantam, 2001); Lora Ann Quiñonez and Mary Daniel Turner, *The Transformation of American Catholic Sisters* (Philadelphia: Temple University Press, 1992), x; David Nygen and Miriam Ukeritis, *The Future of Religious Orders in the United States* (Westport, Conn.: Praeger, 1993); Helen Rose Fuchs Ebaugh, *Women in the Vanishing Cloister* (New Brunswick, N.J.: Rutgers University Press, 1993), 47–50.

21. Bell Hooks, *Talking Back* (Boston: South End Press, 1989). Hooks explains that, in the southern black community in which she was raised, "talking back" meant "speaking as an equal to an authority figure." "Back talking" meant carving out a space to disagree and to have an opinion. In my own research, I have tried to challenge the traditional authoritative and vertical structure of researcher and researched, so creating space where sisters could "talk back" was essential to the interview process.

22. Lorraine Code, "How Do We Know?: Questions of Method in Feminist Practice," in Burt and Code, *Changing Methods,* 13–44.

23. Mary Gordon, "Women of God," *Atlantic Monthly* (January 2002): 58–91. The cover of the magazine featured Audrey Hepburn in her role in *The Nun's Story* (1959), reinforcing once again stereotypical images of nuns from the 1950s as the dominant image of today's "women of God." By contrast, images of real contemporary nuns were relegated to small and sketchily drawn figures located toward the end of the article.

24. Elaine Lawless, "'I Was Afraid Someone Like You . . . an Outsider . . . Would Misunderstand': Negotiating Interpretive Differences between Ethnographers and Subjects," *Journal of American Folklore* 105 (1992): 306. See also Jeffrey Titon, *Powerhouse for God: Speech, Chant, and Song in an Appalachian Baptist Church* (Austin: University of Texas Press, 1988), 13.

25. Bernard McGrane, *Beyond Anthropology* (New York: Columbia University Press), 125.

26. For a good discussion of these issues, see Gary Tomilson, *Music in Renaissance Magic: Toward a Historiography of Others* (Chicago: University of Chicago Press, 1993), 6–9.

27. Donna Haraway, *Simians, Cyborgs, and Women: The Reinvention of Nature* (New York: Routledge, 1991), p. 189.

28. Karen Brown, "Writing about the 'Other': New Approaches to Fieldwork Can End the Colonial Mindset of Anthropological Research," *Chronicle of Higher Education,* April 15, 1992, A56.

Introduction

1. This phrase comes from the announcement of the conference theme ("Healing as a Planetary Agenda") for the Fifth International Conference of Sisters of Earth (2002), an informal network of Roman Catholic religious sisters primarily based in the United States and Canada.

2. In the course of conducting electronic interviews with sixty-five North American Roman Catholic sisters, I additionally corresponded with a number of "green nuns" or "green sisters" in Australia, Ireland, the Philippines, the Netherlands, Peru, and Africa. The responses from these international green sisters and others and the results of visits to international green sisters' earth ministries in these countries will be included in a follow-up book.

3. It should be noted that the use of the word "green" to identify environmentally activist Catholic sisters is not meant to connect them with the political movement in North America and abroad known as the "Greens" or the "Green Party." Instead, it is used more generally to denote a certain degree of sympathetic consciousness toward environmental concerns. Some green sisters very well may have affiliations with the Green Party, but the term "green" is not used in this sense. "Green" is also used as a kind of shorthand in contemporary ecocritical analysis to indicate sensibilities or cultural productions shaped by an ecological consciousness and earth-referent perspective. See Jhan Hochman, *Green Cultural Studies* (Moscow: University of Idaho Press, 1998); and Laurence Coupe, *The Green Studies Reader: From Romanticism to Ecocriticism* (New York: Routledge, 2000). For further discussion of the history and context of the use of the terms "green" and "greening," see the section on "green culture" in Chapter 1.

4. See Carol Coburn and Martha Smith, *Spirited Lives: How Nuns Shaped Catholic Culture and American Life, 1836–1920* (Chapel Hill: University of North Carolina Press, 1999), esp. chaps. 5 and 7; and Lora Ann Quiñonez and Mary Daniel Turner, *The Transformation of American Catholic Sisters* (Philadelphia: Temple University Press, 1992), 126–130. For cross-community examples, see Mary Ellen Leciejewski, "Common Ground: Women Religious Healing the Earth," master's thesis (videorecording), University of Illinois, Springfield, 1995. A summary history of the founding of "Network," the National Catholic Social Justice Lobby, can be found at http://www.networklobby.org (September 10, 2005).

5. The sixty-five sisters were identified and interviewed specifically because of their involvement with earth ministries in North America, so this was by no means a random sampling. These electronic interviews supplemented in-person interviews and field visits. The pool of those interviewed contains both green sisters who are affiliated with Sisters of Earth and those who are not, but all are actively working specifically with environ-

mental concerns. Except for some inquiries in a short demographic and lifestyle section, the questions themselves were open-ended and intended to stimulate conversation and allow room for personal expression. The intent was not to generate a sociological survey.

6. Four of the sisters with whom I conducted electronic interviews were Canadian citizens residing in Canada. One factor that has contributed to a high representation of sisters' earth ministries in the Midwest region of the United States is that this region is where many religious communities still own substantial farmland.

7. Jo Ann Kay McNamara, *Sisters in Arms: Catholic Nuns through Two Millennia* (Cambridge: Harvard University Press, 1996), 324–384 and 489–525.

8. Lucy Kaylin, *For the Love of God: The Faith and Future of the American Nun* (New York: Harper Collins, 2002), 1–11. Eventually, Kaylin features somewhat livelier sisters, but they are few and far between, and this image of decay and atrophy is the reader's first impression of religious sisters.

9. See, for example, Patricia Wittberg, *The Rise and Fall of Catholic Religious Orders* (Albany: State of New York University Press, 1994); Helen Rose Fuchs Ebaugh, *Women in the Vanishing Cloister* (New Brunswick, N.J.: Rutgers University Press, 1993); and David Nygren and Miriam Ukretis, *The Future of Religious Orders in the United States* (Westport, Conn.: Praeger, 1993). For an exception to more pessimistic analyses of the future of Roman Catholic religious orders, see Mary Johnson's discussion of pockets of light and regeneration in "The Reweaving of Catholic Spiritual and Institutional Life," *Annals of the American Academy of Political and Social Science* 558 (July 1998): 135–143.

10. Mary Ellen Leciejewski, electronic interview with the author, March 22, 2002.

11. Roger Finke and Laurence Iannaccone, "Supply-side Explanations for Religious Change," in Wade Clark Roof, ed., *"Religion in the Nineties,* special edition of *Annals of the American Academy of Political and Social Science* 527 (May 1993), 27–39; Roger Finke and Rodney Stark, *The Churching of America, 1776–1990* (New Brunswick, N.J.: Rutgers University Press, 1992); Laurence Iannaccone, "The Consequences of Religious Market Regulation: Adam Smith and the Economics of Religion," *Rationality and Society* 3 (1991): 156–177.

12. Carole Rossi, interview with the author, Plainville, Mass., June 29, 1997.

13. Wendell Berry, *The Unsettling of America: Culture and Agriculture* (San Francisco: Sierra Club Books, 1996), esp. chap. 4.

14. This model is also a major tenet of "permaculture," an approach to agriculture and holistic landscape design that I discuss more in Chapter 6 and which many sisters have implemented in their community-supported gardens. See Bill Mollison, *Introduction to Permaculture* (Tyalgum, Australia: Tagari, 1991), 33–35. Mollison writes that before any sort of human plan is devised for a particular piece of land, one must walk the land, observe, learn its propensities, and then study its biological and social history. "We do not just see and hear, smell and taste, but we sense heat and cold, pressure, stress from efforts of hill-climbing or prickly plants, and find compatible and incompatible sites in the landscape. We note good views, outlooks, soil colors and textures . . . we can sit for a time and notice patterns and processes: how some trees prefer to grow in rocks, some in valleys, others in grasslands or clumps."

15. Ibid., 34.

16. In discussing these dynamics, I frequently refer to the "living landscape" as well as other organic metaphors. The concern of this work is not with how widely these metaphors can be extended into this area of study, although I hope that will be a topic that others take up and discuss. My aim has rather been to discern the best analytical categories for this particular project. Aside from the agricultural content of much of my subject matter, however, I do believe that organic metaphors work as well as they do in religious studies for the same reason they work well across the humanities and social sciences. Religion, like culture and like society, does not exist outside the realm of the living, changing creatures that create it. This realization becomes undeniably clear when the researcher comes face to face with actual living people and practice.

17. Meredith McGuire, *Religion: The Social Context* (New York: Wadsworth, 1997), 119.

18. Robert Orsi, *Thank You, St. Jude* (New Haven: Yale University Press, 1996), xv.

19. Now in his eighties, Berry first developed a following back in the 1970s, when he began mimeographing a series of his papers for interested students and colleagues and later founded the Riverdale Center for Religious Research in the Hudson Valley of New York. Berry had spent a decade in Passionist monasteries, received his doctorate in history, studied in China, traveled the world as a chaplain for the North Atlantic Treaty Organization (NATO), served as president of the American Teilhard Association, and forged a career teaching at Seton Hall, Columbia, and Fordham universities. Sister Miriam MacGillis of Genesis Farm in New Jersey and others of his students recall eagerly awaiting the next installment of Berry's blue mimeographed booklets or "Riverdale Papers" (1974–1983) for their insights into Christian spirituality, comparative religion, and environmental ethics. Most of all, though, these readers of Berry's works were interested in learning more about what he was then calling the "New Cosmology."

20. Thomas Berry, *The Dream of the Earth* (San Francisco: Sierra Club Books, 1988), 66 and 87–88.

21. Brian Swimme and Thomas Berry, *The Universe Story* (San Francisco: Harper San Francisco, 1992), 22–24.

22. See Mircea Eliade, *The Myth of the Eternal Return or Cosmos and History,* trans. Willard Trask (1949; Princeton, N.J.: Princeton University Press, 1991), 3–48.

23. Ibid., 3–6.

24. It should be noted that Berry departs from Eliade in an important respect. Time, for Berry, is not "cyclical," as Eliade described it in the "archaic consciousness," but instead takes the form of a cosmic unfolding of "one-time events." For example, number nine of Berry's twelve principles for understanding the universe states: "The emergent process of the universe is irreversible and non-repeatable in the existing world order." See Thomas Berry, "Bioregions: The Context for Reinhabiting the Earth," *Breakthrough* (Spring/Summer 1985): 9.

25. Scientific estimates of the actual age of the universe have shifted in recent decades, and Berry's work reflects these variations and adjustments over time.

26. Thomas Berry, *The Great Work: Our Way into the Future* (New York: Bell Tower, 1999), 176–180.

27. Benjamin Webb, *Fugitive Faith: Conversations on Spiritual, Environmental, and Community Renewal* (Maryknoll, N.Y.: Orbis, 1998), 38.

28. Berry, *Dream of the Earth*, 198–199. See also Pierre Teilhard de Chardin, *The Phenomenon of Man* (New York: Harper Collins, 1959). In his discussion of the human as a dimension of the cosmos, Berry, a former president of the American Teilhard Association, demonstrates Teilhard's influence on his own work.

29. See the interview with Thomas Berry in Nancy Ryley, *The Forsaken Garden: Four Conversations on the Deep Meaning of Environmental Illness* (Wheaton, Ill.: Quest, 1998), 239.

30. Berry, *Great Work*, 177–180. In these statements about a lost connection to the universe, Berry again echoes the work of comparative religionist Mircea Eliade, who wrote that the "chief difference between the man of the archaic and traditional societies and the man of modern societies with their strong imprint of Judeo-Christianity lies in the fact that the former feels himself indissolubly connected with the Cosmos and the cosmic rhythms, whereas the latter insists that he is connected only with History." See Eliade, *Myth of the Eternal Return*, xiii–xiv.

31. Quoted in Ryley, *Forsaken Garden*, 239.

32. Open-microphone sessions, Sisters of Earth International Conferences, Sinsinawa Mound, Sinsinawa, Wis., July 17, 1998; La Casa de Maria, Santa Barbara, Calif., August 18, 2000; Mont Marie Conference Center, Holyoke, Mass., August 2, 2002; "Sharing the Wisdom" conference speakers, St. Paul, Minnesota, July 14, 2006.

33. Each of these figures received at least three mentions. See Sallie McFague, *The Body of God: An Ecological Theology* (Minneapolis: Fortress Press, 1993); Elizabeth Johnson, *Women, Earth, and Creator Spirit* (New York: Paulist Press, 1993); Ivone Gebara, *Longing for Running Water: Ecofeminism and Liberation* (Minneapolis: Fortress Press, 1999); Charlene Spretnak, *The Resurgence of the Real* (Reading, Mass.: Addison-Wesley, 1997); Mary Southard, "A Dark Time," *Earth Ethics* (Winter 1994), http://www.crle.org/pub_eeindex_win94.asp (July 11, 2006); Paula González, "An Eco-Prophetic Parish?" in Albert La Chance and John Carroll, eds., *Embracing Earth: Catholic Approaches to Ecology* (Maryknoll, N.Y.: Orbis, 1994); Al Fritsch, *Renew the Face of the Earth* (Chicago: Loyola University Press, 1987); Rosalie Bertell, *Planet Earth: The Latest Weapon of War* (London: Women's Press, 2000); Vandana Shiva, *Tomorrow's Biodiversity* (London: Thames and Hudson, 2000).

34. Quiñonez and Turner, *Transformation*, x.

35. In Chapter 1, I write more about this ethic of diversity embraced by Sisters of Earth. Evidence of this diversity, however, was visible in the course of my field work and is also reflected in the responses to the small section of standardized questions on my electronic interviews. I am also indebted to my phone conversations with Sisters of Earth cofounder Toni Nash, during which Nash expressed concern over monolithic portrayals of Sisters of Earth by researchers. For a nuanced discussion of the "common ground" between ecologically minded sisters, see also Leciejewski, *Common Ground*.

36. Peter Berg and Ray Dasmann, "Reinhabiting California," in Peter Berg, ed., *Reinhabiting a Separate Country: A Bioregional Anthology of Northern California* (San Francisco: Planet Drum Foundation, 1978), 217–220.

37. Stephanie Mills, "Foreword," in Van Andruss et al., eds., *Home! A Bioregional Reader* (Philadelphia: New Society, 1990).

38. Gary Snyder, "Re-Inhabitation," in *The Old Ways* (San Francisco: City Lights, 1977); Kirkpatrick Sale, *Dwellers in the Land: A Bioregional Vision* (San Francisco: Sierra Club Books, 1985).

39. See Wes Jackson, *Becoming Native to This Place* (Louisville: Western Kentucky Press, 1993); Deborah Tall, *From Where We Stand: Recovering a Sense of Place* (Baltimore: Johns Hopkins University Press, 1993), 93.

40. Thomas Tweed, *Our Lady of Exile* (New York: Oxford, 1997), 91.

41. This group is formally known as Sisters, Servants of the Immaculate Heart of Mary. For brevity, I will refer to the sisters from now on as "the Monroe IHMs."

42. The term "sustainability" was developed and popularized after the publication of Gro Harlem Brundtland et al., *Our Common Future,* report from the United Nations World Commission on Environment and Development (New York: United Nations, April 1986). Note that in business use, "sustainability" takes on a different meaning, indicating the ability of a business or industry to survive market forces and continue to produce goods and services.

43. Paul Hawken, *The Ecology of Commerce: A Declaration of Sustainability* (New York: Harper Business, 1993), 139.

44. David Orr, "Education and the Ecological Design Arts," *Conservation Biology* 6, no. 2 (June 1992): 162.

45. Janet Ryan, interview with the author, Monroe, Mich., October 26, 2002. Also, the Monroe IHMs' "Long Range Master Plan Integrating Idea" lists under the "vision section" a "renovated Motherhouse and Health Care Center modeling sustainable buildings and methods of care with staff and resident community open to share its learnings and experience of sustainable living broadly with those who come to the campus for short and long periods of time." (See page 1 of the December 6–10 version on the master plan reprinted for the Master Plan Coordinating Council.) The mission statements from Genesis Farm in New Jersey and Crystal Spring in Massachusetts also contain similar goals about modeling an example of sustainable living.

46. Carol Coston and Elise D. García, *The Eagle and the Condor,* PowerPoint presentation on CD-ROM (Boerne, Tex.: Santuario Sisterfarm, 2002).

47. See, for instance, the interview with Miriam MacGillis in Colman McCarthy, "In N.J., Nuns Cultivate a Spiritual-Ecological Link on Genesis Farm," *Washington Post,* October 2, 1993, B6.

48. In this book, the term "conservation" is not used in its "wise use" sense, a utilitarian management approach that advocates planned extraction of natural resources, such as oil, coal, or timber. (See, for example, Gifford Pinchot, *Breaking New Ground* [New York: Harcourt, Brace, 1947].) Instead, in using the terms "conservation" and "conserving," sisters have reclaimed Muir's association of "conservation" with preserving certain aspects of the landscape from being damaged or exploited for material gain. For further explication of this, see Donald Strong, *Dreamers and Defenders: American Conservationists* (Lincoln: University of Nebraska, 1988), chap. 4; Roderick Nash, *Wilderness of the American Mind* (New Haven: Yale University Press, 1967), 129; and John Muir's cri-

tique of "panutilization" masking as "conservation" in *The Yosemite* (Madison: University of Wisconsin Press, 1991).

49. Max Oelschlaeger, *The Idea of Wilderness* (New Haven: Yale University Press, 1991), 172–175.

50. Miriam MacGillis, "Exploring the Sacred Universe," oral presentation, Blairstown, N.J., August 16, 1995.

51. Andrew Dobson, ed., *The Green Reader: Essays toward a Sustainable Society* (San Francisco: Mercury House, 1991), 253.

52. Mary Jo Leddy, *Reweaving Religious Life: Beyond the Liberal Model* (Mystic, Conn.: Twenty-Third Publications, 1991), 147.

53. For a concise articulation of the integration of old and new in Catholic tradition, see the introduction in Phyllis Zagano and Terrence Tilley, eds., *Things New and Old: Essays on the Theology of Elizabeth Johnson* (New York: Crossroad, 1999), xi–xii.

54. My medievalist historian colleague Richard Kieckhefer correctly points out that "classical sources were used (not just preserved) by medieval writers, and many people think the notion of the Renaissance break away from medieval tradition is much exaggerated." Still, popular historical perception would have it otherwise and in this instance is what counts. Richard Kieckhefer, personal communication with the author, November 15, 2002.

55. See, for example, Gail Worcelo, "An Ecozoic Monastery: Shaping a Transforming Vision for the Future," *Loretto Earth Network News* (Spring 2000): 7.

56. Miriam MacGillis, "Letter to Friends of the Farm," Thanksgiving 2002, 1.

57. The sanctuary movement was initiated by Presbyterian minister John Fife and Arizona rancher James Corbett to provide assistance to refugees, mostly from Guatemala and El Salvador, who were seeking political asylum. North American Catholic nuns also played a significant role in aiding and sheltering refugees; for example, three nuns were indicted in 1983 for harboring "illegal aliens." See Robin Lorentzen, *Women in the Sanctuary Movement* (Philadelphia: Temple University Press, 1991); Renny Golden, *Sanctuary: The New Underground Railroad* (Maryknoll, N.Y.: Orbis, 1986); Miriam Davidson, *Convictions of the Heart: Jim Corbett and the Sanctuary Movement* (Tucson: University of Arizona Press, 1988).

58. A booklet made available through the earth literacy programs at Genesis Farm, for example, offers statistics on how the "American Dream" and its unchecked consumption of natural resources has created a "nightmare" for the earth and for third-world populations. See *All-Consuming: Waking Up from the American Dream* (Seattle: New Roadmap Foundation, 1993).

59. Technically sisters are "laypeople," but here I am distinguishing between those who are actual religious sisters and those who are not.

60. See Martin Marty's introduction to Catherine Albanese, *Nature Religion: From the Algonkian Indians to the New Age* (Chicago: University of Chicago Press, 1990), xii.

61. The term "cosmic liturgy" is used in Swimme and Berry, *Universe Story,* 264. The authors conceive of the universe as a "single, multiform, sequential, celebratory event," and use "cosmic liturgy" to "express the awesome qualities of phenomenal existence."

62. In the small-group discussion portion of the 1998 Sisters of Earth conference,

for instance, conference co-organizer Mary Louise Dolan offered the following question for consideration: "Is it time for rhizomes to rise?" Here, Dolan employed French philosopher Gilles Deleuze's image of the rhizome as a metaphor for sisters working on behalf of the earth and ecological concerns. Dolan had read a discussion of Deleuze's work in an interview with deep ecologist Dolores La Chapelle. See Gille Deleuze and Félix Guattari, *A Thousand Plateaus: Capitalism and Schizophrenia*, vol. 2, trans. Brian Massumi (Minneapolis: University of Minnesota Press, 1987); and an interview with Dolores LaChapelle and Julien Puzey in Derrick Jensen, *Listening to the Land: Conversations about Nature, Culture, and Eros* (San Francisco: Sierra Club Books, 1995), 244–247.

63. Deleuze and Guattari, *Thousand Plateaus*, 8.

64. Ibid., 14.

65. Ibid., 15–16.

66. Constantin Boundas, ed., *The Deleuze Reader* (New York: Columbia University Press, 1993), 32.

67. Berry, *Great Work*, 7–11.

68. Joanna Macy, *Coming Back to Life* (Philadelphia: New Society, 1998), 17.

69. Note that these are also Berry's prescription for ways to bring the planet into the "Ecozoic era." See Berry, *Great Work*, 1–11, and *Dream of the Earth*, 210–213.

70. Jon Butler, "Historiographical Heresy: Catholicism as a Model for American Religious History," in Thomas Kselman, ed., *Belief in History: Innovative Approaches to European and American Religion* (South Bend, Ind.: University of Notre Dame Press, 1991), 291.

71. See Wendy Griswold's discussion of active cultural production in *Culture and Societies in a Changing World* (Thousand Oaks, Calif.: Pine Forge, 1994); and Michel de Certeau's challenge to the assumption that consumption is essentially passive in *The Practice of Everyday Life* (Berkeley: University of California Press, 1984), 167–170. In his discussion of "Reading as Poaching," de Certeau argues that far from being passive, the reader actively invents something in texts different from what was intended, creating something new by allowing for a plurality of meanings. "The text has a meaning only through its readers," writes de Certeau; "it changes along with them." Green sisters are likewise "active readers" of theory, bringing their own ways of reading to philosophical, theological, and environmental texts, and changing those texts as they actively translate them into practical applications.

72. Michael Taussig, *Mimesis and Alterity: A Particular History of the Senses* (New York: Routledge, 1993), 10.

73. There is also a branch of ecologically sustainable practice called biomimicry, in which human populations devise ways of living that mimic the earth's ways of sheltering, nourishing, dealing with waste, neutralizing toxicity, and so forth. See, for instance, Janine Benyus, *Biomimicry: Innovation Inspired by Nature* (New York: William Morrow, 1997).

74. James Terrence Fisher, *The Catholic Counterculture in America, 1933–1962* (Chapel Hill: University of North Carolina Press, 1989); Gene Burns, "Studying Political Culture of American Catholicism," *Sociology of Culture* 57 (1996): 37–53; John Van Engen,

"Faith as a Concept of Order in Medieval Christendom," in Kselman, *Belief in History,* 19–67.

75. Susan Mizruchi, *Religion and Cultural Studies* (Princeton, N.J.: Princeton University Press, 2001), x.

1. The Green Catholic Imagination

1. This icon was designed and painted by Sister Bernadette Bostwick of the Green Mountain Monastery in Vermont.

2. This chant was composed by Jan Novotka of Earthrise Productions, Scranton, Pa.

3. See the official Earth Charter web site, http://www.earthcharter.org.

4. "Earth Community" is a composition of Jan Novotka, Earthrise Productions, Scranton, Pa.

5. Thomas Berry, *The Great Work: Our Way into the Future* (New York: Bell Tower, 1999), 11.

6. Mary Southard, interview with the author, La Grange, Ill., December 13, 2001. Other "planters" of Sisters of Earth include Sister Evelyn Sommers (also a member of Southard's community) and Sisters Toni Nash and Mary Louise Dolan—with whom Southard collaborated in 1993 while at Spiritearth, an ecospiritual center then located along the Hudson River in New York.

7. Mary Southard, personal communication with the author, July 18, 2002. In this case, as in many others, sisters' comments on my work, no matter how brief, afforded me greater insight into their ways of seeing. This suggestion that organic metaphor is more suitable when talking about sisters' activities was not uncommon, and so is reflected in my analysis.

8. This figure is calculated both from those listed in the Sisters of Earth directory and from updated information gleaned from personal contacts, phone interactions, and e-mail exchanges.

9. I have found that sisters make frequent use of e-mail for organizational purposes, activism, pooling resources and information, and maintaining personal networks. It is a relatively inexpensive form of communication (a major selling point to those who have taken a vow of poverty) and enables quick and "tree-free" communication.

10. Toni Nash, Sisters of Earth cofounder and organizer, personal communication with the author, November 30, 2001.

11. Business meeting proceedings, Sisters of Earth conference, August 4, 2002.

12. LCWR National Assembly web archives, http://www.lcwr.org/pressreleases/petitionaryprayers.html (November 10, 2005).

13. Mary Ann Zollmann, "Tending the Holy through the Power of Sisterhood," LCWR National Assembly Presidential Address, August 22, 2003, Detroit, Mich., http://www.lcwr.org/pressreleases/zollmann.html (November 10, 2005).

14. Janet Kuciejczyk, CSJ, Corlita Bonnarens, RSM, and Carol Reeb, SSND, "Reverencing the Earth," *Resolutions to Action* 13, no 1 (January 2004): 1. General resolutions

passed by the assembly included an intensified commitment to acts of advocacy for social justice, the opposition of the LCWR to the Free Trade Area of the Americas (FTAA), and a statement decrying the continuing tragic loss of life in Iraq that has accompanied the U.S. invasion of that country.

15. This chant was written specifically for the conference by Sister Suzanne Toolan, RSN, and sung at various points throughout the conference. See Mary Catherine Rabbitt, "Tending the Holy: Reflections on the 2003 LCWR National Assembly," *Loretto Earth Network News* 11, no. 4 (Fall 2003): 1.

16. Louise Riotte, *Carrots Love Tomatoes: Secrets of Companion Planting for Successful Gardening,* 2d ed. (1975; Pownal, Vt.: Storey Books, 1998), 2.

17. Ibid., 181.

18. Ibid., 133.

19. For a discussion of sisters' levels of education, see Lora Ann Quiñonez and Mary Daniel Turner, *The Transformation of American Catholic Sisters* (Philadelphia: Temple University Press, 1992), 5–6. For a breakdown of the educational levels of the sisters I interviewed, see the Preface.

20. Quiñonez and Turner, *Transformation,* 17–19.

21. Ibid.

22. Mary Ewens, "Inside the Convent," in Karen Kennelly, ed., *American Catholic Women: A Historical Exploration* (New York: Macmillan, 1989), 41.

23. See, for instance, Ann Patrick Ware, ed., *Midwives of the Future: American Sisters Tell Their Story* (Kansas City, Mo.: Leaven, 1985); and Lora Ann Quiñonez, ed., *Starting Points: Six Essays Based on the Experience of U.S. Women Religious* (Washington, D.C.: Leadership Conference of Women Religious of the USA, 1980).

24. Chris Loughlin, interview with the author, Plainville, Mass., June 29, 1997.

25. Mary Jo Weaver, *New Catholic Women* (Bloomington: Indiana University Press, 1995), 93–94.

26. Weaver, *New Catholic Women,* 94; and Robert Ellwood, *The Sixties Spiritual Awakening* (New Brunswick, N.J.: Rutgers University Press, 1994), 300–301.

27. See Tamala Edwards and Genesee Abbey, "Get Thee to a Monastery," *Time,* August 3, 1998; Judith Norkin, "Vacations with a Soul," *Philadelphia City Paper,* June 7, 2001, A1.

28. Lauren Artress, *Walking a Sacred Path: Rediscovering the Labyrinth as a Spiritual Tool* (New York: Riverhead, 1995). For an account of the growing popularity of labyrinth walking in Christian churches, see Beverly Hudson, "Soul to Soul," *Los Angeles Times,* August 7, 1995, E1. Note that communities as diverse as the Dominican sisters' community at Sinsinawa Mound in Wisconsin, the Sisters of Saint Joseph at the Mont Marie Center in Holyoke, Massachusetts, and the Passion Sisters' monastery in Clark's Summit, Pennsylvania, all offer outdoor labyrinths for walking meditation to community members and retreat guests.

29. For more about Thomas Merton discussion groups, see John Monczunski, "A Pilgrim's Progress," *Notre Dame Magazine* (Spring 1997): 10–12. Nearly all of Merton's work remains in print. More recently, an encyclopedia of Thomas Merton has even been published. See William Shannon, *The Thomas Merton Encyclopedia* (Maryknoll, N.Y.:

Orbis, 2002). For examples of the continued large volume of work being published on Merton see, for example, Ross Rabri, *Thomas Merton and the Inclusive Imagination* (Columbia: University of Missouri Press, 2001); Robert Inchausti, *Thomas Merton's American Prophecy* (Albany: State University of New York Press, 1998); Robert King, *Thomas Merton and Thich Nhat Hanh* (New York: Continuum, 2001); Lawrence Cunningham, *Thomas Merton and the Monastic Vision* (Grand Rapids, Mich.: W. B. Eerdmans, 1999).

30. Carol Lee Flinders, *Enduring Grace: Living Portraits of Seven Women Mystics* (San Francisco: Harper San Francisco, 1993).

31. See, for example, Victor-Antoine D'Avila-Latourrette, *Twelve Months of Monastery Soups* (New York: Bantam Doubleday, 1998); Irene Psatha, *Sister Irene's Culinary Journal* (Brewster, Mass.: Paraclete Press, 1998); Monks of New Skete, *How to Be Your Dog's Best Friend* (Boston: Little, Brown, 2002).

32. See Burkhard Bilger, "Raw Faith," *New Yorker,* August 19–26, 2002, 150–157.

33. Patricia Lucas, "Diary of Change," in Ware, *Midwives,* 178.

34. Maureen McCormack, "Uprooting and Rerooting," in Ware, *Midwives,* 98.

35. Maureen McCormack, "Seeds of Awareness," *Loretto Magazine* 43, no. 3 (Winter 2001): 9.

36. For a discussion of the "Natural Step," see Paul Hawken, *The Ecology of Commerce* (New York: Harper Collins, 1993), 52–54.

37. Pamphlet published by Network, Washington, D.C., 2002.

38. Carol Coston, "Open Windows, Open Doors," in Ware, *Midwives,* 147. The phrase "life-giving" is an oft-repeated phrase by green sisters, used as an ethical test as to whether something is appropriate. That is, one consciously engages in those practices that are life-giving and eschews those that are not. An environmental analogy can also be made to Aldo Leopold's land ethic, which determined that a thing is right if it "tends to preserve the integrity, stability and beauty of the biotic community. It is wrong when it tends otherwise." Or, from the perspective of Thomas Berry's "cosmological ethic," something is good if it promotes a "mutually enhancing earth-human relationship." See Aldo Leopold, *A Sand County Almanac* (New York: Ballantine, 1966), 237; Brian Swimme and Thomas Berry, *The Universe Story* (San Francisco: Harper San Francisco, 1992).

39. Santuario Sisterfarm's strategy for carrying forward its work ("cultivating diversity") draws inspiration from Vandana Shiva, who writes: "An intolerance of diversity is the biggest threat to peace in our times; conversely, the cultivation of diversity is the most significant contribution to peace—peace with nature and between peoples." Shiva, *Biopiracy: The Plunder of Nature and Knowledge* (Boston: South End, 1997), 119.

40. Pamphlet published by Santuario Sisterfarm, Boerne, Tex., 2002.

41. Carol Coston and Elise D. García, interview with the author, Boerne, Tex., March 4, 2002.

42. For accounts of further post–Vatican II changes and shifts in the lives of religious sisters, see Quiñonez and Turner, *Transformation;* Sheila Murphy, *Midlife Wanderer: The Woman Religious in Midlife Transition* (Whitinsville, Mass.: Affirmation Books, 1983); Lora Ann Quiñonez, ed., *Starting Points: Six Essays Based on the Experience of U.S. Women Religious* (Washington, D.C.: Leadership Conference of Women Religious of the USA, 1980); Ware, *Midwifing the Future,* 2–3.

43. "Personal experiences in nature" garnered forty-eight mentions in total and was rated the most important factor that led sisters to develop a greater ecological awareness. Frequently, a significant experience with nature in childhood was then reawakened by contact with the work of figures such as Miriam MacGillis, Thomas Berry, or Brian Swimme.

44. National Catholic Rural Life Conference, *Religious Congregations on the Land: The Practical Links between Community, Sustainable Land Use, and Spiritual Charism* (Des Moines, Iowa: NCRLC, 1996), 8–36.

45. Although men's communities have more recently made strides in this area, they are still several years behind the work done by sisters' communities. A much smaller organization called Brothers of Earth also holds biennial conferences, but earth ministries have been much less a priority for religious brothers.

46. Sisters of Earth National Conference, Sinsinawa, Wis., July 17, 1998.

47. For more on this subject, see Jeffrey Marlett, *Saving the Heartland: Catholic Missionaries in Rural America, 1920–1960* (Dekalb: Northern Illinois University Press, 2002).

48. Quoted in Timothy Dolan, "The Rural Ideology of Edwin O'Hara," *U.S. Catholic Historian* 8, no. 3 (Fall 1989): 119.

49. Ibid., 120. See also Edwin O'Hara, *The Church and the Country Community* (New York: Macmillan, 1927).

50. Miriam MacGillis, "Food as Sacrament," in Fritz Hull, ed., *Earth and Spirit: The Spiritual Dimension of the Environmental Crisis* (New York: Continuum, 1993), 164.

51. As quoted in Christopher Kauffman, "W. Howard Bishop, President of the Catholic Rural Life Conference, 1928–1934," *U.S. Catholic Historian* 8, no. 3 (Fall 1989): 133.

52. Peter Maurin [Pierre Aristide], *The Green Revolution* (Fresno, Calif.: Academy Guild Press, 1949), 100.

53. Ibid., 93. See also parallels to Thomas Berry's chapter on "The University" in Berry, *Great Work*, 72–85.

54. Debra Campbell, "Both Sides Now: Another Look at the Grail in the Postwar Era," *U.S. Catholic Historian* 11, no. 4 (Fall 1993): 14. Note that the Grail, an international movement of laywomen, began in 1921 in Holland where it was founded by Jesuit priest Jacques van Ginneken. In 1940, Lydwine van Kersbergen and Joan Overboss established the Grail in the United States.

55. Ibid., 20.

56. See, for example, Barbara Ellen Wald, "Wanted: A New Type of Young Woman," *Torch* (April 1943): 3.

57. Mary Jo Weaver, "Still Feisty at Fifty: The Grailville Lay Apostolate for Women," *U.S. Catholic Historian* 11, no. 4 (Fall 1993): 7.

58. Janet Kalven, "Living the Liturgy: The Keystone of the Grail Vision," *U.S. Catholic Historian* 11, no. 4 (Fall 1993): 35.

59. Ibid.

60. Quoted in Campbell, "Both Sides Now," 16.

61. Quoted in ibid., 14.

62. Janet Kalven, "Women and Post-War Reconstruction," in *Catholic Rural Life Objectives* (Des Moines, Iowa: NCRLC, 1944), 28.

63. Steiner founded the system of biodynamic farming, which will be discussed in greater depth in Chapter 6. See Rudolf Steiner, *Macrocosm and Microcosm* (London: Rudolf Steiner Press, 1968).

64. Janet Kalven, interview with the author, Loveland, Ohio, July 28, 1997.

65. Barbara Ellen Wald, "Grail Adventure," *Living Parish* 3, no. 4 (April 1943): 11.

66. Program notes for August 28–30, 1981, Grailville archives, Grailville, Loveland, Ohio.

67. The weekend attracted a wide range of participants, including bioregionalist Frank Traina, who would go on to write and edit one of the first comprehensive volumes on approaches to bioregional education, drawing from Berry's perspectives in order to theorize bioregional pedagogies. See Frank Traina and Susan Darley-Hill, *Perspectives in Bioregional Education* (Troy, Ohio: North American Association for Environmental Education, 1995).

68. Program notes for August 28–30, 1981, Grailville archives, Grailville, Loveland, Ohio.

69. As feminist author Diane Stein defines it, women's spirituality challenges the norms of patriarchal religion in three important ways. The first is that women's spirituality ritual groups ("circles") and other study groups are nonhierarchical. Instead of there being a "high priestess" or "high priest" who holds a fixed position of authority, in the women's spirituality movement each woman is considered to be a leader in the group, in which responsibility for facilitating rituals rotates. The second difference is that ritual circles are generally women-only groups in which the creation of "women's space" for spiritual expression is a key element of the culture. Women are thus empowered in the microcosm of the ritual space to go out and effect change in the wider world. Third, women's spirituality groups emphasize female forms of divinity. These groups argue that not only are female images of the divine more empowering for women (physically, emotionally, and spiritually), but also the absence of images and worship of the divine feminine from a world dominated by centuries of patriarchy justifies "catch-up" time for neglected goddesses. The importance of images of Mary and Sophia to many green sisters reflects a similar gravitation toward images of the divine feminine. For descriptive examples of nonhierarchical women's spirituality circles, see Barbara Walker, *Women's Rituals* (San Francisco: Harper San Francisco, 1990); Diane Stein, *Casting the Circle* (Freedom, Calif.: Crossing, 1990); and Shekhinah Mountainwater, *Ariadne's Thread: A Workbook of Goddess Magic* (Freedom, Calif.: Crossing, 1991).

70. For the importance of Catholic sacramentals, shrines, and relics, see Colleen McDannell, *Material Christianity* (New Haven: Yale University Press, 1995), chaps. 2 and 5.

71. Kay Turner, *Beautiful Necessity: The Art and Meaning of Women's Altars* (New York: Thames and Hudson, 1999), 61–77.

72. Mary Farrell Bednarowski, *New Religions: The Theological Imagination in America* (Bloomington: Indiana University Press, 1989), 143–144. For examples of Catholic women who have become key figures in the women's spirituality movement, see Carol Christ and Judith Plaskow, eds., *Womanspirit Rising*, 2d ed. (1979; San Francisco: Harper San Francisco, 1992); Judith Plaskow and Carol Christ, eds., *Weaving the Visions* (San

Francisco: Harper and Row, 1989); and Charlene Spretnak, ed., *The Politics of Women's Spirituality* (New York: Doubleday, 1982). I want to acknowledge here as well the significant influence of Jewish women's leadership in shaping the women's spirituality movement.

73. Opening Remarks, Sisters of Earth Conference, Holyoke, Mass., August 1, 2002.

74. Charlene Spretnak, "Gaia, Green Politics, and the Great Transformation," in Patricia Wynne, ed., *The Womanspirit Sourcebook* (San Francisco: Harper and Row, 1988), 90. Note that in response to the "essentialist" critique, Spretnak has pointed to recent scientific research on structural and chemical differences between men's and women's brains as further evidence that men and women differ in their ways of knowing and being in the world.

75. For a deconstruction of "gender" as a constructed category, see Judith Butler, *Gender Trouble: Feminism and the Subversion of Identity* (New York: Routledge, 1999). For a deconstruction of "nature" as a constructed category, see Donna Haraway, *Simians, Cyborgs, and Women: The Reinvention of Nature* (New York: Routledge, 1991).

76. For a critique of this point, see Lois Lorentzen, "Bread and Soil of Our Dreams: Women, the Environment, and Sustainable Development," in Bron Taylor, ed., *Ecological Resistance Movements* (Albany: State University of New York Press, 1995). For an example of ecofeminist "essentializing," see Rosemary Ruether, "Toward an Ecological-Feminist Theology of Nature," in Judith Plant, ed., *Healing the Wounds: The Promise of Ecofeminism* (Philadelphia: New Society, 1989), 145–150.

77. Lorentzen, "Bread and Soil," 58–60.

78. See, for instance, Irene Diamond and Gloria Orenstein, eds., *Reweaving the World: The Emergence of Ecofeminism* (San Francisco: Sierra Club Books, 1990); Carol Adams, *Ecofeminism and the Sacred* (New York: Continuum, 1993); Monica Sjoo, *The Great Cosmic Mother: Rediscovering the Religion of the Earth,* 2d ed. (San Francisco: Harper San Francisco, 1991). For an overview of the effects of women's spirituality on American culture, see Cynthia Eller, *Living in the Lap of the Goddess* (New York: Crossroad, 1993).

79. Elizabeth Schussler Fiorenza, *In Memory of Her: A Feminist Theological Reconstruction of Christian Origins* (New York: Crossroad, 1984), 131–134.

80. Elizabeth Johnson, *Friends of God and Prophets* (New York: Continuum, 1999), 40.

81. This part was edited out of the second and condensed version of the Rule of Life, which was prepared for submission to Rome.

82. Zollmann, "Tending the Holy."

83. Berry, *Great Work,* 180.

84. Ibid., 182.

85. For a deconstruction of this argument, see Eller, *Living in the Lap.*

86. See Merlin Stone, *When God Was a Woman* (New York: Harcourt Brace Jovanovich, 1976); and Riane Eisler, *The Chalice and the Blade* (San Francisco: Harper San Francisco, 1987).

87. Andrew Greeley, *The Catholic Imagination* (Berkeley: University of California Press, 2000), 1.

88. There are of course many more characteristics (nature as teacher, nature as mother, and so on) that provide the flourishing field of "ecocriticism" an abundance of material for analysis. (See Laurence Coupe, *The Green Studies Reader: From Romanticism to Ecocriticism* [New York: Routledge, 2000].) For the purposes of this discussion, however, I will concentrate on these five romantic or sympathetic characteristics. Certainly there are also negative and hostile conceptions of nature in the American cultural imagination (like nature as "howling wilderness," nature as "dominion of the devil"), but these could not be appropriately characterized as "green" per se, because the term has come to be used in popular discourse to mean "earth friendly." From the 1960s on, the term "greening" within the rhetoric of American culture has indicated a process by which something, usually an institution or a discipline, adopts a degree of sympathetic consciousness toward environmental issues or concerns. The popularization of "the greening of" phrase began with Charles Reich's look at the 1960s counterculture in *The Greening of America: How the Youth Revolution Is Trying to Make America Livable* (New York: Random House, 1970). More recent publications have followed suit, addressing "the greening of" psychology, theology, law, business, academia, history, ethics, and any number of areas identified as having been previously "un-green."

89. See Jennifer Price, *Flight Maps: Adventure with Nature in Modern America* (New York: Basic Books, 1999) for a discussion of "green culture" and television shows.

90. Ralph Waldo Emerson, "Nature," in Stephen Whicher, *Selections from Ralph Waldo Emerson* (Boston: Houghton Mifflin, 1957), 24.

91. Loren Eiseley, *The Immense Journey* (New York: Random House, 1957); E. O. Wilson, *Biophilia* (Cambridge: Harvard University Press, 1984); Rachel Carson, *Silent Spring* (New York: Houghton Mifflin, 1962); Ursula Goodenough, *The Sacred Depths of Nature* (New York: Oxford University Press, 1998).

92. See Jonathan Edwards, *Scientific and Philosophical Writings* (New Haven: Yale University Press, 1980); John Muir, *My First Summer in the Sierra* (New York: Penguin, 1987); Chief Seattle, *Chief Seattle's Speech, 1853* (Bedford, Mass.: Applewood, 2000); Julia Hill, *The Legacy of Luna* (San Francisco: Harper San Francisco, 2000); Leopold, *Sand County Almanac;* and Annie Dillard, *Holy the Firm* (New York: Harper and Row, 1977).

93. Wendell Berry, "Peace of Wild Things," in Berry, *Collected Poems, 1957–1982* (San Francisco: North Point, 1985), 6; Emerson, "Nature," 24.

94. Edward Abbey, *Desert Solitaire* (New York: Ballantine, 1968); Dave Foreman, *Confessions of an Eco-Warrior* (New York: Harmony, 1991). For a discussion of sport utility vehicles (SUVs), religion, nature, and culture in America, see my article "Nature" in Gary Laderman and Luis Leon, eds., *Encyclopedia of American Religion and Culture* (Santa Barbara, Calif.: ABC-CLIO, 2003).

95. See Richard Slotkin, *Regeneration through Violence: The Mythology of the American Frontier, 1600–1860* (Middletown, Conn.: Wesleyan University Press, 1973); Richard Slotkin, *The Fatal Environment: The Myth of the Frontier in the Age of Industrialization, 1800–1890* (New York: Harper and Row, 1986); Leo Marx, *The Machine in the Garden* (New York: Oxford University, 1967); David Noble, *The Eternal Adam and the New World Garden* (New York: Brazilier, 1968); Perry Miller, *Errand into the Wilderness* (Cambridge: Harvard University Press, 1956); Conrad Cherry, "New England as Symbol: Ambiguity in

the Puritan Vision," *Soundings* 58 (Fall 1975): 348–362; Cecilia Tichi, *New World, New Earth: Environmental Reform in American Literature from the Puritans through Whitman* (New Haven: Yale University Press, 1979); and Karen Ordahl Kupperman, "Climate and Mastery of the Wilderness in Seventeenth-Century New England," in David Hall and David Grayson Allen, eds., *Seventeenth-Century New England* (Boston: Colonial Society of Massachusetts, 1984).

96. David Shi, *The Simple Life: Plain Living and High Thinking in American Culture* (New York: Oxford University Press, 1985); Rebecca Gould, *At Home in Nature: Modern Homesteading and Spiritual Practice in America* (Berkeley: University of California Press, 1995); Jeffrey Jacob, *New Pioneers: The Back-to-the-Land Movement and the Search for a Sustainable Future* (University Park: Pennsylvania State University, 1997).

97. Greeley, *Catholic Imagination*, 1.

98. John Carmody, *Ecology and Religion: Toward a New Christian Theology of Nature* (New York: Paulist Press, 1983), 62.

99. U.S. Catholic Bishops, *Renewing the Earth: An Invitation to Reflection and Action on Environment in Light of Catholic Social Teaching*, November 14, 1991 (Washington, D.C.: U.S. Catholic Conference, 1992). "Modern Catholic social teaching" consists of papal and episcopal pronouncements on social, political, and economic issues since the time of Pope Leo XIII's 1891 encyclical.

100. John Tropman, *The Catholic Ethic in American Society: An Exploration of Values* (San Francisco: Jossey-Bass, 1995).

101. Ibid. See also Max Weber, *The Protestant Ethic and the Spirit of Capitalism* (New York: Charles Scribner and Sons, 1958).

102. Tropman, *Catholic Ethic*, 154–155 and 165–172.

103. Riotte, *Carrots Love Tomatoes*, 7–23.

104. For an articulation of biocentric philosophy, see John Seed, "Beyond Anthropocentrism," in Seed et al., eds., *Thinking Like a Mountain* (Philadelphia: New Society, 1988).

105. Further context and analysis of this message is provided in the Conclusion. For the full text of John Paul II's message, see "Message of His Holiness Pope John Paul II for the Celebration of the World Day of Peace (January 1, 1990), Peace with God the Creator, Peace with All of Creation," http://www.vatican.va/holy_father/john_paul_ii/messages/peace/documents/hf_jp-ii_mes_19891208_xxiii-world-day-for-peace_en.html (December 20, 2005).

106. Alan Cowell, "Pope Issues Censure of 'Nature Worship' by Some Feminists," *New York Times*, July 3, 1993, A1, A4. Biocentric thought within the environmental movement stems largely from "deep ecology," an environmental philosophy first articulated by Arne Naess in 1973 and further theorized in 1985 by George Sessions and Bill Devall. In contrast to "shallow ecologists" who want to save the earth for human-centered, human-serving reasons, deep ecologists assert a biocentric ethic that recognizes the intrinsic worth of other species and their right to exist, regardless of their "utility" to humans. In other words, man is not the crown of creation, and the rest of the life community was not made for humans. Deep ecology embraces a unitive view of earth and

humanity, in which the human self is recognized as part of the larger ecological or planetary self. In other words, "We are the earth." Accordingly, deep ecologists argue that "the anthropocentric core of Western philosophy must be replaced with a new metaphysics, psychology, ethics, and science based upon an expanded sense of the ecological Self." See Arne Naess, "The Shallow and the Deep, Long-Range Ecology Movements: A Summary," *Inquiry* 16 (1973): 95–100; and Carolyn Merchant, ed., *Ecology: Key Concepts in Critical Theory* (Atlantic Highlands, N.J.: Humanities Press, 1994), 8. Freya Matthews's book *The Ecological Self* (1991) similarly explores the psychology of a united earth-human consciousness, and Australian forest activist John Seed has also contributed to the popularization of the deep ecological concept of the "earthself" through his classic cri de coeur (now famous within green circles): "I *am* the rainforest defending itself." See Seed, *Thinking Like a Mountain*, 35–39.

107. Berry, *Dream of the Earth*, 165, 42.

108. Berry, *Great Work*, 27.

109. Dennis Poust, "Despite Growing Environmental Threats, 'Green' Catholics Remain Few in Number," *National Catholic Register*, November 2–8, 1997, 1; see also Pope John Paul II, *The Ecological Crisis: A Common Responsibility*, World Day of Peace Message, December 8, 1989 (Washington, D.C.: United States Catholic Conference, 1990).

110. This is very similar to the arguments made by evangelical Christians regarding the environment. See, for example, Tony Campolo, *How to Rescue the Earth without Worshipping Nature* (Nashville: Thomas Nelson, 1992), 4–5. Campolo claims that New Age "eco-freaks" have taken over the environmental movement with their "strange ideas" and "demonic influence" precisely because Christians have abdicated their responsibility to provide leadership in this area.

111. Poust, "Despite Growing," 10.

112. Drew Christiansen and Walter Grazer, eds., *And God Saw That It Was Good: Catholic Theology and the Environment* (Washington, D.C.: U.S. Catholic Conference, 1996).

113. Walter Grazer, interview with the author, Washington, D.C., July 17, 1997.

114. Ibid.

115. This statement comes from a talk Thomas Berry gave in 1996 at the Foundation for a Global Community's Center for the Evolution of Culture in Palo Alto, California.

116. Grazer interview, 1997.

117. See, for instance, H. Paul Sartmire, "In God's Ecology," *Christian Century* (December 13, 2000): 1300–1305; Mitchell Pacwa, "Catholicism for the New Age," *Christian Research Journals* (Fall 1992): 14; Charles Rubin, "Worshipping Green Idols," presentation to the Philadelphia Society National Meeting, Oak Brook, Ill., April 25, 1998; Beth Roney Drennan, "Paulists' RENEW 2000 Is Just a Front for Call to Action," *Wanderer*, September 24, 1998, 1.

118. For an examination of Catholic sisters' early social and political activism in the United States, see Emily Clark, *Masterless Mistresses: The New Orleans Ursulines and the Development of a New World Society, 1727–1834* (Chapel Hill: University of North Carolina Press, 2002). See also James Kenneally's chapter on the trials and tribulations faced by activist nuns in nineteenth-century America as they dealt with hostile and dom-

ineering bishops, in Kenneally, *The History of American Catholic Women* (New York: Crossroad, 1990), 43–60.

119. This phrase comes from Terry Tempest Williams's interview with Episcopal priest Benjamin Webb in *Fugitive Faith* (New York: Orbis, 1998), 163.

120. Eugene Kennedy, *Tomorrow's Catholics, Yesterday's Church: The Two Cultures of Catholicism* (New York: Harper and Row, 1988), xiii.

121. Quoted in ibid., 7.

122. Carole Rossi, interview with the author, Plainville, Mass., June 29, 1997.

123. Alan Atkisson, "Living the New Story: An Interview with Miriam Therese MacGillis," *In Context* 24 (1990): 26.

2. Standing Their Ground

1. Patricia Daly and John F. Welch, Jr., "God Versus G.E.," *Harper's Magazine,* "Readings" section, reprint of General Electric's shareholder meeting transcript, April 22, 1998 (August 1998): 23–25.

2. Marilyn Berlin Snell, "Sister Action: The Almighty Dollar Meets Its Match in a Dominican Nun," *Sierra Magazine* (May/June 2003): 16–19.

3. Ibid., 18.

4. Patricia Daly, electronic interview with the author, February 23, 2002.

5. Don Kania, "Modern-Day Prophets 'Speak Truth to Power' at Missile Site," *Dominican Life* (2002), http://www.domlife.org/missiles.html (January 4, 2004).

6. Ardeth Platte, telephone interview with the author, January 2, 2006.

7. Quoted in Melissa Jones, "Nuns Sentenced for Plowshares Action in Colorado," *National Catholic Reporter,* August 15, 2003, 5.

8. Plowshares Nuns Press Release, http://cndyorks.gn.apc.org/yspace/articles/plowsharenuns.htm (May 14, 2004).

9. Carol Gilbert, telephone interview with the author, January 2, 2006.

10. Here Gilbert refers to the *Pastoral Constitution on the Church in the Modern World* (*Gaudium et Spes* or "Joy and Hope"), particularly the last of the sixteen documents of Vatican II. Approved in December 1965, this sixteenth document advocates nonviolence as a legitimate Catholic position and affirms the social engagement of the Catholic Church. See Carol Gilbert, "Sentencing Statement," July 25, 2003, http://www.plowsharesactions.org/sentencing_statement%20-%20Carol.htm (May 14, 2004).

11. Ibid.

12. Carol Coburn and Martha Smith, *Spirited Lives: How Nuns Shaped Catholic Culture and American Life, 1836–1920* (Chapel Hill: University of North Carolina Press, 1999), 13. See also, as cited in Coburn and Smith, *Spirited Lives,* Patricia Byrne, "French Roots of a Women's Movement: Sisters of St. Joseph, 1650–1836," Ph.D. diss., Boston College, 1985.

13. Coburn and Smith, *Spirited Lives,* 27.

14. See, in particular, Martin Gilbert's references to the many Roman Catholic religious sisters who sheltered Jewish children in *The Righteous: The Unsung Heroes of the Holocaust* (New York: Henry Holt, 2003), 51, 79–80, 178, 268, 276, 307, 312, 365, 392.

15. Mary J. Oates, *The Catholic Philanthropic Tradition in America* (Bloomington: Indiana University Press, 1995), 46–47.

16. John Fialka, *Sisters: Catholic Nuns and the Making of America* (New York: St. Martin's, 2003), 6. See also Coburn and Smith, esp. chap. 7 (on sisters and nursing in the United States).

17. Rosemary Radford Ruether and Rosemary Skinner Keller, eds., *In Our Own Voices: Four Centuries of American Women's Religious Writing* (San Francisco: Harper San Francisco, 1995), 36–39.

18. For a detailed history of sisters' active participation in racial activism and the Selma, Alabama, civil rights protest, see Amy Koehlinger, "From Selma to Sisterhood: Race and Transformation in Catholic Sisterhoods in the 1960s (Alabama)," Ph.D. diss., Yale University, 2002.

19. Margaret Ellen Traxler, "Great Tide of Returning," in Ann Patrick Ware, *Midwives of the Future: American Sisters Tell Their Story* (Kansas City, Mo.: Leaven Press, 1985), 133.

20. Field journal notes, Santa Barbara, Calif., March 17, 1999.

21. Julia Lieblich, *Sisters: Lives of Devotion and Defiance* (New York: Ballantine, 1992); 225–269; see also Renny Golden and Michale McConnell, *Sanctuary: The New Underground Railroad* (Maryknoll, N.Y.: Orbis, 1986).

22. Marie Augusta Neal, *From Nuns to Sisters: An Expanding Vocation* (Mystic, Conn.: Twenty-Third Publications, 1990), as cited in Lieblich, *Sisters,* 26.

23. Note that the term "bioneer" is borrowed from environmental activist and sustainable agriculture advocate Kenneth Ausubel, who founded the Bioneers Conferences in 1990 to bring together visionaries with diverse backgrounds and interests (environmental design, biological sciences, agriculture, philosophy, art, culture, spirituality, and so on) who are all working toward creative solutions for "restoring and repairing" the earth. See Kenneth Ausubel, *Restoring the Earth: Visionary Solutions from the Bioneers* (Tiburon, Calif.: H. J. Kramer, 1997).

24. Mary Farrell Bednarowski, *The Religious Imagination of American Women* (Bloomington: Indiana University Press, 1999), 6.

25. This phrasing comes directly out of the Second Vatican Council's *Lumen Gentium* or *Dogmatic Constitution on the Church,* November 21, 1964. Chapter 2 of the constitution is entitled "On the People of God" and defines the Church as not the clergy but the "people of God" and calls for greater shared authority within the Roman Catholic Church. See http://www.vatican.va/archive/hist_councils/ii_vatican_council/documents/vat-ii_const_19641121_lumen-gentium_en.html (July 24, 2006).

26. The perspective described here is in keeping with Kenneth Ausubel's emphasis on bioneers as those who repair damage that is already present and focus on the restoration of life systems to health and well-being. See Ausubel, *Restoring the Earth.*

27. Gary Snyder, "Reinhabitation," in his *The Old Ways* (San Francisco: City Lights Books, 1977), 63.

28. Stephanie Mills, foreword to *Home! A Bioregional Reader,* ed. Van Andruss, Christopher Plant, Judith Plant, and Eleanor Wright (Philadelphia: New Society, 1990), vii.

29. Stephanie Mills, *Whatever Happened to Ecology?* (San Francisco: Sierra Club Books, 1989), 51–52.

30. Pope Paul IV, *The Adaptation and Renewal of Religious Life: Perfectae Caritatis,* October 28, 1965, http://www.vatican.va/archive/hist_councils/ii_vatican_council/documents/vat-ii_decree_19651028_perfectae-caritatis_en.html (July 25, 2006).

31. Neal, *From Nuns to Sisters,* 67.

32. Maureen A. Wild, "Profession of Perpetual Vows (August 5, 1990)," as related in an electronic interview with the author, April 10, 2002.

33. Wild interview.

34. For a good basic outline of contemporary understandings and explanations of the vows, see Kathleen Rooney, *Sisters: An Inside Look* (Winona, Minn.: Saint Mary's Press, 2001), 37, 55.

35. Ibid., 6.

36. Neal, *From Nuns to Sisters,* 68.

37. Rooney, *Sisters,* 36. See also *Code of Canon Law,* trans. Canon Law Society of America (Washington, D.C.: Canon Law Society of America, 1983).

38. Bednarowski, *Religious Imagination,* 6.

39. Eugene Kennedy, as quoted in Jeannine Gramick, "From Good Sisters to Prophetic Women," in Ann Patrick Ware, ed., *Midwives of the Future: American Sisters Tell Their Story* (Kansas City, Mo.: Leaven Press, 1985), 227.

40. For a history of the historical struggle for U.S. Catholic women's religious communities for greater self-determination in the face of community interference by U.S. bishops, see Mary J. Oates, "Organizing for Service: Challenges to Community Life and Work Decisions in Catholic Sisterhoods, 1850–1940," in Wendy Chmielewski and Louis Kern, eds., *Women in Spiritual and Communitarian Societies in the United States* (Syracuse, N.Y.: Syracuse University Press, 1993), 150–167.

41. Rooney, *Sisters,* 30.

42. Ibid.

43. Coburn and Smith, *Spirited Lives,* 9.

44. Michael Waldstein, "Charismatic Renewal Movement," in Richard McBrien, ed., *Encyclopedia of Catholicism* (San Francisco: Harper San Francisco, 1995), 300.

45. Rooney, *Sisters,* 43.

46. Elaine Prevallet, *In the Service of Life: Widening and Deepening Religious Commitment; A Series of Presentations on Earth Spirituality* (Nerinx, Ky.: Elaine Prevallet, 2002), 3.

47. Elaine Prevallet, *A Wisdom for Life: A Series of Presentations on Earth Spirituality* (Nerinx, Ky.: Elaine Prevallet, 1995), 34–35.

48. Ibid., 33.

49. Ibid.

50. Ibid., 3.

51. Miriam MacGillis's audiotape series *Reinhabiting Our Backyard* (Sonoma, Calif.: Global Perspectives, 1990) provides an excellent image of dealing first with one's own immediate environment before concerning oneself with other regions, be they topographical or religious.

52. Susan Ross, "God's Embodiment and Women," in Catherine Mowry LaCugna,

ed., *Freeing Theology: The Essentials of Theology in Feminist Perspective* (San Francisco: Harper San Francisco, 1993), 186.

53. Andrew Greeley, *The Catholic Imagination* (Berkeley: University of California Press, 2000), 2–4.

54. For further discussion of the influence of Johann Wolfgang von Goethe on the work of Friedrich Max Müller, see Daniel Pals, *Seven Theories of Religion* (New York: Oxford University Press, 1996), 3. The Genesis Farm (New Jersey) and the Spiritearth (New York) libraries (the latter of which was eventually moved to the Allium Center in La Grange, Ill.), were particularly impressive for their wide spectrum of holdings informed by diverse religious perspectives.

55. Field journal notes, Genesis Farm, Blairstown, N.J., July 9, 1997.

56. Field journal notes, Sisters of Earth Conference, Mont Marie Conference Center, Holyoke, Mass., August 3, 2002.

57. Prevallet, *Wisdom for Life,* 35.

58. Ibid., 35–36.

59. Note the difference between "chastity," which is a state of sexual purity that the Church expects of all Christians (vowed or not) and "celibacy," which is the specific unmarried state in which one gives oneself over to or consecrates one's life to God. Some orders emphasize the language of one over the other, depending on their traditions and constitutions.

60. Miriam MacGillis, personal communication with the author, March 8, 2004.

61. Toni Nash, lecture transcript, "What Are the Implications of Our Commitment for the People of God? Notes for a Talk on the New Cosmology and Religious Vows," Los Angeles, Calif., October 11, 1998.

62. Ibid., 10.

63. Prevallet, *In the Service,* 22.

64. See Diarmuid O'Murchu, *Poverty, Celibacy, and Obedience: A Radical Option for Life* (New York: Crossroads, 1999), 40–48; and *Quantum Theology* (New York: Crossroads, 1997).

65. Nash, "What Are the Implications," 10.

66. Ibid., 1. See also Diarmuid O'Murchu, *Religious Life: A Prophetic Vision; Hope and Promise for Tomorrow* (Notre Dame, Ind.: Ave Maria Press, 1991); and David Abram, *The Spell of the Sensuous: Perception and Language in a More-Than-Human World* (New York: Pantheon, 1996).

67. "EverGreen: What Is It? Where Is It? Why Is It?," pamphlet, Ministry of the Sisters of the Humility of Mary, Villa Maria, Pa., 2002.

68. Barbara O'Donnell, director of EverGreen, Villa Maria, Pa., electronic interview with the author, April 4, 2002; David Shi, *The Simple Life: Plain Living and High Thinking in American Culture* (New York: Oxford University Press, 1985).

69. Barbara O'Donnell, electronic interview with the author, April 4, 2002.

70. Carole Rossi, interview with the author, Plainville, Mass., June 29, 1997.

71. Chris Loughlin, interview with the author, Plainville, Mass., June 29, 1997.

72. Bednarowski, *Religious Imagination,* 6.

73. Janine Benyus, *Biomimicry* (New York: Harper Perennial, 2002); Cathy Mueller, electronic interview with the author, March 1, 2002.

74. Joellen Sbrissa, electronic interview with the author, January 7, 2002.

75. Mary Southard, electronic interview with the author, February 28, 2002.

76. Janet Fraser, electronic interview with the author, February 26, 2002.

77. O'Donnell interview.

78. Brian Swimme and Thomas Berry, *The Universe Story: From the Primordial Flaring Forth to the Ecozoic Era* (New York: Harper Collins, 1992).

79. This combination of McDonagh's work and peace and social justice themes makes good sense, since McDonagh specifically makes the case for "stewardship" (care for the earth) in the context of his ecojustice work with the T'Boli people of the Philippines, whose poor villages have suffered disproportionately from the ravages of rapid tropical deforestation and erosion. See Sean McDonagh, *To Care for the Earth: A Call to a New Theology* (Santa Fe: Bear and Company, 1987).

80. James Conlon, *Earth Story, Sacred Story* (Mystic, Conn.: Twenty-Third Publications, 1994).

81. Names withheld upon request, interviews with the author, April 4, 2002.

82. Ioannes Paulus PP II, *Evangelium Vitae: To the Bishops, Priests, and Deacons, Men and Women Religious, Lay Faithful, and All People of Good Will, on the Value and Inviolability of Human Life* (1995), http://www.vatican.va/holy_father/john_paul_ii/encyclicals/documents/hf_jp-ii_enc_25031995_evangelium-vitae_en.html (January 12, 2006). In particular, see sections 50, 77, 82, 86, 87, 92, 95, 98, and 100.

83. *Genesis Farm 1999 Calendar of Events*, Genesis Farm, Blairstown, N.J.

84. Adrienne Rich, "When We Dead Awaken: Writings As 'Re-Vision,'" in *On Lies, Secrets and Silence: Selected Prose, 1966–1978* (London: Virago, 1980), as excerpted in Maggie Humm, ed., *Feminisms: A Reader* (New York: Harvester Wheatsheaf, 1992), 369.

85. Miriam MacGillis, *Re-Visioning the Vowed Life*, audio series available through Global Perspectives, Sonoma, Calif.

86. Ibid.

87. Bruce Foltz, *Inhabiting the Earth: Heidegger, Environmental Ethics, and the Metaphysics of Nature* (Atlantic Highlands, N.J.: Humanities Press, 1995), 15. Foltz argues that Heidegger's use of inhabitation also involves the ingredient of care—that dwelling, in its essence, involves both relationship to place and caring. Heidegger's work, according to Foltz, communicates "the primacy of the poetic in the task of learning to inhabit the earth rightly."

88. Any conscious connection between Heidegger's theorizing of "inhabitation" and Berg's theorizing of "reinhabitation" is likely inadvertent. Peter Berg is generally credited with having first coined the term reinhabitation (before Snyder in 1977), and when I spoke with Berg by telephone in the spring of 1999 at the Planet Drum Foundation in San Francisco, Berg remarked that although he had read Heidegger, he was not consciously thinking about Heidegger's discussion of inhabitation when he first began theorizing the concept of reinhabitation as it relates to landscape and bioregionalism.

89. U.S. Census Bureau, Washington, D.C., http://www.census.gov/Press-Release/www/releases/archives/mobility_of_the_population/001729.html (June 20, 2005).

90. Deborah Tall, *From Where We Stand: Recovering a Sense of Place* (Baltimore: Johns Hopkins University Press, 1993), 89.

91. Terry Tempest Williams, *An Unspoken Hunger: Stories from the Field* (New York: Vintage, 1994), 135.

92. Helen Rose Fuchs Ebaugh, *The Vanishing Cloister: Organizational Decline in Catholic Religious Orders in the United States* (New Brunswick, N.J.: Rutgers University Press, 1993), 46–60.

3. It Isn't Easy Being Green

1. Annie Dillard, *Teaching a Stone to Talk* (San Francisco: Harper and Row, 1982), 40.

2. Margaret Susan Thompson, ed., *Building Sisterhood: A Feminist History of the Sisters, Servants of the Immaculate Heart of Mary* (Syracuse, N.Y.: Syracuse University Press, 1997), 6–7.

3. Sharon Abercrombie, "The Motherhouse of Reinvention," *EarthLight Magazine* (Fall 2001): 38–41.

4. Sisters, Servants of the Immaculate Heart of Mary, *Mission for the Millennium: The Sustainable Renovation of the Motherhouse of the Sisters, Servants of the Immaculate Heart of Mary* (Monroe, Mich., 2002), 5.

5. Ibid., 4.

6. Ibid., 16. For a more in-depth discussion of strategies for sustainable living, see William E. Rees et al., *Our Ecological Footprint: Reducing Human Impact on the Earth* (Philadelphia: New Society, 1995).

7. Janet Ryan, interview with the author, Monroe, Mich., October 26, 2002.

8. Paula Cathcart, "Transforming Buildings, Land, and Community," a talk given in the "Sharing the Wisdom: How Are We Living the Vision?" presentation section of the Fifth International Conference of Sisters of Earth, Mont Marie Conference Center (situated on the motherhouse grounds of the Sisters of St. Joseph of Springfield), Holyoke, Mass., August 2, 2002. See also Cathcart's synopsis of this talk in "Transforming Buildings, Land and Community," *Loretto Earth Network News* (Fall 2002): 4.

9. Sisters, Servants of the Immaculate Heart of Mary, "The Blue Nuns Go Green," video recording, Monroe, Mich., 2002.

10. Sisters, Servants of the Immaculate Heart of Mary, *Mission for the Millennium,* 9.

11. Quoted in Denise LaPorte, "Partners in Legacy," *IHM Journal* (Fall 2002): 9.

12. Cathcart, "Transforming Buildings," (conference speech), August 2, 2002.

13. Cathcart, "Transforming Buildings," *Loretto Earth Network News,* 4.

14. Cathcart, "Transforming Buildings" speech given at Sisters of Earth conference, August 2, 2002.

15. Ibid.

16. Quoted in LaPorte, "Partners in Legacy," 8. The Great Law of Peace of the Haudenosaunee (the Six Nation Iroquois Confederacy) mandates that tribal leaders consider the effects of their decisions on seven generations to come.

17. "St. Mary Organic Farm CSA: New Name, Old Name, New Season," *Tap Root* 5, no. 1 (July 2002): 2.

18. Sisters, Servants of the Immaculate Heart of Mary, "A New Moment: Mission for

the New Millennium—Earth, Fire, Water, Air, Spirit," program guide for St. Mary Academy Alumnae, October 26, 2002.

19. "Discernment Group Meeting II, October 14–17, 1999," *Monroe Campus Long Range Master Plan Updates* (October 1999), 2.

20. Ryan interview.

21. Sisters, Servants of the Immaculate Heart of Mary Discernment Group Leadership Council, *Monroe Campus Long Range Master Plan Integrating Idea,* October 1999 (reprinted for Coordinating Council, December 2000), 1, 6.

22. Ryan interview.

23. Stephanie Mills, *Whatever Happened to Ecology?* (San Francisco: Sierra Club Books, 1995), 149.

24. Thomas Moore, "Ecology: Sacred Homemaking," in Michael Tobias and Georgianne Cowan, eds., *The Soul of Nature: Celebrating the Spirit of the Earth* (New York: Penguin, 1994), 137.

25. Field journal, Genesis Farm, Blairstown, N.J., August 22, 1995.

26. Sim Van der Ryn and Stuart Cowan, *Ecological Design* (Washington, D.C.: Island Press, 1996), 162.

27. Athena Swentzell, Bill Steen, and David Bainbridge, *The Straw Bale House* (White River Junction, Vt.: Chelsea Green, 1994). Straw-bale construction is also favored by those who are chemically sensitive, since all the building materials are nonsynthetic.

28. Ibid., 25.

29. Ibid., 27.

30. Gail Worcelo, remarks in Straw Bale Hermitage Guest Book, St. Gabriel's Monastery, Clark's Summit, Pa., August 1995.

31. "Hermitages," Prairiewoods Franciscan Spirituality Center homepage, http://www.prairiewoods.org/scripts/services_hermitages.asp (December 20, 2005).

32. Here Miller invokes the language of the body of Catholic social justice teaching, which calls for a "preferential option for the poor." In John Paul II's *Sollicitudo rei socialis,* for instance, he refers to "the option or love of preference for the poor." See Charles E. Curran, *Catholic Social Teaching, 1891–Present: A Historical Theological and Ethical Analysis* (Washington, D.C.: Georgetown University Press, 2002), 183.

33. Tierra Madre homepage, http://www.geocities.com/tmadre (December 21, 2005).

34. Lora Ann Quiñonez and Mary Daniel Turner, *The Transformation of American Catholic Sisters* (Philadelphia: Temple University Press, 1992), 66.

35. See Philip Sheldrake, *Spaces for the Sacred: Place, Memory, and Identity* (Baltimore: Johns Hopkins University Press, 2001), esp. chap. 4, "The Practice of Place: Monasteries and Utopias," 91.

36. Dominican Alliance Ethic Report, http://www.ksdom.org/landethic.html (January 23, 2005).

37. Chris Loughlin, interview with the author, Plainville, Mass., June 29, 1997.

38. "Religious Lands Conservancy Project," pamphlet produced by Crystal Spring Earth Learning Center, Plainfield, Mass., 2002.

39. Carol Coston and Elise D. García, interview with the author, Boerne, Tex., March 4, 2002.

40. Elise D. García, personal communication with the author, May 19, 2006.

41. Wade Clark Roof, "Religious Borderlands: Challenges for Future Study," *Journal for the Society for the Scientific Study of Religion* 37, no. 1 (March 1999): 1–14, quotation on p. 4.

42. Elaine Prevallet, *A Wisdom for Life: A Series of Presentations on Earth Spirituality Presented at a Conference Sponsored by the Loretto Earth Network* (Nerinx, Ky.: Elaine Prevallet, 1995), 39. The Loretto community has been particularly active in environment issues.

43. See the description and specifications of this interview described in the Introduction.

44. Diane Roche, electronic interview with the author, April 4, 2002.

45. Ibid.

46. Michel de Certeau, *The Practice of Everyday Life* (Berkeley: University of California Press, 1984), 40, 32.

47. See Stephanie Mills's introduction to Van Andruss, Judith Plant, and Eleanor Wright, eds., *Home! A Bioregional Reader* (Philadelphia: New Society, 1990), vii. In this passage, Mills refers to a popular book offering easy everyday things people can do to save the earth—see The Earthworks Group, *Fifty Simple Things You Can Do to Save the Earth* (Berkeley: Earthworks Press, 1989). By contrast, radical environmental groups such as Earth First! have countered with their own tongue-in-cheek "Ten Really Hard Things to Do to Save the Planet," which includes suggestions such as filling a knapsack with explosives and blowing up the Hoover Dam.

48. Mills, *Whatever Happened to Ecology?* 5.

49. Workshop advertisement from *Streams: A Newsletter of Crystal Spring Center for Earth Literacy,* no. 14 (Spring 2002): 4, 3.

50. Diane Roche, electronic interview with the author, April 4, 2002.

51. Maureen Wild, electronic interview with the author, April 10, 2002.

52. Ibid.

53. Rose Mary Meyer, electronic interview with the author, March 25, 2002.

54. Mary Southard, electronic interview with the author, March 4, 2002.

55. Elizabeth Kuhns, *The Habit: A History of the Clothing of Catholic Nuns* (New York: Doubleday, 2003), 139–160.

56. Patricia Lucas, "Diary of Change," in Ann Patrick Ware, ed., *Midwives of the Future: American Sisters Tell Their Story* (Kansas City, Mo.: Leaven Press, 1985), 177.

57. *Rule and Constitutions of the Sisters of the Green Mountain Monastery* (Fall 2003), 9.

58. Maureen Wild, electronic interview with the author, April 10, 2004.

59. I also learned from sisters how to simplify one's life by dividing all of one's belongings into three categories: (1) very useful, so must keep, (2) might be useful, so maybe should keep, and (3) not needed, so should donate and recycle. Everything in the second category is to be put in boxes in storage for six months. At the end of six months, anything that you have not used or looked desperately for during that period gets moved into the third category and is donated or recycled. Ideally, a regular "green inventory" like this should be performed each spring. Sisters also recommended Ellen St. James's work to me as a good resource for simplifying. St. James offers strategies not only for declutter-

ing but also dealing with the "stuff" that finds its way into one's house no matter hard one tries to live simply—plastic bags, trinkets, twist ties, ice cream makers, and so forth. See Ellen St. James, *Simplify Your Life: One Hundred Ways to Slow Down and Enjoy the Things That Really Matter* (New York: Hyperion, 1994); *Inner Simplicity* (New York: Hyperion, 1995); *Living the Simple Life: A Guide to Scaling Down and Enjoying More* (New York: Hyperion, 1996); and *Living the Simple Life with Kids* (Kansas City, Mo.: Andrews McMeel, 1997).

60. Field journal notes, July 8, 1996.

61. See the discussion of the "new nun" in M. Charles Borromeo, ed., *The New Nuns* (New York: New American Library, 1967); Leon Joseph Suenens, *The Nun in the World* (Westminster, Md.: Newman Press, 1963); and Bertrande Meyers, *Sisters for the Twenty-first Century* (New York: Sheed & Ward, 1965).

62. Diane Roche, electronic interview with the author, April 4, 2002.

63. Elaine Prevallet, *In the Service of Life: Widening and Deepening Religious Commitment, a Series of Presentations on Earth Spirituality* (Nerinx, Ky.: Elaine Prevallet, 2002), 22; Toni Nash, lecture transcript, "What Are the Implications of Our Commitment for the People of God? Notes for a Talk on the New Cosmology and Religious Vows," Los Angeles, Calif., October 11, 1998, 10.

64. Marya Grathwohl, electronic interview with the author, March 2, 2002.

65. This phrase comes from Charles M. Sheldon's classic nineteenth-century novel *In His Steps; "What Would Jesus Do?"* (Chicago: Advance, 1896).

66. Catherine Coyne, telephone interview with the author, January 17, 2006.

67. Ibid.

68. Nancy Earle, telephone interview with the author, December 20, 2005.

69. Ibid.

70. Note that I acknowledge the use of the term "hybrid culture" by Nestor García Canclini and other cultural theorists to refer to the dangers of hybridity in modernity, especially for economically disadvantaged ethnic cultures that face the danger of losing their cultural identities to an increasingly homogenized global culture. This is not what I am talking about in the discussion of sisters and hybrid vehicles. Here I use the term "hybrid culture" in a less pejorative sense to signify the kind of blending of heterogeneous categories (for instance, "gasoline-powered" versus "electric") that results in creative and alternative solutions beneficial to communities. See Nestor García Canclini, *Hybrid Cultures: Strategies for Entering and Leaving Modernity* (Minneapolis: University of Minnesota Press, 1995).

71. John Burger, "Summit Draft Ignores Successes in Vocation," *National Catholic Register,* January 6, 2002, 1.

72. Roger Finke and Rodney Stark, *The Churching of America, 1776–1990: Winners and Losers in Our Religious Economy* (New Brunswick, N.J.: Rutgers University Press, 1992), 257–263.

73. Laurence Iannaccone, "Strict Churches Make Strong Churches," as quoted in Finke and Stark, *Churching of America,* 261.

74. See Iannaccone, "Strict Churches Make Stronger Churches."

75. Finke and Stark, *Churching of America,* 238.

76. Mary Jo Leddy, *Reweaving Religious Life: Beyond the Liberal Model* (Mystic, Conn.: Twenty-third Publications, 1991), 147.

77. See, for example, Patricia Wittberg, *The Rise and Fall of Catholic Religious Orders: A Social Movements Perspective* (Albany: State University of New York Press, 1994); Helen Rose Fuchs Ebaugh, *Women in the Vanishing Cloister: Organizational Decline in Catholic Religious Orders in the United States* (New Brunswick, N.J.: Rutgers University Press, 1993); Richard Schoenherr, *Full Pews, Empty Altars: Demographics of the Priest Shortage in U.S. Dioceses* (Madison: University of Wisconsin Press, 1993). For contrast, see Mary Johnson, "The Reweaving of Catholic Spiritual and Institutional Life," *Annals of the American Academy of Political and Social Science* 558 (July 1998): 135–143.

78. Albert Camus, *Noces Suivi de L'Eté* (Paris: Editions Callimard, 1955), as quoted in Keith Basso, *Wisdom Sits in Places: Landscape and Language among the Western Apache* (Albuquerque: University of New Mexico, 1996), 143.

79. Paula Kane, "'She Offered Herself Up': The Victim Soul and Victim Spirituality in Catholicism," *Church History* 71, no. 80 (March 2002): 103–104.

80. Robert Orsi, *Heaven and Earth: The Religious Worlds People Make and the Scholars Who Study Them* (Princeton, N.J.: Princeton University Press, 2005), 21.

81. Field journal notes, Casa de Maria, International Conference of Sisters of Earth, Santa Barbara, Calif., August 18, 2000.

82. Rees et al., *Our Ecological Footprint.*

4. "Changeless and Changing"

1. Field journal notes, Weston, Vt., June 21, 2000.

2. Geologists generally date the Cenozoic era as having begun roughly 65 million years ago, immediately after the Mesozoic era. The Cenozoic era is known for being when a wide variety of mammals developed. In the wake of large-scale extinctions and species loss in the last century, Berry speaks about our coming to the end of the Cenozoic era, a period that he hopes will be followed by a more positive human-earth partnership coming to life in what he terms the "Ecozoic era." But he also darkly envisions a path of continued destructive division between humans and earth—a "Technozoic" era during which the state of human relations with the earth community worsens. See Thomas Berry, *The Great Work: Our Way into the Future* (New York: Bell Tower, 1999), 201.

3. Ibid.

4. Green Mountain Monastery, "A Greensboro Welcome," Greensboro, Vt., Fall 2004.

5. Gail Worcelo, personal communication with the author, May 19, 2006.

6. Ibid.

7. This deliberate renaming of the Sisters of Loretto as the Loretto Community was designed to include the sisters' growing number of active comembers who partner with the sisters in their spiritual mission and ministries. In this way, the Loretto Community is one of a number of sisters' communities implementing new models and configurations of religious life.

8. Gail Worcelo, "Stellar Generosity," *Loretto Earth Network News* (Spring 2005): 5.

9. Mary Johnson, "The Reweaving of Catholic Spiritual and Institutional Life," *Annals of the American Academy of Political and Social Science* 558 (July 1998): 138–141.

10. *Rule and Constitutions of the Sisters of the Green Mountain Monastery,* Greensboro, Vt., Fall 2003, 1.

11. "A Celebration in Stone," *Green Mountain Monastery Newsletter,* (Spring 2005): 1. See http://www.greenmountainmonastery.org.

12. Gail Worcelo, personal communication with the author, May 19, 2006.

13. Betty Didcoct, "Choosing Our Roots: Traditional Christian Attitudes Offer Both Problems and Promise for Healing the Earth; an Interview with Thomas Berry," *In Context* (Winter 1984): 28.

14. Sisters of the Green Mountain Monastery, "A Brief History," Weston, Vt., 2003. This document is part of an informational literature packet made available by the monastery to educate others about their foundation and mission.

15. See Sheila Garcia, "Stability and Change: What Benedict's Rule Can Teach Us," *American Benedictine Review* 49 (1989): 71–81; Michael Casey, "The Value of Stability," *Cistercian Studies Quarterly* 31 (1996): 287–301; Michael Kelly, "Reflection on the Significance of *Stabilitas* and *Conversatio Morum* in Benedictine Commitment," *American Benedictine Review* 55 (2004): 251–264.

16. Statement by North American Bioregional Congress, "Welcome Home!" in Van Andruss et al., *Home: A Bioregional Reader* (Philadelphia: New Society, 1990), 170; Judith Plant, "Revaluing Home: Feminism and Bioregionalism," in Van Andruss et al., *Home,* 21–25; Gary Snyder, *A Place in Space: Ethics, Aesthetics, and Watersheds* (Washington, D.C.: Counterpoint, 1995), 183–252.

17. Snyder, *A Place in Space,* 190–191.

18. For a theorizing of emplacement, bioregionalism, and the importance of committed "dwelling," see Kirkpatrick Sale, *Dwellers in the Land: The Bioregional Vision* (Philadelphia: New Society, 1991).

19. Gail Worcelo, personal communication with the author, May 19, 2006.

20. Ibid.

21. *Rule and Constitutions of the Sisters of the Green Mountain Monastery,* 2003, sections 6 and 7.

22. Gail Worcelo, "An Ecozoic Monastery: Shaping a Transforming Vision for the Future," *Loretto Earth Network News* (Spring 2000): 7.

23. For further explorations of these tensions, see Rebecca Gould, *At Home in Nature: Modern Homesteading and Spiritual Practice in America* (Berkeley: University of California Press, 2005); David Shi, *Plain Living and High Thinking in American Culture* (New York: Oxford University Press, 1985); and Donald Pitzer, ed., *America's Communal Utopias* (Chapel Hill: University of North Carolina Press, 1997). For an analysis of the role of gender in U.S. countercultural experiments, see Wendy Chmielewski et al., ed., *Women in Spiritual and Communitarian Societies in the United States* (Syracuse, N.Y.: Syracuse University Press, 1993).

24. Stephanie Kaza, "To Save All Beings: Buddhist Environmental Activism," in Richard Foltz, ed., *Worldviews, Religion, and the Environment: A Global Anthology* (Belmont, Calif.: Wadsworth, 2003), 292.

25. Ibid., 292–293. Kaza's examples of ecosattvas include, among others, such fig-

ures as poet and writer Gary Snyder, antinuclear activist and deep ecologist Joanna Macy, and rainforest activist John Seed.

26. Thich Nhat Hanh and Robert Ellsberg, eds., *Thich Nhat Hanh: Essential Writings* (Mary Knoll, N.Y.: Orbis, 2001), 80–82.

27. Gail Worcelo, "Nonviolence: Reflections on the Mystery of Suffering," *Stauros Notebook* 6, no. 3 (May/June 1987): 1, http://www.stauros.org/notebooks/v06n3a01.html (August 30, 2005).

28. Gail Worcelo, "The Greening of Our Worship," presentation delivered at the Sisters of Earth Conference, Sinsinawa Mound Center, Sinsinawa, Wis., July 17, 1998.

29. Gail Worcelo, "An Ecozoic Monastery: Shaping a Transforming Vision of the Future," *Loretto Earth Network News* (Spring 2000): 7.

30. Gail Worcelo, personal communication with the author, May 19, 2006.

31. Gail Worcelo, "Holy Ground: Where Catholic Tradition and the Universe Story Meet—Reflections from an Ecozoic Retreat," August 22, 2001, http://thegreatstory.org/CatholicMetarelig.html (August 30, 2005).

32. Robert King, *Thomas Merton and Thich Nhat Hanh: Engaged Spirituality in an Age of Globalism* (New York: Continuum, 2001), 3–5.

33. Worcelo, "Holy Ground."

34. Belden Lane, *The Solace of Fierce Landscapes: Exploring Desert and Mountain Spirituality* (New York: Oxford University Press, 1998), 37.

35. Sisters of the Green Mountain Monastery, "Brief History."

36. *Rule and Constitutions of the Sisters of the Green Mountain Monastery,* 2003, section 38.

37. Gail Worcelo, interview with the author, Weston, Vt., June 22, 2000. For this interview, Gail and I bicycled to the home of a neighbor who had invited the sisters to use her pond. Somewhat fittingly, as we sat at the end of an old wooden dock, dangling our feet in the water, Gail spoke candidly about her conscious path to the "edges" of mainstream American culture, captivated by the depth and beauty of the countercultural monastic life and moved by the potential insight into world problems offered by its position of marginality.

38. For further explanation of this concept, see Thomas Berry, "Into the Future," in Fritz Hull, ed., *Earth and Spirit: The Spiritual Dimension of the Environmental Crisis* (New York: Continuum, 1993), 36–37. Berry writes: "There does exist at present a quantum of energy available for a creative movement from the terminal Cenozoic era into the emergent Ecozoic. Yet it will only be available for a brief period of time. Such transformation moments arise in times of crisis that need resolution immediately. So with the present the time for action is passing. The devastation increases . . . A largeness of vision and supreme dedication is needed." The green sisters' mission is rooted in this calling and to responding to what Berry identifies as a limited window for such transformative efforts.

39. After a brief appearance on stage, Berrigan was hidden in one of the theater troupe's oversized puppets in order to help him evade FBI agents in pursuit. Howard Zinn, *A People's History of the United States, 1492–Present* (New York: Harper Perennial, 1995), 479–480; Daniel Berrigan, *The Geography of Faith: Conversations between Daniel Berrigan, When Underground, and Robert Coles* (Boston: Beacon Press, 1971).

40. Gail Worcelo, personal communication with the author, May 19, 2006.

41. I have documented and theorized about women environmental activists' struggles as "edge walkers" (Terry Tempest Williams's term) and pursue this subject more fully in my forthcoming book on "green" women prophets. Working chapters of this book were presented in the following formats: "Ecologies of Hope and Horror: Activist Women, Ecofeminist Science Fiction, and the Prophetic Imagination," presentation to the Annual Meeting of the American Academy of Religion, San Antonio, Tex., November 21, 2004; "The New Green Prophets: Activist Women, Ecotopian Dreams, and American Religion," presentation to the Woodrow Wilson National Fellowship Foundation, Princeton, N.J., October 16, 2003.

42. Section 39, in particular, of The Rule of St. Benedict (composed ca. 530), urges "moderation be observed in all things."

43. Gail Worcelo, personal communication with the author, May 19, 2006.

44. Gail Worcelo, "Holy Ground: Where Catholic Tradition and the Universe Story Meet—Reflections from an Ecozoic Retreat," 7, http://thegreatstory.org/CatholicMetarelig.html (December 1, 2005).

45. Brian Swimme and Thomas Berry, *The Universe Story: From the Primordial Flaring Forth to the Ecozoic Era—A Celebration of the Unfolding Cosmos* (New York: HarperCollins, 1992); Barbara Newman, *Sister of Wisdom: St. Hildegard's Theology of the Feminine* (Berkeley: University of California Press, 1987).

46. Gail Worcelo, "Liturgy of the Cosmos," *Loretto Earth Network News* (Winter 2004), 4.

47. Thomas Berry in an interview with Derek Jensen, "Liturgy of the Cosmos," *The Witness* (September 2002), http://thewitness.org/archive/sept2002/shorttakes.html (September 14, 2004).

48. Worcelo, "Liturgy of the Cosmos," 4.

49. Ibid.

50. Gail Worcelo, "An Ecozoic Monastery: Shaping a Transforming Vision for the Future," *Loretto Earth Network News* (Spring 2000), 7.

51. Gene Burns, *The Frontiers of Catholicism: Politics and Ideology in a Liberal World* (Berkeley: University of California Press, 1992), 154–155.

52. Meredith McGuire, *Religion: The Social Context,* 4th ed. (Belmont, Calif.: Wadsworth, 1997), 119.

53. David Hufford, "Reason, Rhetoric, and Religion: Academic Ideology versus Folk Belief," *New York Folklore* 11, nos. 1–4 (1985): 177–194; Don Yoder, "Official Religion versus Folk Religion," *Pennsylviania Folklife* 15 (1965–1966): 36–52; Donald Byrne, Jr., "Folklore and the Study of American Religion," in Charles Lippy and Peter Williams, eds., *The Encyclopedia of American Religious Experience,* vol. 1 (New York: Charles Scribner's Sons, 1988): 85–100.

54. Terrence Tilley, *Inventing Catholic Tradition* (Mary Knoll, N.Y.: Orbis, 2000), 15, 6.

55. Andrew Greeley, *The Catholic Imagination* (Berkeley: University of California Press, 2000), 79.

56. Worcelo, "Holy Ground," 5.

57. Ibid.

58. Worcelo, "Liturgy of the Cosmos," 4.

59. See Sabina Flanagan, *Hildegard of Bingen: A Visionary Life* (New York: Routledge, 1998), esp. 135–150 and 77–100.

60. Tilley, *Inventing Catholic Tradition,* 148–149.

61. Bernadette Bostwick, telephone interview with the author, January 4, 2006.

62. Charlene Spretnak, "Recovering the Maternal Matrix: Mary as Premodern and Postmodern Cosmology," keynote address delivered to the Fifth International Conference of Sisters of Earth, Mont Marie Conference Center (situated on the motherhouse grounds of the Sisters of St. Joseph of Springfield), Holyoke, Mass., August 3, 2002.

63. Charlene Spretnak, *Missing Mary: The Queen of Heaven and Her Re-Emergence in the Modern Church* (New York: Palgrave Macmillan, 2004), 40.

64. See, for example, Mary Daly, *Beyond God the Father: Toward a Philosophy of Women's Liberation* (Boston: Beacon Press, 1973), 63, 97–99. Daly points, however, to the curious psychology of Mary: although blacks in the United States who are "Uncle Toms" are praised and receive better treatment than others who do not conform to white standards, they are not exalted the way Mary is. Daly also argues that Mary's virginity can be seen in terms of her independence from men and that Mary herself can be reclaimed as a powerful image for women. See also Marina Warner's classic critique of the Mary/Eve virgin/whore dichotomy in *Alone of All Her Sex: The Myth and Cult of the Virgin Mary* (London: Wiedenfeld and Nicolson, 1976).

65. Spretnak, "Recovering the Maternal Matrix."

66. Spretnak, *Missing Mary,* 146–178.

67. Robert Orsi, *Between Heaven and Earth: The Religious Worlds People Make and the Scholars Who Study Them* (Princeton, N.J.: Princeton University Press, 2005), 52, 56.

68. Field journal notes, Mont Marie Conference Center, Holyoke, Mass., August 3, 2002.

69. Ibid.

70. Spretnak, *Missing Mary,* 180–186.

71. Sandra Zimdars-Swartz, "The Marian Revival in American Catholicism," in Mary Jo Weaver and R. Scott Appleby, eds., *Being Right: Conservative Catholics in America* (Bloomington: Indiana University Press, 1995), 217–219. I am also indebted to Sandra Zimdars-Swartz for our correspondence on this topic.

72. Ibid., 236.

73. Ibid.

74. Kristy Nabhan-Warren finds a similar dynamic of local focus to Marian apparitions in her ethnography of Estela Ruiz, a Mexican American woman living in South Phoenix who receives visions of the Virgin Mary. Nabhan-Warren notes the geographic specificity of these visions: "Estela's apparitions are specific to her South Phoenix community, particularly in the Lady's concern for the social welfare of the urban world of South Phoenix." See Kristy Nabhan-Warren, The *Virgin of El Barrio: Marian Apparitions, Catholic Evangelizing, and Mexican American Activism* (New York: New York University Press, 2005), 82.

75. Orsi, *Between Heaven and Earth,* 61.

76. Greeley, *Catholic Imagination,* 91. Greeley echoes Spretnak's observations about the "goddess problem" but casts these associations in a positive light.

77. Monique Scheer, "From Majesty to Mystery: Change in the Meanings of Black

Madonnas from the Sixteenth to Nineteenth Centuries," *American Historical Review* 107, no. 5, http://www.historycooperative.org/journals/ahr/107.5/ah050200141 (December 6, 2005).

78. Gail Worcelo, "Holy Ground," 6. Note that the more standard spelling is "Czestochowa," but "Czestachowa" is also acceptable.

79. See Leonard Moss and Stephen Capannari, "In Quest of the Black Virgin: She Is Black Because She Is Black," in James J. Preston, ed., *Mother Worship: Theme and Variations* (Chapel Hill: University of North Carolina Press, 1982); Stephen Benko, The *Virgin Goddess: Studies in the Pagan and Christian Roots of Mariology* (Boston: Brill Academic, 2003); Janusz Pasierb, *The Shrine of the Black Madonna of Czestochowa* (Rome: Interpress Publications, 1980); and Ean Begg, *The Cult of the Black Virgin* (Boston: Arkana, 1985).

80. Field journal notes, St. Gabriel's Monastery, Clark's Summit, Pa., July 24, 1997.

81. Greeley, *Catholic Imagination,* 95.

82. Green Mountain Monastery Earth Prayer Beads insert, Greensboro, Vt., 2005. See also Sharon Abercrombie, "Rosaries Focus on Sacred Creation," *National Catholic Reporter,* December 13, 2002, 42.

83. In Joan Hutson's *Praying with Sacred Beads,* the author tells the history of prayer beads from the desert fathers' use of pebbles to count prayers (a precursor to the rosary) to the Celtic tradition of rope or fabric tied with prayer knots, and even the Muslim use of beads for counting the sacred attributes of Allah and the Buddhist use of beads to count the 108 earthly desires of mortals. She also features the more recent development of "chaplets" or variations of the classic rosary prayer that focus on specific religious themes or saints. Whatever the variation, Hutson makes the point that ultimately "the use of prayer beads aids contemplative prayer by bringing into use the body, the mind, and the spirit. The feel of the bead in the fingers helps to keep the mind from wandering while the ordered rhythm of the prayers leads one into stillness. Sacred beads are used to slow down the mind to a new level of consciousness where we reclaim our relationship with Spirit." See Hutson, *Praying with Sacred Beads* (Liguori, Miss.: Liguori Triumph, 2000), ix–xiii.

84. Mary Ann Garisto, electronic interview with the author, March 1, 2002.

85. Field journal notes, Genesis Farm, Blairstown, N.J., July 7, 1996.

86. Colleen McDannell, *Material Christianity: Religion and Popular Culture in America* (New Haven: Yale University Press, 1995), 186.

87. Orsi, *Between Heaven and Earth,* 56.

88. McDannell, *Material Christianity,* 186.

89. Ibid.

90. For a history of this phenomenon and the origin of the term, see Donald Hall, ed., *Muscular Christianity: Embodying the Victorian Age* (Cambridge, Eng.: Cambridge University Press, 1994); Norman Vance, *The Sinews of the Spirit: The Ideal of Christian Manliness in Victorian Literature and Religious Thought* (Cambridge, Eng.: Cambridge University Press, 1985); and Michel Kimmel, *Manhood in America: A Cultural History* (New York: Free Press, 1996).

91. It has been pointed out that this addition was somewhat ironic since Pope John Paul II was an intensely "pro-Mary" pope.

92. Annette Kolodny, *The Land before Her: Fantasy and Experience of the American Frontiers, 1630–1860* (Chapel Hill: University of North Carolina Press, 1984).

93. Here I use the term "religious work" in the way that David Chidester has used it to mean the ways in which religion itself is "work" even as it is worked out in and through the play of culture, imagination, and materiality. See David Chidester, *Authentic Fakes: Religion and American Popular Culture* (Berkeley: University of California Press, 2005).

94. See, for example, Fr. Romanus Cessario, "What's Right with the Catholic Church!" *Catholic Dossier* (March/April 1998), http:// www.catholic.net/rcc/periodicals/faith/nov97/whatsright.html (December 6, 2005).

95. For a summary of U.S. Catholic women religious and their struggle for greater community autonomy from the control of U.S. bishops and overseeing clergy, see the chapter on "Ladylike Nuns" and nineteenth-century activism in James Kenneally, *The History of American Catholic Women* (New York: Crossroad, 1990), 43–59.

96. "Stewardship" page, Abbey of Regina Laudis official web site http://www .abbeyofreginalaudis.com/sitelive/index.htm (November 18, 2005).

97. Ibid.

98. "Stewardship and Hospitality" page, Abbey of Regina Laudis official web site, http://www.abbeyofreginalaudis.com/sitelive/index.htm (December 6, 2005).

99. Mary Blume, "A Master Pursues the Secrets of Cheese," *International Herald Tribune,* January 23, 2004, http://www.iht.com/bin/print_ipub.php?file=/articles/2004/01/23/blume_ed3_0.php (September 7, 2005).

100. Field journal notes, Weston, Vt., June 21, 2000.

101. Helen Rose Fuchs Ebaugh, *Women in the Vanishing Cloister: Organizational Decline in Catholic Religious Orders in the United States* (New Brunswick, N.J.: Rutgers University Press, 1993), 95–98, 165–167.

102. See Roger Finke, "An Orderly Return to Tradition: Explaining the Recruitment of Members into Catholic Religious Orders," *Journal for the Scientific Study of Religion* 36, no. 2 (1997): 228, as quoted in Elizabeth Kuhns, *The Habit: A History of the Clothing of Catholic Nuns* (New York: Doubleday, 2003), 163.

103. In his study of Catholic sisters, many of whom are active and involved in ministry, community committees, or other service well into their nineties or even beyond age one hundred, David Snowdon demonstrates the importance of physical activity, spiritually meaningful lives, social support, and intellectual stimulus for maintaining good brain health in old age. See Snowdon's *Aging with Grace: What the Nun Study Teaches Us about Leading Longer, Healthier, and More Meaningful Lives* (New York: Bantam, 2001), 199–219.

104. As quoted in Julia Lieblich, *Sisters: Lives of Devotion and Defiance* (New York: Ballantine, 1992), 288–289.

105. Snowdon, *Aging with Grace*, 38–51.

106. Heather Millar, "Generation Green," *Sierra Club Magazine* (November/December 2000): 36–47. Millar cites statistics showing that in 1990, one in every ten high schools had an environmental club. Within a decade's time, that ratio jumped to nine in ten with the creation of nineteen separate nationwide student environmental organiza-

tions. See also forest activist and tree sitter Julia "Butterfly" Hill's book *The Legacy of Luna: The Story of a Tree, A Woman, and the Struggle to Save the Redwoods* (San Francisco: Harper San Francisco, 2001), the now-classic autobiographical treatise of Generation Green.

107. Field journal notes, Weston, Vt., June 22, 2000.

5. Nourishing the Earthbody

1. This goal is in keeping with Catholic religious sisters' historical commitment to and involvement in antiwar activism, peace actions, and social justice work. See Mary Jo Weaver, *New Catholic Women: A Contemporary Challenge to Traditional Authority* (Bloomington: Indiana University Press, 1995), 71–108; Debra Campbell's chapter on "Reformers and Activists" in Karen Kennelly, C.S.J., ed., *American Catholic Women* (New York: Macmillan, 1989), 152–181; and the more recent national coverage of the imprisoned Dominican peace activist nuns sabotaging nuclear missiles in Colorado. See Melissa Jones, "Nuns Sentenced for Plowshares Action in Colorado," *National Catholic Reporter,* August 15, 2003, 5.

2. Miriam MacGillis, "Food as Sacrament," 159–164.

3. Ibid., 163.

4. Concern with issues of environmental justice, ecoracism, and poverty were especially pronounced at the 2002 Sisters of Earth conference in Holyoke, Mass., when sisters invited environmental justice advocates Eleanor Rae and Jane Blewett to speak to the membership about their work with the United Nations. Sisters have also repeatedly directed me to Vandana Shiva's work on globalization, environmental crisis, and poverty. See Shiva, *Water Wars: Privatization, Pollution, and Profit* (Cambridge, Mass.: South End Press, 2002). See also Uner Kirdar, *Ecological Change: Environment, Development, and Poverty Linkages* (New York: United Nations Publications, 1992); and Laura Westra and Peter Wenz, *Faces of Environmental Racism: Confronting Issues of Global Justice* (Landham, Md.: Roman and Littlefield, 1995).

5. Caroline Walker Bynum, *Holy Feast and Holy Fast: The Religious Significance of Food to Medieval Women* (Berkeley: University of California Press, 1987), 5.

6. Patricia Curran, *Grace before Meals: Food Ritual and Body Discipline in Convent Culture* (Urbana: University of Illinois, 1989), 62.

7. MacGillis, "Food as Sacrament"; and Albert LaChance and John E. Carroll, eds., *Embracing Earth: Catholic Approaches to Ecology* (Maryknoll, N.Y.: Orbis, 1994), xiii–xvi. MacGillis has also spoken about farmers playing "a prophetic and priestly role . . . entering the sanctuary of the soil and engaging the mysterious forces of creation in order to bless and nourish the inner and outer life of the community they serve." (See Coleman McCarthy, "In N.J., Nuns Cultivate a Spiritual-Ecological Link on Genesis Farm," *Washington Post,* October 2, 1993, B6.) Since many green sisters are working with community-supported gardens and engaging in organic farming themselves, they are in effect performing and fulfilling these "prophetic and priestly" roles of working with the life forces to bring nourishment to the community.

8. Thomas Berry, *The Great Work: Our Way into the Future* (New York: Bell Tower,

1999), 48–55; Thomas Berry, *The Dream of the Earth* (San Francisco: Sierra Club Books, 1988), 1–23; Sallie McFague, *The Body of God: An Ecological Theology* (Minneapolis: Fortress Press, 1993).

9. Many of the ethical considerations that permeate green sisters' concerns about food purity are in keeping with Michael Fox's "Ten Commandments of Humane Organic Sustainable Agriculture" as outlined in *Eating with Conscience: The Bioethics of Food* (Troutdale, Ore.: New Sage, 1997), 161.

10. Mary Farrell Bednarowski, *The Religious Imagination of American Women* (Bloomington: Indiana University Press, 1999), 6.

11. There are many and varied complex reasons why green sisters have chosen to remain within the Church as women religious. See Sarah McFarland Taylor, "Reinhabiting Religion: Green Sisters, Ecological Renewal, and the Biogeography of Religious Life," *Worldviews* 6, no. 3 (December 2002): 227–252. "Reinhabitation" is a term borrowed from the environmental philosophy of bioregionalism. I use it to talk about green sisters' commitment to "stay with," reshape, and renew religious life. Briefly, it means that instead of "moving on" from land where damage or harm has been inflicted on the living systems of the planet, one instead "digs in," commits to stay in place, and resolves to work to create more sustainable and healing ways to live in that place. The antithesis of reinhabitation is moving on to pioneer and claim new land elsewhere. One who practices reinhabitation commits to stay "home" and heal the damage in her own backyard.

12. "Invitation to Join the Green Mountain Monastery Companions," pamphlet, Green Mountain Monastery, Weston, Vt., 2002.

13. *Rule and Constitutions of the Green Mountain Monastery* (first draft), Green Mountain Monastery, Weston, Vt., January 19, 2001, 10.

14. Gail Worcelo, personal communication with the author, March 6, 2004.

15. Gail Worcelo, speech to Community of the Sisters of Charity, St. Louis, Mo., April 2000.

16. R. Marie Griffith, *Born Again Bodies: Flesh and Spirit in American Christianity* (Berkeley: University of California Press, 2004), 24.

17. Wioleta Polinska, "Bodies under Siege: Eating Disorders and Self-Mutilation among Women," *Journal of the American Academy of Religion* 68, no. 3 (September 2000): 569–589.

18. Ibid., 569. An example of this is green sisters' recognition of and attention to the problems of environmental illness and environmentally linked cancers and other catastrophic illnesses.

19. Field journal notes, Green Mountain Monastery, Weston, Vt., June 21, 2000.

20. *Rule and Constitutions of the Green Mountain Monastery* (Weston, Vt.: Sisters of the Green Mountain Monastery, 2002), 19.

21. Ibid., 21.

22. Bynum, *Holy Feast and Holy Fast*, 194. It is important to note that—as my colleague Barbara Newman, a medievalist, rightly reminds me—the act of holy fasting among medieval women was arguably also an affirmation and empowering of women's bodies through women's identification of their own bodies with that of Christ.

23. Curran, *Grace before Meals*, 58.

24. McFague, *Body of God,* 19.

25. Water is also an important subject of sisters' activist work. Miriam MacGillis, for instance, has been very active and vocal in her role on the board of Food & Water, a Vermont-based nonprofit that lobbies for stricter quality restrictions on both resources. A video documentary produced by Foundation for a Global Community, *Water: Sacred and Profaned* (1998), which explores the spiritual, practical, and justice dimensions of water, is also a popular resource and teaching tool in sisters' earth literacy centers. As I described more fully in Chapter 3, at Crystal Spring, a Dominican-sponsored earth literacy center in Massachusetts, sisters post small signs over the sinks, the baths, and the toilets, reminding visitors at each use of the sacred dimensions of water and the need for its mindful and reverential consumption.

26. Transcript of audiotaped presentation by Miriam MacGillis with Thomas Berry at the Sisters of Earth conference, Grailville, Ohio, July 1996 (available through Earth Communications, Laurel, Md.).

27. Curran, *Grace before Meals,* 58.

28. Transcript of audiotaped presentation by MacGillis with Berry, Sisters of Earth conference, July 1996.

29. Greta Gaard, "Living Interconnections with Animals and Nature," 1–12; Carol Adams, "The Feminist Traffic in Animals," 195–218; and Marti Kheel, "From Heroic to Holistic Ethics: The Ecofeminist Challenge," 243–271, all in Greta Gaard, ed., *Ecofeminism: Women, Animals, Nature* (Philadelphia: Temple University Press, 1993).

30. See Colman McCarthy, *All of One Piece: Essays on Nonviolence* (New Brunswick, N.J.: Rutgers University Press, 1994), and *I'd Rather Teach Peace* (Maryknoll, N.Y.: Orbis, 2002).

31. Jeannine Gramick, "Animal Rights," *Loretto Earth Network News* 12, no. 4 (Fall 2004): 2.

32. Walter Grazer's anthology, produced by the U.S. Catholic Conference of Bishops, provides detailed articulations of the stewardship model and its limits from a perspective approved by the U.S. Catholic Conference. See *"And God Saw That It Was Good": Catholic Theology and the Environment* (Washington, D.C.: U.S. Catholic Conference, 1996), especially Grazer's introduction and the reprint of Bishop James T. McHugh's "Stewards of Life, Stewards of Nature," 321–326.

33. Gramick, "Animal Rights," 2.

34. This position parallels the traditional monastic practice of abstinence from meat in which meat from quadrupeds was generally forbidden, although flesh from birds was permitted. See Lowrie Daly, *Benedictine Monasticism: Its Formation and Development through the Twelfth Century* (New York: Sheed and Ward, 1965), 207.

35. Berry, *Great Work,* 49. Field journal notes, Thomas Berry fireside talk, Green Mountain Monastery, Weston, Vt., October 18, 2003.

36. Gail Worcelo, presentation to Sisters of Earth Conference, Sinsinawa, Wis., July 18, 1998.

37. Gail Worcelo, electronic interview with the author, January 23, 2002.

38. Worcelo presentation to Sisters of Earth Conference, July 18, 1998.

39. Gail Worcelo, electronic interview with the author, January 23, 2002. The agri-

cultural method called "biodynamics" was devised by nineteenth-century Austrian mystic and philosopher Rudolf Steiner. Farming biodynamically involves taking into consideration the "energies" of the universe, as Steiner puts it, from "the depths of the earth to the heights of the heavens." See, for example, Rudolf Steiner, *Macrocosm and Microcosm* (London: Rudolf Steiner Press, 1968).

40. Sharon Zayac, electronic interview with the author, April 15, 2002.

41. Maureen Wild, electronic interview with the author, April 10, 2002.

42. Field journal notes, "Food as Spirit: Nourishing Soul and Body," workshop with Miriam MacGillis at Spiritearth Center, Sparkill, N.Y., April 12, 1997.

43. Paula González, electronic interview with the author, March 11, 2002.

44. Nancy Earle, telephone interview with the author, December 20, 2005.

45. Field journal notes, "Food as Spirit."

46. Mary Douglas, *Purity and Danger: An Analysis of the Concept of Pollution and Taboo* (London: Routledge, 1966).

47. For further explication of this phenomenon, see for instance Laurence Coupe, ed., *The Green Studies Reader: From Romanticism to Ecocriticism* (New York: Routledge, 2000), 2–3.

48. Theo Colborn et al., *Our Stolen Future* (New York: Penguin, 1997); Sandra Steingraber, *Living Downstream* (New York: Addison-Wesley, 1997); John Wargo, *Our Children's Toxic Legacy* (New Haven: Yale University Press, 1998).

49. Colburn, *Our Stolen Future*, 259–268.

50. See, for instance, Environmental Protection Agency, *Deposition of Air Pollutants to the Great Lakes Waters, EPA-453/R-93–055* (Washington, D.C.: EPA, 1994); W. J. Rogan et al., "Polychlorinated Biphenyls (PCBs) and Dichlorodiphenyl Dichloroethene (DDE) in Human Milk," *American Journal of Public Health* 76 (1986): 172–177; and R. Repetto and S. S. Baliga, *Pesticides and the Immune System: The Public Health Risk* (Washington, D.C.: World Resources Institute, 1996). Doctor Rosalie Bertell, a Gray Nun of the Sacred Heart, has been particularly active in chronicling the public health effects of environmental toxins. She provided expert witness testimony to the noxious effects of radiation during the famous Karen Silkwood trial and also led the Bhopal and Chernobyl medical commissions. See Rosalie Bertell, *No Immediate Danger: Prognosis for a Radioactive Earth* (London: Women's Press, 1985); and *Planet Earth: The Latest Weapon of War* (London: Women's Press, 2000).

51. These figures are according to the Rodale Institute. See Fran McManus, ed., *Eating Fresh from the Organic Garden State* (Pennington, N.J.: Northeast Organic Farming Association, 1997), 12–14; and Paul Rauber, "Miles to Go before You Eat," *Sierra Club Magazine* (May/June 2006): 34–35.

52. Curran, *Grace before Meals*, 49.

53. For an explanation of the related phenomenon of "keeping eco-kosher," see Arthur Waskow, "What Is Eco-Kosher?" in Roger Gottlieb, *This Sacred Earth: Religion, Nature, Environment* (New York: Routledge, 1996), 297–300.

54. Bynum, *Holy Feast and Holy Fast*, esp. chap. 2.

55. Wild interview.

56. See especially the introduction to Carlo Petrini, ed., *Slow Food: Collected*

Thoughts on Taste, Tradition, and the Honest Pleasures of Food (White River Junction, Vt.: Chelsea Green, 2001).

57. Wild interview.

58. Curran, *Grace before Meals,* 108.

59. Miriam MacGillis, "Earth as Self-Nourishing," section of the "Exploring the Sacred Universe" program, Genesis Farm, July 15, 1996.

60. *Fall/Winter 1993 Genesis Farm Newsletter,* Genesis Farm, Blairstown, N.J. Emphasis in original.

61. This concept is also developed in MacGillis's work on "Food as Sacrament." See MacGillis in Hull, *Earth and Spirit,* 159–164.

62. Carol Coston, interview with the author, Santuario Sisterfarm, Boerne, Tex., March 4, 2002.

63. Ibid.

64. "Bread Is Alive!" *Crystal Spring Newsletter* (*Streams*) 5 (Fall 1997): 2.

65. Field journal notes, Crystal Spring Retreat Center, Plainville, Mass., June 28, 1997.

66. For a discussion of Sylvester Graham follower William A. Ghaskins's 1843 testimony on the effects of Graham health reforms, see Catherine L. Albanese's *Nature Religion in America: From the Algonkian Indians to the New Age* (Chicago: University of Chicago Press, 1990), 117.

67. Edward Andrews and Faith Andrews, *Fruits of the Shaker Tree of Life* (Stockbridge, Mass.: Berkshire Traveler Press, 1975), 74.

68. Ibid., 76.

69. Betsey Beaven et al., *The Political Palate: A Feminist Vegetarian Cookbook* (Bridgeport, Conn.: Sanguinara Publishing, 1980), xii.

70. Betsey Beaven et al., *The Second Seasonal Political Palate: A Feminist Vegetarian Cookbook* (Bridgeport, Conn.: Sanguinara Publishing, 1980), xii. See also Kim Chernin, *The Obsession: Reflections on the Tyranny of Slenderness* (New York: Harper Perennial, 1994); and Carol Adams, *The Sexual Politics of Meat: A Feminist-Vegetarian Critical Theory* (New York: Continuum, 1990). Although I found no direct connection between contemporary green sisters and feminist food collectives of the past, several scholars have documented the significant influence of the feminist movement in general on contemporary religious sisters within North America. See Lora Ann Quiñonez and Mary Daniel Turner, *The Transformation of American Catholic Sisters* (Philadelphia: Temple University Press, 1992); Helen Rose Fuchs Ebaugh, *Women in the Vanishing Cloister* (New Brunswick, N.J.: Rutgers University Press, 1993), esp. chap. 9, "Nuns as Feminists"; Ann Patrick Ware, *Midwives of the Future: American Sisters Tell Their Story* (Kansas City, Mo.: Leaven Press, 1985); Miriam Therese Winter, *Defecting in Place: Women Claiming Responsibility for Their Own Spiritual Lives* (New York: Crossroad, 1994).

71. Arlene Voski Avakian, *Through the Kitchen Window: Women Explore the Intimate Meanings of Food and Cooking* (Boston: Beacon Press, 1997), 6.

72. Elise D. García, personal communication with the author, May 19, 2006. Note that the mission of Sor Juana Press (named in honor of the seventeenth-century Mexican nun, scholar, poet, and scientist) is to publish the works of women, especially women of

color and Catholic religious sisters, on topics related to women's spirituality, earth spirituality, permaculture, and other subjects related to (in the words of the directors) "la Tierra, nuestra madre" (the earth, our mother). The Sor Juana Press can be contacted at Santuario Sisterfarm, 28 Hein Road, Boerne, Texas, 78006; telephone: 830-537-4327; http://www.sisterfarm.org.

73. Field journal notes, "Food as Spirit."

74. Mary Southard, electronic interview with the author, February 28, 2002.

75. Miriam MacGillis, "Earth as Self-Nourishing," section of the "Exploring the Sacred Universe" program, Genesis Farm, Blairstown, N.J., July 15, 1996.

76. Field journal notes, Genesis Farm, Blairstown, N.J., December 22, 2001.

77. Barbara O'Donnell, electronic interview with the author, April 10, 2002.

78. Franciscan sister Janice Welle and Josephite sister Ansgar Holmberg have published a tabletop resource of green graces for all twelve months of the year. See Janice Well and Ansgar Holmberg, *Table Graces: Prayers Reflecting the Earth Charter Principles* (La Grange, Ill.: Ministry of the Arts, 2005).

79. Wild interview.

80. Bynum, *Holy Feast and Holy Fast,* 191.

6. "The Tractor Is My Pulpit"

1. Vincent McNabb, *Old Principles and the New World Order* (New York: Sheed and Ward, 1942), as quoted in Miriam MacGillis, "Food as Sacrament," in Fritz Hull, ed., *Earth and Spirit: The Spiritual Dimension of the Environmental Crisis* (New York: Continuum, 1993), 162.

2. Lowrie Daly, *Benedictine Monasticism: Its Formation and Development through the Twelfth Century* (New York: Sheed and Ward, 1965), 208.

3. Miriam MacGillis, "Genesis Farm," *IS* [International Synergy] *Journal* 7 (1989): 14. This is the journal of the Los Angles–based "Essence Institute," an interdisciplinary think tank that promotes sustainability through international collaborative projects. See http://www.essenceinstitute.org (11 January 2006).

4. Marilyn Rudy, electronic interview with the author, March 15, 2002.

5. Marilyn Rudy, personal communication with the author, International Sisters of Earth Conference, Minneapolis–St. Paul, Minnesota, July 15, 2006.

6. Maureen Wild, electronic interview with the author, April 10, 2006.

7. "San Damiano Reflection Center at Michaela Farm, Oldenburg, Indiana," pamphlet, 2004.

8. MacGillis, "Food as Sacrament," 164.

9. Gail Worcelo, "The Greening of Our Worship," presentation to International Sisters of Earth Conference, Sinsinawa, Wis., July 17, 1998.

10. "About FELC," Franciscan Earth Literacy Center homepage, http://www.earthliteracy.org/about.htm (January 3, 2006).

11. Rita Wienken, *Patterns of Wholeness: A Case Study* (Kutztown, Pa.: Rodale, 1996).

12. John Montgomery, "Seeds of Hope to Feed Body, Mind, and Soul," *Fostoria Fo-*

cus, February 6, 2005, http://www.fostoriafocus.com/viewarticle.asp?artID=3239 (January 3, 2006).

13. See Elizabeth Henderson and Robyn Van En, *Sharing the Harvest: A Guide to Community Supported Agriculture* (White River Junction, Vt.: Chelsea Green, 1999). Peter Mann quotes Van En, one of the founders of the CSA movement, as saying, "Eating from a regional food supply would be a real step toward world peace . . . Growing food is the common thread throughout the world, in that everybody eats. It connects everyone across all party lines, all ethnic and religious differences . . . If every place in the whole wide world had its own regional food supply and its own regional food security, the world would be a very different place. It would be different if people just did not have power over others to manipulate them with food." See especially the section on "Food Security and World Peace" in Peter Mann, "Why Homeland Security Must Include Food Security," http://www.foodsecurity.org/homeland_security.html (January 7, 2006).

14. Nancy Earle, telephone interview with the author, December 20, 2005.

15. Mary Ann Coyle, "EarthRise Farm: The Story of a Family Farm," *Loretto Earth Network Newsletter* (Fall 2004): 4.

16. Ibid.

17. Jane Pellowski and Estelle Demers, electronic interview with the author, April 4, 2002.

18. For a full account of the story of St. Francis and the wolf of Gubbio, see Thomas of Celano, *St. Francis of Assisi: First and Second Life of St. Francis, with Selections from "Treatise on the Miracles of Blessed Francis,"* trans. Placid Hermann (Chicago: Franciscan Herald Press, 1963).

19. Mary Ann Garisto, electronic interview with the author, March 1, 2002.

20. Mary Ann Garisto, personal communication with the author, Sisters of Earth Conference, Minneapolis–St. Paul, Minnesota, July 14, 2006.

21. Ibid.

22. See the web site "Ecology Projects of the Dominican Alliance," http://www.columbusdominicans.org/whatwedo/ecology/alliance/alliance.htm (December 15, 2005).

23. Cristina Vavin, "The Green Nuns: Models of Ecological Spirituality," *Catholic New Times,* July 3, 2005 http://www.findarticles.com/p/articles/mi_mOMKY/is_12_29/ai_n15390050/print (January 19, 2006).

24. Miriam Brown, electronic interview with the author, June 3, 2002.

25. Jennifer Wilkins, "Think Globally, Eat Locally," *New York Times,* December 19, 2002, A19.

26. The Sierra Club reports that every hour, America loses 45.6 acres of its highest-quality farmland to subdivisions, shopping centers, strip malls, and roadways. That is 400,000 acres of farmland commercially developed a year or roughly the size of the state of Vermont. See http://www.planning.org/viewpoints/sprawl.htm (January 7, 2006).

27. Elizabeth Walters, "Hope Takes Root: Stopping Hunger and Loving the Earth," Ministries of the Sisters, Servants of the Immaculate Heart of Mary, http://www.ihmsisters.org/future-gardening.html (January 1, 2006).

28. Square-foot gardening is a highly efficient way of gardening that produces a rel-

atively high yield in a small space by using intensively planted raised beds. See Mel Bartholomew, *Square Foot Gardening* (Kutztown, Pa.: Rodale, 1981).

29. Ibid.

30. "Saving City Soil," *Whole Earth* (Winter 1997): 18.

31. Walters, "Hope Takes Root: Stopping Hunger and Loving the Earth," Ministries of the Sisters, Servants of the Immaculate Heart of Mary http://www.ihmsisters.org/future-gardening.html (January 1, 2006).

32. Elizabeth Walters, personal communication with the author, May 20, 2006.

33. Cathy Mueller, electronic interview with the author, March 1, 2002.

34. Cathy Mueller, "From Dreams to Action," *Loretto Magazine* 43, no. 3 (Winter 2001): 5–6.

35. This is reference to James Oppenheim's (1882–1932) poem "Bread and Roses," which became associated with what came to be known as the "Bread and Roses Strike of 1912," when twenty thousand women textile workers walked off the job in Lawrence, Massachusetts. Young women reportedly held up a banner stating, "We want bread and roses too!" This call for both "bread and roses" has been important and repeated theme within the green sisters movement and can be found throughout the literature, materials, garden signage, and educational programs in sisters' earth ministries. In fact, one of the guest houses used to house earth-literacy students at Genesis Farm in New Jersey is actually named "Bread and Roses," and a large copy of Oppenheim's poem hangs over the main table in the dining room.

36. "Links Happen!" EarthLinks official homepage, http://www.eoncity.net/earthlinks (December 31, 2005).

37. Ibid.

38. A complete list of GreenFingers products can be found on the EarthLinks web site, http://www.earthlinks-colorado.org/product.htm (January 3, 2006).

39. Ibid.

40. For much of this information, I am indebted to Susan Leihaur's "Earth Home: A Sense of Place in Oakland," *Earth Light Magazine* (Summer 1995): 14; and to Sharon Abercrombie, "Schools Restore God's Garden: Environmental Education Teaches Students to Cultivate Earth's Beauty," *National Catholic Reporter,* March 22, 2002, 25–27.

41. "Dominican Sisters Garden Project," Dominican Sisters, Congregation of the Sacred Heart, Houston, Tex., homepage, http://www.houstonoorg/index.cfm/menuItemID/191.htm (January 6, 2006).

42. This phrase comes from what is now a classic in environmental studies literature—E. F. Schumacher's *Small Is Beautiful: A Study of Economics as if People Mattered* (London: Blond and Briggs, 1973).

43. For a history of the community-supported garden movement and a guide to contemporary CSGs, see Trauger Groh and Steven McFadden, *Farms of Tomorrow Revisted: Community Supported Farms—Farm Supported Communities* (Kimberton, Pa.: Biodynamic Farming and Gardening Association, 1997).

44. *Welcome to the Community Supported Garden at Genesis Farm!* CSG Handbook, Genesis Farm, Blairstown, N.J., 7–8.

45. Ibid., 7.

46. Sherry Wildfeuer, *Stella Natura 2006: Kimberton Hills Agricultural Planting Guide and Calendar* (Junction City, Ore.: Biodynamic Farming and Garden Association, 2006).

47. See basic guidelines of the biodynamics calendar at http://www.biodynamics .com/advisory.html (January 11, 2006).

48. Donald Worster, *Nature's Economy: The Roots of Ecology* (San Francisco: Sierra Club Books, 1977), 17.

49. Herbert Koepf, Bo D. Petterson, and Wolfgang Schauman, *Biodynamic Agriculture: An Introduction* (Spring Valley, N.Y.: Anthroposophic Press, 1976), 26.

50. See Briane Swimme and Thomas Berry, *The Universe Story: From the Primordial Flaring Forth to the Ecozoic Era* (San Francisco: Harper San Francisco, 1992), 71–79; and Thomas Berry, *The Great Work: Our Way into the Future* (New York: Bell Tower, 1999), 160–163. Note that "interiority" is alternatively referred to as "subjectivity" in some of Berry's work.

51. Sharon Therese Zayac, *Earth Spirituality: In the Catholic and Dominican Traditions,* Conversatio, Dominican Women on Earth series, no. 1 (San Antonio, Tex.: Sor Juana Press, 2003), 43–44.

52. Catherine L. Albanese, *Nature Religion in America: From the Algonkian Indians to the New Age* (Chicago: University of Chicago, 1990). I use "North American" here to describe a larger context because in the ubiquitous identification of "American Transcendentalists," the influence of Emerson, Thoreau, and other Transcendentalists on Canadian intellectuals—as well as the existence of Canadian Transcendentalists—is too often overlooked. Even though we connect Transcendentalism with New England and the United States, it is important to note that Transcendentalists also conducted speaking tours through major Canadian cities in the nineteenth century and that there were significant connections among those in the United States working to relocate slaves to Canada, Canadian Transcendentalists, and abolitionist sympathizers.

53. See Ralph Waldo Emerson, "Nature," in Catherine L. Albanese, ed., *The Spirituality of the American Transcendentalists: Selected Writings of Ralph Waldo Emerson, Amos Bronson Alcott, Theodore Parker, and Henry David Thoreau* (Macon, Ga.: Mercer University Press, 1988), 59 and 63.

54. Stephen E. Whicher, ed., *Selections from Ralph Waldo Emerson* (Boston: Houghton Mifflin, 1957), 182.

55. Miriam MacGillis, "Food as Sacrament," 162–163.

56. "What Is Biodynamics?" pamphlet, Biodynamic Farming and Gardening Association (BFGA), Kimberton, Pa., 1998, 4. See also http://www.biodynamics.com (January 11, 2006). The BFGA is based in Junction City, Ore.

57. See Herbert Koepf, *The Biodynamic Farm: Agriculture in the Service of the Earth and Humanity* (Hudson, N.Y.: Anthroposophic Press, 1989); and Ehrenfried E. Pfeiffer, *A Condensation of Bio-Dynamic Farming and Gardening* (Pauma Valley, Calif.: Bargyla Rateaver and Gylver Rateaver, 1973).

58. BFGA, "What Is Biodynamics?"

59. Koepf, Petterson, and Schauman, *Biodynamic Agriculture,* 206.

60. See Rudolf Steiner, *Macrocosm and Microcosm* (London: Rudolf Steiner Press, 1968), 140–149.

61. Marilyn Rudy, electronic interview with the author, March 15, 2002.

62. Gail Worcelo, electronic interview with the author, January 23, 2002

63. Sharon Zayac, electronic interview with the author, March 15, 2002.

64. Maureen Wild, electronic interview with the author, April 10, 2002.

65. See Steiner, *Macrocosm and Microcosm.*

66. Sydney Ahlstrom, *A Religious History of the American People* (New Haven: Yale University Press, 1972), 1045.

67. Steiner, *Macrocosm and Microcosm,* 94–96.

68. Catherine Albanese, "Narrating an Almost Nation: Contact, Combination, and Metaphysics in American Religious History," *Criterion* 38, no. 1 (Winter 1999): 7. Albanese develops the Roman Catholic and metaphysical movement connection more thoroughly in *A Republic of Mystics and Metaphysicians: A Cultural History of U.S. Metaphysical Religion* (New Haven: Yale University Press, 2006).

69. Catherine L. Albanese, "The Subtle Energies of Spirit: Explorations in Metaphysical and New Age Spirituality," *Journal of the American Academy of Religion* 67, no. 2 (June 1999): 307.

70. Mary Farrell Bednarowski, *New Religions: The Theological Imagination in America* (Bloomington: Indiana University Press, 1989), 40–41.

71. Albanese, "Narrating an Almost Nation," 4, and *A Republic of Mystics and Metaphysicians.*

72. Albanese, "Narrating an Almost Nation," 7.

73. Bill Mollison, *Introduction to Permaculture* (Tyalgum, Australia: Tagari, 1991), 26.

74. The biotic example usually given is the species specific to coral reefs or mangrove ecologies.

75. More than simply literal "objects," Wendy Griswold defines "cultural objects" as "symbols, beliefs, values, and practices." See her *Culture and Societies in a Changing World* (Thousand Oaks, Calif.: Pine Forge, 1994), 11–14.

76. Mollison, *Introduction to Permaculture,* 24.

77. Coston, *Permaculture: Finding Our Own Vines and Fig Trees,* Conversatio, Dominican Women on Earth series, no. 2 (San Antonio, Tex.: Sor Juana Press, 2003), 67, 63.

78. Swimme and Berry, *The Universe Story,* 77–79.

79. Thomas Berry, *The Dream of the Earth* (San Francisco: Sierra Club Books, 1988), 44–47.

80. Coston, *Permaculture,* 36.

81. Mollison, *Introduction to Permaculture,* 24, 25, 3, 178.

82. Louise Riotte, *Carrots Love Tomatoes: Secrets of Companion Planting for Successful Gardening* (Pownal, Vt.: Storey Books, 1975, 1998).

83. Coston, *Permaculture,* 71.

84. Nettie Wiebe, "Farm Women: Cultivating Hope and Sowing Change," in Sandra

Burt and Lorraine Code, *Changing Methods: Feminists Transforming Practice* (Peterborough, Ont.: Broadview, 1995), 137, 144–145.

85. Frieda Knobloch, *The Culture of Wilderness: Agriculture as Colonization in the American West* (Chapel Hill: University of North Carolina Press, 1996), 118–123.

86. Daniel Spencer has made similar connections, although Spencer's research has explicitly centered on the correspondence between the language of weed encroachment and narratives of racial purity in Iowa. See Spencer, "Ecological and Social Transformations and the Constructions of Race: A View from Iowa," Presentation to the Annual Meeting of the American Academy of Religion, San Francisco, November 1997.

87. Mollison, *Introduction to Permaculture,* 49–54, 178.

7. Saving Seeds

1. Field journal notes, International Conference of Sisters of Earth, Minneapolis–St. Paul, Minnesota, July 14, 2006.

2. Robert Mouck, telephone interview with the author, May 19, 2006.

3. Quoted in "Sisters of Providence Tomato Day Features Heirloom Varieties," *Eastern Ontario Agrinews* (August 2002), http://www.agrinewsinteractive.com/archives/article-4234.htm (January 14, 2006)

4. "Heirloom Seed Sanctuary of the Sisters of Providence of St. Vincent de Paul at Heathfield," pamphlet, Heathfield, Kingston, Ont., 2002.

5. For a summary of "greening measures" being undertaken in Canadian sisterhoods, see Cristina Vanin, "The Green Nuns: Models of Ecological Spirituality," *Catholic New Times,* July 3, 2005, http://www.findarticles.com/p/articles/mi_mOMKY/is_12_29/ai_n15390050/print (January 20, 2006).

6. Wilson, "Save Life, Save Seeds," 13; and Mouck interview.

7. "Seed Sanctuary," official web site of the Sisters of Providence of St. Vincent de Paul, Kingston, Ont., http://www.providence.ca/seeds (January 20, 2006).

8. "Heirloom Seed Sanctuary of the Sisters of Providence of St. Vincent de Paul at Heathfield."

9. There are actually several towns that claim the title of "terminus" on the underground railroad, but Kingston clearly has a legitimate claim to this designation as one of the main sites of refuge for escapees. See Ontario Black History Society Archives, http://collections.ic.gc.ca/obho/inximage.html (January 14, 2006); Archives of Ontario, Black History in Ontario, http://www.archives.gov.on.ca/english/exhibits/black_history/life.htm (January 16, 2006); and Peter Raymont, producer, *A Scattering of Seeds: The Creation of Canada,* documentary film series, White Pine Pictures, http://www.whitepinepictures.com/seeds (January 16, 2006)—especially the background on the underground railroad provided in Director Sylvia Sweeney's *Breaking the Ice: The Mary Ann Shadd Story.*

10. Syracuse University Special Collections, "'That Laboratory of Abolitionism, Libel, and Treason': Syracuse and the Underground Railroad," Special Collections Research Center, Syracuse University Library, http://libwww.syr.edu/digital/exhibits/u/undergroundrr/maps.htm (January 15, 2006); "William 'Jerry' Henry's Escape," African

American History of Western New York, 1830 to 1865, http://www.math.buffalo.edu/
~sww/0history/henry.william.jerry.html (January 15, 2006); "Slave Story of September,
1839, Which Awakened Many Abolition Feelings," http://www.math.buffalo.edu/~sww/
0history/leonard.thomas-jane.html (January 16, 2006). Significantly, during the 1830s
through the 1850s at the height of fugitive crossovers into Canada, there were not so
many white members involved in the underground railroad, nor so many persons transported to freedom, as is commonly perceived.

11. Gail Worcelo, speech to community of the Sisters of Charity, St. Louis, Mo.,
April 2000.

12. See Renny Golden and Michael McConnell, *Sanctuary: The New Underground
Railroad* (Maryknoll, N.Y.: Orbis, 1986); and William Westerman, "Religious Folk Life
and Folk Theology in the Sanctuary Movement," *Journal for the Study of Religions and
Ideologies* 2 (Summer 2002), http://hiphi.ubbcluj.ro/JSRI/html%20version/index/no_2/
williamwesterman-articol2.htm (January 20, 2006).

13. This is one of the few places in this book where, for obvious reasons, I have purposely not included identifying details about community affiliation, history, or location.

14. Elise D. García, personal communication with the author, May 19, 2006. See also
"Say No to GMOs! Conference on Genetic Engineering: The Nature of What's to Come,
or Biocolonialism," http://www.saynotogmos.org/ud2004/ujan04b.html (January 14,
2006).

15. Ibid.

16. Carol Coston, "Santuario Sisterfarm's Seed Saving Project," *Loretto Earth Network News* (Fall 2002): 6.

17. "Genetically Modified Organisms—Report 2005 to McDonald's Corporation,"
http://www.iccr.org/shareholder/proxy_book05/WATER%20AND%20FOOD/
GMO_KELLOGG_McDo_5107.HTM (January 15, 2006).

18. Roberta Mulcahy, telephone interview with the author, January 17, 2006.

19. See the "Justice and Earth" page of the Mercy Earth Harmony Network, http://
www.sistersofmercy.org/justice/earth.html (January 20, 2006).

20. Constance Kozel, "Seed Saving," Genesis Farm, Blairstown, N.J., July 12, 1996;
Cary Fowler and Pat Mooney, *Shattering: Food, Politics, and the Loss of Genetic Diversity*
(Tucson: University of Arizona Press, 1996).

21. Marc Lappe and Britt Bailey, *Against the Grain: Biotechnology and the Corporate
Takeover of Your Food* (Monroe, Maine: Common Courage, 1998), 4–12; Luke Anderson,
Genetic Engineering, Food, and Our Environment (White River Junction, Vt.: Chelsea
Green, 1999), 43–56; Martin Teitel and Kimberly Wilson, *Genetically Engineered Food:
Changing the Nature of Nature* (Rochester, Vt.: Park Street, 1999), 84–98.

22. Fowler and Mooney, *Shattering*, 220–222.

23. Carol Coston, "Santuario Sisterfarm's Seed Saving Project," *Loretto Earth Network News* (Fall 2002): 6.

24. For more information on these groups, see the Seeds of Diversity, Canada
"Resource List," http://www.seeds.ca/library/rl/projects.htm; Seed Savers Exchange, 3076
North Winn Road, Decorah, Iowa, www.seedsavers.org (January 20, 2006).

25. Kenneth Ausubel, *Seeds of Change* (San Francisco: Harper, 1994), 13. Note that

Ausubel has now left Seeds of Change, which has recently been bought by megafood conglomerate Mars Inc. The company still sells organic heritage seed stock and nonpatented seeds. For a guide to corporate buyouts of organic companies, see Francine Stephens and Mindy Pennybacker, "The Corporatization of Organic and Natural Foods," *Green Guide* (June 1999): 5.

26. Ausubel, *Seeds of Change*, 20.

27. Jennifer Wilkins, "Think Globally, Eat Locally: How to Protect Food from Bioterroism," *New York Times*, December 19, 2002, A19.

28. Peter Downs, "Bad Seed: Monsanto Sows Trouble on the Farm," *Progressive* (February 1999): 36.

29. For more discussion of this process and legislation that permits the patenting of life forms, see Fowler and Mooney, *Shattering*.

30. Downs, "Bad Seed," 38. "ETC" stands for the "Action Group on Erosion, Technology, and Concentration."

31. Marilyn Rudy, electronic interview with the author, March 22, 2002.

32. Gabriel Mary Hoare, "Keeping Watch on GMOs," *Loretto Magazine* 43, no. 3 (Winter 2001): 3.

33. Gabriel Mary Hoare, "Does Bioengineering Pose a Threat to Our Health?" *Loretto Earth Network News* (Fall 2004): 3.

34. "Biotechnology Statement of the Loretto Community—Affirmed at the Annual Assembly of the Loretto Community, July 1999," http://www.lorettocommunity.org/biotechnology.html (January 12, 2006). Note that this statement was drawn up by the Loretto Earth Network, a group of Loretto sisters and comembers dedicated to working on environmental issues.

35. Merchant writes about the shift in the European agricultural economy in the twelfth and thirteenth centuries as the locus for milling grain moved from individually owned handmills in peasants' homes to large manor-based milling operations. To guarantee a manor a monopoly on milling, for which substantial fees were charged, lords outlawed cottage milling rights and confiscated handmills. See Carolyn Merchant, *The Death of Nature: Women, Ecology, and the Scientific Revolution* (San Francisco: Harper, 1989), 46–47.

36. Nicole Winfield, "Vatican Opens Talks on Biotech Foods," *USA Today*, November 10, 2003, http://www.usatoday.com/tech/news/techpolicy/2003–11–10-biotech-vatican_x.htm statement (January 20, 2006).

37. Jesuits from the Kasisi Agricultural Training Center (KATC) and the Jesuit Center for Theological Reflection jointly opposed the aid in the form of GMO food, citing the long-term effects on small farmers and the self-sufficiency of Zambian agriculture. Bob Abernathy, "Zambia: Genetically Modified Foods," *Religion and Ethics Weekly*, http://www.pbs.org/wnet/religionandethics/week721/cover.html; Peter Henriot, "The Zambia Experiment," *Sojourners* (April 2005), http://www.sojo.net/index.cfm?action=magazine.article&issue=soj0504&article=050423 (January 20, 2006).

38. "Better Dead Than GMO-Fed," *Economist*, September 23, 2002, http://www.economist.com/science/displayStory.cfm?story_id=1337197&tranMode=none (December 1, 2005); Sheikh Chifuwe, "Levy Explains Government Rejection of GM Maize," *Post* (Lusaka), August 22, 2002, http://www.connectotel.com/gmfood/pz220802.txt (De-

cember 6, 2005); Paul Martin, "Greenpeace and Zambia Reject U.S. Claim," *Washington Times,* August 31, 2002, http://www.connectotel.com/gmfood/wt310802.txt (December 6, 2005).

39. See Martino's concluding remarks in the Vatican Archives, http://www.vatican.va/roman_curia/pontifical_councils/justpeace/documents/rc_pc_justpeace_doc_20031111_conclusions-ogm_en.html (July 24, 2006).

40. "Vatican Report Fuels Genetically Modified (GM) Debate within the Catholic Church," on "Earth and Justice," official web site of the Sisters of Mercy of the Americas, http://www.sistersofmercy.org/justice/vatican_gmos.html (January 20, 2006).

41. Seán McDonagh, *Patenting Life? Stop!* (Dublin: Dominican Publications, 2003)

42. Gabriel Mary Hoare, "GMOs and Bio-Devastation," presentation to the fifth annual conference of Sisters of Earth, Fayetteville, Ark., July 16, 2004; Nancy Wittwer, "Seeds Are Changing—For Better or Worse?" in *Loretto Earth Network News* (Spring 2003): 5; Gabriel Mary Hoare, "Make Food, Not War!" in *Loretto Earth Network News* (Spring 2003): 4. On the effects of the "green revolution," sisters also commonly refer to the works of South Asian physicist and ecological activist Vandana Shiva, especially *Stolen Harvest: The Hijacking of the World's Food Supply* (Boston: South End Press, 2000); *Biopiracy: The Plunder of Nature and Knowledge* (Boston: South End Press, 1997); and *The Violence of the Green Revolution: Third World Agriculture, Ecology, and Politics* (Atlantic Highlands, N.J.: Zed Books, 1992).

43. Gabriel Mary Hoare, "Vandana Shiva," *Loretto Earth Network News* (Summer 2005): 6.

44. Field journal notes, Holyoke, Mass., August 3, 2002.

45. Mary Louise Dolan, "Seeds," *Spiritearth Newsletter* (Spring 1994): 3.

46. Mary Louise Dolan, "Going to Seed," *Spiritearth Newsletter* (November 1997): 6.

47. Mary Rhodes Buckler, "I, You: We Are Seeds," *Loretto Earth Network News* (Spring 2003): 3.

48. The "Call to Prayer" is available through Interfaith Declarations and Worship Observance Resources (The North American Conference on Religion and Ecology), 5 Thomas Circle NW, Washington, D.C., 20005. The quotation from the *Chandogya Upanishad* can be found in Elenath Easwaran, trans., *The Upanishads* (Tomales, Calif.: Nilgiri Press, 1987), 186.

49. Gail Worcelo, "Like a Pungent Shrub with Dangerous Take-Over Properties," *Green Mountain Monastery Newsletter* (Winter 2003): 1–2.

50. Brian Bauknight, "Heirloom Seeds," http://www.christumc.net/Web%20Files/Sermons/2003%20Sermons/2003–2–1%20Heirloom%20Seeds.htm (January 18, 2006).

51. Gail Worcelo, "New Monastery, New Beginnings," *Homecomings Newsletter* (1999): 1.

52. Miriam MacGillis, "The Living Earth," presentation in the "Exploring the Sacred Universe" program, Genesis Farm, July 12, 1996.

53. Miriam MacGillis, "Reinhabiting Our Backyards," audiocassette available from Global Perspectives, Sonoma, Calif., n.d.

54. Carol Coston, *Permaculture: Finding Our Own Vines and Fig Trees,* Conversatio, Dominican Women on Earth Series, no. 2 (San Antonio, Tex.: Sor Juana Press, 2003), 73.

55. Miriam MacGillis, "Religious Traditions and the New Story," talk given as part

of the Exploring the Sacred Universe Story Program, Genesis Farm, Blairstown, N.J., August 16, 1995.

8. Stations of the Earth

1. Field journal notes, Sinsinawa, Wis., July 17, 1998.
2. "Morning Body Prayer Guide," pamphlet, Genesis Farm, Blairstown, N.J., 1985.
3. Ibid.
4. See Thomas Berry, "The Ecozoic Era," http://www.lightparty.com/Visionary/EcozoicEra.html (December 15, 2005).
5. See C. G. Jung, *Memories, Dreams, Reflections* (New York: Pantheon, 1963).
6. The Oasis Ministries Center for Spiritual Development in Camp Hill, Pa., for instance, also teaches the morning body prayer with the "Father; Son; Holy Ghost; and God, Mother of All" format. Oasis is an ecumenically Christian retreat center where both Catholics and Protestants go to receive direction in contemplative life and spiritual action; see http://www.oasismin.org/Assets/Morning_Body_Prayer.html (January 26, 2006).
7. Thomas Berry, *The Great Work: Our Way into the Future* (New York: Bell Tower, 1999), 55; Brian Swimme and Thomas Berry, *The Universe Story: From the Primordial Flaring Forth to the Ecozoic Era* (San Francisco: Harper San Francisco, 1992).
8. Field journal notes, Genesis Farm, Blairstown, N.J., August 14, 1995.
9. David Chidester, *Authentic Fakes: Religion and American Popular Culture* (Berkeley: University of California Press, 2005), 80.
10. Patrick Whitefield, *Permaculture in a Nutshell* (Hampshire, Eng.: Permanent Publications, 1993), 4.
11. Bill Mollison, *Introduction to Permaculture* (Tyalgum, Australia: Tagari, 1991), 5.
12. Brady specializes in running art and prayer retreats and in creating spaces for "interactive ecological art/spiritual experiences." As centers such as Genesis Farm have expanded, labyrinths and earth meditation pathways have become a niche market for Brady, whose work has been featured, among other places, at the Cathedral of St. John the Divine in New York City. She is also cofounder of the Tucson-based Earth Angels, an artists' group that fosters "visualizing and creating a positive future for Mother Earth." Today she creates meditative paintings and landscapes in her studio in Oracle, Arizona.
13. Sharon Brady, "What Is an Earth Pathway?" Earth Meditation Pathways brochure, Dover, N.J., 1996.
14. Sharon Brady, *Genesis Life Trail Guide*, Dover, N.J., 1995, 1. Available from Sharon Brady, P.O. Box 5536, Oracle, Ariz., 85623.
15. Octavio Paz, *The Labyrinth of Solitude,* trans. Lysander Kemp (New York: Grove Press, 1961).
16. For a sample text of a "Council of All Beings," see John Seed et al., *Thinking Like a Mountain: Toward a Council of All Beings* (Philadelphia: New Society, 1988). On July 22, 1995, I participated in a "Council of All Beings" held at Genesis Farm. The council process was facilitated by a Vermont ecological musical group called Joyful Noise, and the portion of the council in which all the species meet to discuss the current state of the

earth was held in the woodland stone circle of the Earth Meditation Trail. This created an ideal dramatic setting for an "all-species" council.

17. Gail Worcelo, "Holy Ground: Where Catholic Tradition and the Universe Story Meet—Reflections from an Ecozoic Retreat," 7, http://thegreatstory.org/CatholicMetarelig.html (December 1, 2005).

18. Ioannes Paulus PP II, *Evangelium Vitae: To the Bishops, Priests, and Deacons, Men and Women Religious, Lay Faithful, and All People of Good Will, on the Value and Inviolability of Human Life* (1995), http://www.vatican.va/holy_father/john_paul_ii/encyclicals/documents/hf_jp-ii_enc_25031995_evangelium-vitae_en.html (January 12, 2006), esp. sections 50, 77, 82, 86, 87, 92, 95, 98, and 100.

19. Sharon Brady, personal communication with the author, July 20, 2006.

20. Brady, *Genesis Life Trail Guide*, 5.

21. Phyllis McGinley, from her poem "In Praise of Diversity," in *Times Three: Selected Verse from Three Decades, with Seventy New Poems* (New York: Viking, 1960). I am indebted to JoAnn McAllister for bringing this poem to my attention. See McAllister, "Choosing Wonder: Overcoming the Fear of Mystery Can Lead to the Ecstasy of Discovery," *In Context* (Late Winter 1990): 35.

22. "Stations of the Cross," in Richard McBrien, ed., *Encyclopedia of Catholicism* (San Francisco: Harper San Francisco, 1989), 1222.

23. Andrew Greeley, "Why Do Catholics Stay in the Church? Because of the Stories," *New York Times Magazine,* July 10, 1994, 38–41.

24. One can now, for instance, consult the web-based "World-Wide Labyrinth Locator" to find labyrinths in one's area. See http://wwll.veriditas.labyrinthsociety.org. There are now also numerous labyrinth societies and conventions. See the Labyrinth Society at http://www.labyrinthsociety.org, and Labyrinth Resources at http://www.labyrinthguild.org (January 26, 2006). See also Lauren Artress, *Walking a Sacred Path: Rediscovering the Labyrinth as a Spiritual Tool* (New York: Riverhead, 1995). This book has been seminal in spurring the labyrinth renaissance. Artress has brought copies of the labyrinth from Chartres Cathedral in France into American Cathedrals, such as Grace Cathedral in San Francisco and the Cathedral of St. John the Divine in New York City.

25. Sisters of the Holy Cross, Notre Dame, Ind., "Walk the Labyrinth at St. Mary's," http:///www.cscsisters.org/spirituality/spirituality_labyrinth.asp (January 26, 2006).

26. See Louis Dupré, *The Deeper Self: An Introduction to Christian Mysticism* (New York: Crossroad, 1981).

27. Sharon Brady, "Earth Meditation Pathways," pamphlet, Dover, N.J., 1996. Emphasis in original.

28. Mircea Eliade speaks about the "omphalos" or world "navel" as the "center of the world." See Eliade's *Patterns in Comparative Religion*, 6th ed. (New York: Meridian, 1970), 231–235.

29. Kirkpatrick Sale, *Dwellers in the Land: The Bioregional Vision* (San Francisco: Sierra Club Books, 1985), x.

30. See Michael Vincent McGinnis, Freeman House, and William Jordan, "Bioregional Restoration: Re-establishing an Ecology of Shared Identity," in Michael Vincent McGinnis, ed., *Bioregionalism* (New York: Routledge, 1999).

31. Michael Vincent McGinnis, "Rewilding Imagination: Science, Art, Technology and Policy in Restoration," paper presented at "Borders and Bridges: Exploring Relationships between Humans and Animals," colloquium series, Interdisciplinary Humanities Center, University of California, Santa Barbara, February 1999.

32. Catherine Bell, *Ritual: Perspectives and Dimensions* (New York: Oxford University Press, 1997), 251.

33. Ibid., 251–252.

34. Gail Worcelo, speech to Community of the Sisters of Charity, St. Louis, Mo., April 2000.

35. Crystal Spring Earth Learning Center, "2004 Program Series: Learning Our Place in the Universe Story," program offerings announcement, Plainville, Mass., 3.

36. "Thomas Berry and the Earth's Passion" *Compassion Magazine* (a periodical of the Order of Passionists) (Winter 1998), http://www.cptryon.org/compassion/win98/berryt.html (January 26, 2006).

37. Benedictine Sisters, Monastery of St. Gertrude, Cottonwood, Idaho, "The Passion of the Earth," http://www.stgertrudes.org/Monastery/Passion/passion_of_earth.htm (January 20, 2006).

38. Ibid.

39. Joellen Sbrissa, electronic interview with the author, January 7, 2002.

40. Benedictine Sisters, "Passion of the Earth."

41. Ibid.

42. Andrew Greeley, *The Catholic Imagination* (Berkeley: University of California Press, 2000), 44.

43. See Sisters of St. Joseph of La Grange, Ministry of the Arts, http://www.ministryofthearts.org (January 15, 2006).

44. Greeley, *Catholic Imagination*, 45.

45. Ibid., 46.

46. Betty Daugherty, electronic interview with the author, March 14, 2002.

47. See Sisters of St. Joseph of Lyon, Living Water Spiritual Center, Winslow, Maine, "The Cosmic Walk," http://www.e-livingwater.org/grounds.htm (January 26, 2006).

48. Gail Worcelo, electronic interview with the author, January 23, 2002.

49. Thomas Berry, "Conversations with Thomas Berry," public lecture, Blairstown Academy, Blairstown, N.J., August 19, 1995.

50. Miriam MacGillis led our "Exploring the Sacred Universe" program group in a cosmic walk on the very last day of our program as a culmination of the intensive "universe story" curriculum. Field journal notes, Genesis Farm, Blairstown, N.J., August 25, 1995.

51. Connie Barlow and others involved in the Epic of Evolution Society have used the cosmic walk at their gatherings and conferences. The Foundation for Global Community uses a different "Walk through Time," which is structurally similar and accompanied by large posters. A book on the "Walk through Time" has been published by the foundation and is available through its office at 222 High Street, Palo Alto, Calif., 94301. Leana McCutcheon, director of Clearings Center for Women in New Jersey, incorporates

the cosmic walk into her feminist spirituality and goddess-oriented programs. Artist and Sister of St. Joseph Marion Honors has also developed a series of illustrations for the walk.

52. Miriam Therese MacGillis, "The Universe and the Unfolding Human Journey," *Timeline* (May/June 1998): 11.

53. Thomas Berry, "Bioregions: The Context for Reinhabiting the Earth," *Breakthrough* (Spring/Summer 1985): 9.

54. Marya Grathwohl, electronic interview with the author, March 2, 2002.

55. Miriam Brown, electronic interview with the author, June 3, 2002.

56. Greeley, *Catholic Imagination*, 46.

57. Keith Roberts, *Religion in Sociological Perspective* (New York: Wadsworth, 1995), 95.

58. Clifford Geertz, *The Interpretations of Cultures* (New York: Basic Books, 1973), 113.

59. Mary Southard, electronic interview with the author, February 28, 2002.

60. Catherine Bell, *Ritual: Perspectives and Dimensions* (New York: Oxford University Press, 1997), 252.

61. Rosine Sobczak, electronic interview with the author, February 19, 2002.

62. Caroline Webb, "The Mystique of the Earth: An Interview with Thomas Berry," *Caduceus* (Spring 2003), http://www.ratical.org/many_worlds/mystiqueOfE.html (January 26, 2006).

63. Ibid.

64. Field journal notes, Genesis Farm, Blairstown, N.J., July 9, 1997.

65. Edward Hays, *Prayers for a Planetary Pilgrim: A Personal Manual for Prayer and Ritual* (Leavenworth, Kans.: Forest of Peace, 1989), 75–77.

66. Miriam MacGillis, *Fire within the Fire: Christian Tradition and the New Universe Story,* videocassette available through Earth Communications, Laurel, Md.

67. Field journal notes, Genesis Farm, Blairstown, N.J., June 21, 1997.

68. "Earth Festivals," in *Crystal Spring Earth Learning Center Offerings,* 2000 program schedule, 2.

69. Thomas Berry, "The Spirituality of the Earth," in Susan J. Clark, *Celebrating Earth Holy Days: A Resource Guide for Faith Communities* (New York: Crossroad, 1992), 69.

70. Chris Loughlin, electronic interview with the author, March 18, 2002.

71. "Waterspirit Programs," Stella Maris Retreat Center, Elberon, N.J., http://www.waterspirit.org/programs.html (January 26, 2006).

72. Gloria Stravelli, "At Waterspirit, Every Day Is Earth Day," *The Hub,* April 19, 2002, http://hub.gmnews.com/news/2002/0419/Front_Page/031.html (January 26, 2006).

73. Stewardship of Life Institute, "Celebrate and Proclaim God's Creation," http://www.stewardshipoflife.org/Resources/Update/Update05.04.11.htm; Catholic Conservation Center Calendar, http://conservation.catholic.org/news_and_events.htm; and National Catholic Rural Life Conference, "Green Ribbon Seasonal Calendar," http://www.ncrlc.com/GR-campaign-webpages/GR-Seasonal-Calendar.html (January 26, 2006).

74. Greeley, *Catholic Imagination,* 52.

75. Robert Orsi, *The Madonna of 115th Street: Faith and Community in Italian Harlem, 1880–1950* (New Haven: Yale University Press, 1985), 57.

76. Mary Evelyn Tucker, *Worldly Wonder: Religions Enter Their Ecological Phase* (New York: Open Court, 2003), 9.

Conclusion

1. Sharon Therese Zayak, *Earth Spirituality: In the Catholic and Dominican Traditions,* Conversatio, Dominican Women on Earth Series, no. 1 (San Antonio, Tex.: Sor Juana Press, 2003), 37.

2. Colleen McDannell, *Material Christianity: Religion and Popular Culture in America* (New Haven: Yale University Press, 1995), 132–160.

3. Zayak, *Earth Spirituality,* 37–38.

4. Ibid., 45, 46, 43, 49.

5. Zayac specifically refers to ecologically friendly content in the 1975 Bishops of Appalachia's pastoral letter, *This Land Is Home to Me: A Pastoral Letter on Powerlessness in Appalachia;* the 1980 U.S. Bishops of the Midwest's *Strangers and Guests: Toward Community in the Heartland;* the 1987 Bishops of the Dominican Republic's *Pastoral Letter on the Relationship of Human Beings to Nature;* the 1988 Bishops of the Philippines' *What Is Happening to Our Beautiful Land?;* John Paul II's 1990 World Day of Peace Message, "The Ecological Crisis: A Common Responsibility—Peace with God the Creator, Peace with all Creation"; and the 1991 U.S. Catholic Conference of Bishops document, *Renewing the Earth: An Invitation to Reflection and Action on Environment in Light of Catholic Social Teaching.* See also Zayac, *Earth Spirituality,* 20–36.

6. See Roger Gottlieb, *A Greener Faith: Religious Environmentalism and Our Planet's Future* (New York: Oxford University Press, 2006), 1–12.

7. "The Earth Charter Initiative," official web site of the Earth Charter, http://www.earthcharter.org (December 19, 2005).

8. Bill Jacobs, "New Age versus Christian Environmental Justice," http://conservation.catholic.org/new_age.htm; and "A Cosmos without the Redemption of Jesus Christ?" http://conservation.catholic.org/creation_spirituality.htm (January 7, 2006).

9. See   http://conservation.catholic.org/catholic_conservation_center.htm   and http://conservation.catholic.org/Earth%20Charter.htm.

10. Jacobs, "A Cosmos without the Redemption of Jesus Christ?"

11. Ibid.

12. Carrie Tomko, "Worshipping the Ground We Walk On," *Today's Catholic Reflections,* http://tcrnews2.com/gennewage.html (January 7, 2006).

13. Ibid.

14. See "Excommunication" in Richard McBrien, ed., *Encyclopedia of Catholicism* (New York: Harper Collins, 1989), 500–501.

15. Famous examples of this include the Dominican Inquisitor Friar Savanarola who, some five hundred years after being burned at the stake as a heretic, is now undergoing the process of beatification—the first step to sainthood. Another famous example

is St. Joan, who was condemned to death as a heretic, sorceress, and adulteress, and burned at the stake in 1431. In 1920 she was canonized by Pope Benedict XV.

16. See John Paul II, "Ordinatio Sacerdotalis" (Apostolic Letter), May 22, 1994, http://www.vatican.va/holy_father/john_paul_ii/apost_letters/documents/hf_jp-ii_apl _22051994_ordinatio-sacerdotalis_en.html (January 19, 2006).

17. Bernard Moran, "U.S. Dominican Nun Brings the 'New Cosmology' to New Zealand," *AD 2000* 12, no. 4 (May 1999): 9.

18. Field journal notes, International Conference of Sisters of Earth, July 14, 2006.

19. Robert Ellsberg, *Blessed among All Women* (New York: Crossroad, 2005), 303–304.

20. Sisters of Providence at Saint Mary-of-the-Woods home page, http://www .spsmw.org/cgi-bin/site.pl (July 17, 2006).

21. "Sisters of Providence—Earth Plunge for Women Religious 2006," http:// www.spsmw.org/cgi-bin/site.pl?3208&dwContent_contentID=634 (July 17, 2006).

22. As cited in Mark Lombard, "Vatican Director: Intelligent Design Belittles God," *Catholic Online,* February 2, 2006, http://www.catholic.org/national/national_story .php?id=18542 (February 2, 2006).

23. Ibid.

24. Gail Worcelo, "Discovering the Divine within the Universe," *Journey* (Summer 2000): 9.

25. Michael Rose, "EarthSpirit Rising over Mount St. Joseph," *St. Catherine Review* (July/August 1998), http://acquinas-multi-media.com/catherine/earthspirit.html (January 20, 2006). (As of 2001, *St. Catherine Review* ceased publication.)

26. Bernadette Bostwick, telephone interview with the author, January 4, 2006.

27. Field journal notes, Genesis Farm, Blairstown, N.J., July 9, 1997.

28. Sharon Bard, "The New Story: An Interview with Miriam MacGillis," *Creation Spirituality* 10, no. 13 (1994): 20–21.

29. So strong was the nineteenth-century Theosophical fascination and affinity for Catholic mysticism and sacramentalism that it spawned a Theosophical offshoot in the earlier part of the twentieth century called the Liberal Catholic Church. In 1916, the Liberal Catholic Church was founded by an English Theosophist named Charles Leadbeater and James I. Wedgewood, a bishop in the Old Catholic Church (a group of dissenting Roman Catholics who maintained their Catholic identity but rejected the proclamation of papal infallibility). Together, Leadbeater and Wedgewood created a church that retained the traditional sacraments, the historic ceremonies, and vestments of the Roman Catholic Church but infused those traditions with Theosophical meanings. Because of the metaphysical affinities between Theosophy and Catholicism, Leadbeater and Wedgewood felt they had hit on a divinely inspired and quite reasonable evolution of both traditions. Rudolf Steiner himself was fascinated with Catholic sacramentalism, as were many of the avant-garde thinkers at Brook Farm who in turn gave rise to alternative religious philosophies that would in the twentieth century become repackaged as New Age. See Catherine Albanese, *A Republic of Mystics and Metaphysicians: A Cultural History of U.S. Metaphysical Religion* (New Haven: Yale University Press, 2006).

30. J. Gordon Melton, "Whither the New Age?" in Timothy Miller, ed., *America's Alternative Religions* (Albany: State University of New York Press, 1995), 350.

31. Ibid., 249–351.

32. See Gottlieb, *A Greener Faith;* Bron Taylor's introduction to *The Encyclopedia of Religion and Nature* (New York: Continuum, 2005); Mary Evelyn Tucker, *Worldly Wonder: Religions Enter Their Ecological Phase* (Chicago: Open Court, 2003).

33. See Roderick Nash's chapter "The Greening of Religion" in his *The Rights of Nature: A History of Environmental Ethics* (Madison: University of Wisconsin Press, 1989), 87–120.

34. Roger Gottlieb, *A Greener Faith: Religious Environmentalism and Our Planet's Future* (New York: Oxford University Press, 2006).

35. Roger Finke and Rodney Stark, *The Churching of America, 1776–1990: Winners and Losers in Our Religious Economy* (New Brunswick, N.J.: Rutgers University Press, 1992), 257–263; and Laurence Iannaccone, "Strict Churches Make Strong Churches," as quoted in Finke and Stark, *Churching of America,* 261.

36. Meredith McGuire, *Religion: The Social Context,* 4th ed. (Belmont, Calif.: Wadsworth, 1997), 166; David Bromley, "New Religious Movements," in William H. Swatos, ed., *Encyclopedia of Religion and Society,* http://hirr.hartsem.edu/ency/NRM.htm (January 6, 2006).

37. J. Gordon Melton, "The Fate of NRMs and their Detractors in Twenty-First Century America," in Phillip Lucas and Thomas Robbins, eds., *New Religious Movements in the Twenty-first Century* (New York: Taylor & Francis, 2004), 229–240.

38. Annie Milhaven, ed., *Inside Stories: Thirteen Valiant Women Challenging the Church* (Mystic, Conn.: Twenty-third Publications, 1987), xi.

39. Dolan encountered Deleuze and Guattari's rhizome metaphor in the work of Dolores LaChapelle and Julien Puzey. See Derrick Jensen's interview with LaChapelle and Puzey in Jensen, *Listening to the Land: Conversations about Nature, Culture, and Eros* (San Francisco: Sierra Club Books, 1995), 244–247. Deleuze and Guattari's discussion of rhizomes is laid out in their coauthored work *A Thousand Plateaus: Capitalism and Schizophrenia,* vol. 2, trans. B. Massumi (Minneapolis: University of Minnesota Press, 1987). See also Dolores LaChapelle, *Sacred Land, Sacred Sex, Rapture of the Deep: Concerning Deep Ecology and Celebrating Life* (Durango, Colo.: Kivaki, 1998).

40. Heather Millar, "Generation Green," *Sierra Club Magazine* (November/December 2000): 36–47.

41. McGuire, *Religion,* 238.

42. Although controversial, the solstices and equinoxes are festivals that bring large groups together not only to celebrate the seasons but also to form broad-based networks to work on local environmental issues. A few years ago, Genesis Farm actually had to begin restricting its winter solstice festival to its garden shareholder families because even after extending the festival to two nights, they still had waiting lists of people they had to turn away.

43. Gail Worcelo, electronic interview with the author, January 23, 2002.

44. Mary Southard, electronic interview with the author, February 28, 2002.

45. Kathleen Sherman, electronic interview with the author, April 5, 2002.

46. Marilyn Rudy, electronic interview with the author, March 15, 2002.

47. Thomas Berry, *The Great Work: Our Way into the Future* (New York: Bell Tower, 1999), 1–3.

48. Sharon Zayac, electronic interview with the author, March 15, 2002.

49. Corlita Bonnarens, electronic interview with the author, January 5, 2002.

50. Ardeth Platte, telephone interview with the author, January 2, 2006.

51. Gail Worcelo, "New Monastery, New Beginnings," *Homecoming's Newsletter* (1999): 2.

52. Mary Louise Dolan, "Seeds," *Spiritearth Newsletter* (Spring 1994): 3.

53. Betty Daugherty, electronic interview with the author, March 14, 2002.

54. Carol Coston, "Ecology, Economics, Eggplants, and Earthworms," *Occasional Papers* (Spring 1994): 10.

55. As quoted in Diarmuid O'Murchu, *Religion in Exile: A Spiritual Homecoming* (New York: Crossroad, 2000), vii.

56. Eugene Rochberg-Halton, *Meaning and Modernity: Social Theory and the Pragmatic Attitude* (Chicago: University of Chicago Press, 1986), 109. Emphasis in original.

57. See Raymond Williams, *Culture and Society, 1780–1950* (London: Chatto and Windus, 1958).

58. Williams, as quoted in Rochberg-Halton, *Meaning and Modernity,* 111. Emphasis in original.

59. Ibid.

60. Timothy Fitzgerald, "A Critique of 'Religion' as a Cross-Cultural Category," *Method and Theory in the Study of Religion* 2 (1997): 97.

61. This schema is borrowed from Wendy Griswold's discussion of culture in *Cultures and Societies in a Changing World* (Thousand Oaks, Calif.: Pine Forge, 1994), 7.

62. Rochberg-Halton, *Meaning and Modernity,* 119. I have found this concept enormously useful in my own work on environmentally activist Catholic sisters and organic farming communities. The "living" quality of Rochberg-Halton's "cultivation of culture" not only speaks to the lived dimension of religion, but also provides an apt metaphor for those engaged in "sacred agriculture."

63. Ibid.

64. See, for instance, David Hall, ed., *Lived Religion in America: Toward a History of Practice* (Princeton, N.J.: Princeton University Press, 1997), in particular Robert Orsi's essay on "Everyday Miracles," 3–21.

65. Penny Becker and Nancy Eisland, "Developing Interpretations: Ethnography and the Restructuring of Knowledge in a Changing Field," in Peggy Becker and Nancy Eisland, eds., *Contemporary American Religion: An Ethnographic Reader* (London: Alta Mira, 1997), 19.

66. Fitzgerald, "Critique of 'Religion,'" 96–97.

67. Robert Orsi, *Thank You, St. Jude: Women's Devotion to the Patron Saint of Hopeless Causes* (New Haven: Yale University Press, 1996); Catherine L. Albanese, "Hopeless Cases and Historical Conventions: Reflections on Robert Orsi's *Thank You, St. Jude,*" presentation to the American Academy of Religion, New Orleans, November 1996.

68. Peter Berg and Raymond Dasmann, "Reinhabiting California," in Peter Berg,

ed., *Reinhabiting a Separate Country: A Bioregional Anthology of Northern California* (San Francisco: Planet Drum Foundation, 1978), 218.

69. Bernadette Bostwick, telephone interview with the author, January 4, 2006.

70. Gail Worcelo, "Like a Pungent Shrub with Dangerous Take-Over Properties," *Green Mountain Monastery Newsletter* (Winter 2003): 1–2.

71. Elaine Prevallet, *A Wisdom for Life: A Series of Presentations on Earth Spirituality* (Nerinx, Ky.: Elaine Prevallet, 1995), 35–36.

72. Evelyn Fox Keller, *A Feeling for the Organism: The Life and Work of Barbara McClintock* (San Francisco: W. H. Freeman, 1983), 198, 199.

73. Gail Worcelo, "Discovering the Divine within the Universe," *Journey* (Summer 2000): 9.

ACKNOWLEDGMENTS

This book would not have been possible without the generous gifts of time and resources so freely given by religious sisters. In particular, I would like to thank all the Sisters of Earth who welcomed me at their meetings, took time to speak with me at their ecological centers or in the context of their earth ministries, and corresponded via both conventional and electronic means. Miriam MacGillis has been especially helpful with this project, as have Gail Worcelo, Bernadette Bostwick, Toni Nash, Maureen Wild, Mary Southard, Marilyn Rudy, Maureen Murray, Chris Loughlin, Carole Rossi, Barbara Harrington, Nancy Earle, Cathy Coyne, Roberta Mulcahy, Cathy Mueller, Bette Ann Jaster, Carol Coston, Elise D. García, Mary Ellen Leciejewski, Paula González, Mary Louise Dolan, Liz Walters, Janet Ryan, Nancy Wittwer, Maureen McCormack, Paula Cathcart, Sharon Brady, Jean and Larry Edwards, Lori Gold, and so many others.

At various times over the past decade, this research was supported by a Rockefeller Foundation Humanities Fellowship, a Louisville Institute Fellowship, a Joseph Fichter Award for the Study of Women and Religion, a Society for the Scientific Study of Religion Research Award, and a Humanities and Social Sciences Award from the University of California. I am tremendously grateful to each of these funding sources. Without these grants, field travel, assistance with data gathering, and time for research and writing would not have been possible.

I also want to acknowledge the contributions of my research assistants. With great fortitude for dealing with technical logistics, Terri MacKenzie sent out and retrieved the electronic interview, while elucidating "insider" terminology and abbreviations of women's religious communities. Donna Carpenter provided indispensable assistance with transcribing interview audiotapes. Northwestern students Amanda Downs and Omayr Niazi worked with great enthusiasm to help me track down elusive articles, archival sources, and hard-to-locate texts. Amanda Baugh kindly helped index the book. The Grailville community graciously allowed me to work in their archives.

My colleagues at Northwestern University supported me intellectually through this process. I am particularly thankful for the guidance offered by Richard Kieckhefer, Barbara Newman, Cristie Traina, and Nicki Beisel. My sage mentors Catherine Albanese, Wade Clark Roof, Patricia Cohen, and the late Walter Capps generously gave assistance with the initial stages of what would later evolve into a much larger endeavor. Mary Evelyn Tucker offered valuable counsel at a critical juncture in the project. I am also deeply indebted to Mary Farrell Bednarowski, Catherine Brekus, Roger Gottlieb, Rebecca Gould, Belden Lane, Bron Taylor, and Peter Williams for their comments on the manuscript in its entirety or sections of it.

Editor Peg Fulton was wonderful to work with. Her excitement from the beginning about this project fed my energy to write. I am grateful to her successor, Alex Morgan, for valiantly and gracefully taking over the project after Peg's retirement. Alex's clarity of vision and respect for the material made him a delight to work with. Thank you to all those at Harvard University Press who have made this work possible, including my talented copyeditor, Julie Carlson.

I received personal support for finishing this book from Helen DoBell, who gave spiritual direction and perspective to the writing journey. I am indebted to my sisters, Anne and Martha, for teaching me what it is to be part of a lifelong sisterhood, and to my father, for his love and for his unbridled zeal for my academic accomplishments. Lauren Harrison has been my soul sister for thirty-plus years and inspired me to keep writing. I am especially thankful to my beloved husband, John, and to my baby, Brody, who remind me daily of what is most important in the world. Above all, I am grateful to my mother, Sandy McFarland Taylor, not only for her invaluable comments, contributions, and loving support, but also for introducing me to nature at an early age. My view from her backpack during our daily walks through the Watchung Reservation awakened my wonder at and consciousness of belonging to the larger community of life.

INDEX

Harvard University Press is a member of Green Press Initiative
(greenpressinitiative.org), a nonprofit organization working to
help publishers and printers increase their use of recycled paper
and decrease their use of fiber derived from endangered forests.
This book was printed on 100% recycled paper containing
50% post-consumer waste and processed chlorine free.